AF505909

Contradictions and Limits of Neoliberal
European Governance

Contradictions and Limits of Neoliberal European Governance

From Lisbon to Lisbon

Edited by

Bastiaan van Apeldoorn
Reader in International Relations
Vrije Universiteit Amsterdam, the Netherlands

Jan Drahokoupil
Senior Research Fellow
Universität Mannheim, Germany

and

Laura Horn
Lecturer in International Relations
Vrije Universiteit Amsterdam, the Netherlands

First published 2009 by
PALGRAVE MACMILLAN

Palgrave Macmillan in the UK is an imprint of Macmillan Publishers Limited, registered in England, company number 785998, of Houndmills, Basingstoke, Hampshire RG21 6XS.

Palgrave Macmillan in the US is a division of St Martin's Press LLC, 175 Fifth Avenue, New York, NY 10010.

Palgrave Macmillan is the global academic imprint of the above companies and has companies and representatives throughout the world.

Palgrave® and Macmillan® are registered trademarks in the United States, the United Kingdom, Europe and other countries.

ISBN-13: 978-0-230-53709-5   hardback
ISBN-10: 0-230-53709-X   hardback

This book is printed on paper suitable for recycling and made from fully managed and sustained forest sources. Logging, pulping and manufacturing processes are expected to conform to the environmental regulations of the country of origin.

A catalogue record for this book is available from the British Library.

Library of Congress Cataloging-in-Publication Data

Contradictions and limits of neoliberal European governance : from
   Lisbon to Lisbon / edited by Bastiaan van Apeldoorn, Jan
   Drahokoupil, Laura Horn.
      p. cm.
   Includes bibliographical references and index.
   ISBN 978-0-230-53709-5
   1. Neoliberalism—Europe.   2. Europe—Politics and government.
      3. Europe—Economic integration.   I. Apeldoorn, Bastiaan van.
      II. Drahokoupil, Jan, 1980–   III. Horn, Laura.
   JC574.C656   2009
   320.51—dc22   2008030652

10   9   8   7   6   5   4   3   2   1
18   17   16   15   14   13   12   11   10   09

Printed and bound in Great Britain by

CPI Antony Rowe, Chippenham and Eastbourne

Contents

Tables

Foreword

I congratulate the editors and authors of this important collection of essays on the European political project for producing an innovative and coherent contribution to the renewal of critical political economy. The resulting volume is especially timely. It appears in a critical conjuncture when the limitations of unregulated finance-led accumulation have become evident to everyone from the problems originating in the Anglosphere and their global repercussions. Thus the contributors address the emergence of European integration, the Lisbon Agenda, neoliberal governance projects on the national, EU and supranational scales, and related strategies from the viewpoint of a neo-Gramscian concern with accumulation strategies, state projects, and hegemonic visions and their social bases. Equally importantly, they explore the basic contradictions at the heart of the capital relation, their particular forms of appearance in contemporary Europe in the wider context of a variegated global capitalism and its associated geo-politics, and the emerging economic, legitimacy and social crises of finance-led neoliberal mode of growth. Indeed, a concern with basic contradictions, class conflicts and resistance is one of the defining features of this volume. Nonetheless we should note that most of the contributions are mainly concerned, as the title indicates, with the limits of the European Union political project – whether these are reflected in the Growth and Stability Pact, the Lisbon Agenda, the rejected constitutional settlement, or other forms and sites of governance. This focus is reflected in a recurrent concern with the crisis of mass political legitimacy of the European project and its associated forms of social partnership and (multi-level) governance rather than with the fundamental economic limits of the neoliberal project, whether in its more disembedded Anglo-Saxon form or its more embedded Continental European variants. This focus follows from many contributors' interest in what van Apeldoorn (2002) describes as the socio-economic *content* or underlying social purpose of the European integration process as well as with its institutional form.

This remark is not intended to counterpose a claim about economic determination in the last instance to an alleged one-sided concern with the state, governance and politics. On the contrary, one of the most interesting features of the essays below is their recognition of (a) the importance of capitalist contradictions, conflicts rooted in different roles within the circuit of capital and/or global division of labour and class conflicts, and (b) the dependence of capitalist reproduction on extra-economic structural and institutional supports and specific forms of institutionalized compromise within the power bloc and between it and popular social forces. Nonetheless I do want to emphasize even more strongly than do these essays that the political crises, including the crisis of mass legitimacy, are related to emerging economic problems. These concern not only growing economic inequalities and social exclusion but also the emerging structural crisis at the heart of a variegated world market organized under the dominance of a neoliberal, finance-led accumulation strategy. It is this structural crisis that has become self-evident as the repercussions of the 'sub-prime' crisis (a symptom of more deep-seated problems) have spread in unexpected ways around the world. What is particularly striking about this crisis is that, in contrast to the so-called East Asian crisis in the late 1990s, it emerged in the heartlands of neoliberalism. Whereas the misleading naming of the East Asian crisis disguises the first symptoms of a general crisis *in* the world market by focusing on where they first appeared, the origins of the current crisis provide a much more telling index of the crucial flaws in disembedded or 'pure' capitalism (Husson 2008). Whether or not this leads to a general crisis *of* capitalism does not depend on the economic (il)logic of capitalism alone, however, but on the political, intellectual and moral struggles of the kind that the neo-Gramscian approach favoured by many contributors highlights.

In addition to this widely shared neo-Gramscian approach to critical political economy, several other themes tend to unify the contributions. First, while often pre-disciplinary in inspiration (witness the references to Marxist political economy, Polanyian analyses of the embedding of the market economy in a market society, and neo-Gramscian concern with class fractions, subaltern groups and political, intellectual and moral hegemony), most essays also display a distinctive flare for novel and effective trans-disciplinary analysis, critically combining concepts and perspectives from heterodox work in several disciplines as well as drawing creatively on several emerging inter-disciplinary perspectives. Second, many are not only concerned with the systemic logic (or, indeed, illogic) of neoliberalism – including its more embedded European variants – but also with the more or less active strategic role of specific social forces, whether dominant, sub-dominant or subaltern in establishing, guiding, mediating or resisting this logic. Thus many contributors seek to denaturalize and deconstruct neoliberalism and illustrate the complicity of key social forces – including in Europe itself – in the spread of neoliberalism and, especially, of finance-led accumulation strategies. Third, many essays engage critically with important ontological and epistemological questions and display remarkable methodological self-awareness about research problems in political economy. Key issues include identification of the underlying mechanisms of capital accumulation, its tendencies and counter-tendencies, and their associated contradictions; the complex dialectic of structure and agency and the asymmetrical opportunities for securing material interests that are inscribed in specific economic and political regimes; and the equally complex interaction of internal and external structural constraints and internal and external forces in shaping economic and social policy as well as the success and failure of specific regimes and strategies.

Substantively, the contributions explore the impact of neoliberalism in the fields of economic and social policy, the rearticulation of scales of economic and social policy formulation and implementation (and associated opportunities for scale jumping), and new forms of governance and meta-governance at various scales. This is reflected in the increased importance attached to competitiveness, innovation, entrepreneurship, flexibility, active labour markets, the rescaling and recalibration of governance, the form and content of the failing Lisbon Agenda and its associated Open Method of Coordination, and the manner in which emerging European governance structures are related to more general efforts to establish international regimes and forms of global governance appropriate to a neoliberal order organized in the shadow of American hegemony. But most of the contributions in this volume go beyond mere description of these trends, which are very common in the literature, to resist a 'premature harmonization of contradictions', a concern that is far less common in work on the European Union. Thus, although not always as systematic in their presentation as I would like to see, the essays often highlight the contradictions and tensions at the heart of the European project, economically as well as politically, and reveal the surprising ways in which these contradictions and tensions have manifested themselves. Thus we find references to the uneven development of the European Union, the impact of new Member States' economic and social policies on the capacity of founding members to maintain the European social model, the contradictions built into the Stability and Growth Pact, resistance to the constitutional settlement, and so on. In their different ways and with their quite different foci, therefore, the contributions make a powerful cumulative case for a critical political economy that treats economic and political projects as potentially decisive material as well as discursive forces in social development, without seeing them as essentially arbitrary and wilful acts of power on the part of the dominant fractions or classes and/or political elites and state managers. On the contrary, they demonstrate clearly the economic and political limits of specific projects as these are rooted in the more basic tendencies of capital accumulation in a variegated world market with its complex geo-political and geo-economic dynamics. This is reflected in turn in the contributors' interest in the flanking and supporting mechanisms that have kept the neoliberal project alive in Europe (witness the compromise character of the Lisbon Agenda itself and the recent manoeuvres around the new, post-referendum constitutional settlement) as well as in the role of subaltern forces, social movements and resistance in reinforcing the objective limits to neoliberal globalization and its manifestations and/or repercussions in Europe.

For these reasons, among many others, I congratulate the editors and contributors on this joint work and commend it, as with all other scientific work, to the tender mercies of criticism, subsequent refinement and, of course, further criticism. But I also hope that it will shape political as well as theoretical paradigms and influence current and future debates on the future of the European project in a global world.

Bob Jessop
Lancaster University

Notes on Contributors

Bastiaan van Apeldoorn is Reader in International Relations at the Vrije Universiteit Amsterdam (PhD, European University Institute, Florence). His research interests lie within the tradition of transnational historical materialism, in particular the changing political economy of European governance and, more recently, the rise of a new geopolitics within the context of changing global capitalist social relations. His publications include *Transnational Capitalism and the Struggle over European Integration* (Routledge, 2002), *Transational Historical Materialism: The Amsterdam International Political Economy Project* (*JIRD*, 2004, editor) and *The Transnational Politics of Corporate Governance Regulation* (Routledge, 2007, co-editor).

Andreas Bieler is Professor of Political Economy and Fellow of the Centre for the Study of Social and Global Justice (CSSGJ) in the School of Politics and International Relations, University of Nottingham, UK. His research is predominantly focused on understanding the current struggle over the future economic–political model of the European Union (EU) and the possibilities to resist neoliberal restructuring. He is author of *Globalisation and Enlargement of the European Union* (Routledge, 2000) as well as *The Struggle for a Social Europe: Trade Unions and EMU in Times of Global Restructuring* (Manchester University Press, 2006).

Hans-Jürgen Bieling is Junior Professor for European integration at the Department of Political Science at Philipps University Marburg, Germany. In this context, he also co-directs a research group on European integration (FEI). His main fields of interest are European integration, international and comparative political economy and political theory. His publications include *Gesellschaftstheorien und Zeitdiagnosen* (Westfälisches Dampfboot, 2000), *Euro-Kapitalismus und Globale Politische Ökonomie* (VSA, 2003, co-editor), *Theorien der Europäischen Integration* (VS, 2005, co-editor) and *Internationale Politische Ökonomie: Eine Einführung* (2007).

Dorothee Bohle is Associate Professor of Political Science at Central European University, Budapest. Her main publications include *Europas neue Peripherie: Polens Transformation und transnationale Integration* (Westfälisches Dampfboot, 2002) and a special issue of *Competition & Change* (vol. 11, no. 2, June 2007) called 'State, Capital and Labour: The Political Economy of Capitalist Diversity in Eastern Europe', together with Stuart Shields. Currently, together with Béla Greskovits, she is working on a book project called 'Capitalist Diversity on Europe's Periphery'.

Alan W. Cafruny is Henry Platt Bristol Professor of International Affairs at Hamilton College (USA). For several years a visiting professor at the European University Institute, he is the co-editor of *A Ruined Fortress: Neoliberal Hegemony and Transformation in Europe* (Rowman & Littlefield, 2003) and co-author of *Europe at Bay: In the Shadow of U.S. Hegemony* (Lynne Rienner, 2007).

Jan Drahokoupil is a senior research fellow at the Mannheim Centre for European Social Research (MZES), University of Mannheim. He serves on the Executive Board of the Czech think tank Economy and Society Trust. Jan obtained his PhD at the Central European University in Budapest. His research deals with the politics and political economy of Central and Eastern Europe and Central Asia. His publications include *Globalization and the State in Central and Eastern Europe: The Politics of Foreign Direct Investment* (Routledge, 2008).

Sandy Brian Hager is a PhD candidate in the Department of Political Science at York University in Toronto, Canada. His current research interests lie within the tradition of critical political economy, specifically in the areas of capital theory, global finance and geopolitics. He is the secretary of the Critical Political Economy Research Network.

Laura Horn is Lecturer in International Relations in the Department of Political Science at the Vrije Universiteit Amsterdam. She is a member of the Amsterdam Research Centre for Corporate Governance Regulation (ARCC-GOR); her dissertation focuses on the transformation of corporate governance regulation in the European Union. She has published articles in *New Political Economy* and *Competition & Change*.

Johannes Jäger is Head of the Economics Department at the University of Applied Sciences bfi Vienna. His main research interests are the financial sector and regional economic developments. Geographically the work focuses on Europe and Latin America. His recent publications include: 'New Forms of Global Financial Regulation', *Cahier de la Recherche ISC*; 'Urban Land Rent Theory – a regulationist perspective', *International Journal of Urban and Regional Research*; *Kapitalistische Entwicklung in Nord und Süd* (Mandelbaum, 2007); and 'Land Rent Theory' (in *Encyclopedia of Urban Studies*, forthcoming at Sage Publications).

Henk Overbeek is Professor of International Relations at the Vrije Universiteit Amsterdam. He works in the tradition of transnational historical materialism. His publications include *Rivalität und ungleiche Entwicklung: Einführung in die internationale Politik aus der Sicht der Internationalen Politischen Ökonomie* (VS, 2008), *The Transnational Politics of Corporate Governance Regulation* (Routledge, 2007, co-editor), *The Political Economy of European*

Employment (Routledge, 2003, editor), *Restructuring Hegemony in the Global Political Economy* (Routledge, 1993, editor) and *Global Capitalism and National Decline* (Unwin Hyman, 1990).

Magnus Ryner is Professor of International Relations at Oxford Brookes University. He is the author of *Europe at Bay: In the Shadow of US Hegemony* (Lynne Rienner, 2007, with Alan Cafruny) and *Capitalist Restructuring, Globalisation and the Third Way* (Routledge, 2002), and co-editor of *Poverty and the Production of World Politics* (Palgrave Macmillan, 2006) and *A Ruined Fortress? Neoliberal Hegemony and Transformation in Europe* (Rowman & Littlefield, 2003, with Alan Cafruny).

Arjan Vliegenthart studied political science and history at the Vrije Universiteit Amsterdam and the Freie Universität Berlin. Arjan Vliegenthart has been junior lecturer at the Department of Political Science of the Vrije Universiteit Amsterdam between 2003 and 2005. Currently, he is working within the context of the Amsterdam Research Centre for Corporate Governance Regulation (ARCCGOR) on his PhD on the political dimension of the developments in corporate governance regulation in Central and Eastern Europe. Apart from this, he is a Dutch senator for the Socialist Party (SP).

Acknowledgements

The idea for this edited volume developed during a workshop of the ESA Critical Political Economy Research Network (CPE RN) held at the Vrije Universiteit Amsterdam in September 2006. The CPE RN was set up in 2005 in the context of the European Sociological Association (ESA) as a platform to bring together critical scholarship on the political economy of the European Union and European capitalist economies, to reassert the critical political economy perspective in European social science, and to promote critical and emancipatory scholarship in Europe.

The 2006 workshop was a singularly fruitful experience with many outstanding contributions and discussions. Financial support for the workshop from ESA, the Netherlands Organisation for Scientific Research (NWO), the Netherlands Institute of Government (NIG) and the Amsterdam Research Centre for Corporate Governance Regulation (ARCCGOR) is gratefully acknowledged.

Most chapters of this volume were first discussed as papers at this workshop. We thank all of the participants for their input: Ilker Atac, Martin Beckmann, Claes Belfrage, Paul Boccara, Hubert Buch-Hansen, Sophie Heine, Jeffrey Henderson, Ines Hofbauer, Matthieu Lietaert, Frank Longstreth, Christian Möllmann, Andreas Nölke, James Perry, Or Raviv, Vanessa Redak, Antonios Roumpakis, Stuart Shields, Beat Weber and Angela Wigger.

We want to thank the editorial team at Palgrave Macmillan, which, in spite of rather frequent personnel changes, remained committed to this project. We are grateful to Femke Bink for compiling the bibliography, keeping track of all editorial changes and generally (and patiently) assisting us with this project. *Dank je, Femke!* In the process of editing this volume, we have received valuable feedback from Andreas Bieler on the initial book proposal, and from an anonymous reviewer on the draft manuscript. Moreover, several members of the CPE RN have provided us with comments on the introduction of this volume. In particular, we would like to thank Ian Bruff for his observations. Special thanks is due to Bob Jessop, not only for agreeing to write a highly perceptive foreword to this volume, but also for his continued support of the CPE RN. We would also like to thank Bob for inspiring many of us through his profound theoretical contributions on the nature of the capitalist state and state power. Finally, we also wish to thank the contributors for their flexibility and commitment to the project. The volume benefited considerably from their co-operative approach.

Bastiaan van Apeldoorn (Amsterdam)
Jan Drahokoupil (Cologne)
Laura Horn (Amsterdam)

Abbreviations

AFI	Association for Foreign Investments (Czech Republic)
AmCham EU	EU Committee of the American Chamber of Commerce
AmCham Hungary	American Chamber of Commerce Hungary
ATTAC	Association pour la Taxation des Transactions pour l'Aide aux Citoyens
BCBS	Basel Committee on Banking Supervision
BCCI	Bank of Credit and Commerce International
BIS	Bank for International Settlements
BWS	Bretton Woods System
CAP	Common Agricultural Policy
CCCTB	Common Consolidated Corporate Tax Base
CDA	Christen Democratisch Appèl (Dutch Christian Democratic party)
CDU	Christlich Demokratische Union Deutschlands (German Christian Democratic party)
CEE	Central and Eastern Europe
CFDT	Confédération Française Démocratique du Travail (French Democratic Confederation of Labour)
CFSP	Common Foreign and Security Policy
CIA	Central Intelligence Agency
CIT	Corporate Income Tax
D66	Democraten 66 (Dutch Liberal 'Reform' Party)
DG	Directorate General
DGB	Deutscher Gewerkschaftsbund (German trade union)
DWSR	Dollar Wall Street Regime
EC	European Community
ECB	European Central Bank
ECSC	European Coal and Steel Community
EDA	European Defence Agency
EDC	European Defence Community
EIF	European industry federation
EIRO	European Industrial Relations Observatory
EMCEF	European Mine, Chemical and Energy Workers' Federation
EMF	European Metalworkers' Federation
EMS	European Monetary System
EMU	Economic and Monetary Union
EP	European Parliament

EPSU	European Federation of Public Service Unions
ERT	European Round Table of Industrialists
ESDP	European Security and Defence Policy
ESF	European Social Forum
ESM	European Social Model
ETUC	European Trade Union Confederation
EU	European Union
EUCOB@N	European Collective Bargaining Information Network
FDI	Foreign direct investment
FDIC	Federal Deposit Insurance Corporation
FNV	Federatie Nederlandse Vakbeweging (Dutch trade union)
FSA	Financial Services Agreement
FSAP	Financial Services Action Plan
FSF	Financial Stability Forum
GATS	General Agreement on Trade in Services
GM	General Motors
HEBC	Hungarian European Business Council
HLG	High Level Group of Company Law Experts
HZDS	Hnutie za demokratické Slovensko (Movement for a Democratic Slovakia, Slovak Republic)
ICT	Information and commmunication technology
IIF	Institute of International Finance
IMF	International Monetary Fund
IOSCO	International Organization of Securities Commissions
IPE	International Political Economy
ITUC	International Trade Union Confederation
JVA	Joint Venture Association
LCEC	Lisbon Council for European Competitiveness
NATO	North Atlantic Treaty Organization
ODS	Občansko demokratická strana (Civic Democratic Party, Czech Republic)
OECD	Organisation for Economic Co-operation and Development
OEEC	Organisation for European Economic Co-operation
ÖGB	Österreichischer Gewerkschafsbund (Austrian Trade Union)
OMC	Open Method of Coordination
OPEC	Organization of the Petroleum Exporting Countries
PES	Party of European Socialists
PvdA	Partij van de Arbeid (Dutch Labour party)
PVV	Partij Voor de Vrijheid (Dutch far right party)
QMV	Qualified Majority Voting
R&D	Research and Development

SCO	Shanghai Cooperation Organization
SEA	Single European Act
SEM	Single European Market
SGP	Stability and Growth Pact
SME	Small and medium enterprise
SP	Socialistische Partij (Dutch Socialist party)
SPD	Sozialdemokratischen Partei Deutschlands (German Labour party)
SUD-PTT	Solidaires, Unitaires et Démocratiques (French trade union)
TABD	Transatlantic Business Dialogue
TNC	Transnational corporation / company
TUC	Trades Union Congress
UNICE	Union of Industrial and Employers' Confederation of Europe (now Business Europe)
V4	Visegrád Four
VAT	Value Added Tax
VVD	Volkspartij voor Vrijheid en Democratie (Dutch Liberal party)
WB	World Bank
WEF	World Economic Forum
WSF	World Social Forum
WTO	World Trade Organization

Introduction: Towards a Critical Political Economy of European Governance

Jan Drahokoupil, Bastiaan van Apeldoorn and Laura Horn

Just before this book went into production, the Irish rejected the so-called Lisbon reform treaty, that is, the treaty that after long and arduous negotiations was designed as a substitute for – and containing almost identical institutional reforms as – the European Constitution that had been voted down three years before by the French and the Dutch in the referendums of 29 May and 1 June 2005. Although it is too early to analyse the causes of the Irish 'no', or to predict the precise consequences of this dramatic event (beyond the fact that its planned entry into force of the treaty in 2009 now seems unlikely), it is clear that it is another slap in the face of Europe's political elites, and has brought the European Union (EU) into a new deep crisis after it had barely recovered from the one it faced when the Constitutional project turned out to lack the necessary popular legitimacy.

The sombre mood now reigning in Europe's capitals stands in stark contrast with the mood prevailing around the turn of the century. Then, with a prospective 'big bang' enlargement of ten Member States and the Euro having been introduced in 1999, Europe's political leaders were optimistically seeking to drive the integration project forward, starting the constitutional process, and at their Lisbon summit of March 2000 proclaiming the goal to turn the European economy into the most competitive by 2010. As we are now nearing that 'magical year' (but with the aforementioned objective already abandoned), how should we make sense of the current state of the project of European integration: which key developments and shifts have taken place in the past decade or so, and where are they taking us?

At the level of the global political economy, we must perhaps start by observing how the terror attacks of September 11, 2001, created a window of opportunity for the US neo-conservative project to further the imperial turn in US foreign policy – reflecting as well as contributing to new tensions and rivalries beyond and within the capitalist heartland (Van der Pijl, 2006b; De Graaff and Van Apeldoorn, 2008). These developments are arguably further undermining the legitimacy of global neoliberal governance, a legitimacy which had already been called into question by social forces both within the core and in the periphery in the years before. Next to the geopolitical ramifications, which as yet remain unclear but are bound to be important given the historical linkage (or arguably subordination) of the European project to US hegemony, 9/11 also sparked a worldwide recession after the boom of the 1990s. At the time of writing, Europe seems to be set for possibly an even worse economic downturn as engendered by the global credit crisis originating in the USA. The consequences of this crisis for the (real) European economy are as yet difficult to assess. What we do know is that the recession of the early 2000s deeply affected the European political economy, which had just more or less recovered from the last downturn in the early 1990s – even if unemployment levels in most Member States had remained high. As the European Union had just entered the final phase of Economic and Monetary Union (EMU), the deflationary effects of the Stability and Growth Pact (SGP) really started to make themselves felt, engendering a protracted political battle over the pact. Europe was now divided over both the Iraq war (and foreign policy generally) as well as over what is a core element of its socio-economic governance regime.

Adding to the crisis of confidence was the subsequent anti-climax of the accession of ten new Member States, mostly from the former Eastern bloc. The long-awaited enlargement was in fact greeted with little enthusiasm on either side of the former Iron Curtain. Indeed, whereas in the West the popular complaint arose that the 'new Europeans' were only costing 'us' a lot of money and also threatened to take 'our' jobs, at least in part of the 'new Europe' disappointment has been growing over what the integration into the European and global capitalist market in the end has offered. Although there has been economic development, inequalities have also been growing dramatically, and new forms of social exclusion have arisen. Indeed, with respect to the new Member States the EU is far from living up to its promise of social cohesion as the incorporation of Central and Eastern Europe has arguably turned it into a new periphery for the benefit of West European capital (Bohle, 2002; Holman, 2004b).

The completion of the 'Big Bang' enlargement reinforced the need for the EU to finally get its act together over institutional reform and deal with the business left unfinished in the treaties of Amsterdam and Nice. The Convention presided over by former French President Giscard d'Estaing then stepped up the ambitions by proposing to replace all the existing treaties with a new one – containing a number of important institutional innovations such as an EU president, a foreign minister, more qualified majority voting, but also a commitment to undistorted competition – and to call it a constitution. Although in the end ratified by a large majority of Member States, for instance with a huge popular fiat in Spain, the European Constitution proved highly unpopular in several key Member States – not just in the usual suspect, the UK, but also in France and Germany (although the government of the latter avoided the real test of a referendum). As indicated, the Constitution then met its premature end with the referendums in France and in the Netherlands. Clearly, the treaty which had been designed without any significant involvement of Europe's population but which did seek to interpellate them as *European* citizens, had pushed the limits of the European integration project too far. The fact that the subsequent attempt to salvage as much as one could from the wreckage of the Constitution, but without any longer calling it a constitution, that is, the Treaty of Lisbon, has again been sunk by a majority of the voters of the only Member State that actually held a referendum on the new treaty (i.e. Ireland), is making these limits even more visible.

At least since the early days of the European Coal and Steel Community, until the relaunching of the integration project with the Single European Act (SEA) and the Treaty of Maastricht, the process of European integration has primarily been an elite project. This is also the one thing that analysts from all rival theoretical camps – neo-functionalists and later supranationalists (Haas, 1968; Stone Sweet and Sandholtz, 1998); (liberal) intergovermentalists (Moravcsik, 1998) as well as various critical theorists (e.g. Van der Pijl, 1984; Holman, 1992; Van Apeldoorn, 2002; Bieler and Morton, 2001a) – have hitherto agreed on. Arguably this is now being challenged inasmuch as we are – albeit in a geographically uneven and far from mature manner – witnessing a politicization of the integration process from below (e.g. Hooghe and Marks, 2007a). This is of course not to say that European integration is now no longer an elite project, in the sense that the masses rather than the elites are in the driving seat, but 'the masses' have at least shown their ability to 'hit the brakes'. This has derailed the constitutional project, and now seems to have even led to the demise of the Lisbon treaty that repackaged the intended reforms in a way that it could be somewhat better sold to domestic audiences. Thus, whereas European integration may still be an elite project, it is increasingly a contested project (witness for instance also the transnational battle over and against the Services Directive discussed by Andreas Bieler in this volume). The growing politicization from below expresses an increasing alienation from and scepticism towards the European integration project (Hooghe and Marks, 2007b), which may be seen as a reflection of a more general legitimacy crisis of European governance. In particular, the mass mobilization in two founding Member States against the Constitution may thus have revealed the (potential) political limits of the European integration project in terms of its ability to sustain sufficient levels of mass legitimacy.

In contrast with some other recent approaches (e.g. Hooghe and Marks, 2007a), the central argument underlying this volume is that we can only come to a full understanding of these political limits and their implications for future European governance if we analyse not just the changing institutional *form* but above all the socio-economic *content* or underlying social purpose of the integration process (Van Apeldoorn, 2002).[1] Examining the nature and limits of the European project in this way also necessitates that we do not stop at analysing the structures underlying the current configuration of social forces, but also give due attention to the agency of those social forces, including the agency of resistance.

With respect to the content, the contributors to this volume all share the notion that at least since the end of the 1980s the European integration process has witnessed a thorough neoliberalization. This process did not take place without struggle, and was far from fully structurally determined – indeed, it has to be understood as a *political* project. Into the 1990s it became clear that, with the internal market project safely steered away from its alternative, neo-mercantilist and social-democratic interpretations (Van Apeldoorn, 2002; see also Chapter 1 of this volume) and the 'disciplinary neoliberalism' (Gill, 1998) of EMU being implemented through the Maastricht criteria, European governance had above all become a supranational form of neoliberal governance. The social purpose of the integration process has thus become fundamentally intertwined with a transnational process of neoliberal restructuring.

This neoliberal governance regime, arguably reaching its zenith as a transnational hegemonic project with the Lisbon Agenda, is currently called into question. It is in this context that this book sets out to analyse the nature, contradictions and limits of neoliberal governance in the EU. It builds on, yet at the same time seeks to go beyond, previous critical scholarship on European integration (e.g. Bieler and Morton, 2001a; Cafruny and Ryner, 2003). It goes beyond this literature inasmuch as this is the first volume from a critical political economy perspective that analyses developments and shifts in the political economy of European governance which have taken place since the early 2000s and that we deem critical to an understanding of the current 'state-of-the-Union'. These developments, already briefly sketched above, *inter alia* refer to the changing geopolitical and geo-economic context, the Lisbon Agenda as a new mode of neoliberal governance, the Eastward expansion of the EU, the subsequent deepening marketization, but also to the ensuing contestation and mobilization against (aspects of) the European project, such as manifested in the national resistance against the Constitution as well as several other instances of (trans)national resistance. As indicated, in capturing these developments, and how they are related to broader processes of transnational capitalist restructuring, we adopt a critical political economy perspective, which we will outline in the next section. After that this introduction concludes with an overview of the contributions to this volume.

Towards a critical political economy of European integration

The critical political economy perspective shared by the contributors to this edited volume draws on a variety of critical approaches; in particular, though not exclusively, a neo-Gramscian approach to the socio-economic configuration of the EU. Without seeking to offer a single research programme, our critical perspective is defined by a commitment to a set of common theoretical positions that explain recent transformations of capitalism and capitalist societies. Van Apeldoorn et al. (2003: 20) formulate the essence of such a perspective: '[C]ritical political economy recognizes the power relations, special interests and arbitrariness contained in market forces and civil societal relations . . . and seeks to relate these to state power.'

To locate (some of) the meta-theoretical common ground shared by the contributors, we draw to some extent on the transnational historical materialist perspective and the related critique on mainstream European integration theories. This has been elaborated among others by Bastiaan van Apeldoorn, Henk Overbeek and Magnus Ryner (2003); we also draw on work by several other contributors of this volume (Bieler and Morton, 2001a; Bieler et al., 2006). At the same time we seek to go beyond this existing critical work by stressing what we see as core themes in need of further attention, both on the theoretical as well as on the empirical level. Since the focus of this volume is on presenting research on recent developments, rather than on theory development per se, this section will introduce key concepts and assumptions that are employed in the empirical analyses. Through a discussion of these key concepts of our critical political economy we seek to show how this perspective can further our understanding of the fundamentally asymmetrical power structures in the EU. Building on a critique of 'mainstream' integration theories, we particularly point towards the transnational nature and inherent contradictions of capitalist restructuring in the EU.

A critical political economy perspective takes as an important point of departure the distinction between problem-solving and critical theory (see the seminal article by Cox, 1981). Rather than perceiving social structures as natural states of affairs, they need to be understood in the context of historically contingent, contradictory and open-ended social relations of production. Although the social relations of production are indeed central to the analysis of the social origins of power in capitalist societies, the role of ideology, ideas and identities is crucial in the (trans)formation of social formations (Van Apeldoorn et al., 2003: 36, 2004a: 152).

From a 'critical realist' perspective – which may be taken as the meta-theoretical grounding of the critical political economy we advance here – we stress the dialectical interplay of structure and agency over time in which agency is never pre-social but always operating within the bounds of given social structures. The latter at the same time depend on individual, collective, strategic or less strategic human agency for their reproduction or transformation (Bhaskar, 1979; for an application of this perspective to EU studies, see Buch-Hansen, 2006). Next to this relational conception of structure and agency, another important 'critical realist' meta-theoretical starting point is the notion that (social) reality is stratified and that therefore we need research strategies that are able to probe at the deeper levels of non-observable yet real structures that account for what we observe empirically (see e.g. Sayer, 1992, for the methodological implications of this). Such an ontological depth is indispensable for realizing the emancipatory potential of critical political economy, as it enables us to separate the necessary from the contingent and uncover the underlying structures and power relations that constrain human freedom but can very well be transformed by (collective) human agency.

Towards a critical understanding of politics in the European Union

Although we do not wish to rehearse an already older debate on the 'nature of the beast' (Risse-Kappen, 1996) – whether the EU is merely an international organization as in the intergovermentalist tradition or whether it represents in fact a novel form of political authority that has for instance been dubbed a 'post-Hobbesian order' (Schmitter, 1996) and even a 'post-modern state' (Caporaso, 1996) – we maintain that the state, which in an era of multi-level governance (Hooghe and Marks, 2001) includes institutional structures of the EU, remains the quintessential arena of contemporary politics. The state is the institutional ensemble through which capitalist class rule needs to be effectuated and legitimated, and through which conflicts arising out of its contradictions mediated. In capitalist economies, and those of the EU are no exceptions to this, the state is indispensable to provide, as Van Apeldoorn and Horn (2007a) argue, the institutional preconditions for markets to arise, develop and be reproduced. The question remains whether in the case of the EU the state is still merely or even primarily national, also supranational or, as Etienne Balibar once suggested, in fact *'neither national nor supranational'*. Balibar added that 'this ambiguity does not slacken but deepens over time' (Balibar, 1991: 16). Without pretending to be able to present a theory of the 'European state', we suggest that Balibar was indeed right and that this points to the fundamentally transnational nature (Van Apeldoorn, 2004a) of the European project, or to what Jessop (2007) has theorized in terms of 'multi-scalar' governance.

In order to come to an understanding of EU–European statehood as a multi-level polity we first need a more abstract conceptualization of 'the state'. A conventional distinction would identify three competing explanatory logics for understanding 'the state'. These notorious 'three Is' include (1) social *interests* or domestic coalitions, (2) *institutions* and the state and (3) dominant *ideas*. Particular accounts usually construct explanatory frameworks by combining individual theories. In fact, there is considerable convergence in the 'actually-employed' explanatory logics – as opposed to self-proclaimed theoretical assumptions – among various Weberian, neo-classical and Marxist or neo-Gramscian perspectives.[2] By discussing individual 'competing' explanations, we develop a conceptual framework that the authors of this volume draw on. Our understanding of the state and of policy-making relies in particular on *strategic–relational* state theory as developed above all by Bob Jessop (1990, 2002, 2007; see also Drahokoupil, 2008a). Developed outside (critical) international political economy, this (neo-) Gramscian approach provides a refined conceptual apparatus, which is not only compatible with the concepts employed within the Amsterdam International Political Economy project (Van Apeldoorn, 2004b), but also allows one to combine the 'three Is' into a coherent understanding of the state in transnational political economy. We develop such a conceptualization by discussing major alternative 'theories of the state'.

Social forces, hegemony and the state

Focusing on distributional consequences of policies around which interests mobilize, *interest-based or coalition approaches* assume that politicians exchange policies for political support. At the same time, dominant social groups are able to exert influence on politicians and bureaucrats through various channels, including provision of material support, fraud, corruption, clientalistic relations and other personal ties. The state is thus understood as an arena through which social struggle is waged. In effect, state strategy is likely to reflect interests and preferences of the dominant coalition. There are traditionally two ways to investigate the influence of social interests. First, the deductive approach, such as that of rational-choice institutionalism, starts from identifying groups that are likely to be favoured by a particular policy (e.g. Frieden and Rogowski, 1996). Yet, this is problematic as there is no guarantee that political beneficiaries are a cause rather than a consequence of policy reform. Second, the inductive approach, such as that of pluralism, instrumental Marxism or the radical tradition in American political science, would analyse particular channels of influence through which coalitions of social actors exert influence (e.g. Miliband, 1969; Domhoff, 1996; Thacker, 2000). This approach, too, is not without problems. Policies can represent social interests in the absence of direct influence. Social structure can operate as a constraint on government action through the 'law of anticipated consequences' (Haggard, 1990). What is more, the structural power may make governments 'wish what the dominant actors wish' (Strange, 1988; Nye, 1990). Thus, we understand the state as a *social relation* that reflects the changing balance of forces in a determinate conjuncture (Poulantzas, 1978; Jessop, 1990). The mechanisms that 'condense' or 'reflect' such a balance include not only direct influence or relational power, but also indirect pressures and constraints, or structural power.

Institutionalist and state-centric theories emphasize that the state elite – the executive branch in particular – enjoys considerable autonomy from societal interests in designing and implementing policies and in organizing political support for them (Evans et al., 1985). Others argue that although social interests may play an important role in the period of institutional reproduction, they are less likely to be important for explaining change, and that particularly during times of economic crisis, state actors often enjoy considerable autonomy vis-à-vis social interests, proactively constructing rather than reflecting societal coalitions.

The issue of the autonomy of state managers – or 'the state' – has been plagued by heavy straw-man making. In fact, however, both Weberian institutionalism and structural Marxism emphasize the autonomy of state managers from societal pressures. The Weberian idea of 'corporate coherence', especially as 'embedded' by Evans (1995) and the Poulantzasian notion of 'class wide rationality', are very similar and refer to the same feature of the bureaucratic, as in Weber, or the capitalist, as in Poulantzas, state: the separation of the political from the economic. This provides state managers with considerable autonomy. Yet the seeming contradiction between this formulation and understanding the state as a social relation can be resolved by insisting on considering state managers as a social force, or as another social interest. We maintain, though, that the very institutional position that gives them the autonomy within the *capitalist state* that is structurally separated and thus dependent on 'the economy' and on seeking social legitimacy (to varying degrees) – structures their interests and provides them with important incentives to ally with other social forces. Most notably, since state actors are dependent economically and politically on the (capitalist) economy, they are structurally dependent on those who control the production process – the respective growth segments in particular. Thus the (capitalist) state has an inherent form-determined bias – or what Jessop (1990) has denoted *strategic selectivity* – that makes it more open to capitalist influences and more likely to be mobilized for capitalist policies. It is also important to note that state personnel by no means can be considered as socially isolated: these spheres – often misleadingly separated as 'state' on the one hand and 'society' on the other – are interlinked or embedded through flows of information, people, money, social ties and common social aspirations and identifications.

Institutionalist theories and the strategic–relational approach claim that institutions are constitutive of interests. Moreover, they provide advantages to some groups in pursuing their political goals while imposing constraints on others. The state as a terrain of social struggle is considerably uneven, which has an independent influence on the balance of forces in society. Institutions will also shape the degree of autonomy from other forces enjoyed by the state managers. State autonomy thus cannot be assumed, but must be investigated and explained, so the degree and nature of state autonomy can be understood as a part of an institutional mediation of the balance of forces in society. This can be summarized by characterizing the state as a *form-determined* social relation (Jessop, 1990). An analysis of public policy thus starts from identifying the 'unequal structure of representation' that links a particular policy instance to the balance of forces in a given conjuncture (Mahon, 1977).[3]

Finally, *ideational perspectives* emphasize the importance of ideas in constituting interests and determining ranges of (imaginable) policy options and goals (e.g. Campbell, 1998; Blyth, 2002). They insist on the importance of experts, professional analysts and international organizations producing and disseminating ideas. While neo-Gramscian and relational perspectives also insist on the discursive constitution of reality, they point out that 'ideas do not float in an endless universe of meaning, but are seen as produced by human agency in the context of social power relations, and as such are also linked with the strategic action of social (class) actors ' (Van Apeldoorn, 2002: 19). Ideas or knowledge are shaped within these power relations.

Ideas are essential for constituting political coalitions. They constitute or define interests of social groups. At the same time, they may also seek to legitimate these interests vis-à-vis other social groups. Thus ideational practice is an important element of constituting social leadership. Gramsci has identified various forms of leadership or dominance that can help to secure a social order and function as mechanisms of social integration. These include rule by force, fraud and corruption (Gramsci, 1971: 80). Hegemony is a form of social leadership of rule based on a combination of consent and coercion, with the former being the primary mechanism and the latter 'always looming in the background' (Gramsci, 1971: 169–70). Strategically, hegemony is contingent on developing a 'hegemonic project' (Jessop, 1983, 1990), or what the Amsterdam Project calls a 'comprehensive concept of control' (Van der Pijl, 1998; Van Apeldoorn, 2004b):

> This involves the mobilization of support behind a concrete, national-popular program of action which asserts a general interest in the pursuit of objectives that explicitly or implicitly advance the long-term interests of the hegemonic class (fraction) and which also privileges particular 'economic-corporate' interests compatible with this programme. Conversely, those particular interests that are inconsistent with the project are deemed immoral and/or irrational and, in so far as they are still pursued by groups outside the consensus, they are also liable to sanction.
>
> (Jessop, 1990: 208)

Thus, hegemony includes not only presenting the interests of the hegemonic group as 'the general interest', but also incorporating other (opposing) interests into the hegemonic world view and thus transcending the narrow self-interests of the leading group. In this way, various discourses are articulated into a single hegemonic discourse and some of the social antagonisms are neutralized (Laclau and Mouffe, 1985). The related notion of a power bloc refers to a relatively stable coalition of forces that is brought together by a hegemonic project. Its unity depends on sacrifice of some immediate interests of at least some of its members and on members' commitment to a common world outlook (Jessop, 1990). However stable, a power bloc is not a static coalition, but rather a dynamic process of coalition building that brings together various actors through promoting the hegemonic project in particular places and times.

Ideas, to be effective, have to articulate other (material) elements of social practice. Hegemonic projects, to be successful, need to be organically related to material and ideational constraints and opportunities of the conjuncture. Hegemony does not work as an imposition or negotiation of a consensus. It is a relational moment forging a field of force that shapes social relations in a way that exerts pressures and set limits on achievable social forms. This field of force, or historic bloc (Gramsci, 1971: 366), not only shapes the production of ideas, but also makes some ideas and projects more 'comprehensive' and appealing than others (Williams, 1977; Roseberry, 1994; Kalb, 1997; Smith, 2004a).

In the field of economic policy, to become hegemonic a political project must articulate a feasible 'accumulation strategy'. Jessop summarizes the links between the hegemonic project and accumulation strategy as follows:

> [T]he collective interests of capital are not reducible to the various interests that individual capitals happen to have in common. Far from these collective interests comprising the lowest common denominator of shared interests in the reproduction of the general external conditions of the circuit of capital (such as money and law), they are not wholly pre-given and must be articulated in, and through, specific accumulation strategies which establish a *contingent* community of interest among particular capitals.
>
> (1990: 159, emphasis original)

State actors and the state as a site of social struggles have a major role in formulating and implementing hegemonic projects and accumulation strategies and thus in reshaping the balance of interests in society. The state does not only enjoy considerable autonomy from social interests, but it is also a site where collectively binding decisions are made. Neo-Gramscian approaches have emphasized the role of 'organic intellectuals' (see the chapter by Horn in this volume) and 'cadres' (Van der Pijl, 1998), located both within and beyond the state apparatus, in formulating hegemonic projects, shaping social interests and reworking the 'common sense'. Both intellectuals and state actors constitute autonomous social groups. Yet the structural imperative to respect material constraints in formulating strategies, *inter alia*, links them to other social (class) forces.

In sum, state strategies are produced by social forces within the state in the context of a social struggle for hegemony. Ideas, institutions (most notably, state form) and the relations of production are constitutive of social forces and mediate their relative power and ability to influence state strategies. The notion of a hegemonic project, or of a comprehensive concept of control, denotes a temporary synthesis generated by an ascendant trend in the economy and articulated by set of social forces operating in the context of the state (or a number of states) – translating their class-bound perspective into a general (comprehensive) programme for society as a whole.

Beyond methodological nationalism: towards a scalar political economy of transnational processes

By focusing on 'the transnational' the Amsterdam Project of transnational historical materialism contributes to a wide choir of voices criticizing the deeply entrenched methodological nationalism of mainstream social sciences, international political economy in particular (see Van Apeldoorn, 2004a). We insist that it is impossible to distinguish between 'the local' and 'the transnational' – or 'internal' and 'external' factors – in the real world. On the level of concrete–complex, transnational is local and local is also transnational:

> The local turns out not only to be influenced by the transnational but to be a specific site of the materialization of transnational processes. That is to say, the local is not only transnational, but also, there is no transnational that does not have specific and particular local enactments.
>
> (Glick Schiller, 2006: 9)

In turn, 'the external' is always also internal. Thus, the transnational actors are not external to states as often understood by neo-realist international relations, rather these 'actors by definition operate simultaneously inside different 'national states' rather than 'confronting' those states from the outside' (Van Apeldoorn, 2004a: 146). Yet the concepts of transnational–domestic/local and internal–external cannot be avoided; instead, a different meaning should be forged for them.

We approach this problem from the strategic–relational perspective in the same way as the structure–agency dichotomy that we already discussed above. From the strategic–relational perspective, neither structure–agency, nor local–transnational (nor internal–external) exist in themselves; instead, they constitute through their relational interaction. Thus, structure–agency and the internal–external should be understood relationally to the object of analysis both in space and time. The analysis should thus focus on the dialectical interplay of structure–agency or internal–external factors in real contexts of social and political interaction. In a similar way to the agency–structure dilemma, the local–internal can be brought into the transnational–external and the transnational–external can be brought into local–internal. The former corresponds to uploading and co-optation of locally produced practices and discourses, the latter to different theories of translation, mediation and internalization of transnational influences. Yet, in order to give a proper meaning to local–transnational, internal–external on the level of the concrete-complex, it is necessary to go further so that the distinctions will dissolve. Thus, the transnational–local distinction should be dissolved into locally enacted transnational environment and transnationally constituted local action (see Drahokoupil, 2008a).

Along these lines, the national case studies in this volume study developments on the national level as domestic articulations of transnational processes. At the same time, they underscore the importance of the national scale in producing particular outcomes.

Social forces, hegemonic projects and the state in the EU

Applying our critical political economy more explicitly to the European arena, we understand neoliberal European governance as a political project (not necessarily a hegemonic one), which we comprehend as an integrated set of 'initiatives and propositions that, as pragmatic responses to concrete national and European problems, conceptually and strategically further the process of socio-economic, societal and institutional restructuring' (Bieling and Steinhilber, 2002: 41, our translation). Within Europe it is no longer the national states that exclusively provide the regulatory framework that allows the capitalist market economy to function – rather, increasingly, a key role here is played by the EU and by the process of European integration. In analysing this role we adopt a transnational perspective as outlined above in which the institutional intergovernmental and supranational governance structures of the European multi-level polity are seen as embedded within a transnational political economy and a transnational civil society (see also Van Apeldoorn et al., 2003). Such a political project reflects the agency of a dominant set of *transnational* social and political forces. Concretely, a political project is articulated ideologically through the discursive and political practices of a multitude of (transnational) actors, such as expert groups, associations, lobby groups, think tanks, private forums and planning groups. Through the transnational networks constituted by these actors (Nölke, 2003) certain interests are brought to the fore and come to underpin the EU's policy discourse and shape the content of the regulatory framework it seeks to put in place. Only through an understanding of how the EU polity as a form of state (Cox and Sinclair, 1996) – in its integral relationship between civil society and the state apparatus – is *also* structured and delimited through the very institutional configuration of the polity can the particular manifestation of policies and political strategies be analysed.

From this perspective, then, the European Commission, although indeed an important supranational public actor, whose role as policy-entrepreneur is also underlined by several of the studies collected in this volume, must not be interpreted as an autonomous actor in the way some 'supranationalist' accounts of European integration tend to do (e.g. Stone Sweet and Sandholtz, 1998). Rather, the Commission can arguably be viewed as a key public actor within the EU as a 'multilevel state formation' (Jessop, 2002: 205), and as such embedded in a particular configuration of transnational social forces, and a concomitant (potentially hegemonic) construction and articulation of interests. In its institutional set-up, as well as its practices, the Commission is considerably autonomous from political accountability to broader societal interests; at the same time it constitutes a crucial site for the realization of political projects driven by social forces in the struggle for hegemony in the European Union.

In the current European Union as a system of asymmetric socio-economic governance establishing a 'free space for capital' (Van der Pijl, 2006a: 32), it is in particular those interests bound up with the most transnationally mobile fractions of capital that are privileged (see also Van Apeldoorn, 2002). Put in more structural terms, as a 'multi-level state' the EU can be seen as a condensation of transnational social forces and possessing its own *strategic selectivity*, one that heavily favours the interests of transnationally mobile capital over other interests, including that of labour (see Van Apeldoorn, 2002: Chapter 1; Bieler, 2005b). At the same time this emphasis on the structural primacy of transnational capital must not be taken to imply that political projects, notwithstanding their presentation as coherent programmes, are free from contradictions and therefore uncontested. As indicated, hegemony in a Gramscian sense is in fact never complete, and subordinate groups and classes may always struggle to redefine the terms of the dominant discourse and transform underlying social practices. It is through the analysis of social and political struggle, as well as the compromises necessary to sustain hegemonic projects, that the contours of rival political projects become most clear.

Contesting the neoliberal project: what role and prospect for resistance?

A central focus of our critical political economy perspective is the emphasis on the social struggle underlying the political project of neoliberal European integration. Rejecting pluralist notions of agency on the European level (see Van Apeldoorn et al., 2003: 27–8), we argue that, in order to analyse the potential for contestation of and resistance to socio-economic restructuring, the position and agency of subaltern classes in European governance have to be seen from a perspective that acknowledges the fundamental power asymmetries in the EU. Most critical political economy studies of European integration processes have so far focused on the role of transnational capital (fractions) and the emergence, consolidation and reproduction of hegemonic discourses and 'concepts of control'. This volume seeks to contribute to an understanding of how these hegemonic discourses are actually maintained and disseminated with the support of subaltern classes. At the same time, as for instance the chapter by Bieler points out, it is crucial to look at the agency of subaltern classes in order to be able to conceptualize resistance to and contestation of neoliberal restructuring. Here we follow Cox in emphasizing the emancipatory potential of a critical political economy perspective (Cox, 1981). As Drainville has argued, 'as a political reality, neoliberalism is *both* a broad strategy of restructuring *and* a succession of negotiated settlements, of concessions to the rigidities and dynamics of structures, as well as the political possibilities of the moment' (1994: 166, emphasis in original). This understanding of neoliberalism opens up political space for subaltern classes to contest and challenge neoliberal governance, and engenders a research perspective that takes into account the agency of resistance.

Plan of the book

This book is divided into four parts. The first part focuses on the nature, contradictions and limits of the European neoliberal project at a more general level. In the first chapter, Bastiaan van Apeldoorn analyses the contradictions and limits of what he calls the project of 'embedded neoliberalism', which advances neoliberal marketization at the *supranational* level yet, in seeking hegemony, in the first instance retains a limited embeddedness at the *national* level. However, given this asymmetry within multi-level European governance, the national embeddedness is in effect increasingly hollowed out, thus revealing fundamental contradictions within embedded neoliberalism that in turn play a crucial role in engendering Europe's current multi-level legitimacy crisis. Magnus Ryner then critically examines an important part of the ideological and discursive underpinnings of current European socio-economic governance through a critique of an academic discourse on (the necessity) of welfare state reform on the part of what he calls the 'New Malthusians'. Ryner argues that this social scientific discourse serves a key ideological function in negatively legitimating European order through naturalizing and objectifying social relations, and thus making neoliberal restructuring appear inevitable and lacking a real alternative. In contrast to the New Malthusians' account, Ryner emphasizes the causal importance of EMU and of global restructuring – understood as transitive phenomena and the outcome of a *politics* serving powerful interests – with respect to welfare state retrenchment within the European political economy. The chapter by Alan Cafruny addresses the important global geopolitical dimension of the European neoliberal project, arguing in particular that we have to understand the latter in relation to Europe's persistent subordination to US 'minimal hegemony'. Cafruny here discusses the role of US military power in the development and consolidation of neoliberalism in Europe, analysing in particular the role of NATO expansion of and of the latter's wars over ex-Yugoslavia. Assessing the chances of a European challenge, he concludes that in spite of the current travails of the US empire, economically the EU's autonomy continues to be constrained as a result of its subordinate participation within a neoliberal US-dominated financial order, and that geopolitically the EU has been unable to develop a regional security structure that might underwrite alternatives to Atlanticism and neoliberalism.

In the second part of the book, in-depth discussions of particular instances of neoliberal integration illustrate recent developments and inherent contradictions of this political project. Hans-Jürgen Bieling and Johannes Jäger analyse the process of Basel II banking regulation, in particular the role of the European Union therein. Moving beyond the perception that the EU is merely a passive force in global financial deregulation, Bieling and Jäger identify the driving forces and conflicts in the negotiation and implementation processes of Basel II. The contribution by Sandy Hager analyses the EU's Lisbon Agenda and its relation to changing conceptions of social citizenship. The central argument advanced is that the emergence of a 'neoliberal communitarian' citizenship model under Lisbon contradicts claims made by supportive social and political forces, as well as some academics, that the Lisbon Agenda marks a positive 'turning point' for EU-level social citizenship. In contrast, Hager demonstrates how the Lisbon Agenda is part and parcel of a broader shift away from the Keynesian Welfare State towards a Schumpeterian Workfare Regime both at the member state and EU-levels of socio-economic governance, carrying important implications in terms of the long-term legitimacy and sustainability of the overall EU project. Engaging with Gramsci's concept of the 'organic intellectuals', Laura Horn then discusses the role of transnational expert groups in corporate governance regulation in the EU. Focusing on the work of the High Level Group of Company Law Experts, she illustrates how this particular group of experts came to have such a significant impact on corporate governance regulation, and how their policy recommendations and their function are organically linked to the neoliberal marketization project.

The third part will examine the widening of European governance, in particular analysing the transnational politics of capitalist transformation in Central and Eastern Europe as well as the implications of that restructuring for the overall European project. Arjan Vliegenthart and Henk Overbeek analyse the political struggles over regulating taxation and tax competition on the European level. In particular, they focus on the impact of Eastern enlargement on corporate tax reforms in individual countries and attempts at corporate tax regulation in the EU. They identify an emerging configuration of social forces within the EU, the Euro-liberal bloc, which aimed to use the enlarged European economic space to defend and develop an integrated

European technological-industrial complex, which should ultimately be able to compete with the USA. Enlargement has not only intensified already existing competitive pressures towards the lowering of corporate and income taxes, but also worked to the advantage of a competing, neoliberal, US-oriented camp. At the same time, Vliegenthart and Overbeek identify social contradictions that may partially reverse some of these trends and increasing divergence within Central and Eastern Europe in terms of the accumulation model that is being developed. Jan Drahokoupil's chapter emphasises the importance of domestic – yet transnationally constituted – actors in mediating and conditioning transnational processes and producing particular outcomes, including the expansion and transformation of the neoliberal project. After a critical engagement with neo-Gramscian scholarship on the transition process and state internationalization in Central and Eastern Europe, he analyses the emergence of competition strategies in the region and identifies political, social and institutional support of the competition state. In particular, he argues that transnational power blocs organized around a core social group, the comprador service sector, constitute political underpinning of the competition state. Dorothee Bohle investigates the dynamics and contradictions of the increasing locational competition in the enlarged EU. She argues that Eastern enlargement has reinforced regime competition within the EU and allowed transnational corporations to expand their room for manoeuvre. The fiercest locational competition is however not between East and West, but between the four Visegrád countries. Arguing that the Visegrád countries are the weakest and most vulnerable elements in the embedded neoliberal European constellation, Bohle identifies certain social and institutional contradictions of the variety of competition strategies pursued in Central and Eastern Europe.

The fourth and final part contains two chapters that each – focusing respectively on the national and the transnational level – deal with different manifestations of the rising contestation of, and in some cases outright resistance to, neoliberal European governance. The chapter by Bastiaan van Apeldoorn applies his analysis of the nature, contradictions and limits of embedded neoliberalism as developed in the first chapter to the national level by taking the political economy of the Netherlands as a case study. Examining the political implications of the now manifest limits of the Dutch 'national competitiveness strategy', the chapter focuses on the political economy of the 'No' vote in the Dutch referendum, and argues that the Dutch rejection of the constitution can only be understood in the context of the output failure of embedded neoliberalism. The final chapter by Andreas Bieler even more explicitly focuses on the potential for contestation and resistance to neoliberal restructuring by analysing the role of organized labour within European governance. Looking at whether European trade union organizations have developed into independent transnational actors, his empirical analysis shows that there is indeed an increasingly co-ordinated response to neoliberal restructuring on the European level. Bieler emphasizes the role of trade unions in challenging neoliberal policies at the European level, while at the same time pointing towards the heterogeneity of labour, and the struggle between established and more radical trade unions.

Notes

1. For a critique of the mainstream approaches that focus either mainly on institutional form or explain the content from a pluralist model that simply ignores the fundamental power asymmetries inherent in capitalist social relations, see Van Apeldoorn et al., 2003.
2. These approaches do not correspond to the stylized distinction among ideational, interest-based and institution-oriented explanations. For instance, both rational choice theory and instrumental Marxism employ the interest group logic.
3. Institutionalists have claimed that state autonomy and capacity is dependent on organizational resources available to state managers, on the coherence of state apparatus in particular (e.g. Haggard, 1990). We argue, along with Jessop (1990), that the coherence of the state apparatus is an emergent phenomenon to be explained. To achieve such coherence, state managers must articulate the complex, incoherent and often contradictory ensemble of state institutions by developing a 'state project', which may give some operational unity to the state as an apparatus. As lack of coherence and unity of interest within a state apparatus is a norm, there may be competing state projects attempting to impose contradictory institutional unities.

Part I The Nature and Limits of the European Neoliberal Project

1
The Contradictions of 'Embedded Neoliberalism' and Europe's Multi-level Legitimacy Crisis: The European Project and its Limits

Bastiaan van Apeldoorn

Introduction

The sudden and unexpected death that the European Constitution met in French and Dutch voting booths in the late spring of 2005, and the post-referendum blues that followed it, brought into the open a legitimacy crisis of the European project that had been looming for years, and that arguably will now deepen with the Irish rejection of the Lisbon reform treaty that was intended to replace the failed Constitution. What is in fact a *multi-level* legitimacy crisis – inasmuch as national states find it equally hard to maintain the legitimacy of their policy output and national governments often blame Europe in the process[1] – has called into question the coherence and foundations of the European integration process as a political and socio-economic *project*, which has been guiding the restructuring of state–society relations within Europe's transnational political economy over the past decades.

Next to the political crisis besetting European governance, the European economy has also been rather stagnant since the turn of the millennium – with the more recent cyclical upswing now being threatened again by the rapidly unfolding global credit crisis. The ambitious goal to become the 'most competitive' economy in the world by 2010, set at the Lisbon summit of March 2000 (European Council, 2000), has turned out to be illusory. Arguably, the crisis of European governance and the disappointing (socio-)economic performance of recent years are related inasmuch both are signs of, as well as feed into, a weakening of the European project, both internally, vis-à-vis Europe's populations, and externally, within the global political economy. As argued in the introduction to this volume, the European project in its current form is reaching its limits. A central claim put forward in this chapter is that we can only understand the currently manifest political limits to the European integration project in light of the fundamental contradictions inherent in the *socio-economic content* and related substantive output of European governance.

As I have argued elsewhere (Van Apeldoorn, 2001, 2002) this content may be understood in terms of what I have called 'embedded neoliberalism', reflecting a *hegemonic project* or what we could also call a *comprehensive concept of control* articulated and propagated by – and reflecting as well as mediating the interests of – social and political forces bound up with transnational European capital (see the introduction to this volume for an elaboration of these concepts). Embedded neoliberalism is here seen as a *hegemonic* project inasmuch as it seeks to advance neoliberalism through a strategy of incorporating, and ideologically neutralizing, rival projects.

Analysing the nature of this embedded neoliberal project – focusing in particular on its inherent contradictions and the implications of those contradictions in terms of sustaining the project's necessary levels of mass legitimacy – the main purpose of this chapter is thus to come to an understanding of current neoliberal European governance, and of its limits. This chapter is divided into two main parts. The first analyses embedded neoliberalism as a project in which the freedom of capital and the primacy of markets is ideologically articulated with the subordinate interests of productive capital as well as of organized labour, and seeks to demonstrate how this hegemonic project is expressed in current European Union (EU) socio-economic governance. What made this project hegemonic is also what now lies at the origin of its potential unravelling: the attempt to articulate discursively the goals of 'competitiveness' – defined in neoliberal terms – and 'social cohesion', while in practice promoting the first at the EU level and leaving the latter the responsibility of the Member States. The embeddedness of embedded neoliberalism is thus to be found primarily at the national level while supranational marketization at the same time continues to hollow out that embeddedness. This, then, is at the core of the contradictions of the embedded neoliberal European project.

These contradictions, their class nature and their political implications will be analysed in the second part. As in recent years European governance has become even more thoroughly neoliberal, the incompatibility of the Polanyian principles of 'economic liberalism' and 'social protection' (Polanyi, 1957: 132) have also come more to the fore. In addition, deepening capital market integration and a concomitant project of a marketization of corporate control also highlight the potential contradictions between productive capital and money capital.[2] Examining some of the implications of these contradictions, I argue that they reveal the political limits of the current European project, as they have become manifest in an unfolding multi-level legitimacy crisis and a growing contestation of neoliberal governance. The chapter ends by concluding that we might well be witnessing the unmaking of embedded neoliberalism. Given especially the lack of any coherent alternative on the horizon, however, this unmaking for the moment does not seem to imply an end to European neoliberal governance as such but rather merely a deepening of its political crisis.

Embedded neoliberalism as a transnational hegemonic project

The origins of embedded neoliberalism lie in the twin crises of European capitalism (Boltho, 1982) and of the European integration project. Both reached a new low point in the early 1980s. The subsequent relaunching of the integration process through the internal market programme and the Single European Act (SEA) can be seen as a supranational response to this crisis, but one that revolved around and was mediated through three contending responses or transnational strategic projects. As argued extensively elsewhere (see Van Apeldoorn, 2002), three such rival projects can be identified for the period of the second half of the 1980s and into the first half of the 1990s.

All three projects favoured a relaunching of Europe through a completion of the internal market, but they fundamentally differed on *what kind* of European market it was to be. In the *neo-mercantilist conception*, the project of European integration was first of all conceived as one of creating a big home market – supported by an active industrial policy if necessary protected by European tariff walls –in which 'European champions' would be able to confront successfully the American and Japanese competition. The *neoliberal project*, on the other hand, emphasized the free market aspects of the internal market, a free market that should be open to and fully integrated into the emerging global economy. In contrast, the *social democratic project* – as in particular promoted by the then Commission President Jacques Delors (see Delors, 1992; Ross, 1995) – sought to protect and consolidate the 'European social model' in a supranational regulatory framework.

The first two strategies, those of neoliberalism and neo-mercantilism, have ultimately been most dominant, and can be interpreted as contending strategies on the part of rival groups or 'fractions' within the ranks of Europe's transnational capitalist class. Throughout the 1980s and into the 1990s, the main dividing line within this capitalist elite was between on the one hand a 'globalist' fraction consisting of Europe's most globalized firms – including global capital market actors, that is, financial capital – and, on the other hand, a 'Europeanist' fraction made up by large industrial enterprises primarily serving the European market. The perspective of the former has tended towards neoliberalism, whereas the latter came to promote the neo-mercantilist project.

Although they aspired to become more global, in the 1980s many of Europe's large industrial firms were still more *regional* transnational corporations (TNCs), and these firms dominated Europe's emerging transnational corporations. A major platform for the agency of this class was and is the European Round Table of Industrialists (ERT), founded in 1983. Back then dominated by the neo-mercantilist wing of European big business, the ERT promoted a defensive regionalism, the heart of which was the promotion of a big European home market (see e.g. ERT, 1983, and for a more elaborate account Van Apeldoorn, 2002: Chapter 4). This home market turned into a big success inasmuch as Europe 1992 was both successfully launched and successfully implemented, an achievement for which the ERT could take much of the credit (Cowles, 1995; Fielder, 1997, 2000; Van Apeldoorn, 2000; Balanyá et al., 2003). But the internal market that was created on the basis of the Commission's White Paper of 1985 in many ways did not turn out to be the kind of relatively protected home market that many of the early Roundtable members (of the Europeanist fraction) had envisaged. In fact, the way the internal market programme was implemented only led to a further opening up of Europe's national economies to the global economy (Hanson, 1998). It is hence that the regionalization of the European economy, in the sense of the further integration of its national economic systems, went hand in hand with a further globalization of the European region and the subordination of its economy to global and to a large extent US-centred forces (see Chapter 3 by Alan Cafruny in this volume, and Cafruny and Ryner, 2007a, 2007b). In the transnational struggle over Europe's 'extended relaunch' (Holman, 1992) we can thus observe the rise of a neoliberal concept of control. This struggle had also been fought out within the ranks of Europe's transnational capitalist class in which the Europeanist fraction was slowly losing its dominant position and moreover itself gradually abandoned its earlier neo-mercantilist perspective.[3]

Yet, the neoliberalism that triumphed was not the orthodox neoliberalism that, at least as an ideological project, had become hegemonic in the Anglo-Saxon capitalist heartland, but rather a more continental European-style neoliberalism that became articulated with a 'modernised' social democratic discourse (as in the 'Third Way' discourse of the 1990s, see Ryner, 2002, and Hager and my Chapter 5 in this volume), while also seeking to address the concerns of that part of European capital in need of a more pro-active, though not necessarily protectionist, role of the state. What in fact developed in the 1990s was a synthesis in which neoliberalism attained its hegemony through incorporating elements of the two contending projects, integrating them in such a way that the antagonism of these rival projects was effectively neutralized and the primacy of the neoliberal objective of free markets and free enterprise secured.

I have denoted this synthesis 'embedded neoliberalism' (Van Apeldoorn, 2002: Chapter 5). To some this concept may seem to be a contradiction in terms inasmuch as neoliberalism is a disembedding force (e.g. Holman, 2004a). Indeed it is, and as such embedded neoliberalism must be seen as inherently contradictory, but at the time also as offering the kind of temporary stabilization of these contradictions in such a way that at least at the elite level hegemony could be secured within Europe's transnational political economy. Drawing on Polanyi (1957), embeddedness here refers to the role of the state in sustaining and reproducing markets by in effect protecting society from the destructive effects of the self-regulating market. The term 'embedded' in embedded neoliberalism thus refers to what Polanyi (1957: 132) called the *principle of social protection* 'aiming at the conservation of man and nature as well as productive organization' whereas neoliberalism is associated with the *principle of economic liberalism* 'aiming at the establishment of a self-regulating market'. It is these two opposing principles that embedded neoliberalism thus seeks to combine but it does so, as I will argue below, in a way that in the end fully subordinates the principle of social protection to that of economic liberalism.[4]

Although embedded neoliberalism is essentially neoliberal inasmuch as it constitutes a political project aimed at the restoration and expansion of capitalist class power (Harvey, 2005) through an ideological commitment to the freedom of market exchange and to the absolute exercise of capitalist property rights, it was particularly within the European context that the new neoliberal policy paradigm had to adjust to the persisting traditions of corporatist industrial relations ('social partnership'); social and industrial protection offered by an often interventionist state, and other elements of 'embeddedness'. Hence, the 'embedded' component of embedded neoliberalism addresses the concerns of both the former neo-mercantilists as well as those of the European labour movement and social-democratic political forces.

In contrast to the UK, where neoliberalism was constructed on the *ruins* of corporate liberalism (Van der Pijl, 2006a: 266), the configuration of social forces in *continental* Europe in the 1990s was such that not only organized labour was still *relatively* strong (even if severely battered by three deep recessions and concomitant waves of corporate restructuring since the 1970s), but also that there remained a clearly identifiable, if weakening *productive capital* orientation within the ranks of the European capitalist class.[5] Although the ongoing financialization of capitalism also tends to make a money capital perspective increasingly dominant even among the ranks of European industrial capital (more on this below), at least for a part of that industrial capital (in particular its former Europeanist fraction) still a more pure neoliberalism would also undermine their long-term accumulation prospects inasmuch as policies necessary to enable growth and investment (in productive and technological development), as well as policies to guarantee labour acquiescence, would then tend to remain insufficiently developed. Embedded neoliberalism is the dominant strategic and ideological outlook of Europe's transnational capitalist elite as it has moved away from neomercantilism and towards neoliberalism, but without adopting a pure *laissez-faire* perspective. Embedded neoliberalism is at the same time the outcome of the transnational struggle between the three rival elite projects identified above, and represents a strategy of incorporation on the part of the neoliberal project, neutralizing the opposition from the rival projects.

Thus, the 'embedded' component of embedded neoliberalism addresses the concerns of the former neo-mercantilists as well as those of the European labour movement and social-democratic political forces, but these concerns are in the end subordinated to what has become the overriding objective of 'competitiveness' defined in neoliberal terms of market liberalization and market discipline. Indeed, what can be called a *neoliberal competitiveness discourse* informing EU socio-economic governance in the 1990s in fact became a linchpin in the discursive articulation of the embedded neoliberal hegemonic project. A key actor in articulating and promoting this discourse has been the ERT (see Van Apeldoorn, 2002: 171–8, 2003). Below I argue that the effective subordination of the principle of social protection to that of economic liberalism within the embedded neoliberal concept of control, and therefore the primacy of the disembedding force of neoliberal restructuring, must be understood with reference to the fundamentally asymmetric nature of European governance as it evolved since the 1992 Maastricht Treaty.

Embedded neoliberalism as asymmetric European socio-economic governance

The social purpose of European multi-level governance is revealed if we see how European integration in the past decades has created a *supranational* internal market (and later a monetary union), thus transferring 'policies promoting market efficiencies' to the European level, whereas policies 'promoting social protection and equality' have remained at the *national* level (Scharpf, 2002: 665; see also Scharpf, 1999; Holman, 2004a). As Fritz Scharpf argues, this asymmetry is in fact enshrined in Europe's 'economic constitution' through the doctrines of 'direct effect' and 'supremacy' (Scharpf, 1999, 2002). Within this setting, national states' capacity for restraining the market is subsequently undermined through the economic mechanism of regulatory competition, the competition in order to attract or retain transnationally mobile capital (Streeck, 1996, 1998; Scharpf, 1999, 2002). Adding much to these pressures of policy competition within the single market is the 'disciplinary neoliberalism' (Gill, 1998) of the Economic and Monetary Union (EMU), in particular the monetarism of the European Central Bank (ECB) and the fiscal policy constraints of the Stability and Growth Pact (SGP).

Within these conditions of European asymmetric multi-level governance, socio-economic policy-making is structurally biased towards policies of neoliberal restructuring. Following Bob Jessop (1990, see also the introduction to this volume), we may call this the neoliberal *strategic selectivity* of the current EU as 'a multilevel state formation' (Jessop, 2002: 205). As Scharpf contends: '[I]n principle, the only national options which remain freely available under European law are supply-side strategies involving lower tax burdens, further deregulation and flexibilization of employment conditions, increasing wage differentiation and welfare cut-backs' (2002: 649). Indeed, we may argue, and as I will show for the case of the Netherlands in Chapter 5 of this volume, that the asymmetric governance of the embedded neo-liberal European order makes states adopt supply-side oriented *national competitiveness strategies*, which, rather than offering any shelter from the discipline of the European market, promote a thorough neoliberal socio-economic restructuring. As Becker (2005: 1096) has noted, such strategies tend to produce a kind of 'rat-race economic nationalism' where each Member State seeks to out compete the other by providing the better conditions to mobile capital. Although taking place to varying degrees and in various forms across Europe's 'national models of capitalism' (Hall and Soskice, 2001a), a number of studies (see, e.g. Streeck, 1997; Ryner, 2003; 2007b; Hay, 2004; Martin and Ross, 2004; Becker and Schwartz, 2005) show quite unequivocally that there is a 'common trajectory' (Hay 2004) of neoliberal restructuring in which national welfare states and national policies of social protection have since the 1980s been subject to significant retrenchment, resulting in a recommodification undermining the social purpose of what was once the Keynesian Welfare State (see also Chapter 2, by Magnus Ryner, in this volume). It is only in light of embedded neoliberalism as a *transnational* hegemonic project that we can make sense of this common trajectory.

In sum, then, embedded neoliberalism is an essentially neoliberal project inasmuch as it seeks to organize 'the EU along the lines of the Lockean heartland: a free space for capital, with separate state jurisdictions keeping political sovereignty and democracy away from the larger structure' (Van der Pijl, 2006a: 266). At the level of EU governance, the core of this neoliberal programme is constituted by the political project of marketization, which aims at 'bringing about [and maintaining] the institutional (regulatory) pre-conditions [such as property rights; the free operation of the price mechanism and equal rules of exchange] for markets to arise and develop, thereby extending the market mechanism to new areas of social life' (Van Apeldoorn and Horn, 2007a: 5). At the EU level, then, and notwithstanding some limited 'flanking policies' such as a rather timid industrial policy aimed to placate in particular European productive capital and a mildly redistributive regional policy, the 'embeddedness' of 'embedded neoliberalism' is more symbolic than substantive. At the national level, on the other hand, embeddedness is indeed more substantive but the catch here is that as the process of market liberalization at the European level deepens, the limited remaining embeddedness at the national level is further eroded. This, then, constitutes an inherent contradiction in embedded neoliberalism.

It is this contradiction, emerging out of the asymmetry of European governance, that the so-called Lisbon strategy was supposed to tackle. Below, however, I will argue that in fact the Lisbon strategy has only reaffirmed this contradiction (and asymmetry) as it expresses the embedded neoliberal concept of control *par excellence*, both in form and content (for a similar argument but one that focuses specifically on Lisbon's concept of citizenship, see the contribution by Sandy Hager to this volume, Chapter 5). An analysis of the Lisbon programme, being at the core of EU socio-economic governance since the turn of the millennium, will therefore elucidate what embedded neoliberalism as a hegemonic project for European order has meant in practice.

The 'hegemonic moment' of embedded neoliberalism: the discursive articulation of competitiveness and social cohesion in the Lisbon strategy

Reflecting the rise of embedded neoliberalism, the Lisbon Agenda on the one hand is clearly steeped in the neoliberal competitiveness discourse, while on the other hand also contains elements addressing concerns of the former neo-mercantilist wing of the European capitalist elite as well as of transnational social-democratic forces. However, these concerns are incorporated in such a way that they remain subordinate to the overriding goal of competitiveness defined in a neoliberal way.

The original Lisbon strategy as outlined in the Presidency Conclusions from the 2000 summit calls for a series of economic and social 'reforms', which are deemed necessary in the context of the 'quantum shift resulting from globalisation and the challenges of a new knowledge-driven economy' with which the EU is confronted (European Council, 2000: 1). Discursively linking the exigencies of globalization to the notion of a knowledge economy investing in the latter is seen as a way to strengthen the position of the European economy vis-à-vis global competition. The proposed reforms are, in the words of the European Council, 'part of a positive strategy which combines competitiveness and social cohesion' (European Council, 2000: 2). It is this discursive articulation of the goals of competitiveness and social cohesion that constitutes the ideological core of Lisbon and is also reflected in the EU's 'new strategic goal . . . to become the most competitive and dynamic knowledge-based economy in the world, capable of sustainable economic growth with more and better jobs and greater social cohesion' (European Council, 2000: 2).

On the one hand, the policy discourse in which the Lisbon strategy has been couched clearly appeals to a notion of European distinctiveness vis-à-vis Asia and especially the USA, rejecting the 'unregulated' capitalism of the latter and ideologically clinging on to some notion of a European social model.[6] On the other hand, this strategy does imply, as then Commissioner for Social Affairs, Pádraig Flynn, once put it, that in order to preserve it, the 'European social model' needs to be adapted (*Agence Europe*, 1995: 13). In the words of the High Level Group on the Lisbon strategy (chaired by former Dutch prime minister Wim Kok), it needs to be adapted through a series of structural reforms aimed at *inter alia* 'completing the single market and opening up hitherto sheltered and protected sectors . . . to improve the climate for enterprise and business [and] to secure more flexibility and adaptability in the labour market' (High Level Group Chaired by Wim Kok, 2004: 8). Thus 'social cohesion' is equated with what is called 'modernising the European Social Model' (European Council, 2000: 8), which above all entails the adaptation of workers 'for living and training in the knowledge society', involving among others enhancing 'employability' and the acquisition of new skills as part of 'life-long learning', which should become 'a basic component of the European social model' (European Council, 2000: 8, 10).[7]

The Lisbon Agenda thus tends to define 'the social' mainly in terms of the adaptability of the labour force to the exigencies of competitiveness in a globalized world economy. Although adhering to the notion that labour market flexibility can and should be combined with social security the latter is made dependent on the former. As Sandy Hager also argues in this volume, this reflects the ideology of the 'Schumpeterian Workfare State' (Jessop, 2002), informed by the notion that work is the best way to prevent social exclusion and maintain social cohesion, *and* that a re-commodification strategy is the best way to get people back to work. Combining competitiveness and social cohesion thus involves a shift from the 'old' idea of supranational market-*correcting* regulation (as advanced by the Delorist social democratic project) towards a market-*enabling* strategy (see also Ferrera et al., 2000). The marketization aspect of Lisbon furthermore does not only refer to the labour market but also to services, and most, crucially of all, to capital markets. Indeed, financial market integration was considered by the then Internal Market Commissioner Bolkestein (2000) to be at 'the core of the Lisbon strategy'.

In sum, at the heart of Lisbon we find an articulation of neoliberal competitiveness with concerns of the transnational social democratic projects in ways that effectively subordinate the latter to the former. However, Lisbon at the same time also reflects the incorporation of the neo-mercantilist project. This is most clearly reflected in the ways the Lisbon strategy, as part of its proclaimed goal of promoting the transition to a knowledge-based economy, emphasizes the need for the creation of a 'European Area of Research and Innovation', stimulating in particular R&D within the ICT-sector, including the allocation of some public money through the European Investment Bank. In this context we must note the ideological overlap between the social-democratic and neo-mercantilist projects inasmuch as they both tended, for different reasons and in different ways, to reject the pure *laissez-faire* of economic liberalism in favour of Polanyi's principle of social protection, that is, they were both aimed at the conservation of productive forces (Polanyi, 1957: 132). However, the social protection that the Lisbon Agenda offers is largely symbolic, and what is not merely symbolic has been rendered compatible with, indeed supportive of, neoliberal market liberalization –reflecting the effective neutralization of the neo-mercantilist and social-democratic challenges to the dominant neoliberal project.

In implementing what has been dubbed the 'new European social policy' (Mosher and Trubek, 2003), the 'open method of co-ordination' (OMC) has become the preferred 'new mode of governance' (Eberlein and Kerwer, 2004). The OMC basically substitutes hard top-down Community regulation with 'soft policy co-ordination' through a Commission-led peer review in which Member States's performances are measured against 'best practices' and on the basis of common objectives (e.g. Borrás and Jacobsson, 2004). In this iterative multi-level, multi-actor 'surveillance process' (Mosher and Trubek, 2003: 67), so-called benchmarking has been elevated to be the key policy instrument (see De la Porte and Pochet, 2001; Zängle, 2004). The tool of benchmarking had already been developed and introduced in the 1990s by the industrialists of the Roundtable in conjunction with their promotion of the new competitiveness discourse (De La Porte and Pochet, 2001: 293; Van Apeldoorn, 2002: 176–7; Zängle, 2004: 1). Following earlier ERT publications (ERT, 1994; 1996), the Commission already in 1996, and invoking the inevitability of globalization and 'hence' the need for adaptation, defined benchmarking as a tool for improving competitiveness and with that as 'a tool for promoting the convergence towards best practice' (1996: 16). According to the Commission this involves the global 'comparison of societal behaviour [sic], commercial practice, market structure and public institutions' (European Commission, 1997: 3). It was thus that benchmarking ideologically became an instrument of neoliberal restructuring, and, in a discursive move that Watson and Hay (2003) call 'rendering the contingent necessary', the Commission legitimated this restructuring in terms of promoting competitiveness.

It is significant that it is with respect to the social policy areas bound up with the goal of 'social cohesion' – in particular employment – that EU governance indeed remains limited to policy co-ordination through benchmarking, whereas in the case of several policies deemed critical for achieving 'competitiveness', 'old-fashioned', 'hard' supranational law-making is still preferred, especially in the area of financial market integration.[8] The OMC, then, does not at all challenge the fundamental asymmetry of European governance, and in fact arguably reinforces it. Applying the OMC to the social policy domain reinforces the market liberalization thrust of the European project inasmuch as under the conditions of the regulatory competition induced by the internal market and a deflationary EMU, social policy is structurally biased towards market-enabling rather than market-correcting policies. As indicated, under these conditions any social policy co-ordination is bound to boil-down to a kind of supply-side strategy that supports and facilitates what is euphemistically called the 'adaptation' of societies to the so-called exigencies of European and global competition, thus deepening commodification. The European Employment Strategy, which was launched in 1997 but is now an integral part of the Lisbon strategy, is a case in point: emphasizing 'employability' it rather exclusively focuses on labour market flexibility as the panacea for unemployment (see also Mosher and Trubek, 2003). The Lisbon policy framework therefore helps to promote the kind of national competitiveness strategies that I argued above mediate and effectuate a transnational process of neoliberal restructuring.

Hegemonic articulation and the incorporation of contending social forces

Notwithstanding Lisbon's neoliberal bias as analysed above, what remains crucial about Lisbon in ideological terms is the articulation of neoliberal competitiveness with the objectives of social cohesion as well as its focus on shaping the conditions for a 'knowledge-based economy' (involving some role for public authorities beyond letting the market do its work). It is this articulation that I argue has helped to solidify the bloc of social forces underpinning the emergent embedded neoliberal project. In fact, from the start Lisbon won wide support among Europe's trade unions and from the ranks of the European transnational capitalist class. The European Trade Union Confederation (ETUC) supported the Lisbon strategy in particular because of its 'balanced and integrated approach between economic, social and environmental policies' (ETUC, 2005b; see also ETUC, 2000). In other words, the European trade union movement welcomed Lisbon as a strategy to overcome the asymmetry of European governance. The 'reform agenda' of Lisbon also has been very much welcomed by the ERT, which saw many of its ideas reflected in it. Subsequently – and in light of the noticeable lack of progress – the ERT has devoted much energy to push for the implementation of Lisbon, prioritizing (among others) the areas of innovation, the creation of an integrated European capital market, full liberalization of services and public utilities, deregulation, pension reform and labour market reform (ERT, 2002, 2004b).

To summarize this section, the socio-economic governance regime of the EU as constructed in the 1990s and culminating in the Lisbon strategy clearly represents a neoliberal shift in content that in part has been enabled by the shift in form. Articulating competitiveness with social cohesion, combining the push for financial market liberalization with concerns emanating out of industry, this neoliberal project has manifested itself as an *asymmetrically* embedded neoliberalism. At least at the EU elite level, it was able to attain a hegemonic position in the course of the 1990s. The wide support across the political spectrum, and from both the ERT and ETUC, for the Lisbon Agenda is a testimony to this hegemony while at the same time consolidating it. However, I also argued that since most of the supposed embeddedness remains the responsibility of national states operating under the discipline of regime competition and monetary union, embeddedness in a substantive sense is increasingly eroded. This brings us to examine the extent to which embedded neoliberalism can actually continue to generate and sustain the necessary levels of popular legitimacy. Below, I argue that in this sense embedded neoliberalism has already reached its political limits. Given its inherent contradictions, a multi-level legitimacy crisis of European governance has unfolded. We are thus witnessing the demise of embedded neoliberalism as a hegemonic project.

The contradictions of embedded neoliberalism and its multi-level legitimacy crisis

After an initial success in consolidating embedded neoliberalism as a hegemonic project by providing a rallying point for diverse transnational social forces, Lisbon is now failing rather dismally in sustaining the consent for neoliberal European governance, either at the rhetorical level or as a policy practice. Already in spring 2004, when he was about to leave office, even the then President of the European Commission, Romano Prodi, called the Lisbon process 'a big failure' (Barber and Parker, 2004) and the press of that time was rather unforgiving as well (*Financial Times*, 2004b). Clearly, the Lisbon Agenda was failing in terms of falling far behind its own targets (High Level Group Chaired by Wim Kok, 2004; European Commission, 2005a). But as we shall see below, also key transnational social forces, in particular organized labour, started to distance themselves from Lisbon. The new Commission President, José Manuel Barroso, did make a revival of the Lisbon Agenda his top priority (Barroso, 2004), and, after the recommendations of the aforementioned High Level Group, the new Commission relaunched Lisbon under the new name (a clear recognition of the faltering legitimacy of the old Lisbon strategy) of the 'Growth and Jobs Strategy' (European Commission, 2005b). But as Sandy Hager shows in this volume, by explicitly prioritizing the goal of competitiveness over social cohesion, as well as environmental sustainability (Buck, 2005), hence further downscaling even Lisbon's discursive commitment to embeddedness, the new Commission has, unsurprisingly, not really been able to bolster the strategy's appeal across European civil society. The Lisbon strategy, hence, rather than providing a solution to the European legitimacy crisis that had been looming for years, is actually becoming an expression of that crisis, as well a constituent element of it.

In this section I will argue that the declining legitimacy of Lisbon is in fact part of a more general, and multi-level, legitimacy crisis of embedded neoliberalism as a concept of control for the European integration process. Although the rightward shift of the Barroso Commission is for sure not helping in this regard, I argue that this crisis was bound to erupt in any case due to the contradictions inherent in embedded neoliberalism (and as already manifest in Lisbon from the start, as argued above). The point being that, all along, and in a structural sense, the priority lay with competitiveness defined in neoliberal terms since the embeddedness remained largely restricted to the national level, and thus continued to be under threat from a supranational 'disembedding' neoliberalism. This, then, is what makes it increasingly hard for embedded neoliberalism to reproduce itself politically.

As indicated, at the heart of the contradictions of embedded neoliberalism lies the substantive incompatibility of that what Lisbon seek to unite ideologically, that is, the opposing principles of economic liberalism and social protection. As the project of market liberalization, and its attendant (re-)commodification of social relations, advances, these contradictions become more manifest. The deepening of neoliberal restructuring was subsequently buttressed by the Eastern enlargement of 2004, which has further structurally weakened those social forces (previously) calling for a more substantive embeddedness. As Holman (2004b) argues, the complete underdevelopment of the 'social cohesion' dimension of the enlargement process has tended to turn EU expansion into a mere geographical extension as well as deepening of neoliberal restructuring, and turn Central and Eastern Europe into a 'new periphery' instrumental to the accumulation strategies of European capital, which indeed has been a consistent supporter of Eastern enlargement (ERT, 1991, 1999, 2004a). Not only has Eastern enlargement facilitated Western European TNCs' easy access to cheap labour (Bohle, 2005), this is also, crucially, putting pressure on Western European labour as it further shifts the class balance of power in favour of transnationally mobile capital (see also Chapters 7–9 in this volume by Vliegenthart and Overbeek, Bohle and Drahokoupil).[9]

In sum, the neoliberal restructuring, set in by the relaunched European integration project through the internal market programme and monetary union, reinforced by the marketization drive culminating in the Lisbon 'competitiveness' agenda, and further locked in by the Eastern enlargement, has subordinated the objective of social cohesion to that of a logic of commodification. It is this that has made Lisbon's rhetoric of combining cohesion and competitiveness increasingly hollow, undermining the effectiveness of 'embedded neoliberalism' in unifying contending social forces and in sustaining legitimacy of the European project. Social forces hitherto incorporated into the embedded neoliberal project have in fact started to disengage themselves and come to resist critical aspects of European socioeconomic governance. This applies to both former neo-mercantilist sections of European industry as well as to elements bound up with organized labour and underpinning what used to a supranational social-democratic project.

Limits to the incorporation of industrial capital

Critical in the deepening of the neoliberal dimension of the European integration project – and hence in a weakening of the remaining limited embeddedness – that has taken place since the Lisbon summit is the project of creating a single European financial area that arguably now constitutes the thrust of the ongoing completion of the internal market. This project started with the original internal market programme, but it was only in the 1990s that financial market integration became a key 'political project' of the European Commission, at the heart of the broader European neoliberal marketization project (see Bieling, 2003b; Van Apeldoorn and Horn, 2007a, 2007b). A critical step here was taken with the Commission's *Financial Services Action Plan* (European Commission, 1999b), and subsequently made into one of the priorities of the whole Lisbon Agenda. Within this context, the Commission has also been increasingly turning its attention to the related issue of corporate governance, in particular through a number of initiatives seeking to push Europe towards a more (capital) market-driven form of corporate governance. Framed as an integral part of creating a single and efficient European financial market, which in turn is presented as a *sine qua non* for achieving the competitiveness needed to meet the challenges of globalization, the Commission is in particular seeking to develop an EU-level regulatory framework aimed at promoting what could be called a *marketization of corporate control* (Van Apeldoorn and Horn, 2007a; see also Chapter 6 by Laura Horn in this volume).

These regulatory initiatives, together with the broader programme of financial market integration, can be seen as playing a crucial role in the emergence of a European shareholder capitalism, arguably part and parcel of a more global financialization process (e.g. Aglietta and Rebérioux, 2005). Inasmuch as this further undermines the limited elements of embeddedness still to be found in the present hegemonic project of European socio-economic governance, the limits to which industrial capital can be subordinated to financial capital also start to reveal themselves in terms of industrialists starting to worry about this aspect of the EU's emergent 'model of capitalism'.

On the one hand, top managers of large European industrial firms are increasingly tied to the interests and outlook of financial capital both because industry itself becomes financialized, in the sense that it makes an increasing part of its profits in the financial sector (through derivatives and so on) rather than industry itself – what Nölke and Perry (2007) call profit financialization – but also as the marketization of corporate control (or control financialization, ibid.) incorporates management materially through stock options and the like (Höpner, 2003). On the other hand, this incorporation – and a concomitant rise to hegemony of a money capital perspective over productive capital perspective *within industry itself* – is still far from complete. Some sections of Europe's managerial class continue to resist aspects of it, in particular when Europe's emerging market for corporate control threatens to make them fall victim of a hostile takeover.

In this respect it is noteworthy how the EU's attempts to establish a pan-European market for corporate control is still far from uncontested, as testified by the political controversies that were sparked by the growing wave of (hostile) takeovers taking place across Europe in the past few years as part of an unprecedented merger and acquisition boom (Politi and Saigol, 2006).[10] Even more controversy has been generated recently by the staggering rise of private equity and hedge funds as a new type of owners, adopting an uncompromising financial perspective with regard to their ownership titles. In what over the past two years has become a transnational political debate on the upsurge of these controversial funds, not only representatives of labour (see below), but also some of Europe's top managers have expressed their worries about the short-termism of especially hedge funds.[11] All of this for sure does not yet boil down to any serious resurgence of industrial capital and a concomitant effective challenge to the hegemonic position of financial capital, but it does underline the limits to the latter, with rising tensions as we are now reaching those limits. How these tensions will play out is of course too early to tell, then. It depends in part on whether 'finance-led' growth – which shareholder capitalism can be seen to express – is sustainable in the longer run (Boyer, 2000). As, at the time of writing, the global credit crisis deepens and the assessments of its possible effects on the European economy become more pessimistic (Milne, 2008), the prospects for such sustainability seem to become slim indeed.

Finally, with respect to the incorporation of the former neo-mercantilist wing, we may note that the current commitment to global free trade, and more broadly to the insertion of the European economy into global circuits of production and finance, is not necessarily irreversible. The collapse of the Doha round of World Trade Organization (WTO) trade talks in 2006 and their continuing deadlock and the rise of protectionist sentiments within the EU – especially in France (Bounds et al., 2007) – indeed underline this point. On the other hand, the pro-free trade coalition still holds the clear majority, both among the majority of Europe's politicians and among the ranks of European transnational capital, as well as within the elite of organized labour. Yet, a profound global economic crisis – such as we arguably are currently experiencing – may see the resurgence of (Euro) protectionism on the part of some sections of European industry, and possibly involving a coalition of (segments of) capital and labour. This then might put further strains on the incorporation of the former neo-mercantilist project into the hegemonic project of embedded neoliberalism. The extent to which this scenario might nevertheless unfold also to a significant extent depends on the global context, and in particular on evolving transatlantic relations. The openness of European regionalism is premised first and foremost on the still strong bonds of the transatlantic economy. In other words, whether the project of European integration will continue to be part and parcel of a neoliberal globalization process is not just decided in Europe, either on the part of its political or of its business elites. It will also depend on the geopolitical and geo-economic developments within the global political economy and in particular on how the current contradictions of the 'new imperialism' (Harvey, 2003) of the USA will play out (see also Alan Cafruny's contribution to this volume, Chapter 3).

Limits to the incorporation of organized labour

Turning our attention to the social forces bound up with organized labour, we start with our earlier observation that their incorporation hinges on the successful articulation of the goals of competitiveness and social cohesion. As it increasingly becomes apparent that the former is defined in terms of market liberalization and increased market discipline, whereas the latter is defined mainly in terms of adaptability of workers to market conditions– rather than in terms of protecting workers from the vagaries of that market – this incorporation becomes increasingly hard to sustain.

Although many so-called social-democratic parties have rather converted to much of the neoliberal paradigm, part of European organized labour turns out to be less solidly incorporated into the embedded neoliberal bloc.[12] ETUC for instance has grown increasingly critical of the Lisbon process. Even before the Barroso Commission revamped the Lisbon strategy to focus more one-sidedly on 'competitiveness', ETUC openly expressed its worries that the balance between the 'economic' and 'social' pillars was being lost in favour of a 'pure "business" or "market strategy"', and warned that if 'Lisbon becomes equated with the dismantlement of social Europe, the "ownership" of the Lisbon strategy as such will be refused' (ETUC, 2004: 5; see also ETUC, 2005b). Yet, thus far the ETUC seems still too much wedded to the current European project to take this radical step of disowning the Lisbon Agenda (see e.g. ETUC et al., 2005). More radical criticism, however, comes from outside the elite of European organized labour, in particular from the European Social Forum (Bieler and Morton, 2004b, and Bieler in Chapter 11 of this volume).

The growing disenchantment on the part of trade unions with respect to the output of European socio-economic governance, weakening its legitimacy as labour came to the conclusion that it was not getting their side of the deal (that is, competitiveness *plus* an enhanced social agenda), culminated in 2005 in the struggle over the Services Directive (see also Bieler's contribution to this volume, Chapter 11). As this directive raised the spectre of intensifying regulatory competition in the field of industrial relations, an alliance of trade unions and non-governmental organizations staged large demonstrations against the directive in Brussels in March 2005 and February 2006, after which it was significantly watered down in the European Parliament, in particular by removing the controversial 'country of origin' principle that was at the heart of the original proposal of Commissioner Bolkestein, and which, so ETUC argued, would have led to regulatory competition and social dumping in the service sector, putting downward pressures and wages and working conditions.[13]

We must furthermore note the role of monetary union in straining the allegiance of organized labour to the embedded neoliberal project. As EMU will continue to put more pressure on the national welfare states, this core part of the European project may increasingly come to be seen as endangering the so-called European social model (see also Chapter 2 in this volume by Magnus Ryner, and Cafruny and Ryner, 2007b). These strains manifest themselves above all within the intergovernmental arena, as some governments – in particular France and Germany – have become unwilling to pay the (domestic political) price for sticking to the required budget discipline, especially in a time of economic downturn (such as after 2001). Yet although played out between governments (sometimes in opposition to both the Commission and the ECB), these governments of course do respond to worries about employment and growth on the part of workers – as well as arguably on the part of the less globalized fractions of capital – among their domestic constituencies. After an earlier challenge to the strict rules of the SGP by France and Germany had resulted in 2005 in a reform of the Pact that basically reflected a victory of the latter countries (Benoit et al., 2005), controversies have recently been rekindled by the newly elected French President Sarkozy, who before and after his election campaign questioned both the monetarism and the independence of the ECB and called for a more growth oriented strategy and an EU 'economic government' to counterbalance the ECB (Atkins and Parker, 2007; Hall and Parker, 2007).

Finally, as with industrial capital, the contradictions arising out of the unrestrained financialization of European capitalism that European governance tends to promote – while rhetorically remaining committed not only to the competitiveness of European *industry*, but also to the often invoked 'social dimension' – is also putting limits on organized labour's commitment to the current European project.[14] In fact, these limits have become manifest rather late. Although the marketization of European corporate control and the concomitant rise of 'the new capitalists' has been going on for years, only from the end of 2006 do we see trade unions in Europe seriously starting to question the role of this new form of financial capital, with ETUC secretary general, John Monks, calling on Europe to 'take on the casino capitalists' (Monks, 2007; see also Arnold, 2007). This has to be understood in the context of several notorious cases of hedge fund activism and (attempted) takeovers by private equity and subsequent job-shedding restructuring and followed the trend established earlier by social-democratic politicians like the then chairman of the German labour party (SPD) Franz Müntefering, who had opened the transnational debate by notoriously comparing these (mainly Anglo-Saxon) investors to locusts (Jenkins, 2005). Recently, the Socialists Group in the European Parliament has added its (albeit guardedly) critical voice to this debate (PES, 2007; see also Laura Horn, Chapter 6 in this volume).

Yet in spite of this small political storm gathering over European financial capitalism, regulatory floodgates to the new money capital were opened at the EU level as well as at the national level already some time ago, and there is insufficient political will to close them (Buck, 2007). Of course, one may speculate that an alliance might be forged between elements of industrial capital (and their managers) on the one hand, and trade unions as well as some social-democratic (and Christian-democratic) political forces on the other. At the moment, however, such a cross-class alliance is only present in some individual cases (where for instance workers and management are united in their opposition to a hostile takeover). Nevertheless, although not amounting to anything resembling a coherent resistance, these instances are another indication of how embedded neoliberalism is increasingly running into contradictions that it cannot solve.

Resisting neoliberal Europe

To what extent, then, can we, in light of the above contradictions and tensions, heightened by the deepening neoliberalization of European governance, observe rising popular dissent as a sign of embedded neoliberalism reaching its limits as a hegemonic project? Here we need to keep in mind that embedded neoliberalism was never fully hegemonic beyond the level of transnational elites: that is, it primarily rested on the active consent of transnational *elites*, while this consent tended to be much more passive among Europe's populations in general. There are clear signs that, though with considerable national variation, this passive consent has been weakening in recent years, marking a shift parallel to that which is taking place with respect to attitudes vis-à-vis the EU in general, that is, a shift from a 'permissive consensus to [a] constraining dissensus' (Hooghe and Marks, 2007a).

A general hypothesis as put forward by Liesbet Hooghe and Gary Marks among others is that since the Maastricht Treaty the integration process has tended become much more *politicized* since it has deepened to such an extent that it intervenes much more directly into people's daily lives and more directly enters into the domestic political arena ('Europeanization'), and that with this politicization, the contestation of the European project has risen, with some political parties and other forces effectively mobilizing against European integration (Marks and Steenbergen, 2004; Netjes, 2004; Hooghe and Marks, 2007a). Recent research has shown that Euroscepticism has been on the rise both among Europe's electorates and within the discourse of (populist as well as mainstream) political parties (see Hooghe and Marks, 2007b). My claim here is that in light of my preceding analysis this mass politicization of European integration, which has translated growing alienation into growing rejection and resistance, can be partly interpreted as a legitimacy crisis of the output of (embedded) neoliberal governance. Arguably, the competitiveness strategies or national neoliberal restructuring strategies induced materially and ideologically by asymmetrical European governance are failing to deliver the goods that its citizens have come to expect from both their national and European political institutions. The reason why the integration process is so deeply intervening in citizens' lives, and why this has resulted in rising *negative* attitudes towards the EU, is that the integration process has become bound up with a neoliberal restructuring process that is hollowing out the social citizenship of Europe's populations (see also Chapter 5 by Hager and Chapter 2 by Ryner in this volume; see also Scharpf, 1999).

Although also associated – particularly in the context of the recent as well as possible future round(s) of enlargement[15] – with rising nationalism, xenophobia and other anxieties about national identity, worries about social issues and the (perceived) negative impact of European market integration on for example employment and social security also play a role in the growing popular contestation of the European project. Indeed, the latter may be in part an underlying cause of the former. Thus, the socio-economic dimension – and in particular the perception that Brussels is trying to impose an 'ultra-liberal' model of capitalism that threatens job security, the national welfare state and cherished public services – played for instance a critical role in the discourse of those French social forces that opposed the European Constitution (Cassen, 2005b; Grunberg, 2005; Heine, 2006; Storey, 2006). Indeed, the French and, although in a more mediated way, Dutch rejection of the referendum (see my Chapter 5 in this volume) can be taken as the culmination – together with the aforementioned struggle around the Services Directive – of a growing resistance to a neoliberal socio-economic governance regime. With the Constitution – with its reference to 'free and undistorted competition' (Article 1–2) as one of the fundamental objectives of the Union and its inclusion (in part III) of all the relevant treaty provisions on the single market and monetary union – this regime would have gained in legitimacy (simply by being called a constitution), but it now has been further challenged because of its popular rejection.

Epilogue and conclusion: beyond (embedded) neoliberalism?

The Treaty of Lisbon, signed after protracted and often acrimonious negotiations in 2007 was intended to save as much as possible of the European constitutional project, in particular with regard to the proposed reforms to the EU institutional architecture (that is, creating the post of a Council President, changes of the voting rules, and so on). In this respect, critics were right to claim that the so-called reform treaty was really the Constitution under a different name, and without the references to the perceived symbols (such as anthem, flag, and so on) of an alleged European super state (for a systematic comparison of the two treaties see Open Europe, 2008). This does tend to overlook, however, two important differences, which underline the significance of the aforementioned referendum outcomes. One is that existing treaty provisions regarding EU (neoliberal) socio-economic governance (internal market, EMU) in the Lisbon treaty are no longer elevated to the status of a formal constitution, since it is just another treaty amending previous treaties, rather than a 'constitution' replacing all previous treaties. Second, and maybe as significant, is that the French President, Nicolas Sarkozy, had succeeded – clearly responding to the message signalled by the French 'Non' – in getting the aforementioned clause on 'free and undistorted competition' removed from the EU's list of objectives. The immediate outcry that this sparked both from the Commission as well as from Europe's business elite (including the ERT) – both expressing fears that this might mean that in the hierarchy of policy goals competition would now (be perceived to) rank below Union objectives such as 'employment and social progress' (Buck and Benoit, 2007; Parker and Benoit, 2007) – is telling in this respect. Of course, the future of the new Lisbon reform treaty itself looks very uncertain now that it has been turned down in the Irish referendum of June 12, 2008. Yet, the significance of the above responses to the preceding popular rejection of the European Constitution, still stands. On the other hand, and regardless of the fate of the Lisbon treaty, we should not too quickly conclude that growing resistance to neoliberal European governance is successfully transforming the social purpose of European integration.

Even if the outcome of the latest round of intergovernmental bargaining could be interpreted as a partial victory for some of those oppositional forces, it is not yet heralding a fundamental change of the social purpose of the European project. First, because, as indicated, much of the market-making EU governance framework is already in place and there is hardly a Member State that is seriously willing to challenge those policies. Moreover, the current Barroso Commission, reputed to be the most market-liberal Commission yet, seems rather oblivious to what this chapter has identified as the legitimacy crisis of European governance inasmuch as it tenaciously clings on to its marketization programme. Second, although Sarkozy's recent moves and rhetorics (also against the SGP) do show that also someone who has been seen as the most pro-business French presidential candidate cannot ignore (and might even share) French fears of the current EU as, in Sarkozy's own words, 'a Trojan horse of unfair globalization' (Bounds et al., 2007), there are of course limits to what the French president may achieve on his own (which is not to say that he may yet be instrumental in further eroding the legitimacy of aspects of European neoliberal governance). So far, Sarkozy has only met fierce opposition to most of his plans, particularly with respect to EMU, from almost all of his colleagues. Although we cannot predict how exactly this will play out, arguably the obstacles to a true transformation of the European project are of a rather structural nature. In particular, resistance remains rather fragmented (in part because of how neoliberal restructuring has been successful in for instance further fragmenting the working classes), and is not yet able to coalesce *transnationally* – forming a countervailing power against transnational capital – around a coherent and comprehensive alternative European project. Trade unions by and large remain too tied to the institutions of the national state, finding it hard to transcend their national diversity of interest and ideological outlook (compare Andreas Bieler's contribution to this volume, Chapter 11).

These limits to the limits of neoliberal European governance may yet be overcome, but for the moment we are rather likely to witness a continuation of European neoliberal governance, which has become increasingly less embedded (as its disembedding force at the national level is also starting to take its toll). But with this we are also likely to observe a continuation and indeed a deepening of its legitimacy crisis. As embedded neoliberalism continues to hollow out the (national) non-market institutions in which it is supposed to be embedded, and makes its commitment to the principle of social protection equally hollow, it loses its attraction to those social forces whose incorporation was so critical to its rise to hegemony. This is, as this chapter has argued, precisely what has happened in recent years. In the absence of a coherent alternative, the upshot of this may well be that we will witness a growing rejection of the European project increasingly fusing with rising nationalism, xenophobia and various populisms.

Notes

1. With Scharpf (1999: 6–13) we here refer to 'output legitimacy' as deriving from the *content* of the policies made, or the extent to which citizens support those policies because they effectively solve common problems.
2. In our view, capitalist class formation crystallizes around rival 'capital fractions', where this fractionation is linked both to *scale*, e.g. the distinction between national, European and global capital (Overbeek and Van der Pijl, 1993; Van Apeldoorn, 2002), and, more fundamentally, to *function*, where we may ideal-typically distinguish between the rival perspectives of *money* and *productive* capital (Van der Pijl, 1984, 1998).
3. For an empirical account of this shift and its underlying causes see Van Apeldoorn (2002: 130–42).
4. This then also makes for the principle difference with Ruggie's historical concept of 'embedded liberalism' describing the post-war corporate-liberal world order and its underpinning class compromise in the same way (Ruggie, 1982). However, the crucial difference between embedded liberalism and what I here identify as embedded *neoliberalism* is that whereas in the former liberalism (above all through the subordination of money capital to productive interests) was so attenuated as to actually be amenable to an embedding within non-market institutions and market-correcting policies, in embedded neoliberalism the disembedding force of neoliberalism remains largely intact in spite of the limited embeddedness, which is hence continuously subject to erosion. That (neo) liberalism currently is ultimately not sufficiently restrained and therefore embedded in a more substantive and durable fashion has to do, as I will explain below, with the fact that whereas the 'liberalism' is promoted at the supranational European (and global) level the 'embeddedness' remains stuck at the national level. It is precisely this asymmetry that makes for a crucial difference with embedded liberalism, in which both the European and the international order were set up to protect

national welfare states against international market forces (Van Apeldoorn, 2002: 51–3, 63–5).

5. Productive capital here is not synonymous with industrial capital. Rather, a productive capital perspective can be taken as the ideal-typical perspective of industry inasmuch as industry does what it is *supposed* to do, which is *produce* commodities. The productive capital perspective, being more directly tied to the fate of the populations who live in the spaces where industry is located, and to the states that exercise political rule in those spaces, tends to move away from a pure liberal perspective, which can be seen as the ideal-typical orientation of money capital (which does not face the spatial constraints and is inherently more mobile, see also note ii). Yet in practice industry might, as a result of *profit* as well as *control financialization* (see on this distinction Nölke and Perry, 2007), very well be dominated by a money capital perspective.

6. A quotation from the 2004 report of the High Level Group on the Lisbon strategy illustrates this point well:

> The Lisbon strategy is not an attempt to become a copy-cat of the US – far from it. Lisbon is about achieving Europe's vision of what it wants to be and what it wants to keep in light of increasing global competition, an ageing population and the enlargement. It has the broad ambition of solidarity with the needy, now and in the future. To realise this ambition, Europe needs more growth and more people in work.
>
> (High Level Group Chaired by Wim Kok, 2004: 12)

7. The latter concept had for years been promoted by the ERT (ERT, 1989, 1992, 1995; see also European Commission, 1995b), and fits with the requirements of the new flexible accumulation paradigm and its need for a core workforce that can add functional flexibility to the numerical flexibility provided by the peripheral workers.

8. Thus in 2004 some 70 directives have been adopted under the Lisbon process, mainly in the area of the internal market. Although transposition of these directives has been lagging, most progress has been made in the area of financial market integration under the heading 'Financial Service Action Plan'; see European Commission 2004b.

9. Moreover, the widening to currently 27 Member States has of course only enhanced the institutional difficulties with respect to achieving any kind of positive (social policy) integration (Scharpf, 2002).

10. Here one can for example think of the ultimately successful bid by London-based steel giant Mittal for its Luxembourg-based rival Arcelor (Hollinger et al., 2006), as well as the flurry of takeover activity among European utilities sparking various 'nationalist' responses.

11. They for instance did so at the summit of business associations of the G8 in April 2007 (preceding the real G8). The business leaders called for more transparency over the activities of hedge funds but could not agree on any stronger language, probably because of opposition from the representatives of US and UK employers (De Corbière, 2007; see also the remarks made by Business Europe (formerly UNICE) President, Ernest-Antoine Seillière, in Atkins, 2007a).

12. Although for sure not a monolithic whole and often divided along national lines in as far as labour is organized at all, we may still regard workers as sharing certain basic class interests in opposition to capital. These class interests are neither immutable nor discourse independent (hence these interests are 'discovered' in

practice), yet neither are they independent of the objective position of wage labour within capitalist social relations (that is, the discourse produced is bound to be affected by and related to the *structure* in which agents find themselves). See also Chapter 11, by Bieler.
13. As it is a compromise it would be unjustified to interpret these developments as an outright victory for the forces opposing neoliberal market liberalization, nor does this necessarily spell the end of the Lisbon 'reform agenda'. However, the fact that a compromise was necessary is significant in and of itself. Here, we may note the worries expressed by UNICE about the proposed deal as 'opening the door to the introduction of new restrictions against service providers' (Buck, 2006).
14. On the consequences of the marketization of corporate control for labour see Van Apeldoorn and Horn (2007a: 9–10).
15. In 2005 – the year of the referendums in France and the Netherlands – among the EU-25 future enlargement had the support of 49 per cent, with that figure being much lower in the old EU-15 (European Commission, 2005c).

2
Neoliberal European Governance and the Politics of Welfare State Retrenchment: A Critique of the New Malthusians

Magnus Ryner

Introduction

The history of European integration contains its share of social scientific theories, which although they have proven to be spurious have enjoyed significant prominence because of the politico-ideological functions that they have served. Although already the Empty Chair Crisis of 1965 put into severe doubt the postulated mechanisms of neo-functionalism, this evolutionary theory has remained a compulsory reference point for students of European integration. Undoubtedly this has something to do with the *raison d'être* it gives the EU's supranational institutions and the positive spin it gave to the corporate-liberal Atlanticist Grand Design that united the US State Department, intellectuals like Jean Monnet and attendant social forces in the 1950s (Milward and Sørensen, 1994; Van der Pijl, 1996). A more recent example is the neo-classical liberal economics of the Cecchini Report (European Commission, 1988), with its euphoric predictions about the cumulative static and dynamic effects of the completion of 'Europe 1992'. Despite these predictions being far off the mark, neoliberal economics has provided the rationale not only for the Single Market, but also for its disciplinary structuring in financial and monetary arrangements through the European Monetary System (EMS), the Economic and Monetary Union (EMU) and the reform of European financial services (Gill, 1998; Bieling, 2003a).

In this chapter I argue that what I call the New Malthusian 'politics of retrenchment' literature on the welfare state can be understood in a similar way. Following a set of well-received pieces by Harvard Professor Paul Pierson, New Malthusianism has in recent years become so dominant in welfare and social policy research that it resembles what Kuhn (1962) called a 'normalized' scientific paradigm: it has become accepted as a default explanation of the general 'state of the welfare state'; it defines the research questions that are posed and the concepts used in the interpretation of evidence. This default explanation is no longer considered questionable and it provides the starting point for more pragmatic research to clarify details and to offer policy solutions.

Whether or not this has been the intention of individual social scientists, New Malthusian discourse on the welfare state has come to serve hegemonic-ideological functions for embedded neoliberalism in the interface of the policy fields of European economic- and social-policy multi-level governance as manifested, for example, in the Lisbon Strategy. The ideological function played by neo-classical economics in the 'relaunch' of European integration in the 1980s has already been mentioned. In a second phase, the communitarianism associated with Anthony Giddens increasingly flanked neo-classical economics in the 1990s, and sought to counter some of the legitimation problems that arose from the disappointments of a 'pure' market conception. Hence, the neo-social democratic 'Third Way' was provided with coherence and direction. Indeed, the Summit that set the 'Lisbon Agenda' was very much steeped in Third Way thinking (Ryner, 2002: Chapter 1; see also Chapter 5 in this volume, by Sandy Hager). New Malthusianism is not directly associated with any political project in the way that the Third Way, or for that matter neo-classical economics, has been. Indeed, the austerity and scientific detachment of New Malthusianism offers no euphoric vision of the future. As an ideology, it operates in a subtler but not necessarily less effective manner. As the Third Way has collapsed as a credible political project (in no little part because of its internal contradictions), the New Malthusian rearticulation provides a compelling alternative flank to neoliberal economics. It serves as a more 'depoliticized' rationality, providing direction and legitimacy for Europe's agenda of welfare state retrenchment within a market oriented model of growth, operating within a frame of macroeconomic austerity. It does so, in part, by catering to the fears about the future of a cherished social model by understating the extent of which matters are changing. But, more importantly, it operates as a social scientific ideology in the strict Frankfurt School sense of the term: it naturalizes social relations and attributes to them a sense of objectivity and inevitability. It is by doing so that it provides the existing order with negative legitimation by giving credence to the claim 'there is no alternative'.[1] The power of such negative legitimation can be formidable as it locks in those social forces into the 'embedded neoliberal project' (see Chapter 1 by Van Apeldoorn in this volume), which did not necessarily find Thatcherism or the Third Way ideologically appealing in any positive sense.[2] In the process of doing so, however, New Malthusianism falls short as a social scientific theory as it obscures the power relations, interests and social rationales that underpin the hegemonic project that it – deliberately or inadvertently – legitimates (see Horkheimer, 1939).

In the first part of the chapter I outline the New Malthusian position in general as articulated by Pierson. I then review Hemerijck's (2002) and Rhodes' (2002) application of New Malthusianism to the interpretation of the implication for the 'European social model' of a Single Market as structured by the Economic and Monetary Union (EMU). The argument of the latter, that the EMU facilitates a propitious 'self transformation' of the European social model and hence is (or may be) 'good' for the welfare state, echoes rather clearly the two central theses of Pierson. The first of these is that 'post-industrialism' is objectively exerting structural–functional pressure on 'mature' welfare states, making welfare state retrenchment and reform unavoidable. The second thesis is that such retrenchment and reform is exceedingly difficult to implement, in part because of the acknowledgement that some sort of welfare state is an essential feature of modern society, but also because the welfare state has created such a complex array of social constituencies that it is meaningless to talk about a general 'retrenchment' – rather we should view reforms in terms of more or less rational redistributive bargains. Clearly Hemerijck and Rhodes suggest that the EMU does (or may) facilitate more rationality in that regard. As the review in this section of the chapter unfolds, I begin my critique of the New Malthusian position. While accepting that welfare state restructuring is a highly complex affair, I argue that it is not so complex that we cannot see a general tendency towards retrenchment that threatens the very nature of the conception of social citizenship that has been integral to the European social model and indeed the European bargain that has rendered capitalism and democracy compatible after World War II. In the third section, I return to the economic core of the New Malthusian position to critique it on empirical and conceptual grounds. This sets the stage for my conclusion, where I reassert what the New Malthusians have denied, namely the causal importance of global restructuring understood as a transitive phenomena of a neoliberal politics that serves powerful interests.

Post-industrialism and the politics of retrenchment: The new Malthusianism

According to Pierson, the welfare states of advanced capitalist societies have entered a phase of 'maturity', characterized by diminishing growth, stagnation and indeed 'immovable and irresistible' compulsion towards retrenchment (Pierson, 1994, 1998, 2001b). In pursuit of his argument, he denies any significant causal power to the 'exogenous variable' of 'globalization' by arguing that even in the absence of contemporary transformations towards a global political economy, welfare states would have faced the pressures attributed to transformations towards a global political economy. Pierson offers an 'endogenous' 'counter-factual' to the globalization explanation, namely the 'post-industrial explanation':

> In short, my counter-factual runs as follows: the slower economic growth and related problems associated with rising service employment, the tremendous expansion of governmental commitments, the fiscal demands

stemming from population ageing in countries with mature social programmes, and the restructuring of the households would, by themselves, have generated much of the current turmoil around the welfare state. Had economic openness remained constant over the past quarter-century, governments would nonetheless face increasing inflexibility and intense fiscal pressure, including tendencies towards deficit spending and demands for programme cutbacks and policy reform.

(ibid, 2001b; 83)

At its economic core, this explanation is Malthusian in that it assigns critical significance to a supposedly intransitive tendency towards diminishing economic returns as well as to demographic pressures. New Malthusians attribute this inherent tendency towards diminished productivity and output growth to 'post-industrial' economies characterized by an increased contribution by the 'service sector' to GDP and above all employment. Again, a butt of the argument is directed towards the 'globalization thesis'. On the basis of the 'broad consensus of economists' (ibid, 2001b; 83) one would have expected increased international economic exchange to generate *increased* productivity growth. Instead, the 'OECD world' has experienced a reduction of output and productivity growth over the last 30 years. William Baumol's (1967) theory about the economics of the service economy is held to fit these developments much better. Service industries are by their essential nature unable to match the productivity increases of manufacturing industries. The sort of continuous – and during the Fordist phase quasi-endogenous – increases of output per factor unit employed are not possible, where, as in the case of services, 'it is essentially the labour effort itself we wish to consume' (Pierson, 2001b: 84). There are limits to how many clients a banker can serve, how many patients a nurse can nurse, and how many haircuts a hairdresser can cut – limits that do not apply to the production of manufactured goods under technological change.

Although the service economy may express successful economic development and increased prosperity, Pierson argues that it generates acute problems for the welfare state: growth of revenue depends heavily on the growth of wages and salaries, which in turn are dependent on high productivity growth (Pierson, 2001b: 86) (at a given profit-rate one might hasten to qualify). The decline of productivity generates a 'trilemma' for the welfare state, where it is impossible to combine all three of employment growth, wage equality and fiscal balance (see also Iversen and Wren, 1998). In an economy increasingly characterized by a low productivity service 'sector', employment can, in a capitalist market, only expand on the basis of low wages, as has been the case in the Anglo-Saxon 'residual' welfare states, resulting in marked increases of inequalities. Alternatively, one can – as has been the case in most continental European 'Christian democratic welfare states' – seek to defend high and relatively equal social wages. But this has been at the price of high unemployment as barriers to new service employment are high. A vicious circle is often associated with this development as increased outlays on pensions and unemployment insurance increase payroll surcharges, hence accentuating the problem of high labour costs. Finally, as in the Scandinavian 'social democratic' welfare states, employment may be expanded through public social service provision. Since such provision does not need to be for market profit, it may be rendered compatible with wage equality in relation to the manufacturing sector. However, because of the gap in productivity growth between the public service sector and the manufacturing sector, wage equality can only be maintained if the relative prices of services increase. This, in other words, entails a continuous commitment to tax increases. As the willingness of the tax payer to pay taxes reaches its limits, such service employment can in the long run only be maintained through increased budget deficits (Pierson, 2001b: 87).

This argument about the economic nature of service production is at the very centre of the post-industrial explanation. But it is combined with a set of broader institutional and sociological considerations that point to further amplification of welfare state instabilities and tradeoffs. The first of these is simply the cumulative institutional effect of welfare state growth: a set of politically motivated institutional commitments were made during welfare state expansion. However, these seem to have assumed continued growth and expansion. When the reality of slower post-industrial economic growth sets in at the same time as the relevant programmes mature (for example as the first cohorts with full pension benefits retire) these commitments generate persistent budgetary pressures, a loss of policy flexibility, and they contribute to the increased non-wage costs of labour as a factor of production. The most prominent examples of such commitments are pensions (public expenditure on pensions in OECD countries increased from 4.6 per cent to 8.5 per cent of GDP between 1960 and 1990) and health care (where expenditure increased from 2.5 per cent to 6 per cent of GDP in the same time frame) that together represent two-thirds of social protection outlays (Pierson, 2001b: 88). The second development that is invoked is population ageing and the increased age-dependency ratio. Finally, changes in the household structure and the decline of the 'male breadwinner' family model are invoked, which is associated with increased female participation rates, lower fertility rates and a proliferation of single parent households (Pierson, 2001b: 88–99). The latter development is more ambiguous in its effects on the welfare state than the other developments. Increased female participation rates may serve to counteract fiscal crisis if it is combined with an increase of (service) employment opportunities, since this increases the tax base. On the other hand, low fertility rates exacerbate demographic imbalances and the process of household fragmentation places additional burdens on public social provision and tends to produce additional poverty traps.

What are the political implications of these 'irresistible forces' of structural transformation? In his attempt to answer this question, Pierson combines the aforementioned structural-functionalist arguments with a neo-institutionalist understanding of political processes, which marked his first original contribution to the debate (Pierson, 1994). In that work, he argued that the efficacy of neoliberal and neo-conservative reformers in the 1980s had been very much exaggerated and that the intentions and rhetoric of these had been taken too much at face value. The actual record of implementation suggested much more policy continuity and political resilience of the welfare state. The reason for this is that while diffuse anti-welfarist rhetoric and the promise of tax cuts may be attractive, it is much harder to confront the concentrated group of voters who face tangible losses in any given retrenchment policy. This is exacerbated by the fact that the benefits are diffuse while the costs are tangible. In other words, the welfare state has dramatically changed the context of politics as it has created entrenched socio-political interests with strong stakes in welfare state arrangements that go to the very heart of social reproduction. While Pierson is careful not to argue that his 1994 study of Thatcherite–Reaganite 'aggressive neoliberalism' contains any general answers, he underlines the importance of complexity (and indeed it is this that precludes a general transposition of Reaganite–Thatcherite configuration). Since each type of welfare state has its own institutional configuration and faces different problems (inequality, unemployment or budgetary problems), each configuration will have its own politics. Second, and following the postulation of institutionally induced complexity, the current configuration is not one of 'pro-' versus 'anti-' welfare state. Rather in the current conjuncture of welfare state *reform* one could in the Christian democratic welfare state, for example, imagine common interests between single mothers and long-term unemployed in search of employment opportunities and business interests and public policy reformers.

New Malthusianism and neoliberal European governance

Pierson gives just as little credence to neoliberal European governance as he gives to globalization as a causal power behind welfare retrenchment. With reference to Europe-wide macroeconomic austerity, as institutionally manifested in the EMU, he argues: '[I]t is essential to realize that the broad constraint on government debt/GDP ratios and the implications of rising interest payments would exist in a world without EMU' (Pierson, 2001b: 92).

This argument has been amplified by Martin Rhodes's (2002) and Anton Hemerijck's (2002) analysis of the effect of the EMU on the European welfare state and 'social models'. These authors also follow Pierson's argument on the politics of retrenchment, arguing that the EMU cannot be seen to be part of a neoliberal project that is undermining the European welfare state. Rather, they see EMU as part of a complex politics of necessary welfare state reform, entailing a complex configuration of socio-economic revitalization and redistribution between different welfare state constituencies. Through the EMU, the European 'social model' is undergoing a rational 'self-transformation'. In this regard, the EMU is (or may be) 'good' for the welfare state.

In pursuit of this argument, Rhodes (2002: 311–12) points to the 'remarkable continuity' of social expenditure levels in the 1990s, in relation to previous decades. He also argues that the empirical evidence does not justify the fear of 'social dumping' where economic competition from less developed welfare states in southern (and now also eastern) Europe would compel the northern European welfare states to 'retrench' in a 'race to the bottom'. As a close observer of the Mediterranean, he argues rather that there is evidence of a 'race to the top' insofar the southern welfare states – notably Portugal – have extended coverage to more groups who previously were not protected by a safety net (Rhodes, 2002: 319–20). Furthermore, the EMU and the Stability and Growth Pact (SGP) have increased the *need* and the *scope* for strengthening corporatist collective agreement and industrial relations regimes. The need has increased because this is one of the few areas where nation states can recover some economic policy autonomy. The scope for agreements has also simultaneously increased since the reduction of policy tools under the formal discretion of the state has reduced the agenda of distributive conflict between the social partners.

The conclusion of 'social pacts' also mushroomed in the 1990s throughout the EU, after a decade of corporatist decline in the 1980s (Rhodes, 2002: 324, 327; Hemerijck, 2002: 11–12). According to Rhodes, fiscal consolidation for the purpose of meeting the Maastricht convergence criteria was largely achieved through reduced interest payments, caused by reduced risk premiums that could be 'imported' to previous high inflation countries from the low inflation countries in the EMU core through the common currency backed by the credibility of the SGP. This even had positive demand side-effects via decreasing interest rates. In addition, fiscal consolidation was largely secured on the revenue side. True, corporate taxation rates and employers' contributions were reduced. However, tighter writeoff rules for corporate taxes, and the switching from payroll surcharges to general taxation, increased the tax base. In addition, privatization increased revenue (Rhodes, 2002: 317–18).

These contributions demonstrate that the relationship between the EMU and welfare state retrenchment is complex. For one, the welfare state is an institution, that is, as argued above, intertwined with, and constitutive of, the very being of modern European social order. Hyperbolic claims of an outright 'end' of the welfare state are out of order in the foreseeable future and if nothing else these contributions underline this. Furthermore, in line with arguments about uneven development and 'agglomeration economies' (e.g. by Smith, Rainnie and Dunford, 2001) it is also possible that in some locales the welfare state has been maintained at existing levels and perhaps even expanded. But, the implications for *social citizenship* conveyed by the indicators invoked by, for example, Rhodes are highly misleading. As Esping-Andersen put it in a memorable turn of phrase, 'it is hard to find any instance where social forces have struggled for spending as such' (Esping-Andersen, 1990: 19). In fact, '[E]xpenditure is epiphenomenal to the substance of the welfare state' (ibid.). What matters are rather *effective entitlements*, and the extent to which they correspond to the norms of distributive justice and legitimacy that is contained in the social citizenship accords.

When considered from this point of view, the stability of social expenditure levels may actually be an indicator of significant welfare state retrenchment. This is because from the point of view of prevailing norms of *unchanged* social citizenship there are good grounds to suppose that there should be an *increase* of claims. Here one may well turn some of Pierson's arguments on their head and refer to Europe's ageing population: there has been a marked increase in pensioners ready to make claims on programmes they see themselves as having contributed towards in their working lives. The level of claims has been exacerbated by previous rationalization strategies in Christian Democratic welfare states, based on early retirement. Furthermore, divorce rates have increased markedly, leading to an increase of single parent households (mostly 'headed' by single mothers). This, along with the efforts to increase employment rates and the aspiration of women to become full economic citizens, has increased the demand for family services. It is no wonder that Rhodes' more disaggregated figures point to a marked shift of resources towards areas like these (Rhodes, 2002: 312–13).

Thus from the point of view of social citizenship norms, it makes more sense to focus on the interrelationship of welfare state programmes and what they provide in terms of entitlement. Given the increased demand for, and claims on, these programmes despite fixed resources, we can expect that there has been significant retrenchment. This is indeed born out by the evidence. Using the outstandingly comprehensive comparative data base of social programmes at the Institute for Social Research at the University of Stockholm, Walter Korpi's research shows that there has been a marked reduction of the net replacement rates for benefits received during sickness, work accidents and unemployment in Europe (see also the 'social reforms database' of the Fondazione Rodolfo Debenedetti, 2008). Korpi observes a marked decrease of these rates in the period 1975–95 (Korpi, 2003: 597). This corroborates what one would expect from changes in welfare legislation in countries of the Eurozone, pointing towards retrenchment.

But above all, as Korpi rightly points out, what Hemerijck, Rhodes and the New Malthusians forget is that the end of the full employment commitment and the understanding of employment in terms of 'a right to work' at a certain standard is *in and of itself* a crucial indicator of welfare state retrenchment:

> [U]nemployment . . . [is] . . . a central variable [of the welfare state] . . . because for categories of citizens with labour power as their main basic power resource, the efficacy of this resource in distributive conflict and bargaining is to a major extent determined by the demand for labour and by the level of unemployment . . . [T]he maintenance of low levels of unemployment empowers citizens and is an essential preventative part of the welfare state . . . In western Europe, the emergence of full employment as well as the expansion of social transfers and social services . . . emerged approximately at the same time . . . [C]ontemporaries saw this triplet as constituting a unity, the full employment welfare state, where expanding social insurance and services were combined with unemployment rates below the 3 per cent maximum level set by the British social reformer William Beveridge . . . It was a manifestation of what can be called an implicit social contract between the main interest groups in these countries . . . The return of mass unemployment must be seen as . . . the eradication of one of the corner stones of the Western European welfare states.
>
> (ibid.: 592, 593–4, 596)

In light of this, it is not surprising that inequality levels have also increased or that there also have been serious cutbacks to public services in relation to demand (Clayton and Pontusson, 1998; Beckfield, 2006; Clayton and Pontusson, 1998).[3] It is also not surprising, looking at matters over a longer term time scale, that the almost perfect proportionality of social wage increases with economic growth has been broken, indicating that the wage relation is increasingly defined as a 'market variable' as opposed to a means to disseminate the 'fruits of progress' and to ensure the 'virtuous' Fordist relationship between *inter alia* mass production, productivity growth and mass consumption (Boyer, 1995). When considered against the backdrop of the latter point, it is also doubtful whether the corporatist bargains of the 1990s really represent continuity or even 'self-transformation'. In contrast to previous periods, when the *raison d'etre* of corporatist bargains was to contain price increases at full employment, they are now used in order to secure wage settlements below rates of productivity growth at high unemployment levels. Unions have signed up to these bargains from a position of exceptional weakness in order to increase the probability – but not guarantee – that this will boost employment. This puts serious strain on the 'moral economy' that makes workers join unions in the first place, as unions are perceived to contain rather than increase wages, and as concessions attenuate internal representative structures within unions at the expense of peak-level concertation (Schulten and Ryner, 2003).

When matters are considered at the more disaggregated level of entitle-ment, Hemerijck and Rhodes also concede that there has been significant retrenchment. There has been 'some' increase of inequality, mainly due to increased incidence of ageing, single parenthood and unemployment. Also, while Portugal, Spain and Italy have mainly rationalized in terms of a redis-tribution of entitlements, it is conceded that in France, Germany, Belgium and Austria there have been important changes in entitlements that are more or less directly linked to the Maastricht convergence criteria. In Finland, the Netherlands and Ireland, such changes preceded Maastricht (Rhodes, 2002: 318–22). And, indeed, it is conceded that there clearly have been adverse deflationary effects on employment rates (ibid.: 305). The point they make though is that these are seen as 'necessary' changes, and the EMU has served as a catalyst for this necessary retrenchment in order to put European welfare states on a more secure footing. It is in this sense that the EMU has been 'good' for the European welfare state. In making the case for this necessity, it is exactly the post-industrial constraints discussed in the previous section that are invoked (Hemerijck, 2002: 3–9; Rhodes, 2002: 308, 311 and 318).

Welfare state retrenchment, citizenship and the problem of legitimacy

To insist on a focus on effective entitlements rather than on expenditure levels is important. This is because it is the former that concern the question of citizenship and therefore questions of legitimacy in a democratic order. The welfare state is intimately connected to the rise of social citizenship, redeeming the equality of status as required by political and civic citizenship in a capitalist society and hence with *substantive legitimacy* (Marshall, 1950; Unger, 1976: 193–200). The welfare state reproduces social accords and dis-tributive coalitions that lie at the heart of the European social order. These coalitions are connected to political society through mass parties and their competition and co-operation (Häusler and Hirsch, 1989: 306). In almost the entire eurozone, where Christian Democracy has been hegemonic in the definition of the 'national-popular' after World War II, reproduction and change takes place through the distributive principle of *incomes replacement* and the political principle of *mediation* – 'a religiously inspired, ideologically condensed and politically practiced conviction that conflicts of interests can and must be reconciled politically in order to restore the natural and organic harmony of society' (Van Kersbergen, 1995: 2). Successful political and elec-toral strategies of mass parties have been based on the management of the various dimensions of socio-political cleavages (especially of class, religion and language). Furthermore, the solidarity between welfare state contrib-utors and claimants has been based on this mode of entitlement and political context. However, as economic growth slows, and as welfare state retrenchment proceeds, the scope of such politics of mediation is restricted, thereby reducing the range of social forces that can be integrated into the political mainstream. This in turn requires a change in the politics of mediation itself. Parties are compelled either to redefine the terms of the redistributive coalitions, or to change the politico-economic framework, or sometimes both.

In such a context, it is exceedingly difficult to implement the abstract and uncompromising neoliberal reforms of 'flexibility'. Such reforms contravene the very nature of compromise and mediation, and threaten highly entrenched status groups as well as the claims of social protection of the most vulnerable in society. Electorally, implementing these reforms is a hazardous exercise for political movements whose success has been based on constructing complex and composite coalitions such as the Social Democratic Party (SPD) and, quintessentially, the Christian Democratic Union (CDU) in Germany. French Presidentialism may seem to give the state more 'executive authority' to take 'hard decisions'. However, there are powerful countertendencies: the 'dual executive' nature of the French system; electoral laws that encourage the formation of composite coalitions; and the semi-autonomous status given to professional groups and unions in the management of French social insurance, connected to the 'Jacobin' tradition of street protests when the executive goes 'too far'. As mass protests in 1995 and 2005/6 have shown, French unions and other social movements have developed skills in strategically harnessing such outbursts ('*greviculture*') (Ross, 2004).

In France, for example, the relationship between social welfare, social citizenship and legitimacy is based on a particular meaning of the norm *solidarité*, which corresponds with a concern of counteracting the disintegrative tendencies of capitalism while still harnessing its productive powers. Institutionally, this crystallized into France's particular social accord as expressed first at the foundation of the Third Republic in 1875 and then in post World War II welfare legislation. In the French Republican tradition, *solidarité* and welfare legislation are seen as essential to the elimination of the distinction between 'active' and 'passive' citizenship (where the former was reserved for the wealthy and educated invested with a measure of leisure to participate in the public sphere), which had marred French politics during the first century after the revolution of 1789, a century characterized by a chronic pendulum movement between revolution and reaction, open social conflict and civil war (Beland and Hansen, 2000: 50–1).

The institutions and the dominant norms of *solidarité* correspond to the typical Christian demcratic principle of restoration of social order, albeit with a modernist 'Durkheimean' inflection. As is the case with the latter's concept of 'organic solidarity', it is based on the idea of modern life as characterized by an intrinsic interdependence arising from division of labour and functional differentiation. This interdependence necessitates a system of social protection, founded on the principle of insurance to neutralize the random risks inherent in industrial life (ibid.: 51). Again, the welfare state is not primarily understood in redistributive terms and even less in terms of charity. It is understood to be of central importance to all, as a protection against the vagaries of modern industrial life. Hence, the French welfare state is very much based on social insurance and the principle of income replacement and programmes, while for the most part compulsory, are occupationally differentiated and managed by the social partners. The lack of resonance of recent reform bids towards a more residual welfare state, based on labour market flexibility intended to create jobs for the long-term unemployed while providing them with a modicum of social protection, indicates how deeply entrenched this norm of *solidarité* is in French political society and reform initiatives certainly are not meaningfully understood as a 'self-transformation'.

It is beyond the scope of the chapter to engage in a more comprehensive and general analysis of the political situation in the member states of the euro-zone. Nevertheless, examples abound in Austria, Belgium, France, Germany, the Netherlands and Italy (on the Netherlands see Van Apeldoorn in this volume, Chapter 1). All of these countries exhibit, in greater or lesser degree, the diminished stature of Christian Democratic and Social Democratic politics of mediation and increased fragmentation, the rise of populist mavericks, reduction in voter turnout, ascendancy of personalistic or charismatic leaders and growing volatility and unpredictability of electoral support.

Fallacies in the economics of post-industrialism

Up to this stage, the chapter has outlined the New Malthusian argument about the welfare state and its application to the analysis of the implications of the EMU for the European 'social model'. While accepting that the politics of welfare state reform is complex, it has also critiqued the way in which New Malthusians invoke this complexity to relativize the degree of welfare state retrenchment to the extent that it denies that such retrenchment has taken place. By shifting the attention from expenditure levels to effective entitlements, the chapter has argued that significant retrenchment has taken place. Furthermore, by departing from entrenched distributive principles, such retrenchment poses a serious challenge to the very foundations of legitimacy and norms of solidarity on which European socio-political order is based (for an elaboration, see Cafruny and Ryner, 2007b).

Of course, this argument loses much of its force if the post-industrial economic forces compelling change are as intransitive, objective and unavoidable as the New Malthusians argue. In this section it will be argued that this is not the case. The focus of the discussion will be on output and productivity growth and their determinants. The reason for this is rather straightforward: if annual output and productivity growth in Europe were a couple of percentage points higher, then the constraints of existing welfare commitments, population pressures and changes to the family structure would not be as daunting for the welfare state as New Malthusians make them out to be.

The section begins by pointing to some serious divergences between the New Malthusian argument and the empirical evidence. This in and of itself should make us highly sceptical towards the New Malthusian economic interpretation of 'post-industrialism'. However, without an alternative framework of interpretation, the argument only goes so far. Hence, in a second section the *conceptual* problems of post-industrialism are discussed. This discussion starts with some rather straightforward problems of measurement and then proceeds to more fundamental ontological questions concerning adequate methods of abstraction.

Empirical problems

Even the aggregate figures of the development of output and productivity growth in the industrial countries that Pierson invokes (2001b: 84, Table 3.1) are not as unequivocal as he suggests. Recalling that 'the problem' is supposed to be that the service sector, which is employing an increasing share of the workforce, has an inherently slower rate of growth than the manufacturing sector, Pierson shows that this is indeed the case. What he does not mention, however, are the historical variations over time *in the sectors themselves.* According to Pierson's figures, productivity growth (here measured as the output per person employed), in manufacturing decreased from 4.6 per cent in the period 1960–70 to 3.1 per cent in the period 1971–94. It is true that the corresponding slowdown of productivity growth in services was from 3 per cent to 1.1 per cent. Nevertheless (again, working with Pierson's figures), considering that that service productivity growth in the period 1960–70 was only 0.1 per cent lower than manufacturing productivity growth in 1971–94, one can legitimately ask if it is inherent attributes to manufacturing and services that matter, or if there is something else in the advanced capitalist economies that changed from one time period to the other.

The empirical evidence becomes even more problematic when consideration is given to variations of 'economic performance' as recorded in national accounts between different types of welfare state regime.[4] This evidence does not accord with the predictions of the 'post-industrial trilemma' – see Table 2.1. Theoretically, the USA, as the paradigmatic case of a 'liberal' welfare state with few restrictions to the 'free' operation of the labour market, represents an economy that has adjusted to post-industrialism. To be sure, productivity growth is no longer likely to be high. However, output and employment levels can still be high because labour markets can adjust to low productivity, even without pushing the economy into excessive deficits

Table 2.1 'Post-industrialism' in different types of welfare state: Hypothesis versus empirics

	USA (liberal)	Germany (Christian democratic)	Sweden (social democratic)
Employment rate	High	Low	High
Unemployment rate	Low	High	Low
Labour productivity growth – predicted	Low	High	Low
Output growth – predicted	High	Low	Low
Inflation	Low	Low	High
Budget balance	Balance	Balance	Deficit
Employment rate*	73.1	68.5	71.9
Unemployment rate[†]	5.0	8.0	5.7
Labourproductivity growth[‡]	2.1	1.8	2.2
Output growth[§]	3.2	1.3	2.7
Rate of inflation[¶]	2.1	0.6	1.3
Government balance[‖]	−2.2	−3.9	+1.3

* Average annual percentage of total adult population, 1996–2005.
[†] Average annual percentage, 1996–2005.
[‡] Per hour worked, average annual percentage, 1996–2005.
§ Average annual percentage growth of real GDP, 1996–2005.
¶ Average annual percent increase of the GDP deflator, 1996–2005.
‖ Government net lending as percentage of GDP, average annual, 1996–2005.
Source: European Commission (2006b), Statistical Annex; OECD (2006a), Statistical Annex.

and inflation. This is indeed born out by the evidence. One objection would be that labour productivity growth is not that much lower than in the Fordist period (the average annual figure was 2.4 per cent in 1961–73), and it is questionable whether it warrants such a grandiose explanation as the shift from an 'industrial' to a 'post-industrial' age. Germany, as the paradigmatic case for the Christian democratic regime, at first glance also seems to confirm the New Malthusian thesis: high wages and generous social insurance have stultified service-market expansion, resulting in low employment and high unemployment levels, which also act as a drag on output growth. The budget deficit is excessive, given the emphasis on monetary austerity and fiscal rectitude, but if one adjusts for the costs associated with German reunification it is probably consistent with the fiscal burden on social insurance generated by high unemployment. However, labour productivity growth is a lot lower than what one would expect from an economy based on export-oriented, high value-added manufacturing production. This could, of course, be interpreted as the social market economy performing even worse than anticipated. A less complacent reading would be one that recognizes that this makes the situation more complicated than what the simple theory allows. One might indeed begin to discern alternative interpretations behind German stagnation. One would also remember that the issue of productivity, so central to the hypothesis, also gave grounds for scepticism in the US case.

However, it is the empirical evidence from Sweden, the paradigmatic case of a social democratic welfare state, that delivers the devastating blow. With equally, if not more, highly 'decommodified' labour markets and generous social benefits than the Christian democratic German case, Swedish social democracy empirically confounds the New Malthusian thesis. Its employment, unemployment and output performances pretty much match those of the USA. They are slightly lower but not by much. In addition, productivity growth is actually somewhat higher, and this is at full capacity utilization (European Commission, 2003e). This in and of itself is, of course, not incompatible with the trilemma thesis: in contrast to the Christian democratic state, which depends much more on traditional family networks and charities, a social democratic welfare state has invested massively in a public state-service sector. It also has a highly developed labour market policy system of retraining and reactivation. However, the prediction is that this type of welfare state will face difficulties in containing inflation or budget balances as it tries to maintain public service employment (alternatively, prohibitive tax rates will choke growth). However, it is here that the Swedish case is the most confounding. Inflation rates are well below those of the USA (although not as low as the incredibly low 0.6 per cent of Germany) and government net lending yields an annual average surplus of 1.3 per cent of GDP. Indeed, these rates are probably sufficient to explain any gap in performance between the USA and Sweden with regard to employment and output growth.[5]

Conceptual problems

The claim of the aforementioned is not that the empirical 'facts' establish anything conclusively. Nevertheless, it has been demonstrated that even on the basis of the empiricist rhetoric that the New Malthusians like to deploy, one can, simply by referring to some basic and generally available mainstream indicators, point to some rather elementary problems with the New Malthusian explanation. At the very least, this suggests that there are some fundamental conceptual problems with the New Malthusian account of the post-industrial service sector.

One basic problem is the conflation of the physical volume of production and exchange values.[6] Although Baumol's (1967) argument might have some purchase with regard to physical output, the case is very different with exchange values. The problem is compounded when one, as the New Malthusians do, seek empirical verification of a physicalist argument with reference to measurements that are based on exchange values: Due to the difficulties of aggregating and comparing physical outputs, national accounts measure productivity in terms of the *value* of output over factor input. However, values are expressed in terms of prices and therefore exchange value. New Malthusian discussions symptomatically slip between the two. Although the 'cost-disease' argument is supposed to be one with regard to the tendency of service sector prices to increase *in relation* to manufacturing prices (and hence should rather be a 'price-disease' argument), we are told that the problem is that we are 'bad at' service production (Pierson, 2001b: 85) as if there was something wrong with the production-function of services (which by the very premise of the argument cannot be compared with manufacturing).

Once we follow through the consequence of the fact that the empirical building blocs are exchange values rather than physical values, the New Malthusian intransitive necessities increasingly give way to transitive contingencies, and hence social choice, politics and power. This is made even more apparent when we consider more deeply the problem of treating the notion of the 'service sector' – which entails such diverse activities as catering, health care, education and investment banking – as an abstract category when it is doubtful whether it really has the homogenous attributes that would be required to make this intellectually justified.

If we instead depart from the category of the commodity, as for example Regulation Theory (following the Marxist as well as institutionalist critical engagements with Ricardian economics) does, a different interpretation of the present emerges. The relative prices of different commodities, expressed through the 'general equivalence' of the money form, are central to a regime of accumulation. However, commodity exchange is not simply to be understood as determined by the market equilibrium of supply and demand as generated by free price formation under perfect competition. Rather, this is something that is generated within an institutional context. In no little measure, this is today determined by oligopolistic price setting, which is something that is enjoyed by corporations in *both* the manufacturing and service 'sectors': one would hardly describe investment banking, corporate legal advice and accounting firms as low value added, low wage sectors (nor are we alarmed by price increases of these to the same extent that New Malthusians worry over higher tax rates to support public services). Nor is it the case that value added in these industries is to the result of innovations in the labour process. However, a broader institutional matrix is more directly social and it pertains to the institutionalization of the factor markets that Polanyi (1957) referred to as the 'ficticious commodities' (land, labour, money). The determination of the exchange value of these are inherently political and thus directly a function of the configuration of a mode of regulation underpinned by accumulation strategies and hegemonic projects (Lipietz, 1987; Aglietta, 1998; introduction of this book).[7] Important in this context is, of course, also the social gender contract. When we consider this social contract, it is a misnomer to suggest that the service sector was of less significance in earlier phases of welfare capitalism. It was rather the case that these services were provided without monetary compensation in the household (Pateman, 1988). It should also be pointed out that different welfare states seem to have 'matured' at different rates of social expenditure of GDP. It is hard to find objective reasons behind higher levels of social expenditure in Scandinavia than in continental Europe or America except with reference to the different distributive bargains that constituted the different welfare state regimes in the first place (Esping-Andersen, 1990).

It should be pointed out in this context that there is nothing wrong with using exchange value as the basis of measurement. It would be excessively physiocratic, and contrary to any modern understanding of economics, to suggest that it was. In this context it is also worthwhile to point to the interdependence of manufacturing and services and the fact that service provision may have positive indirect effects on productivity in the manufacturing sector. One obvious and direct example would be good IT consultancy. Other examples would include the education of the workforce. However, childcare and health provision also serve essential reproductive functions as well as essential functions for 'user-producer networks' in national systems of innovation (Lundvall, 1992; Mahon, 2007). No doubt investment bankers, lawyers and accountants would also stress the indirect productive value of their services. Whether all these different service providers are proportionately compensated for their contribution could be debated.

Conclusion

At a juncture in history when the development of the productive forces has put advanced capitalist societies, such as the European ones, in a position potentially to produce a larger mass of surplus in a more humane and ecologically sustainable manner than ever before, the neo-Malthusian counter-intuitive explanation should encounter more resistance than it has hitherto met. Instead, attention should once again be given to distributive questions – over the last three decades (and the neo-Malthusians are totally silent on this) there has been a massive redistribution from wages to profits, and within this category towards rentier profits (Duménil and Lévy, 2001). Attention should also be given to the politics and power relations that have produced such an outcome.

On the basis of this, one can resubmit another explanation to the dearth of productivity growth over the last decades in advanced capitalist – and then especially the European – societies, despite the vast production possibilities opened up by the 'third' informatics–cybernetic industrial revolution. This could be characterized as the 'revenge of the globalization thesis', although 'globalization' is here understood less as an objective necessity imposed by footloose capital than as a neoliberal political artefact – and an artefact where nation-state strategies and differential effects and uneven development still play crucial parts.

Such an account would explain the failure of unleashing the latent potential productivity growth of 'post-Fordism' with reference not to the 'Ricardian' dynamics Pierson used to refute the globalization argument, but rather to 'Kaldorian' dynamics (e.g. Schwartz, 1994), that is, productivity growth as a function of the *ex ante* stable expansion of aggregate demand, providing the basis for further expansion of such demand. Such Kaldorian dynamics have not been adequately unleashed in Europe, because of the particular mode of regulation that has constituted the post-Fordist accumulation regime out of a range of potential alternative trajectories (Lipietz, 1987; Boyer, 2000). This is, for the most part, a finance-led regime that prioritizes shareholder-value, immediate asset yield ratio returns on an attenuated productive capital base. Hence the social and institutional construction of commodity-value chains of equivalence assign priority to rentier profits and their claims of the productive base of the economy to the extent that it permeates accounting practices themselves (Perry, 2006; Watson, 2006). This is flanked by a disciplinary neoliberal macroeconomic stance as institutionalized first through the EMS and then through the EMU that is exactly preventing the sort of expansion of stable demand that would be required for long term 'learning by doing' in accordance with Kaldorian economics (Boyer and Petit, 1991). To be sure, this is a situation characterized by uneven development, where niche strategies can be pursued in small social democratic countries despite all, albeit within unstable and precarious conditions. It also provides the basis for debt and finance-led and neoliberal growth in the USA on the basis of a more predatory form of hegemony (Cafruny and Ryner, 2007b). However, this does not mean that, for example, social democratic alternatives are prevented due to intransitive constraints as much as because of the existing political and power configuration. Wolfgang Streeck, one of the primary – and most subtle – proponents of the New Malthusian thesis, in effect admits this in an analysis of the German situation. Recognizing that, in principle, an expansion of the service sector along Scandinavian social democratic lines provides just as viable way out of the German 'post-industrial' dilemma as an Anglo-American strategy, he and his co-author nevertheless conclude:

> [T]he first priority for the Federal Government is *balancing* its budget, not *expanding* it. The main criterion by which the performance of the Finance Minister is publicly judged year by year is whether his budget meets the targets of the Maastricht stability pact.
>
> (Streeck and Trampusch, 2005: 22)

To spell matters out, this explanation concedes that disciplinary neoliberal governance itself is a central variable in explaining the dearth of output and productivity growth in the European economy, and thereby by extension the crisis of the European social model. In the most recent phase of disciplinary neoliberal governance, this has happened through the very terms of reference of the European Central Bank (ECB) mandate (emphasizing price stability as defined by the ECB itself and by prohibiting any Keynesian lending functions to the ECB), the Maastricht convergence criteria and the stability pact. This has ensured a continuation of the situation under EMS, where the cost of asserting price stability has been a straitjacket on aggregate demand expansion. Although this has been compatible with niche strategies in some economies, the lack of policy flexibility in what is not an optimal currency area has resulted in massive supply and demand shocks in other areas even prompting calls for a renationalization of monetary policy in some areas (for example, Italy). The EMU has also contributed to the stagnation of output and productivity growth, by being based on an acceptance of the global financial architecture as it has been structured by American leadership after the collapse of Bretton Woods. This has assigned market values to financial and rentier capital at the expense of the strengths of European welfare capitalism: diversified quality manufacturing production and social welfare services.[8]

Notes

1. New Malthusian themes are prominent in key passages of recent documents associated with the Lisbon Strategy (e.g. Ferrera, Hemerijck and Rhodes, 2000; High Level Group, 2004: 13–15; European Commission, 2005d: 15), although the vagueness of the language on the 'social model' and hints to the promise of information and communication technology (ICT) technology also allows for different readings. Nevertheless, it is in this context that the hegemonic status of the New Malthusian position in welfare state research is particularly important. With reference to its authoritative knowledge claims, it clarifies how the 'social model' and the potentials and limitations of ICT should be understood.
2. On the concept of 'lock-in' (*Einbindung*) and European trade unions, see Schulten and Ryner (2003).
3. Clayton and Pontusson's piece, which has become a standard reference for critiques of the politics of retrenchment, drew on comparative OECD data on changes P90/P10 ratios up to 1995 for their argument of an increase of (wage) inequality. Updated data on P90/P10 ratios are not readily available. However, UTIP–UNIDO data up to 1999, using the THEIL measure, is consistent with Clayton and Pontusson's argument (Galbraith, 2004). Beckfield's more recent study measures income inequality in the form of GINI coefficients.
4. This comparison is based on the reasonable premise that significant variations especially in labour markets remain, between liberal, Christian democratic and social democratic regimes. In other words, neoliberalization as a process has not gone so far as to produce a state of neoliberal convergence rendering these categories meaningless (Ryner, 2004: 98–9; Cafruny and Ryner, 2007b: 6–7).
5. Similar economic performance can be observed in the other Nordic countries (European Commission, 2003e; Goul Andersen, 2007).

6. In developing this argument, I am greatly indebted to discussions with Paul Lewis at the Department of Political Science and International Studies at the University of Birmingham.
7. This can hardly be denied by the New Malthusians who, contrary to the neo-classical economists, make their argument about wage formation with reference to average productivity as opposed to marginal productivity.
8. For an elaboration of these arguments, see Cafruny and Ryner (2007: chapters 2 and 3).

3
Geopolitics and Neoliberalism: US Power and the Limits of European Autonomy

Alan W. Cafruny

The first decade of the twenty-first century has not been kind to the American superpower. The meltdown in US credit markets resulting from the bursting of the housing bubble in the fall of 2007 has laid the global financial system 'wide open to catastrophic failure' (*Financial Times*, 2008). A disastrous military campaign in Iraq, a bloody and inconclusive holding action in Afghanistan, and growing threats to the super-currency status of the dollar have given rise to predictions of 'terminal decline' (Arrighi, 2005) and celebrations of a European counter-hegemonic project in defence of the European social model (Habermas and Derrida, 2003; Kupchan, 2002; Haseler, 2004; Reid, 2004; Judt, 2005; Leonard, 2005; McCormick, 2007). The 'project for a new American century' seems to have ended almost before it was supposed to have begun.

The role played by US structural financial power in the construction of Europe's neoliberal project has been analysed by a number of scholars (Helleiner, 1994; Gowan, 1999; Seabrooke, 2001; Baker, 2006a; Panitch and Gindin, 2005; Cafruny and Ryner, 2007a; Ryner, 2007a; see also Chapter 4, by Bieling and Jäger, in this book). However, the relationship between neoliberalism and geopolitics has received less attention. In part one of this chapter I discuss the role of US military power as it has served, in tandem with US structural financial power, to consolidate the turn to neoliberalism in Europe. Beginning in the mid-1990s the USA transformed the North Atlantic Treaty Organization (NATO) from a containment-oriented and defensive alliance to an instrument designed to promote the forward expansion of US power across the European continent and into Central Asia. This reinforced Europe's geopolitical dependence on the USA and buttressed neoliberal social forces across the continent.

In the second part of the chapter I consider the long-range possibilities for the USA and Europe in view of growing challenges to US power in both its geoeconomic and geopolitical dimensions. The uncertain status of the dollar as reserve currency is the natural accompaniment to relative industrial decline and the transnationalization of production even as US hegemony has been prolonged through financial deregulation and a resultant series of bubbles. In this context the Bush administration's policy of geopolitical advance and militarization, designed in part to maintain its hold over global energy resources, is a compensatory strategy (Harvey, 2003) that has, however, encountered substantial costs and risks. Nevertheless, despite the deepening crisis of the US imperium, the possibilities for a European challenge are sharply circumscribed by its subordinate participation within a US-led neoliberal transnational financial order and its related inability to develop an autonomous regional security structure.

After the cold war: interregnum and restoration of US coercive supremacy in Europe

US power played a central role in establishing not only the international economic and political structural conditions of Western Europe and its embryonic union, but also the character of its politics, institutions and doctrines. Marshall Plan aid was instrumental in facilitating nascent forms of European supranational integration through the Organisation for European Economic Co-operation (OEEC) and European Payments Union. The European Defence Community (EDC) itself was a response to American pressures for German rearmament; its failure led to direct US control over European 'security architecture' through a garrison of 350.000 US troops, an archipelago of military bases, and the positioning of thousands of nuclear warheads in Western Europe, of which 480 remain in the UK, Germany, Belgium, the Netherlands and Italy (Norris and Kristensen, 2006: 57–8).

Although transatlantic relations exhibited chronic tensions, most notably over what Charles DeGaulle called 'exorbitant' monetary privileges, geopolitical weakness and fragmentation diminished the ability of Western European states individually or collectively to challenge core US interests. The Suez Crisis showed that all decisions concerning the Middle East would be made in Washington, and not in London or Paris. The threat to withdraw troops from Europe reinforced adherence to the dollar gold standard during the 1960s and defeated French attempts to challenge the Anglo-American control of oil markets during the 1970s. By eliminating its only military challenger, the collapse of the Soviet Union presented the European Union (EU) with an opportunity but also a threat. The reunification of the continent appeared to establish a basis for renegotiation of Europe's political role within the transatlantic order, parallel to the formation of a monetary zone of stability.

The Maastricht Treaty codified ambitious plans for a common foreign and security policy alongside Economic and Monetary Union (EMU). As a European constitutional process began to unfold many observers discerned the basis of a nascent 'polity' that was a precondition of genuine economic and geopolitical self-determination: appointment of a high representative for the Common Foreign and Security Policy (CFSP), expansion of the Western European Union, articulation of an European Security and Defence Policy (ESDP) involving a rapid reaction force, agreement on a set of international 'humanitarian' tasks, and the establishment of an EU military protectorate over Bosnia. These developments were reinforced by attempts at transnational consolidation of European defence industries involving collaborative projects such as the eurofighter, and sporadic attempts to institutionalize co-operation through a European Defence Agency (EDA) and multilateral agreements.

Uncertainties among US policy-makers in the aftermath of 1989 also contributed to the expectation of a renegotiated multilateral political-military settlement. Residual cold war instincts continued to influence the policies and attitudes throughout the first Bush administration and during the first years of the Clinton administration, resulting in a sphere of influence policy conceding considerable authority to Europe. During this brief interregnum the USA contemplated the downsizing or even elimination of NATO in favour of European security co-operation in what appeared a replay of the EDC: large-scale withdrawal of US forces to realize a 'peace dividend', and the granting of considerable influence to Russia in Eastern Europe and the former Soviet Union. The sphere of influence policy seemed to accord with the Clinton administration's core project of financial liberalization, globalization and domestic fiscal retrenchment. The first gulf war and the UN-supervised post-war settlement temporarily reinforced these policies, reaffirming US primacy in the Middle East, albeit within the framework of coalition building and a high level of consensus among allies.

War and the expansion of NATO

Despite Secretary of State James Baker's assurances during negotiations with the Soviet Union over Germany's unification that NATO would not be extended 'one inch to the East' (Zelikow and Rice, 1995: 183), the Clinton administration abandoned the sphere of influence policy in favour of a forward strategy designed to expand American power over Europe and to consolidate the position of neoliberal and Atlanticist forces in individual states and in the Eurepean Union (EU) as a whole (Gowan, 1999; Van der Pijl, 2001a). The expansion of NATO was to play a central role in this transformation whose sources were multiple and complex and included fragmentation among the EU powers; growing disarray in South-eastern Europe; the increasing importance of Eastern European economies and labour markets to the world economy; interrelationships of energy security and political stability; and the development of a more confrontational posture towards Russia.

The wars against Serbia played a central role in this transformation. Initially designated as the test case of a common EU policy, the war in

Bosnia (1992–5) would eventually demonstrate that the EU states lacked the cohesion and commitment required to fulfil their nominal ambitions, even in the European space itself, with respect to a security order underpinned by cosmopolitan human rights norms and international law, and would need to rely on American power. Confronted with pressures for structural adjustment arising from international debt exceeding $22 billion, a contraction of export markets in Western Europe, and the return of 'guest workers' from Germany, the individual republics of former Yugoslavia began to pursue their own methods of dealing with the resulting massive economic shocks as communist party leaders in all of the republics underwent a seamless transition to ethnic nationalism, most notably and tragically in Serbia and Croatia. When Serb units of the Yugoslav National Army mobilized in Croatia and Slovenia, the USA accepted European Council President Jacques Poos's proclamation that 'This is the hour of Europe, not of America' (Gardner, 1991). Yet, Germany's recognition of Croatian and Slovenian sovereignty during the Serbo-Croat war provoked serious conflicts with France and Britain. Germany's diplomatic offensive was not linked to a broader strategy of conflict prevention and support for Bosnia, much less a broader diplomatic and political project for regional stability. Once Germany was sidelined, France and Britain offered a plan for *de facto* partition that rewarded and thus further provoked ethnic cleansing and encouraged Croatia to ally with Serbia (Ramet, 1996: 50). Massive human rights violations, the failure of UN forces to protect 'safe havens', and refugee flows to Western Europe generated pressures for a settlement, eventually provoking US military intervention within the framework of NATO and sponsorship of a joint Croat–Bosnian force, and culminating in the cold peace established at Dayton in 1995 (Cafruny, 2003).

Although tentative and somewhat improvisational, the US intervention in Bosnia reflected the transition in US foreign policy to a more expansionist strategy. By 1998 US policy towards South-eastern Europe had begun to cohere. Although the year-long diplomatic prelude to the 1999 air war against Serbia was still marked by diplomatic uncertainty and vacillation, the USA had nevertheless moved towards a more comprehensive project for the region, predicated on the elimination of Russian influence and the establishment of an enlarged security zone under NATO control. The aerial attack on Serbia followed a period of diplomatic manoeuvre establishing a more or less unified NATO stance and a propaganda offensive re-defining the crisis in terms of human rights violations whose severity justified military intervention. At Rambouillet in February 1999 NATO issued an ultimatum to Serbia (and indirectly to Russia) demanding access for NATO military deployments throughout Serbian territory. Serbia's anticipated rejection[1] provided the basis for a 78-day bombing campaign followed by a Serbian capitulation when it became clear that Russia would not provide diplomatic or military assistance. The war demonstrated the limitations of EU foreign and security policy and also greatly diminished Russian influence in South-eastern Europe.

The expansion of NATO's role 'out of area' served to entrench Atlanticist forces throughout the continent, most notably in Germany. Whereas at the outset Britain and France had sought to exclude Germany from the Rambouillet negotiations, as the bombing campaign intensified Germany emerged as a central factor in the war effort. Thus the Blair–Schröder 'third way' economic initiatives, announced at the end of the war, served to marginalize finance minister Oskar Lafontaine's 'compensatory' policies, more in tune with a modernized version of traditional social democracy (Ryner, 2003). They had their counterpart in the ascendance of the Atlanticist vision of European security, which was consolidated through the maintenance of NATO's 'credibility'. Atlanticism was confirmed in Germany by the ouster of Lafontaine, who had linked opposition to the war to alternatives to monetarism and Atlanticism (Van der Pijl, 2001a; Lafontaine, 2000).

Kosovo (along with Macedonia) has implications for the international political economy that are notably lacking in Bosnia and other parts of western former Yugoslavia. US policy since 1992 has recognized the strategic importance of the Western Balkans. As David Gompert, special assistant for national security affairs under the first President Bush wrote:

> The chief American strategic concern during the Bush administration and later under Clinton was to keep the Yugoslav conflict from spreading southward, where its flames could leap into the Atlantic Alliance. Therefore, while the Bush Administration was not convinced of the need to intervene in Bosnia, it took a markedly different attitude towards Kosovo. Washington feared that a Serbian assault against the Kosovar Albanians would consume the entire southern Balkan region in a conflagration that would pit one NATO ally against another. Hostilities in Kosovo would probably spill into Albania proper. This in turn could incite the large Albanian minority in Macedonia and lead to a Serbian or Greek intervention there . . . Whereas the Bosnian war could be contained, conflict in Kosovo could not.
>
> (Gompert, 1996: 136–7)

The importance of the region expanded greatly in the ensuing years as a result of intensifying conflicts over energy resources and the construction of pipelines linking the Caspian Sea Basin to Western Europe and the Mediterranean (Baghat, 2002; Cafruny, 2003). The defeat of Serbia not only served to restore the credibility of NATO and stabilize its eastern flank, an objective that had been recognized as early as 1992, but also paved the way for the establishment of direct US military presence in the region and the concomitant transition from state capitalism to neoliberalism (Freyberg-Inan, 2005). Camp Bondsteel in western Kosovo, built by Haliburton in

1999 as part of a \$330 million contract, is the largest US military base in South-eastern Europe with permanent housing for 7000 troops and forms part of a nearly contiguous arc (excepting only Syria and Iran) of existing or projected facilities extending from the Balkans (Kosovo and Montenegro) to Pakistan. In many other respects the war with Serbia prefigured the subsequent US invasion of Iraq and the Bush doctrine with its emphasis on pre-emption, rejection of the principle of national sovereignty, and abandonment of multilateralism. Faced with Russian and Chinese opposition, the USA bypassed the UN Security Council and deployed humanitarian rhetoric and a NATO mandate as an alternative legal and political justifications for military intervention. The heavy bombing of Belgrade and other Serb cities gave a foretaste of the 'shock and awe' tactics that would be used to subdue Baghdad and demonstrate US military prowess to the world.[2] By the mid-1990s the USA had moved towards a clear policy of NATO expansion in Central and Eastern Europe. Kosovo's 'declaration of independence' in February 2008 established the basis for a full-fledged joint EU–US protectorate.

NATO expansion has paved the way for EU enlargement. Although the Copenhagen Criteria (1993) formally established open-ended commitments to accession for all European countries, enlargement beyond Central Europe contradicted prevailing assumptions concerning the character of the EU. As Chapters 8 and 9 in this volume by Dorothee Bohle and Jan Drahokoupil show, the wholesale expansion of the EU into Eastern Europe created *de facto* centre-periphery relationships under the umbrella of nominal equality. If there are numerous problems in applying the concept of an 'optimal currency area' to the existing eurozone, the concept is even less plausible with respect to an expanded eurozone encompassing Central and Eastern European Member States. The absence of a social dimension (Holman, 2004a) encourages internal labour flexibility and intensifies wage competition. As shown by the contributions by Bohle and by Vliegenthart and Overbeek to this volume (Chapters 8 and 7), enlargement has reproduced a logic of competitive austerity and uneven development in the new Member States. The result has been wholesale abandonment of traditional understandings concerning the *Acquis Communautaire*: lengthy 'transition periods' before allowing the free movement of labour; limitations on new Member States' access to structural and CAP funds; (largely unsuccessful) attempts to limit new members' political influence; and growing resentment. New Member States have adopted economic growth strategies linked to Western European (and US) production chains and predicated on the provision of cheap labour (Bieler, 2002; Bohle, 2005; Dunford, 2005; Ivanova, 2007). German corporations in particular have become increasingly dependent on outsourcing; they are locating a growing share of their production to exploit lower wages in the east (Lorentowicz, Marin and Raubold, 2002); the availability of eastern cheap labour is a central factor in negotiations over wages and working conditions, and taxation (see Vliegenthart and Overbeek, Chapter 7, this volume).

EU enlargement reinforces neoliberalism, but it inevitably produces internal political fragmentation because it grants nominal equality to peripheral states that seek closer relations to the USA both for geopolitical reasons and because of their second-class economic and political status within the EU. As the USA struggles to maintain its primacy over the key sources of energy and transit routes in Eurasia, the development of political influence in Central and Eastern Europe has become a central aspect of foreign policy.

European energy, European security and US power

Intensifying international competition for oil and natural gas as a result of diminishing global supplies and the rapid growth of the Chinese and Indian economies has dramatically enhanced the importance of Eurasia and the 'great game' of geopolitics. Energy security has become a serious concern for European countries. The increasing significance of Eurasian sources of energy reinforces Europe's dependence on the USA. The EU currently imports 50 per cent of its oil and gas, a figure that is expected to increase to 75 per cent by 2030, with most supplies originating in 'geopolitically uncertain' areas in Russia and the former Soviet Union. Germany receives 35 per cent of its oil and 40 per cent of its gas from Russia. Poland and Hungary import more than 60 per cent of their natural gas from Russia (European Commission, 2006a: 1). The indirect impact on the EU of Russia's decision to cut off supplies of natural gas to Ukraine in early 2006 and oil to Belarus in early 2007, alongside Gazprom's bid to expand ownership of Western and South-eastern European gas companies, have dramatized Europe's energy vulnerability.

Although the European Commission has sought to promote energy liberalization, EU energy policy remains at an embryonic stage. There is no single market for energy; two decades after the advent of the Single European Act prices for electricity and gas vary from country to country by as much as 100 per cent (*Economist*, 2006a: 65). Despite the centrality of energy (coal) to the original European Coal and Steel Community (ECSC) there is no EU policy of energy security. According to the European Commission, 'Energy-using countries are starting to see each other as potential rivals for [energy] provision . . . just at a time when Europe imports more energy than ever before. This trend will further accelerate substantially' (*EUObserver*, 2006: 1). The development of intra-European and intra-EU rivalry is evident in Russia's ability to develop long-term bilateral commercial relationships with individual Member States; Italian threats to cut off energy supplies from Italy to Corsica in retaliation for France's bid to block Enel's takeover of Suez by merging it with Gaz de France; Spain's attempt to block the takeover of Endesa by Eon of Germany; Poland's fierce opposition to the proposed German–Russian North European Gas Pipeline (a 1200-kilometre pipeline running through the Baltic Sea and bypassing Polish territory); Poland's subsequent threats to veto the EU–Russian 'Strategic Partnership

Treaty'; French and German opposition to Commission proposals to break up their national electricity companies, Gaz de France and Eon; and Gerhard Schröder's appointment as director of Gazprom following the defeat of the Sozialdemokratischen Partei Deutschlands (SPD) in the elections of September 2005 (Beunderman, 2006: 1). The European Council on Foreign Relations has concluded that Russia is 'picking off individual EU member states and signing long-term deals which undermine the core principles of the EU's common strategy . . . EU member states tend to "Europeanize" their disputes with Russia while they bilateralize their "sweet deals"' (Leonard and Popescu, 2007: 1, 17).

During the mid-1990s the major Anglo-American oil companies made significant inroads into the Russian energy sector. Russia's re-emergence as regional power, signified by the development of nationalism and the state takeover of the Yukos empire, enabled it to renegotiate contracts from a position of strength. Nevertheless, Russia has lost considerable influence in South-eastern Europe and the Black Sea region, which is the source of 50 per cent of EU energy requirements and the centre of transit routes connecting Central Asian and Caspian oil and gas with Western and South-eastern Europe. The US government prevented the construction of Europe's preferred crude oil pipeline from the Caspian Sea through Iran and has supported a network of alternative pipelines financed by Anglo-American firms from Central Asia to Western Europe that bypass Russia (Jackson, 2006).

Energy insecurity greatly increases Europe's dependence on NATO and US military power. US political–military initiatives in Eastern Europe are closely related to the attempt to consolidate power in the Eurasian sphere. As Zbigniew Brzezinski has written,

> Geopolitics has moved from the regional to the global dimension, with preponderance over the entire Eurasian continent serving as the central basis for global primacy. The United States . . . now enjoys international primacy, with its power directly deployed on three peripheries of the Eurasian continent serving as the central basis for global primacy. America's global primacy is directly dependent on how long and how effectively its preponderance on the Eurasian continent is sustained.
>
> (Brzezinski, 1997b: 38–9)

During the last decade the USA has established close bi-lateral relationships with strategically important Eastern European and Central Asian countries. In 2004 Kazakhstan, the largest country in Central Asia with large and untapped oil deposits, joined the NATO-sponsored Partnership for Peace (Bordonaro, 2006: 2). In April 2005 the governments of Georgia, Ukraine, Azerbaijan and Moldova (GUAM) met the USA to promote 'Euro–Atlantic' integration and establish a 'Pax Americana' from the Adriatic to the Caspian region (Power and Interest News Report, 2005: 3–4). The entry of Bulgaria and Romania into NATO cemented relations with the USA prior to their accession into the EU. A similar path still appears possible for the Ukraine. All of the 'new European' states strongly supported the US invasion of Iraq. Poland's role as the key US ally in continental Europe has been confirmed by plans to host (along with the Czech Republic) US anti-ballistic missile systems.

In conjunction with the policy of reformulating the NATO mandate to include 'out of area' actions, the USA has begun radically to transform its military posture by shifting troops and resources from Western Europe – and especially Germany – to the 'arc of instability' linking the Black Sea region to the Middle East. Even as France, Germany and Russia sought to prevent the US invasion of Iraq in the spring of 2003, Romania and Bulgaria publicly stated their willingness to co-operate strategically with the USA. Both countries provided access to their military bases, and eventually sent substantial numbers of troops to Iraq. In November 2005 Romania agreed to the installation of US military bases at Kogalniceanu Airport, near the Black Sea port of Costanta, and Fetesti, 200 miles east of Bucharest, with the provision that US warships would patrol in the Black Sea. Romanian military analyst Cornel Codita observed that the agreement 'allows the USA to move closer to Russia and above all to hot spots in the Middle East' (*Deutsche Welle*, 2005: 2). Similar agreements were made with Bulgaria for the establishment of a base near Bezmer Airfield near the southern border with Turkey (Bordonaro, 2005). These agreements, which were signed in the teeth of popular outcry throughout Europe over revelations of Central Intelligence Agency (CIA) 'renditions' of prisoners to various European countries, signal the formation of strategic alliances between Atlanticist blocs in 'new Europe' and the USA rather than support for an autonomous regional security identity. They will be consummated by extensive economic and military–industrial links to the USA.[3]

Limits of European security and defence policy

The Common Foreign and Security Policy (CFSP) originated in the late 1980s in the context of a Franco–West German project that recognized the need for an integral relationship between monetary and political union. However, the vague language concerning CFSP in the Maastricht Treaty reflected traditional British concerns for the primacy of the transatlantic relationship and the sharp conflicts of interest that developed over German reunification and peolicy towards former Yugoslavia. France has traditionally viewed a common European foreign policy as a means of countering US power, whereas throughout the 1990s Britain and Germany insisted any such defence identity should be within the NATO framework. The Balkan wars, especially the 1999 war with Serbia, demonstrated European dependence resulting from the gap between European and US military capabilities and prompted a renewed commitment to a European Security and Defence Policy (ESDP). At the end of 2005 the EU, with the second largest military force in the world, was conducting seven separate operations in Africa, Iraq, the Caucasus and South-eastern Europe. Having formed a 60,000 troop rapid reaction force the EU was deploying 7000 troops in Bosnia and had conducted more modest interventions in Darfur and the Democratic Republic of the Congo. These peacekeeping or 'constabulary' missions do not, however, signify the development of genuine European global military capabilities or autonomy from the USA. The ESDP has remained limited in part as a result of Britain's traditional commitment to Atlanticism. However, even absent this commitment, the EU remains politically fragmented and unable – in the context of EMU and adverse demographic and growth rates – to develop military capacities that would enable it to approach the USA on a remotely equal terrain.

Franco–German co-operation reached its rhetorical apex at the 'Summit of Four' in April 2003, when Chirac and Schröder followed up a 'joint declaration' of January 2003 calling for joint decision-making with an appeal (with Luxembourg and Belgium) for an autonomous military planning headquarters. These initiatives were predicated on substantial political–military co-operation, but also on the creation of 'Franco–German industrial champions'. Yet, these initiatives collapsed in the context of economic rivalries centred around German resistance to Sanofi-Synthélabo's takeover bid for Aventis, attempts to prevent Siemens from buying parts of Alstom, and de Villepin's concept of 'economic patriotism' (*Economist,* 2004b: 47–7; Parker 2006).

European attempts to develop significant defence industry collaboration have nevertheless been partially successful and will be further encouraged by the formation of the EDA. By 2006 four European firms – BAE Systems, EADS, Thales and Finmeccanica – were among the top ten global armaments firms. Concentration in the European industry was a response to the consolidation of the US defence industry around three large firms – Lockheed Martin, Boeing and Raytheon – and fears that 'European industry could be reduced to the status of sub-supplier to prime US contractors, while the key know-how is reserved for US firms' (European Commission, 2003c: 11). As the chief executive officers of BAE systems, EADS and Thales declared in 2004:

> Industry in Europe is under enormous competitive pressure from the United States. With US defence R & D investment running at around eight times that of Europe's fragmented total, and with substantial growth in the Pentagon's vast procurement budget in a heavily protected national market, American industries are reaching new heights.
>
> (Jones and Larrabee, 2005–6: 63)

Yet, despite these collaborative efforts, European defence capabilities are continuing to fall further behind the USA. The real military capability of the

EU is estimated to be 10 per cent that of the USA (European Commission, 2003c: 5). A relatively high percentage of European defence budgets is devoted to personnel costs, but only 3–4 per cent of European soldiers can be deployed. The European military–industrial complex remains fragmented and technologically backward and there is no single market for defence procurement. Because of the vast discrepancy between American and European defence budgets, European defence firms are becoming more heavily dependent on the highly restricted US market. BAE Systems, Britain's largest defence contractor, is the seventh largest American defence contractor and is considering becoming a US firm (*Economist*, 2006b: 66–7). Further access appears to depend on co-operation with the US military–industrial complex, which prevents them from cutting the Atlantic umbilical cord. For example, the EU's attempts to develop a 'strategic relationship' with China have been blocked by US opposition to the lifting of the EU's arms embargo and European firms' unwillingness to jeopardize limited access to the US market. Added to these factors, the fiscal and monetary constraints of EMU preclude substantial increases in defence spending. While Britain and France have implemented modest increases in their defence budgets, German military spending has decreased substantially in real terms during the past decade (CSIS, 2005: 21).

These considerations provide the context for understanding US governmental and military support for a more closely integrated European defence policy and substantial increases in defence spending, as well as for the European constitutional treaty (*EUObserver*, 2006). Zbigniew Brzezinski has summarized the logic of a 'strong Europe' that is subordinated to the USA with great clarity:

> Europe is America's essential geopolitical bridgehead in Eurasia . . . .
>
> Unlike America's links with Japan, NATO entrenches American political and military power on the Eurasian mainland. With the allied European nations still highly dependent on US protection, any expansion of Europe's political scope is automatically an extension of US influence. Conversely, the United States' ability to project power and influence in Eurasia relies on close transatlantic ties.
>
> (Brzezinski, 1997a: 75)[4]

Despite its tendency to indulge in anti-European and anti-French rhetoric, the Bush administration has strongly supported EU defence integration in order to facilitate common US–EU operations under American leadership (Centre for Strategic and International Studies, 2005). A stronger European defence is viewed as a means of consolidating Atlanticism and expanding the US imperium. The 2006 Quadrennial Defence Review predicts that there will be a 'long war' involving 'long-duration, complex operations involving the US military and international partners, waged simultaneously in multiple countries round the world' (US Department of Defence, 2006: 7, 13). European countries are assigned a central supporting role in this 'transformational' strategy, which includes the NATO-led 'Operation Enduring Freedom' in Afghanistan the planned US–NATO rapid deployment force to be based in Kleiaat, Lebanon, and an 'Individual Co-operation Agreement' with Egypt that serves as the prelude to 'promoting political and military ties with the Euro-Atlantic and the Mediterranean regions' (NATO, 2007: 1). In December 2007 a NATO-sponsored report by former US and Western European high-level military officers called for the adoption of a 'first-strike' nuclear strategy (Centre for Strategic and International Studies, 2007).[5]

Europe, the USA and 'the long war'

By proclaiming the limited utility of military force and the advantages of 'soft power' in the contemporary era proponents of this concept seek to rescue the thesis of a 'European challenge' (Nye, 2003, 2004; McCormick, 2007). Yet, the dual track enlargements of NATO and the EU have entrenched the position of political elites and transnational business interests across Europe linked to the USA and to neoliberalism. Indeed, even if one grants the limited utility arising from 'soft power', the bargaining position that might, in principle, derive from the sheer weight of the European economy is compromised by the neoliberal context in which a (self-limiting) socio-economic project demands adherence to Washington and Wall Street. Europe's geopolitical predicament precludes attempts to establish an autonomous EU power and marginalizes forces in 'core Europe' that favour alternatives to US-led neoliberalism.

It is possible to conceptualize the contemporary exercise of US power in terms of 'domination without hegemony' (Guha, 1992; Arrighi, 2005). Although this formulation is useful in capturing the increasingly parasitic and coercive aspects of US financial and military power, it does not take into account the degree of consensus and common interest among transatlantic (and global) ruling classes – and the growing distance between elites and mass opinion – that is conveyed by the concept of 'minimal hegemony' (Cafruny and Ryner, 2007b). During the post-World War II phase of *integral* hegemony the USA was prepared to make material concessions to its European allies to promote systemic stability and legitimacy. In the present *minimal* phase, by contrast, the USA draws on structural power to pursue more narrowly based policies that externalize social and political problems. The system nevertheless remains hegemonic in a minimal sense because structures and intersubjective norms compel subordinate social forces to consent to the prevailing order. The leading sectors of European capital derive substantial benefits from the prevailing economic and security framework even as their societies experience stagnant growth and high unemployment. German industry pursues a highly profitable export-led growth strategy, heavily dependent on outsourcing in Eastern Europe and capital outflows to the USA. Neoliberalism in Europe does not derive from monetarist dogma alone, but more fundamentally from the concrete interests of powerful actors responding to the opportunities and constraints of a given transatlantic regulatory order.

Terminal crisis?

There are nevertheless clear signs that even this more tenuous and unstable type of hegemony may be eroding. The brutal and costly occupation of Iraq has once again raised the spectre of geopolitical overstretch, antagonizing world public opinion and tarnishing the domestic ideological legitimacy of the Bush administration. The costs of the occupation have been partially defrayed by fiscal deficits that have deepened US dependency on foreign capital. Can US hegemony recover from the Iraqi quagmire, resolve its financial problems, and reconsolidate its position as the leader of a capitalist core? Giovanni Arrighi asserts that the USA stands at the precipice of a 'terminal crisis' resulting from geopolitical overstretch and financial insolvency that is leading to confrontation with China:

> Far from laying the foundations of a second American Century, the occupation of Iraq has jeopardized the credibility of US military might, further undermined the centrality of the United States and its currency within the global political economy, and strengthened the tendency towards the emergence of China as an alternative to US leadership in East Asia and beyond.
>
> (2005: 80)

The crisis presents Europe with a variety of options, including the establishment of closer ties with China or the recasting of the Atlantic order based on Keynesian and social democratic precepts (see also Harvey, 2003: 208–12).

The ability of the USA to attract massive capital inflows has served as the linchpin of the minimally hegemonic order. Yet, the continuation of these inflows has been called into question by trade and budget deficits and the downward pressure on the dollar that has been greatly magnified by the bursting of the housing bubble and subsequent strains in the US financial system. To be sure, a precipitous decline in the value of the dollar would make it more difficult to sustain large US military expenditure and would call into question a concept of economic governance based on consumer debt. In 2004 total securities invested in the USA amounted to $33.4 trillion, or 50 per cent of the world total. The 2006 US current account deficit reached $869 billion or 6.6 per cent of national income; the trade deficit with China was $202 billion. In 2006 US budget deficit was $248 billion or 2.3 per cent of gross domestic product (GDP), representing a substantial decline in relation to 2005; Chinese dollar reserves exceeded $1.3 trillion at the end of 2007 (US Treasury, 2007). Whereas until the turn of the twenty-first century capital inflows were largely private equity funds in the form of foreign direct investment or portfolio investment, during the first years of the new century the composition of these inflows has changed significantly. They are now coming primarily from governments or 'sovereign wealth funds' that are controlled by governments (Goodman and Story, 2008: B1). Hence, there is both a political and market logic to capital inflows. The strength of the dollar once again depends in part on explicit or implicit international pacts, as it did during the middle and late 1960s.

Between 2002 and 2007 the dollar fell by 24 per cent on a trade-weighted basis, with an even greater decline of 41 per cent against the euro (Guha, 2007: 13). Yet Asian investors and governments have continued to increase their dollar holdings, because most of their trade is with the USA and because they maintain undervalued exchange rates in order to continue export-led growth and employment strategies that render them highly dependent on access to the US market. China runs substantial trade deficits with its East Asian trading partners; hence, all East Asian economies, and not simply China, are vulnerable to any decrease in US demand.

Nevertheless, the potential dangers to the dollar are widely recognized, especially as the Federal Reserve responded to the subprime crisis with rate-cutting beginning in the fall of 2007 to avert recession. Notwithstanding mutual dependency between American and foreign central banks, there is broad agreement that the dollar will continue to decline in the coming years, although the pace and extent of depreciation are unpredictable. There is also speculation that China, which has permitted modest appreciations of the renminbi, will continue to diversify its foreign exchange reserves away from the US dollar and government bonds (Dombey, 2007: 5). George Soros has foreseen 'the end of a 60-year period of continuing credit expansion based on the dollar as the reserve currency' (Evans and Strasburg, 2008: 1). Arrighi has concluded that:

> The sinking dollar of the 2000s is the expression of a far more serious crisis of American hegemony than the sinking dollar of the 1970s. Whether gradual or brutal, it is the expression (and a factor) of a relative and absolute loss of the US's capacity to retain its centrality within the global political economy.
>
> (2005: p. 74)

A precipitous decline of the dollar would have serious and unpredictable consequences for the world economy and US society and politics. The US regulatory model has been predicated on high levels of consumption for the middle- and upper-classes, made possible in part by the 'exorbitant privilege' of dollar hegemony, which Kenneth Rogoff has quantified at $300–400 billion annually in recent years (Dombey, 2007; Rogoff, 2008: 1). US income and consumption levels would be hit hard by a combination of tax increases, dollar depreciation and rising interest rates (Duménil and Lévy, 2004b). The USA would also experience a closer relationship between its financial problems and its overall military posture at a time when the difficulties of the Iraqi occupation have encouraged Iranian intransigence and emboldened challengers to US hegemony in Latin America, and when China has made significant political and economic incursions in the Middle East and Africa. As a recent report for the US Council on Foreign Relations noted, 'The economic ramifications of a recession are much-discussed, myriad, and well-known. Less certain are the geopolitical and geoeconomic effects a US downturn might bring, especially at a time that finds other powers on the rise, the price of vital commodities spiking, and US prestige in question' (Teslik, 2008).

New American century?

The manifold economic and political uncertainties of the present period of international relations – marked above all by the extreme volatility of the Persian Gulf region as a result of US occupation – render all predictions about the future trajectory of American hegemony hazardous. Yet, if the war in Iraq and growing financial problems have clearly blown the USA into uncharted waters, the concept of 'terminal hegemony' is imprecise and tells us very little about the nature of a putative 'endgame' and its impact on Europe.

The significance of data on the US current account deficit and capital inflows depends on assumptions about the long-term political and economic strategies of states and financial capital. The USA was until 1989 (and Britain prior to 1914) a net creditor but since 1971 US hegemony has depended more on its central position in global capital markets than on industrial strength or capital outflows.[6] It is almost certain that foreign liabilities will gradually diminish with future dollar depreciations (or Asian revaluations), as they did in 2002 and 2003, and that the US trade deficit will also be reduced. More importantly, the import bias that accounts for these liabilities reflects the dominance of US multinational corporations as well as the relatively high growth and productivity rates of the US economy in relation to Japan and Europe. Sales of US foreign affiliates are three times as great as US exports. MNC investment abroad adds to the US current account deficit. An 'ownership-based' concept of trade would reduce the current account deficit by at least 25 per cent (Farrell, 2005).

Asian (and to some extent European) investors and governments have strong incentives to continue to finance US imports in order to maintain their export-led growth strategies (Eschweiler, 2007: 28). There are substantial complementarities between the Asian growth strategies, the reserve currency status of the dollar, and US consumer-driven capitalism. As David Levey and Stuart Brown write, 'Only a fundamental transformation in Asia's growth strategy could undermine this mutually advantageous interdependence' (2005: 4). With respect to China, moreover, the possibilities for such a transformation need to be assessed within the context of massive and violent absorption of 200 million peasants into urban areas.

There is no scholarly consensus concerning the future status of the dollar as an international reserve currency. Even if the USA experiences a 'worst case' scenario of prolonged recession and massive financial crisis (e.g. Roubini, 2008), a significant erosion of the dollar's status would probably be gradual. Nor is there a likely successor to the dollar at least in the short and medium-term. The dollar remains central to worldwide financial transactions and the USA continues to attract massive amounts of capital in the form of foreign direct investment and portfolio investment. By mid-2007 25.6 per cent of foreign currency reserves were held in euros, up from 19.7 per cent from early 2002 (Atkins, 2007b: 8) but still roughly equivalent to the proportion held by the Ecu, D-Mark and franc in the early 1990s. A switch in the pricing of oil from dollars to euros as called for by some OPEC members would have little more than symbolic importance. At \$13.2 trillion, the USA accounts for 27 per cent of global GDP. By comparison, China's GDP is \$2.7 trillion or 5.6 per cent of global GDP (World Bank, 2007: 24–5). Europe would experience much of the force of such a crisis; evidence from the subprime meltdown has punctured the myth of 'de-coupling' with respect to Europe and may do the same for Asia (*Financial Times*, 2008: 12).

The thesis of euro-dollar rivalry overlooks the massive structural problems of the eurozone that arise from a lack of cohesion. Absent a political or budgetary foundation for monetary union, the neoliberal remit of the European Central Bank (ECB) encourages mercantilism through 'competitive austerity' and thereby reproduces uneven development and interstate rivalry throughout the eurozone (Albo, 1994; Cafruny and Ryner, 2007b). Chronic conflicts over monetary policy and the Stability and Growth Pact makes it highly unlikely that the euro could challenge the key currency role of the dollar (Cohen, 2000; Crouch, 2003; Grahl, 2005; De Grauwe, 2006a, 2006b; Lim, 2006). Although it is possible as Arrighi suggests (2005: 73–4) that the dollar might give way to a multiple reserve currency system (see also *Financial Times*, 2007b: 8), the world economy has never experienced a stable, enduring system of multiple currencies. There is a great deal of evidence that international monetary stability requires hegemonic leadership (Kindleberger, 1973). In this respect, although the USA no longer serves as a net creditor and despite its extractive financial posture, it nevertheless continues to provide significant 'public goods' including 'buyer of last resort', technology transfer and monetary anchor. As the concept of minimal hegemony implies, these 'public goods' relate to a narrower social base than during the more broadly based settlement that characterized the 'golden age'.

To be sure, the costs of the war and occupation of Iraq have vastly exceeded the wildly optimistic initial projections of the Bush administration. The official defence budget request for 2009 is \$515 billion; when supplementary outlays, 'homeland security' and 'black items' are included it may exceed \$1 trillion, a figure that approximates the entire Russian GDP. The US military industrial complex is unique among advanced capitalist states both in terms of scale and political significance. As the domestic manufacturing base diminishes, military Keyesianism is an increasingly important characteristic of the US economy and the political spoils system, and arguably a significant independent variable in the broader causal chain of imperialism (Hossein-Zadeh, 2006). Defence expenditure, disproportionately concentrated in 'red states', buttresses the economic and political-electoral base of the Republican right; hence, military Keynesiansm is central to its core political project of regressive income redistribution.[7]

Control of global petroleum reserves has been central to the exercise of US hegemony since 1945. Strategic primacy in the Middle East – just as in Central Asia – has become increasingly important to the USA at a time of declining supply of oil. Hence the invasion of Iraq represents one part of the more general project of the USA designed to assert geopolitical primacy in Eurasia. Before 2003 the unwillingness to commit large numbers of troops to the Middle East meant that the USA sought through the use of sanctions to keep Iraqi oil off the world market and prevent Iraq from developing commercial relations with rivals. By the late 1990s, when the USA initiated large-scale air attacks, this strategy had begun to break down. Moreover, the September 11 terror attacks showed that further challenges to US authority were arising in Saudi Arabia. The invasion and subsequent occupation of Iraq thus represented an attempt to devise a military solution to these problems. The strength of the Iraqi resistance, the intensity of the civil war, and the sheer ineptitude of the Bush administration have, to say the least, greatly increased the costs and difficulties of this project. At the same time, however, the USA has not relinquished its goal of reasserting its control over Iraqi oil and fortifying a network of permanent military bases throughout the country.

The USA has begun to implement a 'revolutionary grand design in Asia' (Twining, 2007: 15) with a view to containing China, which it has designated as its chief 'strategic competitor'. Since 2001 Japan has made an historic decision to close ranks with the USA against China; the USA has also deepened ties with Australia and South Korea, which will be solidified through the joint deployment of anti-ballistic missiles (Bordonaro, 2006: 2). The hyper-nationalist and neoliberal Koizumi government adopted an extremely provocative stance towards China, including security guarantees with Taiwan, Singapore and India, expansion of naval forces including light aircraft carriers, undertaking joint military exercises with the USA, and sending troops to Iraq (McCormack, 2005; Baker, 2006b: 3). Japan has also launched extensive diplomatic and economic initiatives in Central Asia designed to counteract the influence of the Shanghai Co-operation Organization (SCO) (Len, 2006). In October 2005 the USA and Japan jointly declared their intention 'to develop options and adapt the alliance to the changing regional and global security environment' (Ministry of Foreign Affairs of Japan, 2005). China and Japan have deployed combat planes and ships in disputed areas of the East China Sea with deposits of natural gas. Although Koizumi's successors have been more measured and conciliatory, the basic contours of Japanese policy remain unchanged. In September 2007 Prime Minister Shinzo Abe travelled to Delhi, offering economic assistance if India agreed to anchor an 'Asian arc of freedom' against 'non-democratic' powers as air and naval forces from the 'Quadrilateral Initiative' (US, Japan, India, Australia) began week-long war games in the Bay of Bengal (Ali, 2007: 1; Bajpaee, 2007).

The USA is also seeking to consolidate ties with India, which it considers a 'great power and key strategic partner' (US Department of Defence, 2006, 40) based on support for India's nuclear weapons programme, the developing US–Indian strategic co-operation, the penetration of the Indian armaments market by large US firms, and the complementarities between India's neoliberal reforms and the US service economy (Pant, 2006). The significance of this 'grand design' cannot be over-estimated, especially in conjunction with US advances in Eastern Europe and Central Asia. Standing against these initiatives is the SCO under Sino–Russian leadership. Although the SCO has developed growing coherence, it has not acquired the characteristics of a military alliance and the underlying basis of Sino–Russian co-operation is very weak. Progress towards 'balancing' against the USA at the global level has been halting, and no single competitor has yet achieved regional hegemony.

Conclusion: US power and neoliberalism in Europe

A key premise of this chapter is that US structural power in both its economic and political–military dimensions has been central to Europe's transition to neoliberalism. This does not imply that that European big business, the nation-states, or the EU have played a passive role (or that the transition is fully consolidated or 'completed'). To be sure, neoliberal policies have reflected the preferences of the most powerful fractions of European capital (Carchedi, 2001; Van Apeldoorn, 2002) even as the costs and benefits of these policies have been distributed unevenly among states, regions and segments of labour (e.g. Cafruny and Ryner, 2007b: Chapter 4). Indeed, Ravi Abdelal (2006) has asserted that the liberalization of global finance was accomplished in large part under the day-to-day leadership of French and European officials who were more strongly committed than their American counterparts to establishing multilateral rules in the EU as well as in the OECD and International Monetary Fund (IMF). Yet, his focus on the ideational aspects of policy-making overlooks structural features of American power that, in the context of the problems and internal contradictions of the Bretton Woods system, have shaped the opportunities and constraints available to European capital (see also Chapter 4, by Bieling and Jäger).

Embedded liberalism helped to strengthen political legitimacy and stability by facilitating high growth rates and the expansion of the welfare state. By contrast, structural subordination to the US-led neoliberal order has been highly debilitating for the corporatist or 'Rhineland' systems of Western Europe while (at least until recently) favouring Anglo-Saxon systems modes of regulation. State capacity and legitimacy have been weakened at the national level but not reconstituted in Brussels. Even as the EU has painstakingly established quasi-constitutional *forms* of regional integration over the last two decades it has experienced a *substantive* tendency towards disintegration. The complicity of social and Christian democratic parties with ECB-enforced austerity has encouraged the growth of far right parties and movements. Mercantilism in the form of labour market reforms exacerbates interstate, intra-regional and social inequalities, and thereby precludes substantive regional solidarity – the necessary condition for a 'European challenge' – in favour of a decentralized system of 'multiple Europes' (Agnew, 2001) incorporated into transatlantic circuits of capital and trade as well as NATO. The centrepiece of the German European Council presidency in 2007 was the establishment of a transatlantic free-trade zone. Atlanticism and neoliberalism are indivisible; any attempt to reduce the trend towards liberalization through capital controls – the first precondition of greater regional autonomy – would elicit fierce opposition from Washington and Wall Street as well as from European big business.

The European powers arguably achieved their greatest – albeit limited – autonomy from the USA during the embedded liberal and statist era, long before the advent of supranationalism, 'multi-level' governance, and the euro. De Gaulle's assertion of state supremacy in Luxembourg in 1965 coincided with France's withdrawal from the military wing of NATO, challenges to the dollar-gold standard, and the attempt to forge an independent Middle Eastern policy. As the Franco–German axis has weakened under the pressure of competitive austerity and uneven development, and as the common foreign and defence policy has merged into Atlanticism, ironically it has been left to the Gaullist Sarkozy to enter into a 'hub and spoke' relationship with the USA that will be consummated through France's re-entry into the military wing of NATO, increasing sanctions on Iran, and the construction of a French naval base in the Persian Gulf alongside the

Americans. The increasingly fragile US imperium is casting a widening shadow across Europe.

Notes

1. Appendix B of the Rambouillet Accord granted NATO forces unrestricted access throughout Serbia. As Henry Kissinger noted, 'Rambouillet was not a negotiation – as is often claimed – but an ultimatum' (*Newsweek*, 1999: 22).
2. In 78 days of air strikes NATO forces flew 32,000 sorties and dropped 21,000 tons of bombs on Serbia, Montenegro and Kosovo. Estimates of civilian casualties run from 1000 to 2000 killed and 3000 to 6000 injured. NATO forces did not have a single casualty.
3. The US Committee on NATO, the leading lobby for the expansion of NATO in Central and Eastern Europe, was founded in 1994 by Lockheed Martin vice president Bruce Jackson. Lockheed Martin's $3.5 billion contract with Poland for the F-16 fighter, signed at the end of 2002, cemented close US–Polish relations and served as a template for further US defence industry involvement in the 'new Europe' (Tagliabue, 2002). Jackson, a charter member of the Project for the New American Century, has worked closely with pro-American lobbies in Rumania, Bulgaria, Georgia and Ukraine and recently championed the goal of breaking Gazprom's monopoly on supply and transit to Europe through the construction of an alternate southern transit route for natural gas from the Caspian to Europe (Jackson, 2006: 9–11). When Romanian President Basescu visited Washington in March 2005, Jackson stated that 'the Black Sea is already vital for European energy acquisition, and that it will be even more so in the future' (Power and Interest News Report, 2005: 3).
4. Or as Brzezinski reiterated in 2004, 'An essentially multilateralist Europe and a somewhat unilateralist America make for a perfect global marriage of convenience ... Neither America nor Europe could do as well without the other. Together, they are the core of global stability' (Brzezinski, 2004: 96).
5. The authors are former chiefs of staff Henk Van den Breemen (Netherlands), General Klaus Naumann (Germany), Field Marshal Lord Inge (UK), Admiral Jacques Lanxade (France) and General John Shalisashvili (USA).
6. In contrast to Britain, whose share of world GDP steadily diminished, the USA has retained its share at around 25 per cent, although its composition has become progressively more heavily weighted to services.
7. 'The annual war bill represents only about one cent of the $12 trillion of national income each year, and the total military cost, at most, a nickel. The foundation of US international influence is its large, powerful economy, which can absorb the narrow, resource costs of war and free the US to pursue strategic and security goals' (Holtz-Eakin, 2006: 15).

Part II Case Studies of European Socio-Economic Regulation

4
Global Finance and the European Economy: The Struggle over Banking Regulation[1]

Hans-Jürgen Bieling and Johannes Jäger

Introduction

Within critical IPE, there is an overall consensus that the process of financial deregulation is driven by the so-called global Dollar Wall Street Regime (DWSR). Succeeding the Bretton Woods System (BWS), which orchestrated international financial and monetary relations during the post-war decades, this new regime is fundamentally different in quite a few respects (Gowan, 1999: 19–38). First, the regime is mainly based on two pillars – a *de facto* dollar standard and Wall Street, synonymous for a liberalized and very attractive US financial market – which mutually reinforce each other. Second, the DWSR represents less a negotiated and quasi-legal regulatory framework, but rather a particular material power structure underpinning the neoliberal priorities and rules of international monetary and financial relations. And, finally, by promoting financial liberalization worldwide the regime facilitates the penetration of other economies by foreign capital in order to incorporate them into the domestic capital circuit of the USA (Seabrooke, 2001; Cafruny and Ryner, 2007b: 24–5).

Although not all scholars agree with Gowan's analytical approach, the dominant role of the USA in global financial markets is almost undisputed. This applies to the overall power structure as well as to the particular institutional and regulatory framework that promotes and directs the globalization of finance (Helleiner, 1994; Lütz, 2002; Baker, 2006a). More recently, however, this view has been challenged by Rawi Abdelal (2006). He argues that the USA promoted financial liberalization only through ad hoc measures and bilateral negotiations, while European policy-makers were much more eager to codify the rules for financial liberalization and regulation within a broader multilateral framework. From our point of view, his argument that the EU and its Member States represent a very active force in global finance is only partially convincing. On the one hand, it is right to assume that, in contrast to highly indebted countries, which have no other choice but to follow the neoliberal rules prescribed by global finance, the

EU and its Member States play a significant role (Becht and Da Silva, 2007). However, most differences between the US and the EU are rather differences in policy *style*, but less in *substance*. The European approach to the regulation of global capital markets is, in principle, broadly in line with US objectives. This is partly due to the penetration of the European economy by US capital (Panitch and Gindin, 2003), but partly also the result of the ongoing transition toward a finance-dominated regime of accumulation within the EU itself.

Given this contradictory constellation, the question remains whether there is a particular European approach towards financial regulation and how its content and power should be assessed. Moreover, it is unexplained to what extent rule-shaping at the international level should be conceived as part of a deliberative, but contested, EU strategy to accelerate the implementation of neoliberal (de-)regulation internally. In order to address these questions, this chapter focuses on the negotiation and implementation of the Basel II agreement that became effective in the EU in January 2007, and is definitely binding in 2008. For the last years, the new banking regulation has been at the centre of discussions about new forms of global financial regulation. In this context, we argue that within the EU the forces that are in favour of financial liberalization, such as the Commission, the European Central Bank (ECB) and transnational financial corporations, seized the Basel II negotiations as a further opportunity to promote the transition toward the Anglo-Saxon model of capitalism. Therefore, complementary to other initiatives of financial integration – Economic and Monetary Union (EMU) and the Financial Services Action Plan (FSAP) (Bieling, 2003b) – Basel II can be seen as an additional step to strengthen the role of analysts, rating agencies and investment firms and to deepen the overall financialization of the European economy. At the same time, however, this process also has provoked opposition, for example on the part of productive capital, particularly small and medium-sized enterprises (SMEs) as well as on the part of small-scale or public banks. At least partially, they have been able to negotiate some concessions in order to smooth pressures of intensified competition. Despite some elements of European 'compensatory neoliberalism' (Ryner, 2002) Basel II is likely to consolidate the hegemony of global finance. It will not only accelerate the integration of the European economy into the global DWSR, but also further weaken the former bank-based continental models of European capitalism.

To provide a more comprehensive understanding of these developments the paper starts with an outline of a critical IPE perspective that pays heed to both changes within the global financial structure as well as the European dynamics of financial integration and regulation. After these more general reflections the next sections deal explicitly with the Basel II agreement. The second section identifies the driving forces and main interests behind Basel II. Furthermore, the central conflicts of the bargaining process and the agreed compromises will be analysed. In this context, the focus will be mainly on the interaction of social forces and institutions in the EU and the USA. Finally, the third section discusses the economic consequences of the new banking regulations for the financial sector as well as for productive capital within the EU. This should enable us to assess to what extent the Basel II Accord represents a further step toward neoliberal deregulation.

Global finance and the European economy

To understand how the negotiations of the Basel II Accord are located in the overall processes of financial globalization and capitalist development this chapter draws on the work of both regulationist and neo-Gramscian scholars (see the Introduction to this volume). Both approaches are complementary and offer valuable insights into the emergence of specific forms of financial (de-)regulation and their relation to prevailing strategies of capitalist accumulation. Instead of interpreting financial (de-)regulation as the product of either anonymous systemic developments or neoliberal ideology alone, both regulation theory and neo-Gramscian IPE emphasize the contradictory and contested nature of the whole process. By avoiding a dualistic understanding of the structure-agency problem, both approaches highlight certain specific aspects of global and European transformations. While the regulationist approach is particularly interested in whether the Basel II Accord – as part of a multilevel regulatory framework – corresponds to the emergence of a finance-dominated regime of accumulation, neo-Gramscian IPE examines above all how the accord is shaped by international and transnational strategies, conflicts and power relations.

From a regulationist point of view, the globalization of finance and European integration has brought about fundamental changes of both the prevailing modes of political regulation and capitalist accumulation. Many scholars have interpreted these changes as indicators of a transition from a Fordist towards a finance-dominated regime of accumulation.[2] Of course, monetary and financial issues have also been important in the Fordist age. Within the Bretton Woods framework, however, they were quite strictly regulated at the global and national level. It has since become clear that the emergence of the DWSR – and the promotion of financial liberalization and (de-) regulation as well as the strengthening of securities markets – has a profound impact on the overall mode of capitalist reproduction (Boyer, 2000; Grahl, 2001; Van Apeldoorn and Horn, 2007a). A few tendencies: the privileging of a shareholder value conception, which triggers extensive changes of corporate governance; the privatization of pensions and public infrastructure, which both undermine elements of solidarity within national societies; or the disciplinary pressures of capital on national governments to lower corporate taxes, curtail public spending and investment and renounce active anti-cyclical economic intervention.

Within academic debates it is still contested, however, how far the finance-dominated regime of accumulation has progressed and consolidated. So far, there seems to be only a rather vague consensus that the processes of finance-led restructuring are both an important feature of present capitalism and promoted by global and European developments. In this context, by and large, global developments are defined by the so-called DWSR (Gowan, 1999). It refers to the emerging global monetary and financial structures after the break down of the Bretton Woods system of fixed exchange rates and politically controlled capital markets. Compared with this old regime, which provided national governments with a certain degree of economic, financial and monetary autonomy, the DWSR is less generous. Its main features are open capital markets, floating exchange rates and the worldwide supremacy of the US dollar. The most influential forces determining the rules of this regime are the US Treasury Department, the Federal Reserve and the private financial firms located in Wall Street. The relation between them is characterized by personal exchange, close working relations and similar aims. Besides, the centre of the DWSR, the 'Wall Street-Treasury Complex' (Bhagwati, 1998: 10–11), is closely linked with international organizations such as International Monetary Fund (IMF), the World Bank, the World Trade Organization (WTO), the Bank for International Settlements (BIS) and the Basle Committee, or the International Organization of Securities Commissions (IOSCO). All these fora and institutions not only support the principle of unrestricted capital mobility, they also are the most important proponents of the 'Washington Consensus' – the view that free trade, open financial markets, currency convertibility, domestic structural adjustment and neoliberal reforms provide the only successful way for economic development.[3]

In some respects the DWSR also contains institutional and legal dimensions. Its functioning is facilitated by a range of mutually approved financial regulations. More important, however, is the material basis of the regime, which causes other governments to follow its rules. This is mainly due to the predominant economic power of financial and non-financial US corporations and the still fairly undisputed role of the US dollar as the world's leading currency, which places the Wall Street and the Treasury at the centre of financial networks. Most international credit is denominated in dollars, US banks are the most important international creditors, and, as the Basle Accords reveal, the standards of international regulation and supervision are strongly determined by the US authorities. Moreover, the dominant role of the dollar and control over the IMF and World Bank minimizes the risk for US-based financial operators while enabling the US government to pursue its 'America first' approach and exploit all seignorage of the global key currency (Gowan, 1999: 25–30).

The emergence of the DWSR therefore implies that the 'integral hegemony' of the 1950s and 1960s, based on a broad and high-level consensus within the Euro-Atlantic area, is superseded by a kind of 'minimal hegemony'. According to Alan Cafruny and Magnus Ryner (2007b: 20):

> minimal hegemony describes an international system in which important contradictions have developed between the interests of the ruling and subordinate groups. The hegemon is no longer strong enough to systematically devise policies capable of serving general interests. The system is unstable, but coercion is minimized because subordinate groups and, crucially, the elites who might potentially represent them, are too weak and disorganized to consolidate a counter-hegemonic bloc, especially since the immediate material interests of some within the potentially rival elite may be served by the prevailing order.

Generally, other economies are incorporated into the DWSR in two ways. One way is that of *disciplinary subordination* – of total exposure to the global financial operators and thereby to the vagaries of global financial markets. This path is taken by economies unable to follow a self-determined path of development. Relying on foreign capital and investment, they often accumulate huge foreign debts. As a consequence, they have then almost no chance to resist various pressures – by private creditors, the US government and the IMF and World Bank – to remove national barriers to the free flow of funds, to give full rights of operation to foreign financial investors, and to redesign national financial systems according to external requirements. The other form of incorporation is that of achieving the position of a *privileged junior partner*. This seems to apply to the European Union. Backed by the Single European Market (SEM) and the EMU, the EU has considerable bargaining power in international forums and organizations such as the G7, the G20, the Basle Committee, the IOSCO, the Financial Stability Forum (FSF) or the World Trade Organization (WTO). It is therefore not simply a 'regime taker', but to a certain degree also a 'regime shaper'.

Apart from some conflicts, the European approach to the regulation of global capital markets is, however, broadly in line with US objectives. This can be explained by two developments. The first development is the ongoing integration and interpenetration of the US and EU economy (Hamilton and Quinlan, 2005). In the light of the close links of US financial firms to the City of London, and intensified transatlantic business co-operation based on a huge flow of foreign direct investment, the considerable role and political influence of US business inside the EU, for example through the EU Committee of the American Chamber of Commerce (AmCham EU), is hardly surprising. Next to the co-operation between supervisory authorities in the area of financial market regulation there are further examples of institutionalized business co-operation, such as the Transatlantic Business Dialogue (TABD) (Cowles, 2001) or the establishment of the Financial Leaders Group, which strongly supported the Financial Services Agreement (FSA) negotiated in the follow up of the General Agreement on Trade in Services (GATS) talks (Sell, 2000). These and other dimensions of intensified transatlantic business co-operation have been crucial for the promotion of global rules favourable for the liberalization of trade, finance and investment.

The second development that allowed for a general convergence of American and European views was the profound transformation of the process of European integration (Ziltener, 1999). During the post-war decades, European integration served above all to facilitate government action in order to shelter and stabilize the national Fordist models of capitalism. In the course of the 1980s and 1990s, however, it then changed its purpose and character. The core economic projects – the Single European Market, EMU, Eastward enlargement and financial integration – show very clearly that the new European regionalism is increasingly determined by a neoliberal agenda. This means that the EU represents less and less a political arena supportive of fairly encompassing government regulation. On the contrary, it should rather be seen as an additional lever promoting a competition-oriented reorganization of domestic labour market and welfare regimes (Bieling and Deppe, 2003). This shift in operation and orientation of European arrangements and governance structures can be seen as an expression of a 'new constitutionalism', seeking to 'separate economic policies from broad political accountability in order to make governments more responsive to the discipline of market forces and correspondingly less responsive to popular-democratic forces and processes' (Gill, 1998: 5).

The process of constitutionalizing neoliberal principles in the EU was strongly influenced and shaped by transnational forces, above all financial and non-financial firms which developed an increasingly global orientation (Van Apeldoorn, 2002). Although the privileged role of transnational business can hardly be denied, also other forces – domestically oriented firms, trade unions, social movements, think tanks, journalists or non-governmental organizations (NGOs) – became more and more involved in European debates and regulatory decision-making (Bieler and Morton, 2001a). The EU represents, therefore, a new kind of a 'transnational historic bloc' based on cross-border accumulation, multi-level regulation and a selective transnationalization of civil societies. The particular modes of transnational co-operation were not only decisive to accelerate financial integration, they were also conducive to strengthening the rule setting capacities of the EU at the international or global level, for instance in the negotiations on the renewed Basel Accord. Nevertheless, this does not imply that there is only one single European voice in this process. On the contrary, there are still diverging views and conflicts between national governments that are responsible for the reproduction of their respective models of capitalism. In this context, governmental strategies are strongly influenced by the relative strength of different fractions of capital, above all money or financial capital and productive capital (Van der Pijl, 1984: 8–20). While money or financial capital prefers a liberal-internationalist 'concept of control', productive capital is much more in favour of state-monopoly tendencies. In addition to this distinction, another dividing line – between globally and therefore more market liberal oriented capital fractions and domestically (regionally) oriented fractions of capital, more sensitive to the social embeddedness of finance and production – seems to have certain explanatory power (Van Apeldoorn, 2002).

Struggle over Basel II

A critical political economy perspective seems to be appropriate to highlight some – often ignored – aspects of global banking regulation. First, it directs the attention towards transnational strategies to orchestrate global banking regulation. Second, it shows that the Basel II Accord represents a major shift in socioeconomic and socio-political power relations as part of the proceeding internationalization, financialization and marketization of banking activities. And finally, it points out that the Basel II agreement has a strong yet contested and contradictory impact on the general mode and the criteria of capitalist reproduction.

Driving forces behind banking regulation

The end of the Bretton Woods system and the erosion of 'Atlantic Fordism' have triggered the internationalization of banking activities. In this context, commercial transactions became more risky and revealed an obvious lack of banking supervision. It was not simply the failure of individual banks, such as the German Bankhaus Herstatt or the US-American Franklin National Bank, but above all the general difficulty of British supervisors to collect sufficient information on the overall activities of foreign banks operating in the City of London, and therefore the danger of a cross-border domino effect of those bank failures, which prompted the Bank of England to urge for co-ordinated co-operation at an international level (Kapstein, 1994: 44). This initiative was generally welcomed by the G10 and led to the establishment of the Basel Committee on Banking Supervision (BCBS) at the BIS in 1974. Besides representatives of the G10, Luxembourg, Switzerland and Spain joined the Committee, which at that time still was called Basel Committee on Banking Regulations and Supervisory Practices. Although there had already been *ad hoc* co-operation among the G10 central banks at the BIS, the new institution enabled a permanent arena for co-operation (Wood, 2005: 45). The main aim of the Committee was to ensure that no foreign bank would sidestep supervision. Already in 1975 the supervisors agreed on the Basel Concordat, which laid down some basic principles that international co-operation should follow, for example, joint responsibility of host and parent authorities, comprehensive implementation, home country control of solvency issues, supervision of liquidity by host authorities, and a system of information transfers. All these principles were negotiated in a rather informal atmosphere; and they were only partially and incrementally transposed into national laws.

The limits of the Concordat became evident in the context of the international debt crisis in the early 1980s. The debt crisis represented a severe danger for the US financial system as US banks have been the principle creditors for Latin American countries, but did not dispose of sufficient bad debt reserves (Lütz, 2002: 188–9). Hence, in 1984 the talks on a new agreement on banking regulation and supervision were resumed within the Basel Committee again. It took until July 1988 that central bankers of the G10 agreed on the Basel I Accord, above all on the definition of certain minimum capital requirements.[4] In general, the Accord struck a balance between regulatory and competitive concerns. According to Kapstein (1994: 105) the negotiations were regarded as very successful for two reasons:

> First, although many central bankers had expressed concern over the erosion of capital levels in commercial banks, they entered the multilateral negotiations with conflicting definitions of what actually constituted bank capital, and how much capital banks should be required to hold. Second, national differences in capital adequacy requirements were being exploited by banks as a source of competitive advantage in the financial marketplace; all other things being equal, banks with relatively low capital requirements could charge less for their services and still give shareholders a satisfactory return. The Basle Accord reduces the scope for this type of 'regulatory arbitrage' and helps level the playing field on which international banks must compete.

Hence, Basel I can be seen as an attempt to stabilize the international financial system by creating a sort of level playing field for international banks. At the same time, however, the emerging regulation should not simply be understood as a functional necessity. Rather, it needs to be emphasized that it was above all US regulatory authorities that sought not only to strengthen the international banking system, but also to prevent a loss of international competitiveness of US banks (Strange, 1998: 160–1). To reach both goals the US managed to convert minimum capital standards into global rules:

> It must be remembered that the prime motivation for the Accord [Basel I] came from US regulators trying to protect the competitiveness of their banks, in particular in the face of Japanese banking dominance.
>
> (Wood, 2005: 131)

The new international banking regulation forced banks to increase substantially the amount of equity capital in relation to their liabilities. This contributed to the stabilization of individual banks and thereby of the international banking system in the context of an increasingly volatile global economic environment, characterized by the ongoing processes of financial deregulation and innovation. Until the early 1970s, financial systems were nationally controlled and rather segmented. Since then, they have become increasingly transnationalized, de-segmented and marketized (Underhill, 1997: 42). This metamorphosis indicates that eventually the transition towards a finance-dominated regime of accumulation was not inhibited by the Basel I Accord. The Accord only provided necessary regulations to temporarily stabilize the banking system. At the same time, players in international securities markets such as investment and pension funds and rating agencies gained in importance because they were not included in the Basel I Accord. Effectively, this also had an impact on the operation of banking, as particularly commercial banks became more engaged in trading with shares and securities. In the context of 'disintermediation' and 'off-balance securitisation', 'the increasing practice of removing assets from a bank's balance sheet through the use of innovative debt securities made the Basle I's assessment of risk held by banks out of touch with market practices' (Seabrooke, 2006: 144).

The discussion in the run-up to Basel II and the period of official negotiation

The first attempts to develop Basel II date back to the mid-1990s. It was the experience of repeated banking crises – for example of the Bank of Credit and Commerce International (BCCI), the British Barings or the Japanese DAIWA bank – and the apparent failure of regulation that brought back a broad discussion about the international financial architecture (Langley, 2002: 151–2). Within this context, the overall discourse focused on the assumption that Basel I had to be reformed because of inadequate and risk-insensitive capital coverage and other technical problems. Hence, already in 1996 Basel I was modified in order to incorporate market risks. Nevertheless, it was the simple rules of Basel I that were pushing banks away from higher quality lenders and towards more risky ones because of standardized risk-weightings (Wood, 2005: 124).

Officially, the intention of the reform was to prevent such undesired banking practices by introducing more risk adequate regulations for calculating minimum capital requirements. The proposals for a renewed Basel Accord were again elaborated by the Basel Committee. Behind the scenes, however, transnational financial forces developed a much more pro-active political strategy. In general, since the mid-1990s, large international banks demanded less rigorous and more market-oriented regulations (Lütz, 2004). They complained about the too rigid nature of the Basel I Accord and suggested a more flexible calculation approach, which takes better account of the specific risk portfolio of individual credit institutes. For several years, large international banks – many of them based in the US – have been pushing for a New Capital Accord allowing them to measure risk on their own and, hence, to reduce the levels of minimum capital. The Institute for International Finance (IIF), representing about 350 banks, was one of the main advocates of the new regulations (Underhill, 2004). The banks urged a reduction of the required minimum capital to obtain higher profits. Their claims became even more comprehensible against the background of generally decreasing regulatory capital in the second half of the 1990s (Wood, 2005). Nevertheless, it took several years to convince the Basel Committee to replace, in part, external regulatory standards by internal modelling.

The official period of negotiation started with an outline provided by the BCBS in 1999. The proposed framework was based on three pillars (Basel Committee, 1999). The first pillar revised the 1988 Accord's guidelines for minimum capital requirements. The simple rules were replaced by an advanced framework taking into account more closely each bank's actual risk of economic losses by allowing internal modelling. The second pillar recognized the necessity of exercising effective supervision of bank's internal risk assessments. The third pillar enhanced market discipline by demanding a higher degree of organizational transparency.

The initial proposal included the main demand of the banking sector to allow banks to evaluate regulatory capital themselves, besides the use of external ratings. At the same time, pressured by the German government the Committee recognized that these ways of determining minimum capital requirements were not a viable option to all banks:

> With regard to minimum regulatory capital requirements, the Committee is building on the foundation of the current Accord, which will serve as a 'standardized' approach for capital requirements at the majority of banks. . . . For some sophisticated banks, the Committee believes that an internal ratings-based approach could form the basis for setting capital charges, subject to supervisory approval and adherence to quantitative and qualitative guidelines.
>
> (BCBS, 1999: 5)

Despite these different options, it was already obvious at the start of the negotiations that Basel II would mainly be beneficial for large-scale banks. Only large banks would have the capacity to opt for the internal ratings-based approach and, hence, to save minimum capital, while small-scale banks would have to rely on more expensive standardized methods. This disadvantage was only partially compensated by the option of external ratings of risk assessment. Such suggestions met above all the demands of US-based banks, which – unlike the banks elsewhere – already applied external ratings as a common practice.

Pressure to allow for internal modelling of credit risks came, however, not only from the large-scale banks themselves. Other firms within the financial services sector proved to be an important ally, because the technically complex forms and models of risk assessment and risk management obviously increased the demand for their specific services. Against this background, representatives of the financial services industry played an important role in legitimizing the new rules. They produced numerous studies and papers all demonstrating the putative economic benefits of the new regulations. In this way, the Basel II negotiations were framed by a particular political discourse, which represented the new arrangement as an important step to overcome traditional forms of relationship banking and to establish adequate forms of modern risk management much more in line with the shareholder-value orientation of the dynamic segments of the corporate sector (see the paradigmatic study by PWC, 2004). In a similar vein publications by other firms such as McKinsey highlighted the possibilities for banks to increase profits by adopting Basel II. They left no doubt that this required spending on financial and technical advice (Buehler et al., 2004).

In addition to credit risk (loss of payments of debtors) and market risk (changing rates of interest and so on), the BCBS proposed taking operational risk (for example technical miscalculations, fraud) into account in determining regulatory capital. Although many of the demands of large-scale banks have been considered in the proposal, the latter aspect was heavily opposed by banks because they did not want to hold minimum capital to compensate for this type of risk. An intensive process of discussion and negotiation followed. Initially, the Committee intended to leave the overall amount of minimum capital unchanged on average:

> The Committee is committed to ensuring that any review of the Accord should meet the following supervisory objectives: the accord should continue to promote safety and soundness in the financial system and, as such, the new framework should at least maintain the current overall level of capital in the system.
>
> (BCBS, 1999: 4–5)

Eventually, operational risk remained in the Accord. At the same time, however, banks were expected to hold a lower minimum amount of capital (PWC, 2004). This shows that the BCBS had to compromise on its original intention to maintain the overall amount of minimum capital on average.

During the negotiations, the position of European banks towards the new Accord was far from uniform. While large-scale banks welcomed the possibility of internal modelling, small-scale and public banks frequently opposed the new type of regulations. This was particularly obvious in the case of Germany and Austria, where small and public banks complained about the high costs of Basel II and tried to convince regulators and national governments to defend their interests. Of course, in general, banks have the possibility to apply the standardized approach and, hence, to avoid in part excessive internal modelling. In the end, however, small and medium-sized banks feared disadvantages because in any case Basel II implies a variety of extra costs for them because of the absence of economies of scale. As they have to distribute the additional administrative costs of Basel II to a smaller number of clients, they become relatively less competitive. Furthermore, extra costs are caused by the re-organization of the traditional process of credit lending, which has to be adapted to the new rules.

Irrespective of these problems for small and medium-sized (public) banks, the European Central Bank and the European Commission have been in favour of the principles of the renewed Basel II Accord (European Commission, 1999a). They launched a consultation process and tried to convince all parts of the banking industry of the benefits of the new Accord. In the end, the basic structure of the Accord remained unchanged. Nevertheless, the BCSC had to make some concessions on two fronts. On the one hand, large-scale banks had been able to pressure national negotiators and the BCSC to agree on some minor changes further reducing the overall burden of capital requirements (BCBS, 1999, 2004a, 2004b).

On the other hand, small and medium-sized companies fearing that the original Basel II proposal would restrict their access to credit also managed to receive certain offsets. They were above all represented by the German government, given the prominent role of small public banks and the tradition of relational banking in this country. In October 2001 the German government announced that it would oppose any future European Union banking legislation based on Basel II. Moreover, Italy and Japan articulated similar fears about Basel II. The BCBS responded by suggesting new risk weighting measures for SMEs. Eventually, SMEs and banks related to them achieved a substantial modification of the original rules, which enabled a preferential treatment of SMEs. However, the USA and Great Britain – an important driving force within the EU – secured that this modification did not result in direct disadvantages to large banks or other sectors of the economy. In the end, the original character of Basel II was maintained. Basel II represents a further step towards the US and British preference for market discipline (Wood, 2005: 141–58). The European approach, hence, is characterized by these tensions between the continental models of financial sector regulation as defended by Germany and Anglo-American principles pushed forward by the UK.

Unequal implementation

In principle, the Accord represents a kind of soft law (Tabb, 2003: 176). This means that the regulations only become legally binding if they are transposed into national law. However, this has not taken place in a uniform way. In the USA, only approximately 20 of the largest banks will be subjected to modified new rules. For the rest of the industry, by and large, Basel I regulations are supposed to continue to be effective as Basel 1A regulations. The US decision was taken in response to pressure from smaller US banks for which Basel II would have caused high administrative costs but few benefits. Obviously, small and medium-sized banks in the USA will benefit from this national decision, because they are now able to avoid the high administrative costs related to Basel II. As a consequence of the US interpretation of Basel II, several newly industrializing countries such as China and India announced that they would not force their banks to apply Basel II standards (Wood, 2005: 145–6). While China will not adopt Basel II, India among around 100 other countries in the world is willing to do so, although in a modified form. The discussion in the USA about the implementation of Basel II is still ongoing. Financial supervisory authorities feared too sharp a reduction in capital requirements for large banks with possible detrimental effects to the stability of the financial system. This scepticism is expressed among others by Sheila C. Bair, Chairman of the Federal Deposit Insurance Corporation (FDIC):

> The US has taken a lot of heat for its cautious approach to Basel II implementation, but what we have seen in the credit markets this year [2007] fully vindicates the US approach. . . . Models are a helpful risk management tool, but they are not always a reliable predictor of credit responses; and they should never be expected to predict the effects of a sea change in lending products.
>
> (Global Risk Regulator, 2007b)

Therefore the implementation was postponed until the second quarter of 2009 when a three-year transition period should be started. As a consequence, large US banks claim that this causes a relative (temporary) disadvantage to them (Global Risk Regulator, 2007a).

Within the EU the implementation of the Basel II framework follows a rather different logic. Although the BCBS meant to apply the Accord to internationally active banks only, the EU – the European Commission, the Council and the European Parliament – made the rules binding for all banks with a renewed Capital Requirements Directive in 2006. This decision had been preceded by a variety of amendments – such as the obligation for banks to explain their rating decisions to SMEs – which were incorporated in the Commission's proposal (European Parliament, 2005). All these amendments, however, have not changed the fundamental character of Basel II. The EU still argues that the Basel II regulation should be applied to the whole banking sector irrespective of the size and scope of individual financial institutions in order to guarantee a so-called level playing field:

> Measures to co-ordinate credit institutions should, both in order to protect savings and to create equal conditions of competition between these institutions, apply to all of them.
>
> (European Parliament, 2006: L177/1)

This decision reflects the priority of competition, compared with industrial policy, within the EU; and it implies that the EU uses the new international credit rules to transform the banking sector in a much deeper way than the USA. At least in this sense, the Basel II Accord is not to be considered as a one-dimensional unilateral project of the USA, even if it is likely to extend the hegemonic position of the USA in global finance.[5] In this context, it is important to note that the new forms of regulation can only, in part, be explained through the particular strategies of different capital fractions as outlined above. They are also substantially framed by broader discourses on liberalization, competition and transparency, all consistent with the requirements of the DWSR. Overall, the hegemonic strategy of global finance – promoted by an alliance of financial players and (inter)state institutions such as the Basel Committee and the European Commission – proved to be successful in achieving its goals on the international level. Nevertheless, a closer look on the related struggles on the national level shows that the specific outcomes of regulation differ. At least partially, they also provoke some forms of 'soft' or 'modest' resistance.

Impact on the European economy

Eventually, as part of the overall multilevel structure of regulation, the Basel II Accord is likely to have a strong impact on how the European economy is organized. In principle, it will reinforce the dynamics of competitive restructuring which have been set going since the re-launch of European integration from the mid-1980s onwards, and which have spurred transnational finance-dominated strategies of accumulation via the Single Market, EMU and financial integration. By promoting financial market reforms, labour market deregulation, a dismantling of national welfare regimes and the privatization of the public infrastructure, the EU should become closer to the US model (Grahl, 2004: 293). The general strategic orientation of all these changes was clearly expressed by Frits Bolkestein (2001), the former Commissioner responsible for the single market:

> No-one is forcing the European Union to become more competitive than the United States in nine years time. But if that is what we really want, we must leave the comfortable surroundings of the Rhineland and move

closer to the tougher conditions and colder climate of the Anglo-Saxon form of capitalism, where the rewards are greater but the risks also. If we spurn the means we must lower our sights lest we lose credibility and become ridiculous. So we must force ourselves to carry out those microeconomic supply side structural adjustments we decided upon in Lisbon.

This strategic orientation has generated quite a few problems and contradictions, which also have been articulated politically in the run-up to the Basel II Accord. Eventually, the transition towards a finance-dominated regime of accumulation involves a profoundly changed finance-production nexus, which is likely to erode the traditional productive strengths of continental models of capitalist development. Until the 1980s these strengths were based on rather co-operative relationships between banks, companies and workers conducive to long-term modernization and incremental innovation (Hall and Soskice, 2001a: 39–44; Amable, 2003: 85–92). This is undermined by the Commission's strategy to homogenize regulatory requirements in the banking sector without taking institutional differences in the varieties of capitalism into account. The implicit argument is that intensified European and global competition will make the financial sector more competitive and increase the overall economic efficiency. This position of the European Commission is expressed clearly by the Director of Internal Market and Services Directorate General, Jörgen Holmquist (2007):

> And one area where we must do better is transnational burdens. This is true for the implementation of Basel II and also for other areas. The challenge for the EU and US will be to reduce transatlantic regulatory burdens, to bring down regulatory barriers across the board – from banking to insurance, from securities to corporate governance. This is the way to create new opportunities for business and more potential for investment and growth on both sides of the Atlantic.

Given the fact that the strategic priorities of international investors, credit institutions and transnational corporations are increasingly geared towards securities markets, traditionally rather co-operative relations between production and finance disintegrate. Not only corporations quoted at the stock exchange, but the whole European economy, including many small and medium-sized companies, seem to be under a stronger adaptive pressure, which is likely to be enforced by Basel II. A few tendencies may illustrate this.

First, unlike Basel I, the new capital accord is primarily based on the market mechanism. The fact that banks are allowed to calculate regulatory capital requirements on their own means a substantial transformation of banking regulation. Because of this, strategies of banks are assumed to become more risk sensitive but at the same time more short-term oriented.

Although Basel II does not directly enforce individual risk-adequate pricing, banks are increasingly changing their behaviour. Hence, the new regulations are supposed to have considerable impact not only on credit lending but also on pricing strategies and, therefore, on the availability of capital for different sectors of the economy (Jäger, 2004; Kader, 2005; Jäger and Redak, 2006). Conditions for loans will increasingly depend on individual risk. In comparison to well-rated corporations, firms that are dependent on credit money and have a rather bad rating will face higher financial costs. This effect will only be offset, in part, by the changes of the rules referring to SME. In general, Basel II makes weaker firms less competitive and promotes a stronger centralization of capital. Although large banks benefit from this, the situation has comparatively worsened for smaller commercial banks, co-operative banks and savings banks whose business relations are more long-term oriented and mainly with SMEs. It is foreseeable already now that under the new regulatory Basel II framework they will have to provide for higher capital reserves than globally operating banks capable of applying internal approaches to calculate minimum capital requirements (King and Sinclair, 2003).

Second, to compensate for the difficulties when borrowing from smaller banks, many medium-sized companies are increasingly inclined to raise capital from financial investors. This, in turn, provides the opportunity for private equity funds aiming at very high profit rates – in the German debate they are therefore characterized as 'locusts' – to tap new investment areas. They increasingly buy into medium-sized companies in order to restructure them within a rather short-term period of three to five years. After a significant reduction of production costs – through outsourcing, dismissals or lower wages – the restructured companies are sold again at substantially higher prices (Rügemer, 2005).

And finally, as Basel II will generally strengthen the role of analysts, rating agencies and investment firms, it will also further promote the shareholder value concept. Already now, the shareholder value orientation of transnational corporations has a profound impact on the relations within the production chain. In order to meet profit goals and to fulfil the expectations of shareholders, focal corporations tend to exert stronger pressures on component suppliers to obtain cheaper intermediate products. As a consequence, formerly close and long-term relationships between companies give way to intensified and more short-term processes of cost competition (Dörre and Brinkmann, 2005).

In general, the modification of the monetary constraint that takes place with Basel II will have an important impact on the patterns of accumulation. The new Accord might cause a higher degree of stability in normal times but the risk of systemic crises will probably increase as well. This is shown dramatically by the so-called sub-prime mortgage crisis, which is linked to a systematic bias in the estimation of risk by banks and rating agencies. Basel II not only increases the extended use of these type of techniques but is supposed to deepen cyclical lending of banks and, hence, to make economic development more volatile. Moreover, Basel II as a pure microeconomic approach to financial stability is far from sufficient to prevent financial crisis (Boyer, 2005). This implies that higher costs of bank failure in times of crisis will have to be borne by the public – in other words by the wage earners – as their contributions make for the biggest part of public earnings. The installation of the 100 Mio. USD Super Fund backed in a first step by the US government in the context of the sub-prime crisis represents just a recent example of how costs of financial failures may have to be borne by the public.

All the above tendencies are indicators that the finance-dominated regime of accumulation leads to a fairly comprehensive marketization of the whole economy. One impact of this is that the productive and innovative capacities of continental European systems are impaired due to shortened managerial planning intervals and intensified cost competition. This is the case at least if innovation is not only seen as the outcome of individual invention, but as a social process in which many actors – public institutions, scientists, engineers and also workers – are involved (Amable, 2003: 85–92; Deutschmann, 2005). This means that new ideas and products and improved forms of production are mostly generated by innovative networks whose operation requires a particular co-operative environment (Lazonick, 2003: 27–34). Normally, these networks for innovation function very well, if the actors dispose of sufficient resources (financial commitment), if they are protected against outside intervention and external insecurities (strategic control) and if there are some guarantees that they will benefit from the innovation generated by themselves (organizational integration). Nevertheless, the prevailing neoliberal approach to strengthen the finance-dominated regime of accumulation by the promotion of a market and competition oriented regulatory framework – which the Basel II Accord is part of – is obviously detrimental to these requirements. The rather poor economic performance of continental European models of capitalism during the past decade supports this view (Bieling, 2006a; Cafruny and Ryner, 2007b: 43–61).

Conclusions

The dominant patterns of accumulation and global financial regulation have undergone substantial changes since the breakdown of the Bretton Woods System. The chapter dealt with the question whether there is a particular European approach to international financial regulation by focusing on the struggle over Basel II. Although the new Accord was established within the context of processes of financial integration at a European level, it was shaped considerably by US-based banking capital and discourses inscribed in the DWSR. The analysis of the processes based on a neo-Gramscian extension of regulationist perspectives has demonstrated the existence of contradictory interests between different fractions of capital and, in particular, the role of transnational forces. In this sense, Basel II should not be regarded as a one-dimensional process of neoliberal restructuring but to some extent contingent. For example, some modifications of the original proposal were particularly beneficial for SME and public banks. The modifications that do not harm other banks were achieved in a bargaining process mainly pushed by the German government. Nevertheless, the US hegemony and the related discursive dominance of the neoliberal principles of the DWSR played a crucial role in shaping the struggle over banking regulation.

Moreover, the chapter tried to explain to which extent rule-shaping at an international level should be conceived as part of a strategy of EU-based forces to accelerate neoliberal deregulation. It was shown that financial capital within the EU, particularly in the form of large banks, is likely to benefit most from the rules of the DWSR and US pressures to modify the Basel Accord. They have been fairly successful to shape the agenda of European and global institutions – such as the Basel Committee – in order to transform financial regulation in line with the requirements of the Anglo-Saxon model of capitalist reproduction. By doing this, large banks and institutional investors successfully strengthened their relative position compared with other fractions of capital. This indicates that although the EU has become a more pro-active player in international financial regulation, this should not be confounded with any emancipation from the US model. Indeed, the EU is far from defending an alternative financial structure or a completely different regime of capitalist accumulation. On the contrary, EU legislation subjects all banks within the EU to the renewed Basel II Accord.

Regarding the overall impact of Basel II on the process of accumulation within the European economy it was argued that the Accord expands market-oriented forms of regulation with respective consequences for the economic structure. The new Capital Accord will advance finance-led strategies of accumulation and, hence, will favour or disfavour different fractions of capital. On the one hand, one can assume that the new rules will restrict the provision of credit money for economically weaker SMEs. On the other hand, large banking capital and large (transnational) productive capital seems to be strengthened. It is rather doubtful whether this corresponds to the traditional mode of innovation in the long run. Instead, in the EU tensions between the structural monetary constraint and (productive) strategies of accumulation seem to intensify.

In the process of development of the Basel II rules – although heavily disputed among different fractions of capital – there was almost no opposition of subaltern classes. Framed by the hegemonic neoliberal discourse on a more market-oriented assessment of credit risks the negotiations and decisions were termed to be 'technical'. In general, no reasons for broader political participation were seen. For the time being, there are no signs that the hegemonic forces which benefit from the financialization of the European economy will redefine their strategic priorities. This might only be the case if the problems and contradictions of a finance-led restructuring – particularly the social and economic costs – are politically articulated more forcefully. This would presuppose that not only one specific regulation such as the Basel II Accord but the operation of the whole economy is questioned by a broader alliance of – counter-hegemonic – forces.

Notes

1. The paper is part of a research project on the transformation of global finance funded by the Jubiläumsfond of the Austrian Central Bank OeNB.
2. The assumption of an emerging finance-led regime represents a departure from former regulationist analyses. Although the former work was mainly focusing on the reproduction of labour – the wage-consumption nexus, the particular class compromise between capital and labour and Keynesian welfare state intervention (Aglietta, 1987; Lipietz, 1987) – more recent writings highlight above all the very important role of money and financial markets for capitalist development (Aglietta, 2000; Chesnais, 2004).
3. Since the late 1990s, as a result of major financial crises in Asia and Latin America, the 'Washington Consensus' has been questioned as a result of the absence of effectiveness and democratic legitimacy (Higgott, 2000). The so-called Post Washington Consensus aims at more effective regulation to improve the transparency and stability of financial systems. In substance, however, this new consensus represents only a 'Washington Consensus Plus'.
4. The Accord defined a general 8 per cent minimum capital reserve to safeguard credits. In addition to this, the G10 agreed on a standardized approach to calculate the specific risks of different kinds of credits depending on their short or long-term nature or the presumable solvency of debtors.
5. Moreover, in a global perspective developing countries will probably be negatively affected even without necessarily introducing the Basel II standards in their countries. International credit flows to these countries are assumed to become more expensive and, in part, even more volatile. Furthermore, internationally active banks are supposed to benefit relative to local banks based in the Global South. This result is not really surprising, because developing countries have not played a noteworthy role in the shaping of the rules of Basel II (Eichengreen, 2003: 36–7; Griffith-Jones, 2003; Metzger, 2006).

5
'New Europeans' for the 'New European Economy': Citizenship and the Lisbon Agenda

Sandy Brian Hager

Introduction[1]

This chapter analyses the European Union's Lisbon Agenda and its relation to changing conceptions of citizenship in general, and social citizenship in particular. The guiding assumption made here is that citizenship, conceived in simple terms as the concept defining the rights and responsibilities of civil society to the state and vice versa, is not static but instead bound up with and dialectically related to broader struggles over socio-economic restructuring (see also Purcell, 2002). Although these processes have certain transformative effects on the rights and responsibilities of citizenship, at the same time rights and responsibilities entrenched in prior social struggles can have an impact on, and even limit the degree of such change. If, as Chantal Mouffe (1992: 225) suggests, 'the way we define citizenship is intimately linked to the kind of society and political community we want', and if in turn, as Bryan Turner (1993: 12) submits, 'whatever forces push modernization forward also develop and expand citizenship', then an examination of citizenship should us provide with a clearer indication of the underlying 'social purpose' of these processes.

The Lisbon Agenda, for its part, represents the notion of socio-economic transformation and restructuring *par excellence*. Introduced in the spring of 2000 at the European Council meeting in the Portuguese capital, the Agenda is noteworthy for its now oft-cited calls for a 'radical transformation of the European economy' to make the EU into the most 'competitive and dynamic knowledge based economy in the world' by 2010 (European Council, 2000). The articulation of the Agenda's initial twin goals of economic competitiveness/growth and social cohesion/protection is intended to settle the historically 'conflictual and contradictory encounters' between capital accumulation and social welfare at the EU level (Hansen, 2005: 1). Perhaps most importantly, the attainment of Lisbon's goals is said to reciprocally lead to and in turn be bolstered by the creation of 'more and better jobs' in the union. The declaration made by the European Roundtable of Industrials (ERT) (2001b: 3) that the EU would require 'new Europeans' to match the 'new European economy' as envisioned in the Lisbon Agenda points to the significance of the interface between citizenship and restructuring.

Although the existing literature on the Lisbon Agenda tends to focus on its effects for the institutional form of EU governance (for example the introduction of the open method of co-ordination to various policy domains), this chapter develops an alternative approach, grounded in *transnational historical materialism* (see Overbeek, 2000), which emphasizes the concrete relations of power that underpin the Lisbon Agenda as a strategy for socio-economic restructuring. The Agenda is conceived of here as a project representing the hegemonic interests of the transnational fraction of the European capitalist class. Special concern is placed here on the discursive underpinnings of this class project, and the role of class *agency* in structuring the EU political arena, particularly the European Commission, where the Lisbon Agenda is selected, sustained and ultimately replaced. This requires that we interweave the analysis of institutional form with a consideration of the socio-economic content of the Lisbon Agenda (Van Apeldoorn, 2002), attempting not only to describe *how* EU governance has been transformed by this strategy, but also to *explain* who benefits from it and what kind of EU it seeks to promote (Holman, 2004a).

The central argument made here is that the emergence of a 'neoliberal communitarian' citizenship model under Lisbon contradicts claims made by supportive social and political forces, as well as some scholars, that the Lisbon Agenda marks a positive 'turning point' for EU-level social policy and social citizenship. These findings also run counter to claims that the *asymmetries* of regulation and citizenship in the EU will be overcome with Lisbon. Instead, it is argued that the Lisbon Agenda and the knowledge-based economy that it invokes are part and parcel of a broader shift away from the Keynesian Welfare State towards a Schumpeterian Workfare Regime, both at the Member State and EU levels of socio-economic governance (Jessop, 2002; Van Apeldoorn, 2003). Thus central to the Lisbon Agenda is an increasingly commodified conception of citizenship rights, where traditional Marshallian social citizenship associated with the Keynesian Welfare State is gradually replaced by private responsibilities associated with workfare regimes. Crucially, I explain how this shift been intensified since the shift in early 2005 to a streamlined 'growth and jobs' agenda under the Barroso Commission.

In unfolding this argument, the remainder of the chapter will be structured as follows. First, a transnational historical materialist approach to citizenship will be briefly outlined and interwoven with a discussion of the historical background to EU citizenship prior to the Lisbon Agenda. Second, an outline and critique of the existing 'Third Way' literature on the Lisbon Agenda and its relation to social citizenship at the EU is offered. This then sets the stage for an alternative argument, which points to the emergence of a 'neoliberal communitarian' citizenship model in the Lisbon Agenda policy discourses of the transnational capitalist class, and the European Commission under Romano Prodi (1999–2004) and José Manuel Barroso (2004–). The paper then concludes by discussing the social contradictions engendered by the Lisbon Agenda's neoliberal communitarian citizenship model, as well as forms of resistance that are emerging to contest these dynamics in the EU political arena.

Conceptualizing citizenship, contextualizing Lisbon: a transnational historical materialist approach

The purpose of this section is to briefly outline the contours of a transnational historical materialist (hereafter THM) approach to citizenship that will underpin the remainder of the chapter (see also the Introduction to this volume). In order not stray too far from the subject matter at hand, some empirical grounding will be provided to this conceptual framework by interweaving it with a discussion of the 'extended re-launch' of the EU integration process (1987–99) when formal European citizenship was first introduced in the Maastricht Treaty (1992). This treatment will then in turn to serve to give the historical context leading up to the Lisbon Agenda, allowing us to better grasp the conditions that led to calls for the EU's 'radical transformation'. In the chapter's introduction a definition of citizenship was offered (as the concept defining the rights and responsibilities of civil society to the state and vice versa), and a claim was made that citizenship is situated in a dialectical relationship with broader processes of re-structuring and socio-economic transformation. Yet these two observations leave unanswered two fundamentally important questions that must be tackled before delving into the subject of citizenship: what actually constitutes 'the state', and what are the forces driving the state through transformation and re-structuring?

As was made clear in the volume's introduction, THM approaches view the state as a site of political struggle whereby competing class strategies, referred to as 'hegemonic projects' or 'concepts of control', vie for power over society. It is therefore concepts of control competing for comprehensiveness or hegemony which propel the state through processes of transformation and re-structuring, attempting to overcome the narrow ruling class interests from which they originate to unite together a constellation of 'divergent views, identities and interests' (Van Apeldoorn, 2002: 30). As heuristic and ideal-typical analytical tools, concepts of control capture the unity of what Regulation Theory has deemed the 'regime of accumulation' and 'mode of regulation', yet goes beyond it at the same time by adding crucial dimensions of international politics and transnational class struggle (Van der Pijl, 1998: 51). Although firmly grounded in the 'material' realm, concepts of control can also be regarded as 'discursive mediations of crisis', which in times of economic and/or political turmoil 'seek to give meaning to current problems by construing them in terms of past failures and future possibilities' (Jessop, 2002: 92). The 'new visions, projects, programmes and policies' (ibid.) that concepts of control entail are thus underpinned by uneven 'discursive struggles' that frame the trajectories of re-structuring, attempting above all to address structural contradictions and crises tendencies that are internal to capitalist development.

The 'extended re-launch' of the EU integration process (approximately 1987–99) serves to highlight this conceptualization of the state and the forces behind socio-economic re-structuring. After nearly two decades of 'Euro-pessimism', the re-launch of the EU integration process ushered in a new socio-economic order for the EU based on an 'embedded neoliberal' concept of control. Bastiaan van Apeldoorn (2002; see also his Chapter 1 in this volume) has documented how the outcome of embedded neoliberalism was the result of struggles between the discursive mediations of three rival projects for Europe's re-launch: supranational social democracy, neo-mercantilism and neoliberalism. Although all three projects reached a consensus that the structural crises plaguing European capitalism(s) since the early 1970s required a supranational response (a partial 're-scaling' of state functions to the EU level), they differed greatly in their views over what content the re-launch should entail. While the embedded neoliberal order was based on certain compromises accommodating the views of subordinate projects (e.g. the Maastricht Social Chapter and EU-level infrastructure and R & D policies) (ibid., 2002: Chapter 5), we should not overlook the neoliberal content of the re-launch and its social purpose of facilitating 'the primacy of global market forces and the freedom of transnational capital' (Van Apeldoorn, 2001: 82; see also Grahl and Teague, 1989). In fact the eventual emergence of the embedded neoliberal order was inextricably bound up with the ideological re-orientation of transnational European capitalist class away from its neomercantilist perspective towards, by the end of the 1980s, a perspective associated with neoliberalism (Van Apeldoorn, 2002). Through the platform of the ERT, transnational European capital, in its close co-operation with the European Commission, succeeded in making a neoliberal conception of 'global competitiveness' the overarching goal of EU governance (Van Apeldoorn, 2003).

As also argued by Bastiaan van Apeldoorn in this volume (see Chapter 1), what makes the embedded neoliberal concept of control of the re-launch especially significant in this regard is the *asymmetry* it creates in the modes of regulation of EU's evolving multi-level governance polity. Asymmetrical regulation is not only indicative in this sense of the bias towards negative integration and the lack of meaningful social policy at the EU level, but also, as Otto Holman explains (2004a: 716) implies that 're-regulation at the EU-level in terms of single market and monetary integration causes deregulation at the national level in social terms'. In a broader historical context, then, embedded neoliberalism does not arise out of thin air but instead offers itself as a 'solution' to the structural crises of national European capitalism(s) by seeking to dismantle the remnants of the capital-labour compromise underpinning the nexus of Fordism–Keynesianism that was hegemonic during the 30 'glory' years of the post-war corporate liberal era (1945–75) (Holman and Van der Pijl, 1996).

With this clarification of 'the state' (or better yet 'statehood') as a site managing capital accumulation and class struggle, it now becomes clear that the essential function of citizenship, in managing the relationship between state and civil society, is to *legitimate* the configurations of class relations that constitute the primary purpose of state activity. In other words, the composition of citizenship and especially social rights, as the 'constituent element of citizenship' and the 'cement of social cohesion' (Aglietta, 1998: 64), act as a bridge between accumulation and regulation, between narrow economic and general interests. The very notion of citizenship in this sense, framed in a discourse of equal status for purportedly equal political subjects, can be seen as a key battleground for rival concepts of control and their pursuit of hegemony. Emphasizing the centrality of citizenship to ruling class strategies should not, however, necessarily suggest an instrumentalist reduction of citizenship to a 'top-down' tool of legitimation. In taking a dialectical approach, the realization of social citizenship rights in the corporate liberal period (see Holman and Van der Pijl, 1996) entailed, for example, a clash between the 'bottom up' working class struggle for social protection and a 'top down' ruling class response to maintain hegemony.

This brings us back to the re-launch of the EU integration process, and most importantly to the introduction of the formal introduction of European citizenship as a legal category in the Maastricht Treaty (1992). The social purpose of European citizenship as the EU institutions themselves recognize has always been geared towards bolstering legitimacy by instilling a sense of belonging to the deepening and widening EU project; to 'supplement and complement the rights conferred by national citizenship' (Council of the European Union, 1997) by partially re-scaling citizenship by creating new and compatible identities to accompany the partial re-scaling of state function to the embryonic EU social body (Grahl and Teague, 1994; Scott-Smith, 2003).

The actual content of European citizenship introduced at Maastricht was reflective of the content of Europe's re-launch, so much so that it almost exclusively comprised provisions for facilitating the completion of the internal market. This 'socially-thin' market citizenship presented in Maastricht marked an extension of rights to complement and enhance already existing negative market integration (the free movement of people to complement the free movement of goods, services and capital), yet at the same time the extension of social citizenship rights associated with positive integration at the supranational level occurred only to facilitate labour mobility (Hansen, 2000). Even the Amsterdam Treaty (1997), in spite of its so-called 'rights agenda' (see Smith, 2004b), exposed the limits of European citizenship by providing only modest additions, including provisions allowing Member State nationals to receive correspondence from EU institutions in each of the (then) 12 official EU languages and an ambiguous section on the promotion of education. This revealed itself perhaps most forcefully within the field of employment policy, where a meaningful EU-level response, in the form of social rights, to the crisis of structural unemployment was cast aside in favour of promoting the citizen's *duty* to become 'employable' and 'adaptable' in the face of labour market flexibility (Barnard and Deakin, 1999: 359–60).

Just as we can argue that the rise of embedded neoliberalism in Europe's re-launch instilled a pattern of *asymmetrical regulation*, so too did it result in the formation of an *asymmetrical citizenship*. The emphasis on negative integration at the EU level not only prohibits the formation of (social) citizenship rights at the EU level, but also leads to a dismantling of the national social rights of citizenship that were built up in EU Member States in the corporate liberal era. Nationally constituted social rights, which were central to T. H. Marshall's classic formulation 'Citizenship and Social Class' (1992), provided the coherence, legitimacy and hegemony of Fordism and the Keynesian Welfare State under corporate liberalism by instituting, among other things, extensive collective bargaining arrangements, mass consumption norms and universal welfare services (see also Jessop, 2002, and Magnus Ryner, Chapter 2 of this volume). With the re-scaling and re-structuring of regulation in Europe's extended re-launch, attempts have been made to concomitantly re-scale and re-structure citizenship regimes in the EU away from the remaining vestiges of their Marshallian orientations towards a model more in line with the supposed exigencies of embedded neoliberalism. This largely *deconstructive* and *top-down* exercise was more concerned with eroding the post-war Marshallian model than with constructing a coherent model of its own; it was more about subordinating citizens' pan-European rights to the freedoms of transnational capital (see Smith, 2004b).

It therefore goes without saying that the limited nature of EU citizenship has as a result ineffectively addressed the very issues of EU legitimacy it was set up to solve (Scott-Smith, 2003). This is significant since, as Etienne Balibar (2004: 162–3) argues, the main obstacles (or as Balibar would have it, 'impossibilities') preventing the realization of a democratic and legitimate European citizenship have been the lack of an 'extension of social rights and . . . possibilities for intervention in the regulation of the economy' at the European level (for a similar argument, see Lipietz, 1993). It is within this multi-level context that we come to better understand the relative limitations that the formal introduction of European citizenship faced during the re-launch, failing to stem the growing crisis of EU legitimacy embodied, for instance, in the widespread apathy towards European Parliament elections, or the growing popular resistance to the austerity of Economic and Monetary Union 'convergence criteria' in France (see also Chapter 1 by Van Apeldoorn in this volume).

Beyond asymmetrical regulation/citizenship? The Lisbon Agenda and embedded neoliberalism

What makes the Lisbon Agenda so interesting and significant in this regard is the degree of optimism it initially invoked among a broad base of social and political forces, including trade unions and social non-governmental organisations, that it would solve these asymmetries of regulation and citizenship. Although the Presidency Conclusions of the Lisbon European Council 2000 meeting reveal an overarching concern to boost competitiveness, pledges were also made to promote social cohesion and 'modernized' social protection, as well as addressing the EU's unemployment epidemic by boosting employment rates from around 60 to 70 per cent. The theme of combining goals of competitiveness with other compromises has an obvious affinity with embedded neoliberalism (see Van Apeldoorn, Chapter 1 in this volume), yet this does not mean that we should brush aside the Lisbon Agenda as 'more of the same'.

In many respects, the Lisbon Agenda marks an important new juncture in EU socio-economic governance in invoking the promise of an 'information society' and a 'new knowledge-based economy' with a new growth model based on information and communication technology (ICT) (for an overview, see Boyer 2004). Significantly, the potential successes of the new economy were said to hinge on the acceleration and deepening of financial market integration in the EU, which would 'play an essential role in fuelling new ideas, supporting entrepreneurial culture and promoting access to and use of new technologies' (European Council, 2000). Thus taking cues from the successes of the growth of ICT in certain areas of the USA (e.g. Silicon Valley), and the upswing in US stock markets right before the turn of the millennium (Duménil and Lévy, 2004a: 64), many held faith that the EU could rival and overtake the more competitive economies of the USA and East Asia, while at the same time promoting 'capitalism with a human face' underpinned by the values of the so-called European Social Model (ESM) (Van der Pijl, 2006b).

For certain scholars, the broad political consensus reached at the Lisbon European Council meeting was to mark a positive turning point for EU-level social policy and associated matters of social citizenship (for an overview of this position, see Wincott, 2003). According to Maurizio Ferrera, Anton Hemerijck and Martin Rhodes (2000), some of the staunchest supporters from the academic community, the Lisbon Agenda represents a substantive effort by the EU to address the asymmetries of the integration process through a pragmatic 'Third Way' plan that balances economic reform with a serious dedication to creating a 'Social Europe', a new moment beyond the obsolescent 'corporate liberal' and turbulent 'embedded neoliberal' eras (see the contributions by Van Apeldoorn in Chapter 1 and Ryner in Chapter 2 to this volume). Lisbon's significance is to be found in its innovative refining of 'soft law' mechanisms in areas of social policy, which offer a balanced compromise between 'EU intervention via directives and the alternative (given the long history of blockages in the Council) of leaving policy instruments in the hands of the Member States' (Rhodes, 2000: 2–7). This tackling of asymmetry in governance also brings with it a 'unified account of equality and responsibility', which Rhodes (2000: 2–7) argues 'bridges the traditional concerns of egalitarians and conservatives by embracing both the individual and collective rights and responsibilities of citizens'. In terms of social citizenship, the Lisbon Agenda's focus (through the open method of co-ordination on areas such as social inclusion and pensions has the potential to 'nest' EU-level social rights as a counterweight to negative integration (Ferrera, 2005: Chapter 5, 2006: 10).

This 'Third Way' position on the Lisbon Agenda, despite being highly influential both politically and academically, raises a number of questions about its underlying assumptions about EU integration and governance. Can the asymmetries of regulation and their supposed 'solutions' be reduced to institutional infighting whereby national governments 'jealously guard' social policy domains while supranational institutions seek to wrestle them away? Furthermore, are critics of the asymmetrical and socially thin character of EU citizenship, as Maurizio Ferrera (2005: 243, 2006: 10) would suggest, mere 'perfectionists' who do not set 'an appropriate yardstick' for assessing the institutional basis for EU-level social rights? In returning to our conceptual framework, these scholars could be criticized for focusing solely on the institutional *form* of the Lisbon Agenda while neglecting its socioeconomic *content*: failing (or unwilling) to question its social purpose by asking what social forces benefit from the Lisbon Agenda and *what kind* of EU they promote (Van Apeldoorn, 2002; Holman, 2004a).

When viewed through the lens of THM we come to radically different conclusions about the Lisbon Agenda and its relation to citizenship. As the lynchpin of an (ever-transforming) embedded neoliberal concept of control for transnational European capital, I will now seek to demonstrate how the Lisbon Agenda entails an unequivocal thrust towards intensifying commodification of social citizenship norms in the EU. I will show how the hegemonic articulation of a 'neoliberal communitarian' citizenship model in the Lisbon Agenda discourses of the ERT, in alliance with other elements of transnational capital within the cadre class, has become a key reference point for the European Commission's policy debates regarding the Lisbon Agenda and its relationship to citizenship. While the policy-making debates of the Prodi Commission emphasize the social compromises of this hegemonic articulation, the Barroso Commission, in its streamlined and revamped 'growth and jobs' Lisbon Agenda, advocates a more 'disembedded neoliberal' project reflecting more narrowly the interests of transnational capital. With this shift in the EU's political society, I will conclude by exploring how the conflicts and contradictions of the Lisbon Agenda and 'neoliberal communitarian' citizenship have come to a fore, in turn stimulating the formation of potential 'concepts of resistance' and a 'bottom-up' struggle for European (social) citizenship.

Transnational capital and 'neoliberal communitarian' citizenship

While recognizing the widespread optimism and broad consensus that the Lisbon Agenda initially garnered across the EU, we should be careful to identify the role of the ERT in its origins. Just as in earlier years where it had taken advantage of its 'privileged relationship' with the European Commission, the ERT's role in the formulation of the Lisbon Agenda was no different. In fact, much of the substance of the strategy set forth in Lisbon builds directly on the recommendations of the ERT's Competitiveness Advisory Group (Van der Pijl, 2006b: 34–5). As one document tracking the chairmanship of Morris Tabaksblat exclaimed, the ERT (2005: 74) found it 'very satisfying' to see that much of its lobbying efforts for structural reforms to make the EU more competitive in the global economy had been reflected in the final Lisbon Agenda text.

Yet this interpretation of the initial influence of the ERT risks oversimplifying the nature of the Lisbon Agenda as both a *project* and a *process*; while the original document produced at the Lisbon European Council meeting does indeed reflect the hegemonic project of transnational capital, the Agenda itself is not a static and coherent plan to be merely implemented by EU institutions and Member State governments as it is. As a process, the broad and oftentimes vague terms like 'economic competitiveness' and 'social cohesion' or 'social protection' are highly contested with a variety of interpretations, especially within the context of the different 'varieties of capitalism' in EU Member States. The Lisbon Agenda should be viewed as a dynamic, conditional and malleable strategy that will only find precise meaning once other social actors begin to espouse their own interpretations of it.

For transnational European capital, these interpretations and contestations are mediated through planning bodies such as the ERT, and other elements operating within what Kees van der Pijl (1998: Chapter 5) calls the cadre class, such as the Lisbon Council for European Competitiveness (LCEC) and the World Economic Forum's Lisbon Review, which were established in the aftermath of the 2000 Council meeting.[2] Central to transnational capital's views is a discursive mediation of crisis that portrays the Lisbon Agenda as a response to 'globalization', an inevitable and agent-less external economic constraint:

> The future prosperity of Europe is coming under enormous strain. Unless urgent action is taken on long awaited and long overdue structural reforms, Europe risks paying a heavy price in terms of future economic

growth, job creation and its ability to compete successfully in global markets.

(ERT, 2003: 1–2)

At the beginning of the 21st century, as we move from the industrial age to a networked, knowledge-based economy, our current Social Model is in desperate need of modernization. At a time when flexibility and speed are engines of economic growth and wealth creation, our current system breeds inertia and gridlock ... Our economy, too, has ground to a screeching halt, leaving us puzzled about Asia's and North America's ability to grow out of recession while we sputter along in endless debate, seemingly unable to return to the forefront of the global economy where we belong.

(LCEC, 2004: 1–2)

In the words of the LCEC executive director Ann Mettler (2005), the Lisbon Agenda should mirror the re-structuring undertaken by the most successful EU Member States, those 'that have learned to meet the challenges, and reap the opportunities of globalization, rather than wage a futile and destructive fight against it'. The stubborn resistance of the EU (to technological innovation, labour market flexibility and social welfare cuts) becomes a key factor in explaining the current crisis.

European citizens, for their part, play a key role in the realization of transnational capital's view of the Lisbon Agenda reforms required in the new European economy. As noted by the ERT (2001b: 6), 'the education, personal qualities, attitudes and behaviour of Europe's citizens are essential ingredients for success'. In appealing for 'new Europeans' to accompany the 'new European economy', transnational capital calls for active citizens that accept that they 'are not born with a God-given right to one of the world's highest standards of living' (LCEC, 2004a: 3), that realize that prosperity hinges on competitiveness in the global economy, and acknowledge that 'everybody has a vital stake in, and must make a significant contribution to, the economy and well-being of society' (ERT, 2004a: 3). This conception of the new 'active citizen' in the Lisbon Agenda brings with it a new understanding of rights and responsibilities. In terms of responsibilities of the citizen, this involves an emphasis on the role citizens themselves have in the realization of Lisbon reforms. Citizens are responsible for changing their own attitudes to:

bring a spirit of enterprise to life as an employee and a citizen. Not necessarily in the sense of developing and pursuing business ideas, although Europe certainly needs more business entrepreneurs, but definitely in terms of developing a capacity for creativity, innovation, flexibility, team work and intellectual curiosity. Such an individual must be capable of taking charge of his or her employment destiny. Lifetime employment will not soon disappear, but it will be less relevant for many people. In pursuing other preferences and opportunities, they will need, among other things, to be able to identify emerging employment opportunities and to acquire necessary training for them.

(ERT, 2001b: 4)

Accordingly, the ideal citizen is envisioned as a self-reliant 'risk-taker', a 'life-long learner', an 'entrepreneur' and an 'innovator'. Those citizens that are unwilling to take this responsibility on themselves to adopt more competitive attitudes are regarded as complacent, and too '[a]ccustomed to social safety nets and an assured standard of living' (ERT, 2004c: 6). Active, responsible citizens are those that take sight of their individual interests by increasing their own 'employability', and that are no longer 'reliant' on Marshallian social rights of the welfare state.

In making sense of this position, we see that transnational capital's embedded neoliberal concept of control is discursively underpinned by what can best be described as a 'neoliberal communitarian' citizenship model. In his analysis of EU employment policy, Hans-Jürgen Bieling (2003a) describes neoliberal communitarianism as a fusion of neoliberalism with a communitarian element that attempts to countervail the most harmful effects of neoliberal deregulation and restructuring not by re-invigorating the social rights of the Keynesian national welfare state but through attempting to 'activate the state' in strengthening (private) community networks (ibid.: 53). As a model of citizenship, neoliberal communitarianism signifies a movement away from 'unconditional social citizenship entitlements' (Ryner, 2002: 15) towards an emphasis on providing Schumpeterian-style labour market policies that offer opportunities for skill upgrading and life-long learning so that citizens will be 'willing to *accept more public duties and social responsibilities*' (Bieling, 2003a: 65; emphasis in original). Thus central to neoliberal communitarian citizenship is a Schumpeterian emphasis on a 'workfare' form of citizenship in which 'flexibility' and 'adaptability' on the part of the workforce have . . . come to be seen as the panacea for Europe's unemployment problem' (Van Apeldoorn, 2003: 114).

The embrace of workfare is captured in the view that the purpose of the EU should merely be to maintain 'a healthy economy and a flourishing job market' (LCEC, 2004a: 3), which in turn ensures that 'if a citizen is laid off, he or she can be confident that new employment opportunities can be found within a reasonable time' (LCEC, 2005: 3). Unemployment is as a result considered 'a moral problem of the individual who is unemployed' (Ryner, 2002: 10) who has a personal responsibility 'to make sure they qualify for employment (whatever the changes in the structure of the labour market)' (Overbeek, 2003: 27). In order to gauge to what extent this neoliberal communitarian view of citizenship has ascended to hegemonic status in the EU, we must analyse the degree to which it has been adopted in the main policy-making debates of the European Union. Thus we now turn to a discussion of these debates within the European Commission, the EU institution tasked with the primary responsibility of fulfilling the Lisbon Agenda's strategic goals.

The Prodi Commission (1999–2004) and the Lisbon Agenda: a passive revolution

The EU Commission under the leadership of President Romano Prodi (1999–2004) upholds the sense of optimism that surrounds the original Lisbon Agenda text. Like transnational capital, the Prodi Commission treats global-ization as an inevitable, agent-less process. Yet while the ERT and LCEC speak of globalization's threats, the Prodi Commission takes an optimistic approach to the 'quantum shift' of globalization, where the Lisbon Agenda has the potential to mark a new 'renaissance for Europe': '[t]here is very little for Europe to fear from increased globalization, indeed there is everything to gain if we look to past and present experience' (Diamantopoulou, 2000). In many ways the Prodi Commission's views of the Lisbon Agenda mark a con-tinuation of the embedded neoliberal compromise, one that seeks to balance the starkly neoliberal stance of transnational capital with a discourse of social protection and cohesion that has a less than direct association with the Keynesian National Welfare State and 'Social Europe' as envisioned by former Commission President Jacques Delors. This dualism comes out most force-fully in the speeches of the various Commissioners. Frits Bolkestein (2001), Commissioner for the Internal Market and Taxation, on the one hand argues that the EU 'must leave the comfortable surrounding of the Rhineland and move closer to the tougher conditions and colder climate of the Anglo-Saxon form of capitalism, where the rewards are greater but the risks also'. Meanwhile Commission President Romano Prodi (2000a, 2000b) speaks of a 'just balance between economic reform and social cohesion' whereby 'action to create a dynamic economy is only one side of the equation. It must be balanced by equally determined action to promote social inclusion and solidarity.'

This attempted compromise is furthermore reflected in the Prodi Commission's discourses on citizenship, where neoliberal workfare concep-tions of citizenship are accompanied by references to social rights. The ten-dency towards workfare is demonstrated in the (recurring) assertions that 'a job is often the best protection against exclusion' (European Commission, 2002b: 12). This portrayal of citizenship limits citizens' rights to job train-ing and skills development or life-long learning, while also increasing citi-zen responsibilities, as the attainment of employment leads to greater social cohesion and protection. However, even the Commission's acceptance of a need for greater labour market flexibility is tempered with a social rights discourse. President Prodi (2000b) makes this clear in arguing that '[t]he labour market needs to be flexible certainly: but people need to be able to plan their lives, and should not be the victims of shock redundancy'. There is clearly an element of social rights that calls for a social dimension for the EU's Lisbon Agenda, which will 'ensure adequate social protection for those who cannot [work]' (European Commission, 2003b) and that faces up to the fact that 'you can't have a fair society without fair pay' (Prodi, 2001b).

Perhaps most significantly, and in glaring contrast to transnational capital's neoliberal communitarian conception of citizenship, is the passive role of the citizen envisaged by the Prodi Commission within the Lisbon Agenda reforms. Although Prodi (2001a) exclaims that he wants 'the future of Europe to be firmly in the hands of its citizens' and that the EU 'must explore ways of getting the citizens genuinely involved in EU policymaking', the citizen is generally not conceived as an active actor when it comes to the socio-economic transformation under Lisbon. Instead the Commission describes how the EU and its Member States are responsible for Lisbon Agenda reforms that work towards '*giving* people new skills for the new economy' (Prodi, 2001b; my emphasis) and that '*bring* our fellow citizens greater prosperity' (Prodi, 2003; my emphasis). The notion that the EU's young citizens 'must be taught how to thrive in a world becoming increasingly complex and subject to change' (European Commission, 2000: 16) and that the EU itself 'must encourage risk-taking and the spirit of enterprise' (ibid.) does not lend itself to an active conception of citizenship that is associated with the neoliberal communitarian citizenship model.

In any case, making sense of the Prodi Commission's ideas on citizenship requires us to think in theoretical terms about the significance of this passive conception of the EU's subjects. Using Gramsci's thought, the Lisbon modernization project as understood by the Prodi Commission is best thought of as a 'passive revolution' (Gramsci, 1971: 106–20). Gramsci used the term, as Walters and Haahr (2005: 88) explain, 'to theorize a particular process of socio-political transformation: one where states undertake leadership and modernization tasks whose overall function is to stabilize the socioeconomic order'. Hence, the EU's tasks of socioeconomic transformation, according to the Prodi Commission, are placed solely into the hands of the EU's political society, as citizens become the beneficiaries of the leadership role taken by the EU institutions and Member State governments. Casting the relationship between Lisbon and citizenship in terms of rights and responsibilities, the Prodi Commission focuses primarily on an ambiguous rights-based conception of citizenship, with the burden of responsibilities falling on the EU and its Member State governments.

The Barroso Commission and the Lisbon Agenda (2004–): growth and jobs with active citizenship

In early 2005 the newly appointed Barroso Commission, acting in unison with Member States in the conclusions made at the Spring European Council in Brussels, presented a plan to 're-launch' the Lisbon Agenda in a stream-lined form that focuses on raising employment and economic growth in the EU. This need for revision was attributed to everything from the September 11 terrorist attacks in the USA to the dot.com bubble burst to a general economic downturn in the eurozone, to a concern with the general failures of the Lisbon Agenda under the Prodi Commission.

Thus the aura of optimism framing the Lisbon Agenda under the Prodi Commission was replaced by a strong discursive mediation of crisis under Barroso. Although the Barroso Commission insisted that this re-launched focus on growth and jobs did not mean that the EU was abandoning its commitment to social cohesion and the ESM, the plan proved to be highly controversial and seemed to confirm their suspicions of the newly appointed Commission, especially President Barroso, as too 'business friendly' and bent on shifting the EU to the right (*Irish Times*, 2004). In what has proven to be perhaps the most controversial statement of his brief tenure thus far, President Barroso (2005e), in a speech to the EU parliament, equated the three Lisbon Agenda goals to his three children in arguing for the need to help the EU's 'sickened' economy:

> It is as if I have three children – the economy, our social agenda, and the environment. Like any modern father – if one of my children is sick, I am ready to drop everything and focus on him until he is back to health. That is normal and responsible. But that does not mean I love the others any less!

Even though the above statement has proven to be to the extreme end of Barroso Commission's ideas concerning the Lisbon Agenda (it certainly has not been repeated), a new sense of urgency, and indeed crisis, marks the turning point of the Barroso Commission's streamlined focus on growth and jobs. In particular, it appears as to mark at least a partial 'disembedding' of the compromises of the embedded neoliberal concept of control, in favour of a more intensified neoliberal approach to socio-economic governance.

Acting on recommendations made by the EU-commissioned High Level Group hired to carry out an independent mid-term review of the Lisbon Agenda, the Commission claims that in light of the EU's recent failures to attain its Lisbon Agenda goals and to adapt to ever increasing competition, an ageing population and slow growth, a shift in focus is needed to make the Agenda relevant under changed circumstances. Indeed as the High Level Group made clear in its Lisbon Agenda report, 'time is running out', and in light of the 'new economic situation' that has developed in the EU since the Lisbon Agenda was created in 2000, the EU needs to take drastic measures to update the Lisbon Agenda to reflect the current pressures (High Level Group Chaired by Wim Kok, 2004: 6). As a result, the Commission justifies the move to growth and jobs by prioritizing the role of higher employment and economic growth in securing social protection and inclusion. In essence, the argument moves away from the idea that social inclusion and economic growth and jobs are mutually reinforcing goals, towards an assertion more in line with transnational capital, that the EU needs 'a dynamic economy to fuel our wider social and environmental ambitions' (European Commission, 2005b: 4):

> Growth is a necessary condition for effective solidarity. Without growth, without a dynamic economy, there will be no sustainable development, no future pensions and no response to the pressures on our quality of life.
> (Barroso, 2005a)

The shift in focus to growth and jobs brings with it a change in the citizenship ideas of the Commission. What comes across in quite stark terms in the High Level Group's mid-term review of the Lisbon Agenda is a criticism of the EU's passive conception of the citizen's role under the Prodi Commission. In formulating a shift to focus on growth and jobs, the High Level Group states quite clearly, and in somewhat paternalistic terms, that the EU's citizens' role needs to be re-thought with Lisbon's re-launch:

> The need for reform has to be explained especially to citizens who are not always aware of the urgency and scale of the situation. 'Competitiveness' is not just some dry economic indicator that is often unintelligible to the man in the street; rather, it provides a diagnosis of the state of economic health of a country or a region. In the present circumstances, the clear message must be: if we want to preserve and improve our social model we have to adapt it: it is not too late to change. In any event the status quo is not an option. Engaging and involving citizens in the process has two mutually reinforcing attractions: it in effect seeks public support by giving people elements for debate and it leverages that support to put pressure on governments to pursue these goals.
> (High Level Group Chaired by Wim Kok, 2004: 44)

The Barroso Commission for its part recognises that the EU has 'failed to mobilise support around the idea of what Europe can be' (Barroso, 2005b), and addresses these criticisms in its documents and speeches related to the shift to growth and jobs. There is therefore a constant effort on behalf of the Commission to make the citizen an active actor in the Lisbon Agenda reforms. The sense of urgency for reform associated with the shift to growth and jobs thus brings with it a more active conception of citizenship, as the Commission adopts the idea that success in instituting substantial change requires that citizens have a 'stake in the success of these reforms' (Barroso, 2005a), and that Lisbon 'gives a real sense of ownership' (Barroso, 2005c). The failure of Lisbon to this point is at least partly attributed to the passive role for citizens envisioned by the Prodi Commission, and in making the case for reform to focus on growth and jobs the Barroso Commission follows the High Level Group in calling for a more active citizen that takes an active role in the urgently needed reforms.

Thus we find that the shift to growth and jobs entails not only a more active role for the citizen, but also reflects the neoliberal communitarian and Schumpeterian notion that limit social rights to the skills and education related to making increased 'employability':

> The political challenge to offer citizens a credible 'new deal' allowing them to embrace more flexibility in return for social inclusion systems that effectively help them to master change and partake in prosperity, whilst offering adequate security and solidarity – including between generations – is crucial but has not yet been answered.
>
> (European Commission, 2005b: 15–16)

As a result, the Barroso Commission advocates a 'new deal' between citizens and governments focusing on re-defining 'social inclusion systems' away from the socialization of risk associated with the welfare state, towards a commodified and individualized system whereby the individual's pursuit of employment (through upgraded skills and life-long learning) leads to greater social cohesion and provides the material basis for continued social expenditure. The EU is thus tasked with the responsibility of providing an adequate supply of jobs to its citizens, and 'maintaining a worker's ability to find a job' (Špidla, 2005). Citizen rights become limited to the right to obtain more skills and better education, so that 'workers and enterprises' alike 'become more adaptable and labour markets more flexible' (Barroso, 2005d). The active and responsible citizen is thus indispensable in the reforms associated with more growth and jobs:

> The impact of changes can be limited by sustained investment in developing workers' skills, thereby enabling them to cope with change: a well-trained worker is better able to find a new job in the wake of unavoidable restructuring.
>
> (Špidla 2005)

Towards concepts of resistance: the social contradictions of the neoliberal communitarian citizenship

It is remarkable to note how the ideas of the Barroso Commission towards the Lisbon Agenda and citizenship bear a striking resemblance to the views of the transnational capitalist class. Indeed, since the introduction of Lisbon in 2000, this class has consistently advocated a 'streamlined' version of the

Agenda that strongly resembles the re-launched Lisbon Agenda presented by the Barroso Commission in 2004. The Commission's streamlined Lisbon Agenda has been enthusiastically embraced as an answer to their own demands, with LCEC President Paul Hofheinz (2005) affirming that 'without economic growth, our social system will collapse'. Adding to this, Hofheinz chides critics of Lisbon's re-launch as 'dangerous demagogues' for arguing that 'efforts to improve the economy will lead to a less social Europe'. The discursive re-definition and ultimate subordination of traditional social democratic ideas, such as social solidarity, social rights and full employment to the commodifying logic of neoliberal restructuring, starkly contradicts the assertions made by certain scholars that the Lisbon Agenda marks a sort of positive turning point for EU-level social citizenship. Rather than solving the asymmetries of regulation and citizenship, the strong ideological alliance between transnational capital and the Commission in the Lisbon Agenda instead serves to intensify and deepen these tendencies.

At the same time, however, the intensifying shift towards disembedding the embedded elements of the neoliberal concept of control and the concomitant rise of a Schumpeterian-inspired neoliberal communitarian citizenship model engenders a new set of conflicts, tensions and contradictions. In capturing these dynamics it is worth returning to Marshall's thoughts on the centrality of social rights to modern capitalism. Despite all the relevant criticisms directed towards his original formulation (for naïve evolutionism, Euro-centrism and patriarchal tendencies), Cafruny and Ryner (2007b: 85) explain how Marshall did touch on something crucial in suggesting 'that it is only when risks of destitution and insecurity associated with industrial capitalist society are eliminated, or at least substantially mitigated, through the social rights provided by the welfare state that the broad mass of the population can fully obtain the status required to effectively exercise civic and political citizenship'. Therefore the 'active' element in neoliberal communitarian citizenship is not really active at all, in the sense that the subordination of social citizenship rights serves to also jeopardize the citizen's ability to exercise those civil and political rights that underpin the supposed 'active' element implied within citizenship. This has the potential to induce an 'exhaustion of society' whereby 'the entire weight of the social contradictions of modern capitalism is to be borne by the individual, who has no social rights at all to claim "without responsibilities"' (Ryner 2002: 19). Indeed, as Ryner (2002: 20) argues, it is hard to comprehend how one could expect that a citizen should be a 'heroic, competitive, flexible and mobile individual who at the same time is a nurturing parent, rooted in a community, in which he/she has time and energy to invest civic involvement'.

With all this in mind there is no reason to believe that a neoliberal communitarian conception of citizenship will render 'the exhaustion of society as a consequence of intensified capital accumulation . . . a thing of the past' (Bieling, 2003a: 71). Indeed, it must be emphasized that there are absolutely no guarantees that the neoliberal communitarian citizenship model will be 'internalized' by the citizens themselves. At the current moment it appears as though many of the compromises holding together the embedded neoliberal concept of control may be falling apart in light of the Barroso Commission's relaunch of the Lisbon Agenda. It is no coincidence that the Lisbon Agenda's 'failures' to this point have emerged hand in hand with growing resistance to the EU project, culminating in the rejections of the EU constitution in France and the Netherlands (on the latter see Chapter 10 by Van Apeldoorn in this volume). The same trade unions and social NGOs that enthusiastically embraced the Lisbon Agenda as a route to EU-level social protection and cohesion are now speaking out against the narrow economic objectives of the streamlined focus on growth and jobs (ETUC, 2005b; Platform of European Social NGOs, 2005; on European trade union strategy see also the contribution by Bieler to this volume, Chapter 11). This position is underpinned by efforts to strengthen the social rights dimension of the Lisbon Agenda, through lobbying for transnational frameworks for social policy ranging from pan-European 'co-determination' rights for workers to a minimum citizen income to protect EU citizens against social exclusion and poverty.

Whether or not these counter-movements truly represent a counter-hegemonic struggle away from neoliberal communitarian citizenship, or whether they will be somehow drawn into reformist posturing and drained of their radical content, are left to be determined. The ideological alliance between the EU Commission and transnational capital points to a relatively broad-based, materially powerful bloc of forces; yet at the same time, broad-based social movements are challenging the legitimacy and 'common sense' of this bloc, seeking to stem the intensifying commodification of ever more areas of social life, and at the same time suggesting that the notion of social rights within a 'Social Europe' may still be of relevance. Thus somewhat paradoxically, the struggles against the 'top-down' imposition of EU citizenship are already being countered by nascent 'bottom-up' struggles for an alternative citizenship model; one that speaks for EU citizens against the model that created this identity in the first place. The trajectories of this movement will be determined by its abilities to formulate a coherent alternative concept of resistance with an alternative citizenship model based on a more democratic and egalitarian vision of transnational society.

Notes

1. I would like to thank an anonymous reviewer, the volume editors and the participants from the Critical Political Economy workshop at the Vrije Universiteit, Amsterdam, for their insightful criticisms and suggestions. Thanks are also due to Peo Hansen and Julian Germann for their comments on an early draft. The usual disclaimers apply.

2. The Lisbon Council is a Brussels-based think tank established as an 'informal network of economists, business people and ordinary citizens' lobbying EU and Member State institutions for Lisbon reforms to create a 'more competitive Europe'. Although it portrays itself as a champion for the interests of small and medium-sized enterprises *against* big business, its interests are very much bound up with those of the most powerful transnational corporations, both 'industrial' and 'financial'. A glance at its list of supporters (available at http://www.lisboncouncil.net), including ExxonMobil, IBM, ING Group, Microsoft, Allianz Group, Morgan Stanley, Oracle, Royal Dutch-Shell, Tesco and more confirms this.

6
Organic Intellectuals at Work? The High Level Group of Company Law Experts in European Corporate Governance Regulation

Laura Horn

> *Our mandate was to make recommendations on a modern regulatory framework for company law in Europe; basically to point out a new direction for the future development of company law in the EU.*
>
> (Winter, 2004: 98)

Introduction

In 2002 a report by seven company law experts significantly changed the trajectory of corporate governance regulation in the European Union. After the defeat of the European Commission's proposal for a Takeover Directive in the European Parliament in July 2001, the High Level Group of Company Law Experts (HLG), chaired by Dutch company law professor and legal adviser for Unilever, Jaap Winter, set out to 'point out a new direction for the future' of European company law and corporate governance (Winter, 2004: 98). The Commission, in its 2002 Takeover Directive proposal (European Commission, 2002a) and the ensuing Company Law Action Plan published in 2003 (European Commission, 2003d), followed most of the recommendations and issues raised by the HLG. Arguably, the role and influence of the HLG was far more extensive than just the provision of nitty-gritty company law expertise to figure out the very details of new proposals. Rather, by setting policy options and recommendations in a framework that entailed a considerable shift towards a more market-based corporate governance regulation (see Van Apeldoorn and Horn, 2007a, 2007b), the group significantly shaped the parameters of the corporate governance debate in the European Union. This raises the question of how it was that these seven experts could have such an immense impact on a regulatory field that, after all, is of fundamental redistributive consequence within the socio-economic restructuring in the EU.

This chapter argues that in order to understand the role of the HLG we need to move beyond studies of expert knowledge in the policy-making process that focus mainly on the *mode* of governance and a categorization of expertise, to an approach that also problematizes the actual *content* of the experts' recommendations. On the basis of a discussion of Gramsci's notion of the 'organic intellectual', the chapter argues that the *social function* (Gramsci, 1971: 9) of experts in processes of socio-economic restructuring is crucial indeed. This entails acknowledging the inherently problem-solving character of expertise involved in policy-making processes. Rather than questioning the logic of policy proposals and regulatory frameworks, expert groups are commissioned to provide effective solutions to legislative deadlocks and to cut through conflicts by shifting the debate to different issues. The outcome of the consultation of expert groups more often than not consists in clear-cut policy recommendations, which influence the policy-making process in that they prioritize certain options over others, and leave out particular policy options – which the experts do not consider viable – altogether.

The chapter proceeds as follows. After a brief overview of some of the main concepts and perspectives employed in the literature on the role of expert knowledge, in particular the concept of 'epistemic communities' (Haas, 1992), a neo-Gramscian perspective on the transformation of corporate governance regulation in the EU is discussed. Here, the focus is on the role and work of the HLG, on the basis of document analysis and interviews conducted with several members of the HLG, as well as other actors involved in the policy process.[1] The concluding section then discusses some of the implications of the increasing role of the HLG and other expert committees in corporate governance regulation in the EU.

Perspectives on the role of expert knowledge

In European integration studies, the role of expert committees in a variety of settings has predominantly been discussed in the context of the 'democratic deficit' discussion (for an overview see Radaelli, 1999) – most of all because of the alleged 'technocracy' in the EU.[2] This is also the result of the nature of European integration – rather than aimed at (re)distributive, 'positive' integration, most regulatory policies in the EU are geared towards increasing the efficiency of the integration process (Majone, 1996). As Radaelli argues, 'this makes them suitable for discussion and negotiation in expert circles, whereas distribution kindles the passions of politicians, political parties and mass opinion because of its impact on the class structure' (Radaelli, 1999: 759).

However, conventional theories of European integration are rather inadequate for trying to conceptualize the role of these expert groups in EU governance. Whereas (liberal) intergovernmentalism notoriously does not perceive any significant influence of private groups on the policy-making process (other than at the national level), supranational institutionalist accounts at least recognize the function of expert groups. As Fligstein and

Stone Sweet argue, 'the Commission has an interest in co-opting "experts" – knowledge based and industry-specific elites – into the policy process, to help draft new and assess existing legislation and to help legitimize legislation that is proposed' (Fligstein and Stone Sweet, 2002: 1225). Yet the interests and substantial involvement of these experts are not problematized or questioned at all. Rather, the literature focuses on the functional aspects of expert groups in European governance. The institutional and organizational austerity of the Commission and other EU bodies appears to be the favourite explanation for the consultation and commissioning of external expert groups:

> Permanent understaffing of the Commission has an important impact on the functioning of the institution. It explains why the Commission regularly hires consultants and stays in permanent contact with the private sector. The understaffing makes the proper functioning of the institution dependent on external resources.
>
> (Bouwen, 2001: 24)

The argument that the Commission, because of its limited staff resources, simply cannot deliver all the specialized expertise required in the policy-making process (Verdun, 1999: 309; see also Radaelli, 1999) and thus has to consult external expertise is, of course, plausible. It is overstretched, though, to the extent that it tends to obscure other reasons for the setting up of expert groups in order to shape the policy-making process.

With regard to the involvement of expert knowledge in the various legislative stages in the EU, the Commission's strong demand for expert groups stems from its role in initiating and drafting legislative proposals (Bouwen, 2002: 379). This, again, certainly holds as a viable argument. Yet it is often assumed that the involvement of external expertise is inherently beneficial not only to the effectiveness of the policy-making as such, but also to the legitimacy of these proposals. As Bouwen (2001: 27) argues, 'expertise enables the commission to deal with policy problems in an efficient and effective way and thereby increases the output legitimacy of the institution'.

Among the variety of theoretical concepts and empirical studies dealing with the role of information and knowledge, the advocacy coalition approach (Sabatier, 1998) has focused explicitly on the role of scientific information in public policy processes. Advocacy coalitions comprise 'people from a variety of positions (elected and agency officials, interest group leaders, researchers) who [1] share a particular belief system – i.e. a set of basic values, causal assumptions and problem perceptions – and who [2] show a non-trivial degree of co-ordinated activity over time' (Sabatier, 1998: 115). While this approach moves beyond a focus on state and public actors by taking the role of journalists, think tanks and academics into account, it shares the ultimately descriptive outlook of most approaches to the role of knowledge in the policy process, as it does not seek to explain where and how these 'belief systems' emerge. Neither does the advocacy coalition offer an explanation of why certain advocacy coalitions seem to be more successful in terms of providing information in the policy process.

Epistemic communities

The notion of an epistemic community as a 'network of professionals with recognized expertise and competence in a particular domain and an authoritative claim to policy-relevant knowledge within that domain or issue-area' (Haas, 1992: 3) has had a great impact on the way the influence of expert knowledge in political processes has been conceived. Haas argued that the primary concern of using this conceptual tool is explaining 'the political influence that an epistemic community can have on collective policymaking, rather the correctness of the advice given' (Haas, 1992: 23). The involvement of epistemic communities in policy-making processes, it is argued, 'narrow[s] the range within which political bargains can be struck' (Adler and Haas, 1992: 378). Yet the content and underlying purpose of these ideas is not in any way subject to further analysis. Rather, the form and mechanisms through which epistemic communities exert influence on policy-making bodies is taking place stands at the centre of attention (policy innovation, policy diffusion, policy selection and policy persistence, and policy evolution as learning; see Adler and Haas, 1992).[3]

This focus on the *form* of epistemic communities, and the *mechanisms* through which they exert influence, however, obscures the social function and the *content* of the expert involvement. The ideas and conceptions through which epistemic communities influence and shape policy proposals seem to be exogenous to the expert community in that they appear to be formed within a political vacuum. Epistemic communities seem to be standing outside or above the continuous contestation, struggle and compromise that constitute political processes. On the one hand it is acknowledged that:

> members of an epistemic community share intersubjective understandings; have a shared way of knowing; have shared patterns of reasoning; have a policy project drawing on shared causal beliefs, and the use of shared discursive practices; and have a shared commitment to the application and production of knowledge.
>
> (Haas, 1992: 3, footnote 5)

Yet, just how, on the other hand, these ideas and causal beliefs are formed is left out of the equation. It appears as if 'ideas' in the epistemic community approach are perceived as neutral, isolated from material interests. This is a serious shortcoming, since it renders the epistemic communities approach unable to account for the social function these ideas, and with it the role of epistemic communities, necessarily assume.

The epistemic communities approach does acknowledge, however, that the role of expert knowledge might depend on other factors than just the expertise it brings with it, and that this expertise can be instrumentalized (Adler and Haas, 1992: 381). Also, as Verdun points out, 'not all expert committees *automatically* form an epistemic community. Rather, the notion of an "epistemic community" requires the members to have a commitment to a political goal and to interpret their knowledge in such a way that it support their goal' (Verdun, 1999: 320). It is this link between the political goal and the recommendations and advice advocated by the expert groups that needs to be studied in order to understand the role of expert groups. Adler and Haas, however, very unambiguously insisted on a close reading of their concept by arguing that 'epistemic community should not be mistaken for a new hegemonic actor that is the source of political and moral direction in society. . . . Epistemic communities are neither philosophers, nor kings, nor philosopher-kings' (Adler and Haas, 1992: 371).

Although it is not being argued that expert knowledge takes on the form of a hegemonic force per se, by being part of (hegemonic) discourses and reproducing and validating them, epistemic communities cannot be perceived as detached from social structures and context. As Gramsci argued, 'philosophy cannot be divorced from politics . . . the choice and the criticism of a conception of the world is also a political matter' (Gramsci, 1971: 327).

The following section now turns to the Gramscian concept of the 'organic intellectuals' in order to elicit whether this notion provides answers to some of the problems raised in this discussion on the role of knowledge in political processes.

A neo-Gramscian perspective – organic intellectuals

From a critical transnational political economy perspective that focuses on the socio-economic content of the integration process as an outcome of political and ideological struggles within a transnational political arena (see the Introduction to this volume; also Van Apeldoorn, 2002; Cafruny and Ryner, 2003), the role of experts groups in the transformation of corporate governance is essentially political, rather than a question of expertise and technical detail. Yet, although the emerging literature of neo-Gramscian accounts of European integration processes acknowledges the importance of 'organic intellectuals' in shaping and 'framing' ideological elements of the hegemonic project of market integration (see, for instance, Bieler and Morton, 2001a; Van Apeldoorn et al., 2003: 19–20; Bieler, 2005a), little research has been conducted on actual manifestations of 'organic intellectuals'. Most research has indeed concentrated on the more visible transnational actors and their (unmediated) influence on European governance (for instance, the European Roundtable of Industrialists or the World Economic Forum; but see Bieling, 2005 on 'transnational discourse coalitions') rather than on the role of organic intellectuals as such. This is an unfortunate neglect, as the concept is so central to neo-Gramscian perspectives. As Van Apeldoorn et al. (2003: 37) point out: 'more than anything else, the notion of organic intellectuals and their role in cementing and spreading the ideas of the historic bloc bring into view the importance of agency'.

As Gramsci argued, 'all men are intellectuals . . . but not all men have in society the function of intellectuals' (Gramsci, 1971: 9). Expert knowledge has to be seen within the context of the configuration of social forces struggling for a hegemonic position. Organic intellectuals serve the 'social function' of

> bringing about not only a unison of economic and political aims, but also intellectual and moral unity, posing all questions around which the struggle rages not on a corporate but on a 'universal' plane, and thus creating the hegemony of a fundamental social group over a series of subordinate groups.
>
> (Gramsci, 1971: 182)

In this understanding, they play a crucial role in formulating and spreading the ideological and strategic concepts of any given political project. At the same time, they help to define and articulate the contours and interests of a social group, and:

> every social group, coming into existence on the original terrain of an essential function in the world of economic production, creates together with itself, organically, one or more strata of intellectuals which give it homogeneity and an awareness of its own function not only in the economic but also in the social and political fields.
>
> (Gramsci, 1971: 5)

Gramsci contrasts the notion of the 'organic intellectual' with what he called 'traditional intellectuals'. This distinction is crucial here, as it marks the difference between a perception of experts as providers of (technical) knowledge – in Gramsci's words 'the expression of that social utopia by which the intellectuals think of themselves as "independent", autonomous, endowed with a character of their own . . . and an understanding of organic intellectuals as an "organic category of every fundamental social group"' (Gramsci, 1971: 7–8, 15).

The question whether intellectuals are, indeed, class-bound, or rather, 'free-floating' or a class in themselves is of obvious importance for an understanding of the role of knowledge in political processes. Drawing on Alfred Weber, Karl Mannheim famously claimed that intellectuals constitute a 'relatively classless stratum which is not too firmly situated in the social order, *freischwebende Intelligenz*' (Mannheim, 1976: 138). This 'free-floating' nature of intellectuals afford them the 'ability to attach themselves to classes to which they originally did not belong, [and] was possible for intellectuals because they could adapt themselves to any viewpoint and because they and they alone were in a position to choose their affiliation' (Mannheim, 1976: 140). The Gramscian notion of the 'organic intellectuals' clearly rejects this perception of intellectuals as unanchored – as Gramsci argued, the 'most widespread error of method seems to me that of having looked for this criterion of distinction in the *intrinsic nature of intellectual activities*, rather than in the ensemble of the system of relations in which these activities (and therefore the intellectual groups who personify them) have their place *within the general complex of social relations*' (Gramsci, 1971: 8, emphasis added).[4]

For an understanding of expert groups as in the context of this chapter, however, this debate is misleading inasmuch as the role of organic intellectuals cannot be perceived as an *immediate* translation and articulation of class interest. As Gramsci clarified, 'the relationship between the intellectuals and the world of production is not as direct as it is with the fundamental social groups but it is . . . "mediated" by the fabric of society' (Gramsci, 1971: 3). That is to say, to recognize an 'organic intellectual' when you see one, their function in engineering and reproducing a particular political project, rather than their own class position and class consciousness, is crucial. The 'organicity' (what Gramsci called '*organicitá*') of intellectuals is thus not an *intrinsic* quality, but rather a 'function of their function', that is, contingent on the *content* of their work and impact.

One of the main criticisms brought forward against particular schools of neo-Gramscian thought is that they implicitly assumed that elites are 'structurally literate'. As Drainville argues, 'they read structural dynamics, constraints and imperatives, and invent fitting political projects. The assumption of elite literacy takes as its starting point Gramsci's notion of intellectuals as "an organic category of every fundamental social group" equipped with a special function of cohesion' (Drainville, 1994: 109). Yet although the function of the 'organic intellectual' is indeed to (re)produce, consolidate and disseminate the particular discourse and policies of a given socio-economic configuration, this does not necessarily mean that they are indeed 'reading structural constraints'. Assuming that 'organic intellectuals' are *the* driving force behind a political project, and skilfully navigate between structural dynamics to advance the cohesion of a political project would mean to ignore the fact that 'organic intellectuals' are never uncontested. While, certainly, the position of official expert groups is often less politicized than that of intellectuals diverging from the mainstream,[5] the outcome of their work is always contingent and has to be seen in its historical context. Rather than benefiting from 'structural literacy', it is the hegemonic position of the political project which they are organically linked to which provides them with a position which is favourable to their recommendations and policy advice.

So far, the concept of the 'organic intellectuals', despite its theoretical significance, has remained rather elusive in empirical studies. While the classification of expert actors in 'epistemic communities' can be achieved following the rather parsimonious principles of the concept, the notion of 'organic intellectuals' as discussed by Gramsci implies such a vast category of actors that it seems a complex task to establish empirically whether they are in fact organic intellectuals, and if so, which social group they are organically linked to. The concept does not make for a generic notion for expert groups; however, in the following it will be shown how it can be employed to understand the role of expert groups in the particular context of corporate governance regulation in the European Union.

Corporate governance regulation in the European Union

Corporate governance, that is, those practices that define the power relations within the company and the way, and to which purpose, it is run (Van Apeldoorn and Horn, 2007a: 211), is one of the central aspects in the capitalist mode of production (see the seminal text by Berle and Means 1991; for a critical perspective of recent developments see e.g. Aglietta and Rebérioux, 2005). In the context of European market integration, the regulation of corporate governance is a crucial part of what Van Apeldoorn and Horn have called the 'marketization of corporate control', the process through which who controls the corporation and to what purpose it is run becomes increasingly mediated by the stock market, that is, through the share price as the regulative mechanism (2007a: 217). To this aim, the European Commission, in concert with some national policy-makers as well as a broad alliance of European-level associations, has sought to develop an EU-level regulatory framework aimed at the development of a European market for corporate control. The market for corporate control (Manne, 1965; see also Windolf, 1994), where the commodity traded is control rights tied to a company's shares, is assigned an ever greater role in the external governance of corporations.

In contrast to the early decades of European integration, where corporate governance issues were mainly discussed in the context of company law, the Commission's initiatives with regard to corporate governance regulation are now increasingly framed in the context of single market integration and liberalization, above all the Financial Services Action Plan (FSAP). This implies a shift from a regulatory regime aimed at the harmonization of company law – with corporate governance still perceived as mainly a policy issue pertaining to company law – through public intervention and regulatory practices, to an increasingly market-regulated and market-based corporate governance system, the goals of which are defined in terms of financial efficiency and competitiveness (Van Apeldoorn and Horn, 2007b). The 2003 Company Law Action Plan of the European Commission very much illustrated this shift.[6] As the former Commissioner for the Internal Market, Frits Bolkestein, argued in 2003, 'the responsibility of the regulator is to set up the framework, which then enables the markets to play their disciplining role in an efficient way' (Bolkestein, 2003).

In the following, the role of the High Level Group of Company Law Experts in this process will be examined. After a brief outline of the Group's composition, establishment and mandate, the reports made by the HLG and the impact they had on corporate governance regulation will be discussed.

The High Level Group of Company Law Experts

The High Level Group of Company Law Experts (HLG) was set up in summer 2001 by the European Commission's DG Internal Market to provide policy recommendations for the trajectory of company law and corporate governance regulation in the EU. The HLG comprised seven members, with all but one being company or corporate law professors at European Universities.[7] According to the Commission, the group had been 'selected on the basis of their competence in company law and the Commission's desire that the members should have broad experience of the various legal and economic systems in the EU' (European Commission, 2001a). The group's mandate was to give general recommendations on company law issues, yet its mandate was narrowed and became more significant after the defeat of the Takeover Directive in the European Parliament.

Proposals for a European Takeover Directive in form of draft directives by the Commission had repeatedly been questioned by the Council and the European Parliament (EP). When in July 2001 an agreement had finally been reached between the Commission and the Council, the EP rejected the proposal with a tied vote of 273 to 273 (see Skog, 2002, for an overview of the legislative history of the Takeover Directive). This meant a serious legislative setback for the Commission, which had been the main driving force behind the proposal. In September 2001, it announced that it had commissioned the HLG to advise the Commission on the drafting of a new proposal. Frits Bolkestein argued that the Commission wanted to get 'top quality independent advice from leading European experts in the first instance on pan-European rules for takeover bids' (European Commission, 2001a). The schedule for the group was to come up with a report on the Takeover Directive by the end of 2001, with a second mandate to issue a broader report on more general matters of company law by mid-2002.

The HLG began its work on 11 September 2001 and its final report, 'Issues related to Takeover Bids', was presented to the Commission on 10 January 2002. The report was warmly welcomed by those in corporate governance – the chairman of the International Corporate Governance Network found 'the Winter group a very sensible way forward', and the *Financial Times* even hailed Jaap Winter, the chairman of the HLG, as the 'new guru of European corporate governance'.[8] The Commission proposal on a Takeover Directive did not take up all the policy recommendations of the HLG, but as the Commission argued in its revised Directive proposal, it was nonetheless 'following the logic of the Winter report' with regard to fundamental policy choices (European Commission, 2002a).

In reaction to the new proposal, the European Parliament commissioned an expert report of its own. Two company law experts were asked to 'provide the EP with the information needed in order to properly evaluate the Commission's new proposal' (European Parliament, 2002: 9). This expert report is remarkable in that it constitutes the only instance in the legislative process of the Takeover Directive in which the rationale underlying the Takeover Directive was questioned; as the report pointed out, 'the idea underlying the directive, namely that takeovers are sensible from an overall economic point of view, and that European legislation to facilitate takeovers is therefore necessary, could perhaps be disputed in its very foundations'. Yet at the same time, the report acknowledges that a discussion of this underlying rationale would be 'certainly outside the scope of this report' (ibid.: 13).

After a long legislative process, the Takeover Directive, albeit in a compromise form, was finally approved by the EP in December 2003, and came into force in April 2004.[9] The HLG, meanwhile, presented its broader report, 'On a Modern Regulatory Framework for Company Law in Europe', in November 2002. This report essentially constituted a blueprint for the Commission's Company Law and Corporate Governance Action Plan in 2003 (see below). The HLG did not publish any other reports after 2002; the majority of its members now participate in the European Corporate Governance Forum or the Corporate Governance Advisory Group, expert groups established by the Commission in 2004 and 2005, respectively.

Composition

The HLG was essentially a private expert group. That is, despite being commissioned by the European Commission, the group was not actually accountable to any public body. While a representative of the Commission was present at the group's meetings, the Commission did not interfere with the Group's work.

The initial idea behind forming an expert group on corporate governance was to give a new impetus to the general debate on company law, which had come to a standstill in 2000 over the debate on the Takeover Directive.[10] The members of the Group were carefully selected on the grounds of their expertise in company law, in particular because of their 'international' perspectives. Apart from one member, all members of the High Level Group were closely familiar with, and had an affinity to, Anglo-American company law.[11] At the same time, the members of the HLG all had broad practical experiences, and capital market expertise. This is a crucial factor for the Group's standing – rather than just on academic merit, their authority was also based on their understanding of actual corporate governance practices.[12]

In the context of corporate governance regulation in the EU, the composition of the HLG comes as no surprise. Given the political struggle over corporate governance, the Commission had put together an expert group that was more than likely to advocate regulatory measures broadly in line with the Commission's market-liberal plans. Yet despite the obvious orientation of the High Level Group, its legitimacy, and content of its recommendations was not questioned at all by participants and actors in the policy-making process. Expert knowledge more often than not, and certainly when involved in policy-making processes, has a distinctly problem-solving approach. Rather than questioning existing social and material relations, expert groups provide policy options that deal with the problems emerging from these structures and the social struggles that are taking place in them. Not only in the HLG, but also in the increasing number of other expert platforms and discussion groups on the issue of European corporate governance, critical activity is limited to attempts to find 'best practices', benchmarks and market-based control mechanisms, which are supposed to ensure that corporate scandals like Enron and the like will not happen again.[13] Thus, the problem is not seen in the system itself, but rather with policy failures in it.[14]

'Reframing' European corporate governance – mandate and policy recommendations of the High Level Group

The role of the HLG needs to be discussed by taking into account its policy recommendations, and how these found their way into the Commission's new proposal. The HLG's mandate was to come up with policy recommendations for the Commission's new proposal on the basis of the June 2001 agreement that was rejected by the EP. Although it was assumed that the group be occupied with finding solutions and policy options for the EP's main objections against the old proposal – that is, the lack of a level playing field in the EU with regard to the board neutrality rule, employee protection and the lack of a level playing field with the US – in fact the experts effectively only tackled the first of these objections. Rather, their mandate included the definition of the notion of an 'equitable price' to be paid to minority shareholders and the right for a majority shareholder to buy out minority shareholders ('squeeze-out right').

The mandate's terms of references did not specify particular measures or procedures for bringing about a level playing field, as demanded by the EP. As Mülbert points out, 'by choosing particular guidelines . . . the Group made fundamental policy decisions of its own choosing' (Mülbert, 2003: 5).

The HLG recommended policy instruments that made their market liberal stance quite clear. Notably, with regard to takeovers, the HLG argued that

> the availability of a mechanism for takeover bids is basically beneficial. Takeovers are a means to create wealth by exploiting synergies and to discipline the management of listed companies . . . which in the long term is in the best interests of all stakeholders, and society at large.
>
> (High Level Group 2002: 4)

This clearly indicates a particular view of the role and purpose of a company, and the mechanisms advanced to ensure these reflected this thinking.

Winter acknowledged the shift towards an increased orientation towards capital market law, rather than the traditional company law outlook that had been dominant in European Union company law. He argued that although, formally, the Takeover Directive is a directive on company law and part of the company law harmonization process, 'at the same time, it seeks to regulate an important element of the functioning of capital markets . . . *many features of the draft directive have been driven much more by capital market concepts than by company law thinking* . . . The reach of capital market law over subjects that traditionally fall within the realm of company law is expanding' (Winter, 2004: 106, my emphasis). This represents a significant shift in the underlying perception of on which grounds and to which ends company law should be shaped. Capital markets follow considerably different imperatives than company law, in particular with regard to the transnational nature of capital and the distinctly national configuration of company laws in the European Union. The shift from the strive for harmonization towards market-based policy instruments or even regulatory competition can be seen within this context, and is indeed quite remarkable. In 1973 the then authoritative textbook on European company law argued that 'the virtual unification of national company laws in all essential aspects . . . is a deliberate act of policy on the part of the Community. In fact, it is a political act necessitated by the desire to accomplish the aims of the Community' (Schmitthoff, 1973: 89). The HLG, in contrast, 'has been very reluctant to suggest new projects for harmonization of company law at the EU level' (Winter, 2004: 109).

The HLG advanced a strategy that rejected the traditional harmonization approach in favour of the integration of national company laws into a presumedly efficient (transnational) market. According to the experts, company law and respective capital and securities markets 'must be integrated on a European level to enable the restructuring of European industry and the integration of European securities markets to proceed with reasonable efficiency and speed' (High Level Group, 2002: 22–3). Rather than harmonized regulation of company law, in the context of this market-oriented outlook, the HLG emphasizes the role of disclosure as a regulatory tool. This rests on the assumption that 'where markets are "informationally" efficient, in so far as information is reflected in the prices, disclosure serves to ensure that securities are correctly priced, in that they reflect the intrinsic value of the issuer and, in turn, given the role of securities-trading markets in allocating capital, that capital is allocated efficiently' (Merkt, 2004: 10).

The most far-reaching recommendation by the High Level Group entailed a so-called 'break-through rule', that is, a provision that would render pre-bid defences such as multiple voting rights and voting caps void in the case of a takeover.[15] These company law features are structural rather than merely technical barriers (like for example poison pills or other tools that the target management could use to make a bid more costly) and thus considerably more far-reaching. While the discussion about the Takeover Directive had mainly been about the board neutrality rule and several other provisions, the HLG's introduction of the break-through rule into the discussion redirected the focus towards this new issue. In this vein, 'the goal of the break-through rule is the same as the overall rule of the Takeover Directive – to transform control of listed EU firms into a commodity available for purchase throughout (and outside) the EU' (Coates, 2003: 3). While the break-through rule, as well as the board neutrality rule, are both subject to an opt-in provision in the final form of the Takeover Directive, the HLG's intervention has arguably shifted the debate towards more controversial points, while previously discussed issues, and the more fundamental question of whether this particular perception of company law was indeed uniformly accepted, were left out of the discussion.

Impact and implications

The recommendations above were in no respect binding for the Commission, and yet it followed them to a large extent. As Winter recounts, 'the HLG went to some length to explain that the primary purpose of company law and the EU's involvement in it should be to facilitate the running of efficient and competitive business enterprises across the Union' (Winter, 2004: 111). Although the Commission did not take over *all* of the recommendations of the HLG, it based its new draft proposal for a Takeover Directive on the group's report, and drew on its second report for drafting its Company Law Action Plan. Due to the political process and negotiation that followed the Commission's revised proposal for the Takeover Directive, it would be futile to seek to establish the impact of the High Level Group empirically by comparing the group's recommendation with the final policy documents. Rather, counterfactual argumentation might help to make this point clearer here. In a situation of legislative deadlock and struggle over the trajectory of company law, the Commission very likely would have not been able to advance its initiative for the liberalization of company law and corporate governance without the clout lent to its proposals and plans by the (academic) authority of the High Level Group. What is more, the work of the

HLG helped to articulate and project a coherent set of policy initiatives. In this regard, it is crucial to acknowledge their function 'in directing the ideas and aspirations of the class to which they organically belong' (Gramsci, 1971: 3). Although shareholder protection is being advanced as one of the general policy objectives, ultimately it is the interests of a particular set of shareholders, namely transnationally mobile investors, that are being promoted through the marketization of corporate control. The participation of the members of the High Level Group, as well as of the other expert groups, in conferences, workshops and consultations, serves to disseminate and consolidate a consensus on fundamental policy options with regard to corporate governance in the European Union. Although the Commission has stepped up its consultation procedures in this policy area, the increasingly scientific discourse on corporate governance (in particular due to the shift towards financial market objectives) serves to further isolate the discussion and make expert involvement seem indispensable.

Recent developments and implications

The HLG has not been incidental. Rather, in the last couple of years, there has been a proliferation of expert groups in the area of single market integration, such as the European Corporate Governance Forum, the Corporate Governance Advisory Group or various expert groups with regard to financial market governance and alternative investment.[16] Increasingly, the participants for these experts groups are recruited from outside academia – a trend the High Level Group has already indicated with its academic-cum-practitioner members. Yet despite the intention to bring together a 'diversity of views' in these expert groups, there seems to be an in-built bias in that labour and other potentially more critical actors are severely under-represented in these expert groups. In fact, the increased number of expert groups, and their elevated position in the policy-making process have recently led to criticism from the European Parliament and from organized labour. A report by the Party of European Socialists (PES) with regard to two reports on a European framework for investment funds, argues that it is 'deeply concerned by the strong bias in many of the analyses of the report' (PES, 2007: 4). Consequently, the PES has established its own group of experts in this area – notably academics and trade union representatives who are critical of dominant discourses in the corporate governance discussion in the EU. The fact that the 'organic intellectuals' of the left are now trying to take the stage is a formidable illustration of the politics of expertise.

An awareness of the role of organic intellectuals, Gramsci's 'permanent persuaders' (1971: 10) articulating a certain understanding of socio-economic processes, is important in order to understand the recent changes and developments in corporate governance in the European Union. At the same time, this awareness renders it possible to formulate and advance alternative understandings of socio-economic governance in general, and corporate governance in particular. The role of expert groups in creating and (re)producing popular consent and credibility for policy choices, and in bringing about and consolidating consensus between the various social forces entangled in the power configurations of a hegemonic project, is crucial with regard to a critical understanding of European integration processes. Although the contestation of the Commission's expert group has been very recent, the establishment of alternative 'organic intellectuals' nonetheless demonstrates the battle of ideas about socio-economic governance on the European level, and therefore indicates that the hegemonic position of the neoliberal integration project is indeed increasingly being challenged.

Notes

1. Interviews have been conducted between May and December 2006 with members of the HLG, European Commission officials, members of other expert committees as well as other actors associated with corporate governance regulation. All interviews are on file with the author.
2. Technocratic policy is associated with a policy process wherein knowledge takes precedence over other resources (Harcourt and Radaelli, 1999: 109).
3. The beauty of the epistemic communities approach is its straightforward criteria for categorizing and analysing the role of epistemic communities, and thus its empirical applicability. As Haas argues, 'the research techniques for demonstrating the impact of epistemic communities on the policy making process are straightforward but painstaking. With respect to a specific community, they involve identifying community membership, determining the community members' principled and causal beliefs, tracing their activities and demonstrating their influence on decision makers at various points in time, identifying alternative credible outcomes that were foreclosed as a result of their influence, and exploring alternative explanations for the actions of decision makers' (Haas, 1992: 34).
4. In contrast to a perception of intellectuals as (to a certain degree) bound to a social class of some sort, Bourdieu argues that the 'myth of the organic intellectual, so dear to Gramsci' (Bourdieu, 1989: 109) prevents intellectuals from 'taking up the defense of their own interests' (ibid), thereby assuming that intellectuals constitute a class in and for themselves. This class-ness of intellectuals, he argues, has as its 'first objective [. .] to work collectively towards a notion of their own interests and towards the means necessary for the protection of their autonomy' (Bourdieu, 1989: 103).
5. On this, see Beat Weber (2006) 'Das umkämpfte Feld der Wirtschaftsexpertise WirtschaftsexpertInnen und Wirtschaftspolitik im gesellschaftlichen Wandel' Linksnet, available at http://www.linksnet.de/artikel.php?id=2234
6. available at http://ec.europa.eu/internal_market/company/official/index_en.htm# communications
7. These members were Jaap Winter (NLNetherlands), José Maria Garrido Garcia (Spain), Klaus Hopt (Germany), Jonathan Rickford (UK), Guido Rossi (Italy), Jan Schans Christiansen (Denmark) and Joëlle Simon (FRFrance). Jaap Winter was asked to chair the group because of political sensibilities of the larger Member States.

8. Alistair Ross Goobey (Chairman of the International Corporate Governance Network) in the *Financial Times*, 16 June 16 2003 (Daniel Dombey (2003). The long march to shareholder democracy: The challenges facing the Brussels edict on corporate governance are great', Financial Times FT Report; Paul Betts (2003) 'Europe's capitalists survey a level playing field', *Financial Times*, 31 May 31 2002.

9. The implementation of the Takeover Directive, however, has been slow, and most Member States chose not to implement the controversial breakt-through rule (with the exception of the Baltic Member States). See the Commission's implementation report at here http://ec.europa.eu/internal_market/company/takeover bids/index_en.htm (last accessed 13 July 2007).

10. Interview Member member of the High Level Group, 11 December 2006.

11. One member of the HLG expressed this quite drastically, arguing that 'the most important single contributor to the change in the way in which these issues [company law, LH] are looked at in Europe has been the involvement of German professors in the United States Law and Economics Circuit', Interview interview member of the High Level Group, 18 October 2006.

12. Interview with a member of the High Level Group, 6 November 2006.

13. As Gramsci argued, 'critical activity is reduced to the exposure of swindles, to creating scandals, and to prying into the pockets of public figures' (Gramsci, 1971: 164). The discussion about executive remuneration and the various corporate scandals seem to validate this statement.

14. In fact, membership in an expert group brings several advantages with it. Apart from the academic recognition (with the expert groups being a platform for ideas) and the personal satisfaction that comes with from being involved (as one member of the High Level Group said, 'we just wanted to take Europe forward'), most of the experts also have a professional interest in furthering cross-border transactions and the need for more expertise in the corporate governance process, since they are most likley to gain from an increase in M&Amergers and acquisitions and takeover activities.

15. For an overview of pre-bid defensive barriers, see the annex of the 2002 High Level Group report.

16. For more information on the European Corporate Governance Forum and the Corporate Governance Advisory Group, see http://ec.europa.eu/internal_market/ company/modern/index_en.htm (last accessed 13 July 2007).

Part III   The Widening of Neoliberal Governance: Transnational Capitalism in Central and Eastern Europe

7

Corporate Tax Reform in Neoliberal Europe: Central and Eastern Europe as a Template for Deepening the Neoliberal European Integration Project?

Arjan Vliegenthart and Henk Overbeek

Introduction

European tax issues have consistently made headlines in the financial press since the ratification of the Single European Act in 1985. Discussion focused on tax competition (particularly in the area of company taxation) in general, and on so-called harmful practices in particular. With Eastern enlargement of the European Union (EU) a fact after 2004, however, the debate over issues of taxation has acquired a new dynamic. Most of the new Member States, especially in Central Europe and the Baltic, have proved to be tough opponents of any EU move towards tax harmonization, they have been in the forefront of fiscal policy innovation (with several introducing flat tax systems), and more generally enlargement seems to have altered the balance of forces in the EU at large with respect to fiscal policy.

Some observers have concluded from this that Central and Eastern Europe (CEE) in fact functions as a sort of 'template' for fiscal reform in the EU (and beyond).[1] This suggestion raises a number of questions. What exactly is meant by 'template': is this a reference to a process of cross-border policy learning, or are policies tried out first in CEE to be introduced EU-wide later? And what about agency in this context: is this template function consciously used by specific actors? If yes, who are these actors, what are their objectives, how would this fit in a more general picture? Or does the 'template' function really refer simply to a specific way in which pressures of globalization work themselves out in the EU context?

In this chapter we want to answer some of these questions by exploring the impact that the 2004 enlargement has had in the area of EU tax reform. We focus on one policy field in particular, namely that of corporate taxation. On the European level, corporate taxation has been the most discussed and debated tax area during the 1990s. On the one hand France and Germany have argued repeatedly in favour of harmonization of corporate taxes in an attempt to eliminate alleged unfair tax competition by new (and some old) Member States. On the other hand Ireland, the UK and several new Member

States have fiercely opposed any change in the status quo. Moreover, it has been a field in which the new Member States have been very active. The controversy between the current French President Sarkozy and especially Estonia over the role of the European structural funds in the light of low corporate taxation in Central and Eastern Europe is but one telling example. Also the European Commission has been active in the field of corporate tax reform for over a decade even though it lacks any formal competence in this area. It gave up its initial attempts to work towards full harmonization after defeat of its proposal to introduce qualified majority voting for tax issues during the Nice Summit of December 2000. Since then it has been engaged in a more modest project to introduce a common consolidated corporate tax base (CCCTB) by 2008.

This chapter aims to assess the impact of the 2004 enlargement on the ongoing policy discussion on tax reform in the EU. Doing so to some extent means breaking new ground in EU studies. Most of the studies on EU enlargement concentrate on the consequences for the applicant states (Nugent, 2004: x). With some exceptions (Meardi, 2002, 2004, 2006; Moravcsik and Vachudova, 2003; Kvist, 2004; Nugent, 2004 and Marginson, 2006), studies focusing on the consequences for the whole EU are still rare. There are some studies on the reform of industrial relations within the wider EU (Meardi, 2002) and the consequences for the Common Foreign and Security Policy (Haba, 2004). With Merrill Lynch, we consider this dominant one-sided focus inadequate: 'The mistake has been to think in terms of how west Europe was going to transform the east, rather than how east Europe was going to transform the west' (Merrill Lynch, 2004).

Moreover, these studies do not theoretically specify the relationship between the old and new members in the enlarged Union. In our contribution we are inspired by studies of the enlargement process that emphasize the dialectic between transnational influences in CEE on the one hand, and domestic dynamics on the other (e.g. Holman, 2001; Shields, 2003, 2004a, 2007; Bohle and Husz, 2005; Bohle, 2006; Drahokoupil, 2008a), thus transcending the limitations both of more traditional comparative approaches (which tend to assign exclusive causality to variations in internal conditions) and of dependency approaches (tending to assign primary causality to external factors). However, in this specific case, we take a slightly different perspective. Although paying particular attention to the role of the 'new Member States' in Central and Eastern Europe, we do so within the framework of analysing the EU in its entirety, rather than primarily being concerned with the relationship between the 'old' and the 'new' EU (or the impact of one on the other). The aim is to gain a better understanding of how enlargement and the accession of new Member States have affected EU-level processes: how various social forces are able to strengthen their position in domestic arenas by forging alliances at the EU level, how transnational private and public actors influence the position of governments, and how the overall process of neoliberal market making in the Single European Market is affected by enlargement.

The rest of this chapter is structured as follows. In the second section we will build on the introduction to this volume by the editors and develop some theoretically informed concepts to guide our analysis, focusing on the issue of taxation in the context of European integration, and more specifically the Single European Market. In the third section we will turn to make a concrete analysis of European tax reforms, first during the years of the Accession process (1990–2004). Here we highlight that the EU has partly shaped the new tax systems in CEE, but also that these countries increasingly began to influence the EU-wide debate on tax reform. In the fourth section we turn our attention to developments in the years since Accession became a fact. The introduction of low direct (corporate) tax rates in CEE to some extent spurred the already existing trend of lowering corporate tax rates. Moreover, enlargement strengthened the camp of those social forces that oppose the introduction of a common European tax base, which is seen by some as a first step to stop tax competition in the EU. In the conclusion we will put these developments in the broader context of European integration as a project of neoliberal restructuring.

The EU neoliberal model and the role of tax reform

The trajectory of European integration is structured by the existence of more or less coherent sets of strategies (comprehensive concepts of control) in the areas of socio-economic governance and international orientations (see the introductory chapter to this volume; also Overbeek, 1990: 26). In the concrete historical context of post-Cold War Europe we distinguish three comprehensive concepts of control vying for dominance in the EU.

First, there is a *Euro-mercantilist orientation* (which we may also dub 'regulated capitalism' after Pollack (1998)). This orientation, particularly strong in the 1980s and early 1990s, aims to insulate European capital from the pressures of globalization by protectionist measures aimed at keeping out American and Japanese competitors (exemplified by the French measures in the 1980s against the import of cheap Japanese video recorders). The main pillars of support are those European manufacturing firms that have their main basis (in terms of assets and employment) in the EU and primarily compete on the European markets. Many of these firms have the character of 'national champions', disproportionately French (e.g. Alcatel Alstom, Générale des Eaux, Peugeot: see Van der Pijl, 2006a: 264). In the area of corporate tax policy, this project involves the strongest drive towards harmonization. The offensive to counter 'harmful tax competition' was led from these corners. In the late 1990s the main protagonists of such 'regulated capitalism' in EU politics were the German Finance Minister Oskar Lafontaine and his French Socialist counterpart Strauss-Kahn. With Lafontaine's defeat and subsequent departure from office, the camp of EU-level regulated capitalism was severely weakened. On occasion this position is still represented – albeit much weaker than before – by the German and French governments and other states with a Europeanist orientation, as well as different segments of national capital and of traditional organized labour (especially the German trade union movement).

On the opposite side of the spectrum we distinguish a straightforward *neoliberal globalist orientation*, which rejects any attempt to 'regulate' European capital (or to create a form of Euro-Keynesianism) and advocates the near absolute freedom of capital to accumulate. The neoliberal fraction has a strong pro-US orientation and resists any attempts to turn the European integration project into a vehicle for Euro–American rivalry. This orientation expresses the specific interests of mobile European capital competing directly on the global markets (primarily financial and commercial interests plus the international oil and gas sector): we may think of such corporate interests as Royal Dutch Shell, BP, British Gas, Allianz, British Telecom, Glaxo and Nestlé as well as global finance and services capital (the City of London) (see Van der Pijl, 2006a: 264). Politically the British government primarily represents this orientation, and it is often supported by organizations of highly skilled labour. In this orientation, the sovereignty of capital is seen to be best served by unfettered capital mobility, rejection of any EU-level regulation or harmonization of corporate taxation and consequently maximum tax competition between Member States.

The third position that can be distinguished is in a sense an intermediate one: this *'Euro-liberal' orientation* argues that there should be a prominent role for the European political level (the Commission in particular) in establishing and guaranteeing a 'level playing field' by actively initiating and supporting a process of market-based convergence within the EU. This project is clearly a liberal project in the sense of underwriting the primacy of open markets in a globalizing world, but it advocates a key co-ordinating role for European institutions in order to strengthen the competitive position of Europe-based globally competitive productive capital vis-à-vis its non-European rivals. This orientation is expressed very clearly by the Lisbon Agenda, which aims to shape the Single Market into a veritable rival to the USA (thus expressing also an undercurrent of offensive inter-imperialist rivalry that is absent from the two orientations previously identified). In terms of the configuration of social forces behind this position, we may tentatively distinguish a bloc being led politically by the (majority of the) European Commission as well as majorities in some key member state governments (Germany in particular) and supported by transnational–EU (internationally competitive from strong European base) manufacturing industry (dubbed 'Euro-contender capital' by Van der Pijl (2006a: 264), who mentions corporations like Daimler-Benz, Fiat, Volkswagen, Unilever and Deutsche Bank) as well as by parts of the established trade union movement.

When looking at the corporate tax issue, this 'Euro-liberal' position favours the elimination of obstacles to intra-EU mobility of productive capital, thus enhancing the ability of EU-based firms to deepen their continent-wide internal division of labour and take advantage of the low cost of skilled labour in the new Member States while simultaneously reducing their transaction costs.

As we shall see later, it is the second – neoliberal – orientation that has increased its strength after EU enlargement. In their desire to attract foreign investments and to emulate the Irish example while also being pushed in that direction by transnational capital and by domestic *comprador* elements linked to transnational capital (see Vliegenthart and Overbeek, 2007 for elaboration of this point; also Chapter 9 in this volume by Drahokoupil), the new member state governments have largely adopted the same stance as the British government and forcefully oppose any attempts to harmonize corporate taxation.

Tax harmonization in the EU

In the 1970s, in the context of the first surge of ideas for a monetary and economic union as a means to break the deadlock in European integration, which resulted from the Luxemburg Compromise of 1966, early initiatives to harmonize taxation in the European Community (EC) were easily defeated when the plans to introduce monetary unification failed. EC competence with respect to taxation thus remained mostly restricted to indirect taxation. The value-added tax (VAT) was harmonized in 1977 (Grahl and Teague, 1990: 35–7). In 1992 agreement was reached on the establishment of a 15 per cent minimum VAT rate as well as on the harmonization of various excise rates, including the abolition in 1 July 1999 of intra-EU duty free sales (Dinan, 1999: 364–5).

When considering direct taxation, the discussion focused mostly on the taxation of savings income (not to be further discussed here) and on corporate taxation. The Single Market project aims to eliminate all obstacles to the free and unhindered movement across internal borders of goods, services, capital and labour. One of the major complications in the free mobility of capital in the Single Market is the existence of 27 different national systems of taxation.[2] This state of affairs constitutes a barrier to the free mobility of capital and labour. However, it also, perhaps contradictorily, presents capital (and to some extent highly skilled labour) with the possibility to exploit differential tax regimes to its own advantage, profiting from (and feeding) a process of tax competition between Member States.[3] Since 1990 the implementation of the Single Market thus increasingly gave rise to attempts somehow to streamline the taxation of corporate profits. This process may be divided in two phases, each characterized by a different emphasis in the debates, a different alignment of social forces and hence also a different outcome.

The first phase may be characterized as a struggle between the Euro-mercantilist (or Euro-Keynesian) project attempting to revive essential structures and experiences of post-war corporate liberalism at the EU level and the globalist neoliberal project. In 1990 a first step in the renewed effort to place taxation on the European agenda was taken with the agreement on a common system of taxation applicable to mergers, divisions and transfers of shares involving companies of different Member States as well as to parent companies and subsidiaries of different countries. Nevertheless, the continued existence of differences in systems of corporate taxation within the EU also continued seriously to complicate cross-border EU mergers (Chown, 2000: 106–7). The issue of direct tax harmonization was subsequently put on the political agenda by two documents published by the European Commission in 1996 in which it surveyed the development of tax systems in the EU and discussed a number of possible ways to increase co-operation in the taxation field (European Commission, 1996a, 1996b). In particular, the Commission noted that the mobility of capital in the Internal Market is obstructed by the existence of multiple tax jurisdictions, which complicates the cross-border activities of Europe's multinational companies. A related topic heavily discussed in the 1990s (not in the least by Oskar Lafontaine during his short-lived tenure as German Minister of Finance) was that of 'unfair' tax competition. In the run-up to the December 2000 Summit, the Commission forcefully pressed for harmonization of corporate taxation (Commission Européenne, 2000). However, after the failure in Nice in December 2000 to reach agreement on extended qualified majority voting for fiscal issues, the Commission had to settle for a more pragmatic course concentrating on the practical issues surrounding the completion of the internal market. The deadlock resulting from Nice (and confirmed later in the final text of the ill-fated Constitutional Treaty) had ironic traits. The British government (supported by among others the Irish and the Austrians) blocked progress in the Europeanization of tax policy primarily because of the fear that such progress would follow the lines advocated by the French and the German governments aimed at imposing minimum rates of corporate taxation, if not the elimination of all tax competition (which had brought the Irish and the London City such enormous advantages). But by blocking any European decision-making in the area of corporate taxation, it also blocked progress in eliminating the fiscal obstacles to creating a 'level playing field' for cross-border investment activity by transnational corporations.

The second phase followed with repeated attempts by the European Commission to unlock the impasse by coming up with a new strategy aimed to reconcile key parts of the liberal and the mercantilist camps. In 2001 it produced a *Communication* detailing a strategy to eliminate the fiscal obstacles to capital mobility in the Internal Market without compromising national sovereignty in setting tax rates (European Commission, 2001b). It began by pointing out that tax *rate* differentials are more effective than tax *base* differentials in the competition game, and that it would consider the *level* of taxation a matter for the Member States. However, it argued that differences in the tax base had to be eliminated: business cannot operate freely in the Single Market and the EU cannot hope to achieve its ambitions to surpass the USA as the world's most dynamic economy (its 'Lisbon goals') unless all fiscal obstacles to capital mobility are removed. The Commission proposals were applauded by the European Round Table of Industrialists (ERT), which argued that 'consolidation of corporate tax bases in the EU should be the main strategy towards a, tax-wise, fully functioning Internal Market' (ERT, 2001a) and by BUSINESSEUROPE, the European confederation of industries. The most comprehensive statement to date by the Commission repeated these points, adding that the creation of the European Company Statute from 2003 and the application of the new international accounting standards from 2005 were both lending a new urgency to its proposals (European Commission, 2003a). The Commission argued that the adoption of a CCCTB would be the only way to achieve these objectives.[4] It stated further that political obstacles (a euphemism for the British and Irish intransigence) prevented it from implementing a CCCTB, but that if the Member States would not agree on some way of implementing a CCCTB, they would be forced by the European Court of Justice, which was considering a number of key cases in this respect (European Commission, 2003a: 4–6). It then ended by identifying the Nice Treaty 'enhanced co-operation' procedure as a possible way of moving forward without agreement from all Member States (European Commission, 2003a: 27; European Commission, 2004a; see also Groenendijk, 2006). Notwithstanding strong and persistent opposition, the Commission to date remains committed to introducing the necessary draft legislation in 2008 (Kovács, 2006).

European tax reforms during the accession process

Eastern enlargement of the European Union was a cornerstone of the European neoliberal order being constructed between the Treaty of Maastricht and the Big Bang enlargement of 2004 (see Bieler, 2000; Bohle, 2006; also Holman 2001; 2004b). The accession process in fact, by means of the so-called Copenhagen criteria and the convergence criteria for the Economic and Monetary Union (EMU), gave the European economic constitution force of law in countries that were still in some cases many years from possible membership. On the other hand, existing institutional differences as well as divergent political dynamics in the countries of CEE refracted the EU influences differently. The accession requirements left a deep imprint on the reconstruction of administrative and legislative structures (including in that sense the new fiscal architecture) in Central Europe after the collapse of the communist regimes.

The early years

During the early years of transition in CEE (1989–94) various Western actors inundated the post-Communist governments with 'advice' regarding the exigencies of establishing private property and a market economy (Vliegenthart and Overbeek, 2007). In most sectors, especially with regard to privatization, the advice was unanimously in favour of a big bang approach; in the field of fiscal policy, however, 'Western expert advice was solidly in favour of an evolutionary tax reform strategy' (Martinez-Vasquez and McNab, 2000: 276). The Western policy agenda furthermore favoured the introduction of a VAT and an income tax on individuals in combination with the elimination of high import duties and export levies in order to open up the economies to the world market (Martinez-Vasquez and McNab, 2000: 277). Until December 2002, the objective of ultimate full membership of the EU for countries in CEE was not explicitly stated, but aid to CEE from an early date on stood in the light of the de facto expectation of full membership. Countries further eastwards also received considerable Western technical assistance but missed the political carrot of EU membership that tipped the balance in favour of profound taxation reforms (although some of these countries later joined the flat tax movement – see the next section).

Towards enlargement

In the 1995 White Paper on EU enlargement the Commission explicitly addressed the issue of taxation. It concluded that some progress had already been made in this field 'precisely because the system had the advantage of starting from scratch' (European Commission, 1995a: 27). During the accession negotiations the topic of taxation took up a whole chapter. The process by which the European Commission influenced the domestic tax debates in the region has been well discussed by Hillary Appel (2006). She finds that 'tax policy reflects much less traditional domestic variables, like the strength of particular interest groups or the ideological orientation of the presiding political leadership, than the international imperatives associated with regional and global economic integration' (Appel, 2006: 43). In fact, many of the social forces within the different countries were not too sorry about the agenda pushed forward by the Union (Appel, 2006). Appel recalls that at least two ministers of finance actually were rather happy with the way the EU acted as it made it easier for them to overcome domestic opposition to these plans. The forms of intergovernmental self-restraint (Wolf, 2000) are not unfamiliar, as also other states have at occasion actively sought the support from international agencies such as the IMF, the World Bank and the EU to tip the national balance of power in favour of neoliberal reforms. Given the price for non-cooperation – the exclusion from EU membership – domestic elites were very reluctant actively to oppose EU proposals with regard to taxation policy. CEE governments were in fact quite responsive to the ideas and demands of the European Commission. Overall, Appel concludes that 'the goal of EU membership and the global competition for attracting mobile capital have curtailed the autonomy of East European states to set their own tax policy' (Appel, 2006: 30).

The accession process

After the first wave of tax reforms in the mid-1990s came a second round that further abolished the existing mismatches between the situation in the applicant states and EU demands. Here, special attention was paid to the indirect taxes, such as the VAT, which of course is part of the *Acquis*. EU regulation became the focal point under which reforms were introduced, shaped and defended. It proved to be a very effective disciplining force. By the end of the 1990s the tax systems of the CEE and Baltic states were to a considerable extent compatible with EU regulation and demands (Bönker, 2003: 523–5). As Easson concluded at the time, 'EU rules are already having an impact in those countries that are in the first rank of applicants for membership, even if the main impact seems to have been to produce an unseemly scramble to have a comprehensive set of tax incentives already in place by 1999' (Easson, 1998: 197).

In her discussion of the taxation landscape in the new EU Member States in the years before accession, Luca Gandullia (2004) identified four important differences with the average situation in the EU-15: lower personal income tax rates, lower corporate tax rates, higher indirect taxes and higher social contributions (details can also be found in various other sources (e.g. Groenendijk, 1999; European Parliament, 2003). First, with regard to income taxation, the systems are less progressive than in the old EU-15 and account for a much lower share of GDP and of total tax take (see Table 7.1). The Baltic States introduced flat-rate tax systems in 1994 and 1997 (see the next section for details). In Poland the effective personal income tax rate was almost flat. Second, with regard to corporate taxation the statutory tax rates are very low compared to the old EU-15 (see Table 7.1 for details of developments in later years). Third, in comparison with the old EU-15 the new Member States rely more heavily on indirect, consumption-based, taxes (see Table 7.1). Finally, the tax burden on labour (in the form particularly of social contributions) has in contrast with the other forms of taxation in the region continued to be at the level of the early years of economic transformation (Table 7.1).

Notwithstanding the general convergence between the preferences of national governments in CEE and those of the EU (Commission) since the

Table 7.1   Main taxes in the general government revenue structure (% GDP, 1996)

	Czech Republic	Estonia	Hungary	Poland	Slovenia	EU-15
Total tax revenue (including social security contributions)	39	36	36	40	45	41
Personal income tax	5	4	6	9	7	11
Corporate profit tax	4	2	2	3	1	3
Social security contributions	16	11	14	11	17	12
VAT/sales tax + excise taxes	12	13	15	15	20	12
Various other taxes	2	6	0	2	0	4

Source: Based upon IMF World Economic Outlook, May 1998, p. 105 and modeled after Groenendijk, 1999: 25–6.

early 1990s, there have also been occasional clashes, and these clashes are particularly instructive in showing the configuration of social forces informing the positions of the national governments in CEE during these years. Böröcz (2004) has specifically pointed to the case of a conflict between Hungary and the Commission in the late 1990s. The Hungarian government was dedicated to a more radical programme of tax reforms than intended by the Commission. Its proposals for tax reduction and tax holidays for foreign capital pushed the neoliberal taxation concepts further than the Commission appreciated. As a result Commissioner Monti and the Hungarian government clashed at several occasions on how far these reforms should be allowed to go. Monti considered the specific tax concessions granted by the Hungarians to foreign capital as state aid, and thus as illegal and harmful. A detailed study by Dorothee Bohle and Dóra Husz (2005) has demonstrated that it was in fact a select group of (mostly European) multinational companies (notably Audi, Philips, Siemens, Flextronics and General Electric) that pushed the Hungarian government to defend these far-reaching tax concessions against the pressures of the Commission (and of the German government in the background). More generally, government positions in CEE in these years are strongly influenced by a particular configuration of interests: incoming foreign capital (primarily assembly line production and second tier banks controlling the financial sector) with their domestic *comprador* allies (see Vliegenthart and Overbeek, 2007).

In another Central European case, the Polish Minister of Finance Balcerowicz (for many years allied with transnational interests, see Shields, 2003, 2004a, 2007) in 1998 introduced tax reforms that would make Poland 'the emerging leader of the Tax Avant-Garde' (Burba, 1999). It consisted of systematic cuts in corporate tax rates as well as substantial cuts in personal taxation, countered to some extent by a higher VAT. The plans of Balcerowicz to cut corporate tax rates enjoyed broad support domestically, but this time also received support from the European Commission (the plan to cut tax rates across the board would not violate EU competition rules). His plans were vetoed by President Kwaśniewski, however, who saw no need for this because 'the overwhelming majority of those who would benefit most from the reduced rate are not investors and do not create new jobs' (Kwasniewski quoted in Hunter and Shapiro, 2000: 81).

The final negotiations on the taxation chapter took place between November 1999 and March 2002, involving very intense discussions between EU officials and domestic policy makers over the transposition of the Acquis into the domestic juridical system. The outcome of the process was that the CEE countries when they entered the Union had tax systems that resembled those in the EU-15 in key respects yet diverged in several ways, not only from the EU-15 but particularly also between the Central European countries (Poland, the Czech Republic and Hungary) on the one hand and the Baltic states and Slovakia on the other. In the first group overall revenues from taxation and taxation rates were higher than in the second group. The overall revenues as a percentage of GDP in the second group were all under the level of Ireland, which has the lowest revenues of the old EU-15 measured by percentage of GDP (Bönker, 2003).

European tax reforms after the big bang

Towards a CCCTB

The alignment of forces in the debate about the common consolidated tax base proposed by the EU Commission for introduction in 2008 has undergone a dramatic shift with enlargement. Nearly all of the new Member States (not only in CEE but also of course the traditional tax havens Malta and Cyprus) have joined the camp of Britain and Ireland in opposing the CCCTB. Estonia and Slovakia, especially, have explicitly opposed the Commission's plans. The Slovak Minister of Finance Ivan Mikloš even threatened to withdraw his support for the European Constitution, arguing that it would pave the way for tax harmonization (*EUObserver*, 3 March 2006). The Czech Republic has recently joined these two countries in their opposition. Czech Finance Minister Miroslav Kalousek called the most recent proposals of the German government to tackle harmful tax practices 'not a very happy move . . . Obviously, I cannot forbid anyone their activities but they should then be prepared that some countries would oppose them if they go against their national interest' (*EUObserver*, 27 February 2007). Lithuania and Latvia are also rather sceptical about the proposals for the harmonization of the tax base but have not been as harsh on Commissioner Kovács as the other two new members.

The flat tax revolution in CEE

In 1994 Estonia became the first of the countries in the region to introduce a flat tax system.[5] It replaced existing income tax brackets varying between 16 per cent and 33 per cent to a single rate of 26 per cent, also applying this rate to corporate income tax. In the region of former communist Europe, Estonia was followed by Lithuania, Latvia, Russia, Ukraine, Slovakia, Georgia, Romania and Macedonia, while Serbia introduced a semi-flat tax system. There were ongoing discussions in Poland, the Czech Republic and Hungary about the possibility of introducing a flat tax system. Thus, by 2005 it seemed as if the flat tax revolution was about to conquer large parts of the world (*The Economist*, 2005; Rabushka, 2005; Slate, 2005; Keen et al., 2006). The most recent state of affairs is reflected in Table 7.2, which confirms the trend to ever lower rates of taxation (several countries having lowered their flat rates after they were first introduced).

The discussion on the advantages and disadvantages of flat tax systems is complex, and cannot be fully resolved here. Hyper-liberal proponents (such as the Heritage Foundation; see Mitchell, 2005) argue that flat tax systems are fair (because every dollar of income is taxed in the same way), effective (more people actually pay taxes), raise state revenue and are conducive to economic growth. Opponents argue that progressive taxation is fair (because the richer you are the greater your proportional contribution to society's needs can be), and that flat tax systems increase inequality and reduce state revenue.

Empirically, none of these statements can be verified, primarily because the effects of introducing a flat rate cannot be isolated: inevitably various other reforms are introduced simultaneously (for example strengthening the tax collection system, increasing penalties for tax evasion), and certain alleged effects (economic growth) might easily be explained by a number of other factors. All studies show, for instance, that state revenue in those countries introducing flat tax systems has been stable or even increased. However, most of this effect can probably be explained by a broadening of the tax base (abolishing deductions), and to the effect of raising VAT rates. In a recent IMF Working Paper (Keen et al., 2006) one can find a thorough and nuanced discussion of these and other aspects (heavily criticized by the right, see Mitchell, 2007). The authors at least document one important point. Indeed, in nearly all cases, the lowering of direct taxation occurring with the introduction of the flat tax is accompanied by a rise of the rate of indirect taxation (VAT) (see Table 7.2), which, as is generally recognized, is detrimental for people with lower incomes who spend a greater proportion of their income on goods for immediate consumption.

Against the background of increasing global tax competition generally, and the successful experiments in CEE specifically, different Member States of the EU-15 have also continued to lower their corporate taxation rate. 'After failing to force eastern Europe into submission, some western countries decided

Table 7.2　Tax systems in post-socialist Europe

	Year of introduction	Personal Income tax rates		Personal Income tax revenues % of GDP		Corporate Income taxes		Corporate Income Tax Revenue % of GDP		Indirect taxes	
		Before reform	In 2007	Year before reform	Year after reform	Before reform	In 2007	Year before reform	Year after reform	Year before reform	Year after reform
Estonia	1994	16–33	22	8.5	8.1	35	22	4.8	3.5	11.1	13.3
Georgia	2005	12–20	12	2.7	2.5	20	20	1.6	1.9	8.1	11.0
Latvia	1997	25/10	25	5.4	5.6	25	15	2.0	2.4	12.6	12.5
Lithuania	1994	18–33	27	5.0	5.4	29	18	5.3	2.5	6.2	6.3
Romania	2005	18–40	16	3.0	2.3	25	16	2.7	2.4	10.2	10.9
Russia	2001	12–30	13	2.4	2.9	30	24	5.5	5.8	8.6	9.9
Slovakia	2004	10–38	19	3.3	2.6	25	19	2.8	2.4	9.8	11.4

Source: Calculated from: Keen et al., 2006: 46 and *The Economist* 2007.

they might try to copy the flat tax regimes applied in some new member states', the *Financial Times* wrote (2004a).

Though none of the EU-15 members has actually introduced a flat tax, tax reforms in some of the old EU Member States were announced with explicit reference to enlargement and to the increasing competition of the new Member States in the East. This is probably most clearly demonstrated in the case of Austria. In January 2005 the Austrian government lowered corporate taxes by 9 per cent in a tax reform that also included allowances for losses from foreign subsidiaries and big research incentives. It explicitly referred to its geographical position, on the borders of Slovakia, as one of the reasons for its reduction of corporate tax rates (*Financial Times*, 2004a: 10). But other governments too apparently feel increasing pressure to reform their tax systems. According to Merril Lynch (2004: 3–4), enlargement has 'provided Germany with a sort of jolt that is often needed for reform', which in practice would lead to a reshuffle of the taxation burden from the corporate sector to the employees. Peer Steinbrück, Finance Minister of the German Grand Coalition between Social Democrats and Christian Democrats, recently launched a new plan to cut corporate taxes by more than 8 per cent to 30 per cent, whereas the same government increased the VAT rate as of 2007. In Finland the discussion of tax reduction has entered the policy debate, especially in light of the Estonian flat tax system (*Financial Times*, 2007a: 11).

These developments have received both praise and criticism from various corners. On the 'positive' side, Tommaso Padoa-Schioppa, Member of the Executive Board of the ECB, has applauded the developments in the new Member States and pointed out that the old EU-15 states might well learn something from their Eastern neighbours, stating that if

> lower tax rates in the new Member States were to put pressure for tax reform in the euro area, as the lower tax rates in Ireland have already done, this could only be for our benefit. Arguments about unfair tax competition should not be used as a smokescreen to distract attention from what every citizen in the euro area knows: that tax regimes need to change, and fiscal pressure has to fall
>
> (ECB, 2004)

From the corporate world EU Member States are also urged to follow the kind of tax reforms implemented in the Baltic and Central European States. According to *The Economist*, quoting several businessmen, the new member states will lead the old member states into substantial tax reform both 'by hard necessity and the power of example' (*The Economist*, 2004a).

The European Commission initially saw enlargement as an additional argument for the harmonization of the corporate tax base: adding ten new Member States also meant adding ten additional national fiscal systems complicating the mobility of capital even further. In its communication to the European Parliament, it wrote that the 'imminent enlargement of the EU will accentuate the problems further. There is, therefore, *no reason to cast doubts on the basic rationale of the Commission strategy* and the Commission confirms its commitment thereto' (European Commission, 2003a: 4, emphasis in original).

Yet, the role of the CEE countries as the new avant-garde of tax reforms has not gone unchallenged. In particular, France and Germany have complained that the current tax system in some of the new Member States can only be maintained because of the financial support these countries receive through the Structural Funds. Shortly after their entrance into the Union, then French Minister of Finance Nicolas Sarkozy threatened that France would 'propose that new member countries that have their taxes under the European average will not be eligible to draw from the EU structural funds' (*Slovak Spectator*, 2004b). The former Estonian Prime Minister Juhan Parts actually fuelled this debate when he explicitly related the EU structural funds to low tax rates in a speech at the Natolin Research Centre for European Studies in Warsaw. According to Parts, 'Structural funds and business friendly tax rates are two sides of the same coin – they are both targeted at economic growth and realising the full economic potential of a country' (Parts, 2004).

The link between tax cuts and structural funds is obviously not the real argument. The real argument is that low corporate taxes are luring investment away from the German and French economies. It is very doubtful that this claim is justified, however. We know from a lot of research that location decisions by TNCs are based on many factors (wage rates, quality of infrastructure, quality of public governance and so on) of which corporate tax rates are only a minor one. A much more real effect of the ongoing tax competition race is, as we have seen, the shift from direct to indirect taxation with its inegalitarian distributional effects. However, this effect is much less a cause for concern for the neoliberal Sarkozy and the quasi neoliberal Merkel governments, or for neoliberal forces in CEE, which openly applaud this effect. As Peter Papanek, the neoliberal spokesman of the Slovak Finance Ministry told the *Slovak Spectator* (2004a), business does not allow for higher tax rates on both corporations and incomes. Therefore the EU should help to pay for the upgrading of the Slovak infrastructure. Moreover, as part of the reform programme and an attempt to reallocate government revenues, revenues are increasingly extracted from indirect taxes. 'Our tax reform shifted the tax burden from direct to indirect taxes and introduced order and healthy economic logic to our tax system' (Papanek, 2004).

Nevertheless, recent developments in some of the Central European countries are casting doubt on the longer term sustainability of flat tax systems. These doubts do not concern the 'technical' aspects: it is clear that flat tax systems are financially sustainable (Hong Kong has had a flat tax system since 1947). The doubts concern the political sustainability of the system.

There has been political upheaval very recently about flat taxes in Slovakia (EurActiv, 2007), Slovenia (Lagace, 2007) and the Czech Republic (Czech Radio, 2007). In all cases the discussion revolves around questions of social equity. It is sometimes suggested that a flat tax system may be appropriate for 'emerging economies', but less so for more developed industrial economies with extensive welfare states (e.g. Anderson, 2006; *The Economist*, 2007). In such more complex and mature, and less dynamic, economies flat tax systems might suffer from a lack of legitimacy.

Taxation and the contradictions of the neoliberal hegemonic project in the EU

This chapter has shown that tax competition has been an issue in EU discussions since the mid-1990s. Tax competition exists, especially in the area of corporate taxation. Corporate tax rates (both statutory and effective) have been falling consistently throughout the Organisation for Economic Co-operation and Development (OECD) area since the onset of the current wave of globalization in the early 1980s. This 'fact' has led to debates within the EU to deal with tax competition (especially forms of competition that were deemed to be 'harmful') since the mid-1990s. Initially, the struggle against tax competition was conducted by a coalition of Euro-mercantilist forces advocating 'regulated capitalism' at the European level; concretely with respect to corporate taxation these forces pushed for tax harmonization and the introduction of majority voting on tax issues. Eventually, the Euro-mercantilist camp was severely weakened with the political death of Oskar Lafontaine, and it was dealt a final blow at the Nice Summit in 2000. The neoliberal project was victorious and pushed for further liberalization and deregulation.

Since then, we witness attempts to reconstruct a viable configuration of forces to counter the neoliberal hegemony in the EU. In the context of ongoing neoliberal globalization, of the end of the Cold War with its subsequent realignment of political forces internationally as well as domestically, and of the economic restructuring in Europe following the opening up of Central and Eastern Europe, we have identified the contours of an emerging new configuration, which we have called – for lack of a better term – the 'Euro-liberal' bloc. Supported by a range of internationally competitive (but Europe-based) manufacturing conglomerates (many of the members of the European Round Table of Industrialists), and politically spearheaded by the European Commission and the new German and French governments, these forces aim to use the enlarged European economic space to defend and develop an integrated European technological–industrial complex that should ultimately be able to compete with the USA (as well as with the great industrial powers of Asia). The struggle to introduce a CCCTB, considered essential for the purpose of enabling these conglomerates to truly organize their R&D and manufacturing activities on a continental European scale, can be seen as a key component of this project, which continues to be taken forward in spite of strong neoliberal resistance.

What role has enlargement played in this development? To what extent can we argue that the new Member States of the EU are serving as a 'template' for further neoliberal reforms in the EU, if we survey the field of corporate taxation? Our answers to these questions are inevitably tentative, given the fact that enlargement is only four years behind us and that many of its consequences are still taking shape. Let us consider five points on which we feel we can draw some conclusions from our analysis.

First, enlargement, including the period during which these countries were not members of the EU but were nevertheless in the process of opening their markets as part of the implementation of the Acquis, has prompted a process of industrial restructuring on a Europe-wide scale, allowing key sectors of West European business to take advantage of the low wages and relatively high skills of the Central European labour forces (see also chapter 8 in this volume, by Bohle). This aspect has strengthened the position of 'contender capital' in the EU, and to a certain extent also stimulated the emergence of competitive manufacturing industries, particularly in the Visegrád countries.

Second, however, transition and enlargement have also attracted large flows of foreign capital into the region that is not linked directly to West European transnational productive capital. The influx of assembly industries (for instance the invasion of a long list of Asian car producers) producing for the West European markets and of foreign banking capital has tremendously strengthened the position of a *comprador fraction* in the emerging Central European bourgeoisies (see also chapter 9 in this volume, by Drahokoupil).

Third, specifically in the area of company taxation, our findings point in the direction that the process towards EU membership of the CEE economies and their eventual entrance into the Union have reinforced and exacerbated existing developments within the old EU-15. Enlargement has not in itself caused tax competition to emerge: it already existed well before accession. However, enlargement has in fact intensified the competitive pressures towards the lowering of corporate and income taxes. The low-waged and relatively well-educated CEE labour forces can moreover be seen as a structural catalyst for reform in, among others, Germany, Austria and France. The role of the new Member States in the current struggles over European tax reforms is thus embedded in the dynamics of the European integration process, especially the ongoing process of deepening the European Single Market and the EMU. These European developments moreover are themselves rooted in a process of neoliberal globalization and deepening global tax competition. In this respect it is a truly transnational and nested phenomenon, a process that takes place *simultaneously* at different levels in which the national level can no longer be ontologically privileged over others, and in which developments at one level serve as catalysts for (or constraints on) the dynamics at other levels.

Fourth, politically speaking enlargement has strengthened the already existing camp of opponents of any kind of European tax harmonization or even the introduction of a common corporate tax base that in principle would not at all eliminate tax competition between Member States. In the struggle for hegemony between the neoliberal bloc and the 'Euro-liberal' bloc, enlargement has definitely worked to the advantage of the neoliberal, US-oriented camp (see on this point also Chapter 3 in this volume, by Cafruny). This, however, does not mean per se that the struggle has been decided.

On the contrary: a fifth and final point of conclusion must be that the most recent developments in the Visegrád countries suggest the possibility of a partial reversal of this last effect of enlargement. The emerging debate on the social sustainability of the neoliberal flat-tax system may well be an indication of increasing divergence within CEE in terms of the accumulation model that is being developed. In this volume, Bohle argues that in the Viségrad countries we see the gradual emergence of what they call 'embedded neoliberalism', which is based on a strong manufacturing base. This might be linked to the notion that a flat tax system is best geared to the needs of emerging economies, but that more mature industrial economies need a more developed and more strongly solidaristic welfare state to maintain social peace. If this is indeed the case, we may expect the ongoing struggle between the two comprehensive class projects (neoliberalism and 'Euro-liberalism') for the future trajectory of the EU to become even more complex and intense. Eventually, such a tendency will also strengthen the hand of the European Commission in its attempt to introduce the CCCTB, which European 'contender' capital so needs.

Notes

1. The apostles of tax liberation entertain the expectation that the CEE countries are carrying the torch in a tax revolution that is on the verge of engulfing the old Europe (EU-15) as well (e.g. Laar, 2005; Mitchell, 2007). The Director of the Harvard Business School Europe Research Center, Vincent Dessain, concludes that CEE, especially Estonia and Slovakia, 'are in fact already serving as models for other countries that are considering adopting a flat tax' (quoted in Lagace, 2007: 2). Tax Commissioner Kovács similarly concludes that the 'decrease in corporate tax rates has accelerated with the accession of the new Member States' (Kovács, 2006: 10). See also *The Economist*, 2004a, Tommaso Padoa-Schioppa of the European Central Bank in ECB, 2004, and Merill Lynch, 2004.
2. The term 'tax system' refers to the whole of the types of taxes to be levied (income tax, capital gains tax, VAT, etc.). 'Tax base' refers to the specific sets of goods, services, elements of income and so on to which each of these taxes applies (whether interest income from savings is taxed under the income tax or not, whether foodstuffs are subject to VAT or not, whether interest paid is deductible or not). 'Tax rate' refers to the percentage of the income (or turnover) that is being levied as tax. Tax competition can (and will) normally take place both in the sphere of the tax base (e.g. favourable amortization rules) as well as in the tax rate sphere

(e.g. reducing the statutory tax rate on corporate profits). This explains why the differential between statutory tax rates and effective tax rates (after calculating the effects of regulations regarding the tax base) can vary strongly from country to country (see Bellak et al., 2005).

3. Constraints of space do not allow us to go into the question of tax competition in great detail here. Related to that issue, two questions are important: does tax competition occur and does it matter one way or the other? A recent survey provides convincing evidence of a downward trend both of statutory rates (official tax rates before deductions and tax holidays etc.) as well as of effective tax rates (Griffith and Klemm, 2004). Between 1982 and 2003 average statutory tax rates in the OECD countries fell from some 48 per cent to below 35 per cent (with the gap between the highest and the lowest rates narrowing considerably (ibid., p. 8). Effective tax rates for profitable projects declined from on average approximately 45 per cent in 1982 to around 34 per cent in 2003. De Mooij (2005) is one of many studies (see also Griffith and Klemm, 2004; European Commission, 2001b) to conclude from these trends: 'If capital becomes more mobile and the EU fails to co-ordinate, tax competition will put a severe strain on corporate tax policy and probably even on the effective taxation of capital income more generally' (2005: 296). It therefore seems quite clear that tax competition in the area of corporate taxes does indeed occur. However, does that matter? The answer is not straightforward. It may matter in terms of deflecting investment flows; it may matter in terms of falling government revenue; or it may matter in terms of a shift in the structure of taxation. Steffen Ganghof (1999) has presented the most thorough analysis of the impact of competitive pressures on tax policy in the OECD countries. He begins with the observation that tax differentials have a small impact on manufacturing businesses (where labour costs are a much more important consideration), but a much greater impact on financial and commercial companies. In the case of personal income, likewise, the impact on labour income (excluding highly skilled labour) is much weaker than on income from financial assets. So different fractions of capital profit differentially from tax competition: money capital profits much more than productive capital. Second, Ganghof argues that (*ceteris paribus*) governmental tax revenues decrease as a consequence of increased fiscal competition, but that there are various strategies that states may mobilize to counteract falling revenue. In addition to action taken by states, there are also certain countervailing pressures operating in the global economy, which keep tax competition under control. In this respect Ganghof concludes that we see a 'medium-term stability of average budgetary outcomes' (Ganghof, 1999: 46), which means states are capable of maintaining their revenues notwithstanding increased competitive pressures arising from globalization. Third, however, the outcome of the mobilization of counteracting tendencies by governments is to change the structure of taxation into a more controversial (=inegalitarian) direction. There is a shift from direct to indirect taxation, as well as a shift from taxes on mobile sources of to taxes on immobile income. The result is an increasing tax burden on low incomes, a lower tax burden on high and/or mobile sources of income and growing inequality in the distribution of after-tax income.

4. In such a system companies have a choice of either applying the consolidated tax base to calculate their total tax obligations (which would then be distributed according to an agreed apportionment formula), or to pay taxes in each of the member states concerned separately according to national law.

5. In a flat tax system, all income brackets and most or all allowances and deductions are abolished and one unitary rate of taxation is applied to all taxable income, thus abolishing the progressivity of taxation that is so characteristic for welfare state capitalism. The flat tax normally applies to both personal income and company income, although the rates may vary for these types of taxation. In some cases the same rate also applies to indirect taxation (VAT).

8
Race to the Bottom? Transnational Companies and Reinforced Competition in the Enlarged European Union

Dorothee Bohle

Introduction

Starting with the world economic crisis of the 1970s, European integration underwent a fundamental change. Historically, European institutions mainly secured the diverse national development paths without interfering with the domestic market order. This changed with the main integration projects since the 1980s. With the Internal Market, European Monetary Union and the Lisbon Strategy a new mode of integration has been established, which aims at enhancing competitiveness of the Member States, and the European Union (EU) as a whole. By directly taking over certain state functions as well as by reshaping significantly the framework in which nation states operate, the EU has enhanced regime competition between different national systems of governance.

The new mode of European integration has allowed transnational companies (TNCs) to expand significantly their room for manoeuvre. On the one hand TNCs have direct access to all levels of European decision-making. This stands in contrast with the much more limited access domestically oriented enterprises and trade unions have to the European level. On the other hand, the increased regime competition allows TNCs to play off Member States against each other when it comes to their investment decisions.

Eastern enlargement of the EU has increased the competitive pressure within Europe (see Vliegenthart and Overbeek's analysis in Chapter 7 of this volume). The East European newcomers are significantly lagging behind in terms of economic development and social standards. Observers have expressed fears about the newcomers spurring a race to the bottom of wages, social standards and corporate taxes. As a result of their radical transformation from state socialism towards capitalism under the supervision of the EU, these countries are said to have settled on a regime strongly reminiscent of the Anglo-Saxon model of capitalism, with its highly deregulated labour markets, and comparative low levels of social protection. Their semi-peripheral position, moreover, has made Eastern Europe strongly dependent on foreign investment. In order to attract investors, the region competes with low wages, pronounced labour market flexibility and low corporate taxes. Eastern Europe thus is said to reinforce the competitive pressure on the old Member States.

This contribution seeks to evaluate the dynamics, limits and contradictions of the increasing locational competition in the enlarged EU. It shares the basic assumption that eastern enlargement has reinforced the room for manoeuvre for TNCs and strengthened the competitive pressure in the European economic area. At the same time, it cautions against a too simplistic understanding of European countries being engaged in a 'race to the bottom' where those countries closest to the neoliberal ideal outperform the rest in terms of attracting investment. Such a view is inadequate for two reasons. First, it underestimates the capitalist diversity in Eastern Europe, and cannot explain why it is not the most neoliberal regimes of the region that exert the strongest competitive pressures on Western Europe. Second, the simplistic race to the bottom thesis underestimates the contradictions of further deregulation.

The second section of this chapter outlines the theoretical framework underlying my analysis. I will elaborate on Karl Polanyi's central idea of a double movement of liberalization and countermovement guiding the dynamics of capitalism and offer an interpretation of contemporary forces and strategies of the countermovement in comparison to the one analysed by Polanyi.

The third section characterizes the current mode of European integration and the privileged role TNCs have acquired in it. It argues that despite the neoliberal turn European integration has taken since the 1980s, its neoliberalism is still more embedded socially and institutionally than the US model of capitalism (as discussed in more detail by Van Apeldoorn in Chapter 1 of this volume). The fourth section analyses the models of capitalism that have emerged in Eastern Europe as a result of their transformation and integration into the European order. It will be shown that the Baltic states – Estonia, Latvia and Lithuania – have embarked most consequently on a purely neoliberal transformation path, whereas Slovenia resembles closely the small West European neo-corporatist states. The development path of the Visegrád Four (V4) – Czech Republic, Hungary, Poland and Slovakia – has been shaped most thoroughly by TNCs. It can be conceptualized as a semi-peripheral form of embedded neoliberalism. The fifth section demonstrates that in contrast with the race to the bottom thesis, it is not the neoliberal Baltic states but rather the Visegrád countries, that exert the strongest competitive pressures on Western Europe. The sixth section turns towards the locational competition among the V4 and explores the tendencies towards a race to the bottom. The final section concludes by asking about resistance and limits to further liberalization and deregulation.

Theoretical background: the new great transformation

The changes on the European (and global) order over the last decades are reminiscent of the earlier, nineteenth-century 'great transformation' towards liberal capitalism. As in the nineteenth century, the 'self-regulating market' provides the utopia under which state elites and business groups rally in order to create the international and national institutions that would perpetuate the liberal economic order. As a consequence, incompatibilities between the capitalist world economy, democratic polities and the pursuit of social welfare have resurfaced to a degree unknown in the post World War II period. In this context, I find it useful to build on the insights of Karl Polanyi's *The Great Transformation* to analyse the dynamics and contradictions of the contemporary liberalization movement. Polanyi's central claim is that the 'the idea of a self-regulating market implied a stark utopia. Such an institution could not exist for any length of time without annihilating the human and natural substance of society, it would have physically destroyed man and transformed his surroundings into wilderness. Inevitably, society took measures to protect itself' (Polanyi, 1957: 3). Thus, ever since the idea of liberal capitalism asserted itself, market societies have been governed by a 'double movement' or by 'two organizing principles': on the one hand the principle of economic liberalism that guides the establishment and institutionalization of the self-regulating market, and on the other hand 'the principle of social protection aiming at the conservation of man and nature as well as productive organization' (Polanyi, 1957: 132).

   Polanyi's concept of second organizing principle of society, or the countermovement, bears some similarities with Marx's analysis of class struggle and the emancipatory role of labour. Similar to Marx, he sees the countermovement stemming from the commodity character of labour that can't be anything but fictitious. Treating labour (as well as land and money) as commodities disrupts the social and cultural ties that make up human community as much as it destroys the environment and productive organizations. The countermovement emerges as a reaction to these dangers. There are, however, also differences. Most importantly, first, for Polanyi, rather than relations of production, it is the process of extension and deepening of market relations, which generates the countermovement. Silver defines the 'Polanyi-type of unrest' (as opposed to the Marx-type) as 'the backlash resistances to the spread of a global self-regulating market, particularly by working classes that are *being unmade* by global economic transformations as well as those workers that benefited from established social compacts' (2003: 20, my italics). Silver's adaptation of Polanyi's countermovement as backlash resistance is in my view useful for the current European context, which is to a large extent about the *unmaking* of an industrial proletariat, and the *retrenchment* of the welfare state.

Second, even if in the historical context of the nineteenth century it is labour whose interest is closest to society's need of protection against the perils brought about by economic liberalism, labour is not the only social force that drives the countermovement. Polanyi analyses the countermovement as a spontaneous one, coming from all quarters of societies, including forces of productive capital, and the state itself (Polanyi, 1957: 141–2).

As I will show below, I believe that Polanyi's theoretical figure of a double movement captures well main features of the current process of European integration and its limits. However, the transportation of this figure from the context of the nineteenth and early twentieth century to contemporary capitalism requires some reflection about how the contemporary nature of the forces of the countermovement and their strategic options differ from the earlier one. Three major differences come to mind. First, with transnational movement of persons and capital, which are core elements of the European order, the boundaries of what used to be nationally constituted societies have become increasingly permeable. This increases the range of actors of the countermovement, as well as the range of their strategic options. With reference to actors it implies that in certain respects transnational capital can also become a force of the countermovement for actors. This refers mostly to productive capital, which, as Polanyi explained, also frequently demands 'protective legislation . . . and other instruments of intervention' (ibid.: 132). As to the strategic options, transnationalization has important consequences. Polanyi's historical account of the countermovement mostly relies on the manifestation of 'voice' – to use Hirschman's (1970) term – with industrialists, landed aristocracy and most importantly labour voicing their concerns and asking for protective state legislation.

Hirschman's model knows only the alternatives of voice and exit.[1] Even taking only these two options into account, it is clear that exit is a much easier option for both labour and productive capital in the current European order than it was 100 years ago. In addition, as Ferrera (2005: 28–36) points out, Hirschman's original model has one shortcoming in that it treats the two patterns of voice and exit as alternative behavioural options. However, each of these options has their own opposite: silence vs voice, and staying vs exit. Also, although Hirschman was mostly concerned with insiders, outsiders might also have a say. Based on these extensions, the following typology of strategically relevant options of the contemporary forces of the countermovement can be built (Table 8.1).

The point of Table 8.1 is that it allows one to explore the wider varieties of strategic options forces of the countermovement currently have (light grey cells) in comparison with the period of early industrial capitalism and early democratization (dark grey cell). First, voice from outside is an option for some forces of the countermovement, most notably for TNCs. Second, vocal exit is an option for capital, while silent exit has become an important option for labour. Finally, silent staying in – abstention in elections – has

Table 8.1   Extending Hirschman's model: Strategic options of the countermovement

Vocality	Insiders		Locality — Outsiders	
	Exit	**Staying in**	**Staying out**	**Entry**
Silence	Silent exit (*emigration*)	Silent staying in (*abstention during elections*)	Silent staying out	Silent entry (*immigration*)
Voice	Vocal exit (*productive TNCs*)	Voice from within (*most important strategic option of Polanyi's countermovement*)	Voice from outside (*productive TNCs*)	Vocal entry

Source: Adapted from Ferrera, 2005: 30.

become much more wide spread than it was during early democratization, when especially labour used their newly acquired right to vote extensively.

Table 8.1 also allows us to think in more detail about the relation of the state and the forces of the countermovement. Historically, while always accountable to capital, the state nevertheless turned out to be a central ally of industrial labour in the fight for embedding capitalism. Currently, the state has become much more accountable to the demands of the most contradictory forces of the countermovement, namely productive TNCs, while at the same time it is much less exposed to demands of labour.[2] This is reflected in labour's strategic choices. Silent exit or silent staying have become an important strategy for labour at the expense of voice – be it in the form of strikes or class voting.

I do not intend to offer an explanation for labour's increasing silence. However, one important point is worth mentioning. This is that the most important force of the countermovement as analysed by Polanyi, namely *industrial labour*, has lost its centrality. While Polanyi analysed the role of industrial labour in the phase of its ascendancy, today we witness its decline. As a consequence, on the one hand other groups of labour, such as public sector workers, have become important in the countermovement (see Bieler, Chapter 11 in this volume). On the other hand, labour as a whole seems to lack common foundations of status, dignity, solidarity and vision that would be comparable to their nineteenth-century counterparts. All in all, labour as a force of the countermovement is much more fragmented and disintegrated compared with the turn of the last century.

Below, I will draw on Polanyi's figure of a double movement to analyse the main features of the current process of European integration and the social limits to liberalization.

Embedded neoliberalism in Europe

The new mode of European integration

Critical literature has long insisted on the qualitative change of European integration since the 1980s (for detailed analysis, see Van Apeldoorn's Chapter 1 in this volume). In the first decades after World War II, European economies could pursue diverse development paths, which reflected national compromises in respect to economic efficiency and societal goals in the social, cultural or environmental areas. European integration exerted only limited pressure for Member States to open their economies, and was compatible with high and diverse levels of national market protection. In the aftermath of the world economic crisis of the 1970s, however, European integration took a quite different, neoliberal character. Central to the new mode of integration is that it contributes to reshaping national regimes with the aim of advancing the overall competitiveness of the European economic space. Three integration projects have been essential to this aim: the European Single Market, the Economic and Monetary Union (EMU) and the Lisbon strategy. The single market project's aim has been to thoroughly deregulate and liberalize the Member States' economies in order to open up domestic markets to international competition, and thus create an integrated European economic space. The Maastricht Treaty with its centrepiece of EMU aims at the constitutionalization of macroeconomic stability and a single European currency. The convergence criteria established under the Maastricht Treaty impose strong constraints on Member States' fiscal and monetary policies and indirectly promote privatization as a resource for budgetary revenues. A strong euro is considered essential in the international currency competition (Altvater, 1996). Finally, the European Council in Lisbon designed a comprehensive long-term strategy that integrated the earlier projects with the aim to 'make the EU the world's most competitive and dynamic knowledge based economy in the world' (European Council, 2000). The Lisbon Strategy stresses active policies in the areas of innovation, technology, research and development, infrastructure and industrial upgrading. It also seeks to spell out a social dimension of European integration, which, as Sandy Hager argues in this volume (Chapter 5), is characterized by a workfare orientation. Employability, skill upgrading and lifelong learning have become new foci of EU's activities in the social realm (Jessop, 2003).

The changing form of European integration reflects the priorities of major business groups, who have tried since the crisis of Fordism to escape the confines of the domestic markets and national compromises. It is widely acknowledged that the major integration projects of the EU were strongly influenced by the European TNCs (Van Apeldoorn, 2002; Balanyá et al., 2003). These forces, in close co-operation with representatives of the European Commission, have often bypassed national governments in designing the next steps of European integration. The strategic selectivity (Jessop, 1990: 149–52) of the European governance system favours TNCs over other social forces. Trans-national companies have access to both European and national levels of government, and benefit from the lack of a European public, democratic accountability and the fact that European decision-making processes often lack transparency (Wissen, 2005). In contrast, domestically oriented business groups as well as trade unions can only access more marginal European institutions and are moreover fragmented along national lines (see however Bieler, Chapter 11 in this volume). Moreover, the increased regime competition triggered by the major integration projects allows TNCs to play off Member States against each other when it comes to their investment decisions. In a kind of virtuous circle, therefore, each new major integration project of the EU reinforces transnational capital's room for manoeuvre.

Limits of deregulation

Although the new mode of European integration has a strong neoliberal character, the EU is often depicted as an alternative to the ultra-liberal US capitalism. Representatives of this position point to the stronger welfare states, lower social inequality, and the more co-operative nature of relations between capital and labour (Hall and Soskice, 2001b; Pontusson, 2005). Major EU actors themselves stress the significance of the 'European social model', which distinguishes the EU from the USA and is at the same time a major factor of Europe's competitiveness.

To contrast the 'social' European capitalism with the 'liberal' US–American is not totally convincing, as it underestimates the repercussions of neoliberal restructuring in Europe (e.g. Bieling, 2006b). Nevertheless, it seems plausible that for the foreseeable future, differences between the two models of capitalism will remain. This is so because European capitalism offers forces of the countermovement to liberalization better institutional legacies and more points of intervention than US capitalism.

First, research on welfare state reforms has convincingly argued that retrenchment does not follow a linear logic. Retrenchment is most pronounced in those countries, where the welfare state was the least institutionalized – the liberal market economies. In contrast, highly developed welfare states have typically generated broad societal support that excludes radical retrenchment (see e.g. Pierson, 2001a). This is not to say that welfare state retrenchment has not advanced over the last decades. Rather, the point I want to make is that as welfare states are stronger entrenched in most European countries than the USA, there are reasons to expect that its retrenchment will be met with more resistance (see also Chapter 2 in this volume, by Ryner).

Second, as pointed out by the research on varieties of capitalism (Hall and Soskice, 2001b; Iversen, 2005), European capitalism relies strongly on economic sectors that require more long-term and consensual agreements between banks, labour and capital, as well as social security systems that allow workers to invest in industry-specific skills. To put it differently, sectors of the 'old economy' are still much more central to European capitalism in comparison with the USA. This is confirmed by the composition of the ERT. The majority of its members represent still industrial companies of the car, steel, food or related industries.

Third, in contrast with the USA with its integrated domestic market, a unified European capitalism is still in the making. In this context, nation states tend to support domestic players to position themselves on the transnational market, and protect them against too aggressive foreign competition, as for instance against hostile take-overs. At the same time, different governments seek to make their national territory as attractive as possible for TNCs. Attracting TNCs is not necessarily always compatible with the ideal of a neoliberal, competitive market order and a lean state. More often than not, industrial TNCs ask rather for economic protection. As Palan argues:

> The new period of globalization displays market strength and confidence of capital and, yet, it is a period also characterized in business literature and magazines as extremely hazardous and difficult . . . Contrary to the belief, the ideology of neoliberalism and open markets is not necessarily an unadulterated business ideology, unless one accepts the proposition that 'business likes competition'. It is far more appropriate to say that business likes competition when it suits – which is a rare occurrence indeed – business likes no doubt an efficient and flexible labour market, business does not mind at all competition among governments in the provision of sweeteners, subsidies and other incentives . . . But business, as a general proposition, does not like competition.
>
> (2006: 258)

It is realistic to assume that business' quest for economic protection of the kind Palan is referring to is more successful in Europe than the USA not only because of the integrated nature of the US domestic market. In addition, the European multi-level governance system offers enterprises – as well as other social forces – many more 'veto points' than the US American federalism.

All in all, the changes of European capitalism over the last decades can be analysed as an ongoing process of double movement in the Polanyian sense. The movement towards liberalization is supported by state elites and TNCs. However, it is only financial TNCs and institutional investors that would support full liberalization of European capitalism (see Bieling and Jäger in Chapter 4 of this volume). Industrial TNCs' ambitions are more contradictory – while they seek the opening of markets for themselves, they simultaneously seek the protection of national governments against their competitors. Thus, some of the actions of industrial TNCs can be characterized as 'countermovement'. In addition, domestic capital, trade unions and supporters of the welfare states all resist at different points in time the thrust towards liberalization. As a result, the current form of the European socio-economic order can be conceptualized as 'embedded neoliberalism' (Van Apeldoorn, 2002). This order is fundamentally different from the post-war order of 'embedded liberalism' (Ruggie, 1982), in which detailed regulations and generous welfare states thoroughly mitigated the impact of market forces and offered economic security to most members of society. The embeddedness of neoliberalism is much more limited: it is based on institutional inertia and selective and contradictory resistance against liberalization. At the same time, it is mostly industrial TNCs who profit from limitations of the market mechanism, which paradoxically helps their expansion (for a thorough discussion of embedded neoliberalism see Chapter 1 by Van Apeldoorn in this volume).

What is the role of eastern enlargement of the EU in this double movement of liberalization and protection? Critical literature as well as public opinion see enlargement as another lever towards deregulation and liberalization of European capitalism (see also the contribution by Vliegenthart and Overbeek in Chapter 7 of this volume). In a nutshell, the critical view on the future of European capitalism can be summarized as follows: on the one hand, it is institutional investors, investment banks or hedge funds – so aptly dubbed locusts by Franz Müntefering, the former president of the German Social Democratic Party – , that destroy the traditional model of capitalism with its long-term and patient relationships among corporations, their banks and employees from above (Beckmann, 2007). On the other hand, the East European newcomers to the EU initiate a race to the bottom in terms of wages, working conditions and taxation, which challenges European capitalism from below. How adequate is this latter view? In order to answer this question, first a look at the varieties of East European capitalisms is in order.

Neoliberalism, embedded neoliberalism and neo-corporatism in Eastern Europe[3]

Enlargement has allowed the EU to expand the core elements of its market order to Eastern Europe. Early on, the candidates had to liberalize their external trade and introduce the internal market regime. During the preparation for membership, the EU closely monitored macro-economic development, monetary and budgetary policies, privatization policies and administrative reforms. In addition, the candidates were urged early on to seek compliance with the criteria for the introduction of the euro. Three factors have so far contributed to the fact that capitalism in Eastern Europe is less embedded than in Western Europe. First, as Grabbe (1999: 17) argues, the EU accession has promoted a policy model, where 'the thrust of the agenda is neoliberal . . . The socio-economic system they implicitly promote has a more "Atlantic" than "Rhenish" or "Latin flavour"' (see also Bohle, 2006). Second, during the first decade of transformation, neoliberalism was very attractive for most East European reform makers. This is because it offered the most radical and convincing critique of the delegitimized socialist system (Szacki, 1995). At the same time, trade unions and left-wing social forces emerged as weakened from the break-down of Socialism (Greskovits, 1998; Ost, 2005). Third, the East European societies are strongly dependent on capital imports, a fact that has been reinforced by their rapprochement to the EU (Bohle, 2006). However, as will be demonstrated below, not all East European states have managed or desired to attract 'embedding' industrial capital on a similar level.

The accession process has not led to convergence among its East European members. Although the EU and its most powerful actors, the TNCs, have strongly contributed to shaping the development paths in the region, they have not done so from the beginning on. The legacies of the communist system and the initial reform strategies were similarly decisive. As a consequence of the interaction of all three factors, three models of capitalisms have emerged in Eastern Europe: a neoliberal type in the Baltic states, an embedded neoliberal type in the V4, and a neo-corporatist in Slovenia (for a more detailed analysis see Bohle and Greskovits, 2007).

Pure neoliberalism in the Baltic states

Thus, it is the Baltic states that have embarked on the most radical regime change (Feldmann, 2001). Quick withdrawal of the state from the economy, fast liberalization of foreign trade, and equally rapid privatization drove their transition strategy closest to the neoliberal ideal type of comprehensive and radical reforms (EBRD, 2001). In terms of their welfare states and social standards, the Baltic regimes appear among the most unequal and least socially inclusive not only in the region, but in Europe as a whole (Bohle, 2007). Social expenditure per gross domestic product (GDP) is extremely low with an average 13 per cent, while the EU average is around 28 per cent. Not only is the welfare state in the Baltic countries stripped down to a bare minimum, but in general, the Baltic states abstain from state interference in the economy. The extreme liberal trade regimes, institutionalized early on, are a case in point. Another indicator for this are state subsidies to the economy, where again the Baltic states stand out in an overall European comparison by the meagre amount of subsidies granted (Bohle and Greskovits, 2007). Finally, a major thrust of Baltic reforms has been the institutionalization of macroeconomic stability. Relative to their GDP, the Baltic countries operate by far the smallest fiscal states of the region and keep relying on the most restrictive monetary institutions, currency boards. The Baltic states not only have the least generous welfare states within the EU, but in addition, organized labour has equally been all but completely marginalized. Trade union density as well as collective bargaining coverage is among the lowest in Europe (Visser, 2004).

The radical reform path in these states was closely linked to their political priority of cutting all ties with the Russian economy. EU accession and integration in the European political economy has partly mildly corrected, and partly reinforced domestic politic choices (Lindstrom, 2005). The EU, together with the World Trade Organization (WTO), has insisted on trade barriers to be raised again, and improving the standards of social (and democratic) inclusion has become an issue in the accession negotiations. Overall, however, EU priorities in the region are in line with the Baltic reform priorities, and EU accession therefore could mostly serve as a factor locking in earlier institutional choices.[4]

Neo-corporatism in Slovenia

Diametrically opposite to this is the socio-economic regime that has emerged in Slovenia over the past decades. Slovenian transformation was built on a consensus among all major forces of society – employers, employees, experts, major political parties. The Slovenian welfare state is the most encompassing in the region, and its industrial relation system stands out for its high trade union density, high level of collective bargaining coverage, and the centralization of collective bargaining (Stanojevic, 2003). Although Slovenia accepted the general framework of macroeconomic stability, it was also clear for the reformers that this 'alone would not facilitate a successful transition to a capitalist economy' (Lindstrom, 2005: 23). Trade liberalization and privatization was carried out gradually, and the Slovene reform elites relied heavily on domestic forces, including labour, in the privatization process. Slovenia opened its economy to foreign ownership and control only very reluctantly and gradually and, against explicit advice of the EU, kept its strategic sectors in national hands (Lindstrom and Piroska, 2007).

Dependent embedded neoliberalism in the Visegrád countries

The Visegrád countries occupy an intermediate position between the neoliberal Baltics and neo-corporatist Slovenia. Although these countries all embarked on a thorough path of liberalization, privatization and deregulation, their strategies were more gradual than the Baltic countries. The most distinguished characteristics of the Visegrád's model of capitalism is the significant role of foreign direct investment (FDI) not only in sectors that secure market control (infrastructure, finance, trade), but also in the export oriented manufacturing sector. Hungary very early on settled on a path of foreign dominated accumulation. In contrast, the Czech Republic, Slovakia and Poland all initially attempted to secure broad domestic ownership in the economy. Ultimately, however, the privatization policies in these countries have become subordinated to the cause of attracting FDI (Bohle, 2002; Drahokoupil, 2007b, and see also his Chapter 9 in this volume). Attracting FDI in the major manufacturing sectors entails important state activities. In contrast with both Slovenia and the Baltic countries, the Visegrád countries have developed a wide variety of instruments in order to attract FDI and thus to upgrade their industrial bases. These include instruments towards further liberalization as well as measures geared towards economic protection. Thus deregulation of the foreign investment regime has been combined with tax exemptions, direct subsidies for specific investments, import protection, building of infrastructure, investments in skills, and reforms of the labour code towards more flexible regulations. Trans-national companies have been crucial in shaping these policies. Ever since their entry to the V4, they successfully demanded import protection, which led to the de-liberalization of the trade regime. Thus the EBRD finds that for the early transition period, '[i]n Poland, FDI-intensive industries have average tariffs on imports that are 66 per cent higher than in manufacturing as a whole. The corresponding figure for Hungary is 10 per cent, but Hungary uses quantitative restrictions more heavily than Poland. When non-tariff barriers are taken into account, the strong link between high protection and high FDI also appears in Hungary' (EBRD, 1994: 137). The *Financial Times* comments dryly: 'Ironically, Western multi-nationals have become eastern Europe's most effective lobby for protection and their efforts to link investment commitments to guaranteed markets have become all the more intense as local demand has fallen below expectations.' (*Financial Times*, 1992, cited in EBRD, 1994: 137) Available evidence suggests that each bigger capital intensive investment in Eastern Europe in the early 1990s led to strong and successful lobbying for import protection, as well as significant tax holidays (EBRD, 1994; Balcet and Enrietti, 1997; Bartlett and Seleny, 1998).

The focus of the Visegrád states' support to TNCs has changed over time. With the EU accession process, import protection and tax holidays levelled off, as the EU asked the applicant countries to fulfil the requirements on common external tariff and state aid. Instead, the Visegrád countries switched to tailor made incentive packages, which include preferential treatment in acquiring land, cash benefits, investments in the infrastructure and training of the labour force, and committed themselves to a thorough deregulation of the labour codes (see below).

'Embedding neoliberalism' through investment incentives is a highly contradictory affair. On the one hand, this state activity has indeed allowed the Visegrád countries to transform their industries into modern and competitive sectors. This achievement stands out if compared to the experience of the Baltic states, where radical reforms and the minimal state led to a dramatic de-industrialization (Table 8.3). In addition, wage increases are substantive in an East European comparison, and it is especially the big transnational firms that pay high wages. At the same time, labour market flexibility is the highest among the East European countries. Moreover, especially in Poland and Slovakia it seems that foreign-led restructuring of the economy does not 'trickle down' to the whole society. Poland and Slovakia have the highest long-term unemployment rates and among the highest unemployment rates in the EU. In contrast with the Baltic states, however, the governments of the Visegrád countries have tried to compensate the social risk (Vanhuysse, 2006). Social spending per capita is significantly higher than in the Baltic states. At the same time, in these countries it was repeatedly tried to institutionalize tripartite systems, although these arrangements were contested, and unstable (Ost, 2000).

All in all, the socio-economic regime that emerged in the V4 is best described as the East European variant of embedded neoliberalism. Their state activities are most compatible with the new mode of European integration. In contrast with the minimal Baltic states, these countries seek actively to improve their locational conditions. In contrast with Slovenia and many West European countries, state activity is almost exclusively geared towards attracting foreign capital rather than preparing domestic capital for the European and global competition. This priority reflects the dependent nature of capitalism in the V4. The decisive question is how sustainable a strategy that attempts to embed neoliberalism by attracting FDI can be in the long run. This question will be taken up below.

Table 8.2 summarizes important features of the socio-economic regimes of the new EU Member States.

Table 8.2   Socio-economic indicators of the East European capitalisms

	Index of economic freedom (2006)	State expenditure (% of GDP, 2003)	State aid (% of GDP, 2003)	Social expenditure (% of GDP, 2003)	Gini (2002)
Neoliberalism (Baltic states)	2.1	34.1	0.3	13.4	33
Embedded neoliberalism (Visegrád)	2.3	45.6	1.9	20.4	28
Neo-corporatism (Slovenia)	2.4	48.2	0.7	24.6	22
Germany	2.0	46.8	0.9	27.2	28.3

Sources: Adapted from Bohle and Greskovits, 2007. Column 1: Heritage Foundation; 1 is the 'freest', 5 the most regulated economy, Heritage Foundation Index of Economic Freedom available from www.heritage.org. Column 2: EBRD Transition Reports for CEE countries, OECD in Figures 2005 for Germany. Columns 1 & 2: Eurostat, Statistics in Focus Reports (various issues, available at ec.europa.eu/eurostat). Column 5: European Commission Report on Social Inclusion for CEE, UN Human Development Report 2005 for Germany, European Commission, Annual Joint Report on Social Protection and Social Inclusion (various issues).

Race to the bottom? I: Locational competition between Eastern and Western Europe

Who competes?

Which are the East European countries that exert the strongest competitive pressure on Western Europe? According to the proponents of the race to the bottom thesis, it should be the Baltic states with their low taxes and salaries, their limited social expenditures and minimal states. The Baltic model of capitalism has indeed found much appreciation among relevant neoliberal economic fora and think tanks. Thus, the World Economic Forum (WEF) ranked the new EU Member States in respect to their fulfillment of the EU Lisbon Agenda, according to which the EU is to become the world's most competitive region within a short period of time. WEF found Estonia the most and Latvia the third most competitive of the East European countries. Both countries lie ahead of all four Visegrád countries. Only Lithuania lags far behind, in sixth place (Blanke and Lopez-Claros, 2004).

According to a number of other indicators, however, the Baltic tigers seem much less impressive. Their GDP in 2003 was still below the level of 1989. Although they attract high levels of FDI (especially Estonia), these investments typically go into service sectors like financial intermediation, transport or trade. These investments are not motivated by competition on labour or social standards, but by market control. In terms of manufacturing, it is the traditional sectors like wood and food processing, textile and clothing that attract most FDI. The traditional nature of the competitiveness of the Baltic states' economy is furthermore reflected in their commodity exports: They mostly export raw materials and traditional industrial goods. Even within the limited amount of more high tech manufacturing exports, like electronics, these countries specialize in the lowest value-added segments (Table 8.3; see also Dulleck et al., 2004; Tiits, 2006). This picture is confirmed by a recent study of the European Industrial Relations Observatory (EIRO) on relocation of production to Eastern Europe (Blažienė, 2006; Eamets and Philips, 2006; EIRO, 2006; Karnite, 2006).

All in all it is not the Baltic states with their neoliberal profile that exert strong competitive pressure in the enlarged EU, but rather the Visegrád countries, which as a result of their generous investment incentives are successfully attracting FDI also in their manufacturing sectors. Moreover, these countries have attained similar export structures to the developed European countries. They export to the West what the West exports to the rest of the world: electronics, cars and car components, machinery and equipment goods, pharmaceuticals, and chemical goods. If there is a race to the bottom in terms of social and tax standards, it should originate from these countries. Is this indeed the case?

Table 8.3   Indicators of Eastern Europe's competitiveness

	GDP (2004, 1989=100)	Average growth rate of industrial output (1992–2003)	FDI (stock 1989–2003, per capita)	Complex manufacturing FDI stock per capita (2002–4, US$)	Complex exports 2003 (% of total commodity exports)
Neoliberalism (Baltic states)	97	-1.5	1,641	77	26
Embedded Neoliberalism (Visegrád)	124	4.6	2,581	744	53
Neo-corporatism (Slovenia)	126	1.0	1,647	198	49

Sources: Adapted from Bohle and Greskovits, 2007. Columns 1–3: EBRD Transition reports, various volumes. Column 4: calculated on the basis of national foreign investment agencies data. Column 5: based on COMTRADE database of UN Statistics Division (available at comtrade.un.org); complex exports are products coded 5 (chemicals) and 7 (machinery and equipment) in Standard International Trade Classification (SITC) classification.

Effects of eastwards relocation on the German economy

In order to answer this question, I will turn to the effects of eastwards relocation of production on the German economy. Among the West European countries, Germany is most strongly exposed to eastern competition. Moreover, its 'model of capitalism', described as co-ordinated by the varieties of capitalism literature (Hall and Soskice, 2001b), is prone to liberalization, should a race to the bottom indeed occur.

For a number of reasons it is impossible to give a precise account of the overall effect of the increasing competition from and relocation to the East on the institutional settings of the Western countries. Data collection on relocation is difficult, its effects are hard to isolate from the effects of other instances of restructuring, and it is next to impossible to come to terms with secondary effects like new job creation in new sectors due to relocation. The following elaboration therefore has to be treated with some caution, as it is no more than a tentative approximation to the question.

According to the most recent European Restructuring Monitor Report (Storrie with Ward, 2007), the scale of job losses associated with relocation to the V4 is not important. Between 2003 and 2006 Germany lost around 1 per cent of its total employment due to restructuring. Out of this, only 7 per cent of the job losses are due to relocation of production, and out of these again only a portion – albeit a significant one – are the result of relocation to Central Eastern Europe.[5] The limited degree of relocation notwithstanding, it can be argued that relocation has started to impact on the German model of capitalism, for a number of reasons. First, there is a significant sectoral concentration of relocation.[6] It is particularly important in the motor vehicle industry, which accounts for almost half of all the relocated jobs. In addition, the telecommunication industry is strongly affected. Relocation in these sectors is motivated by cost-saving and to a lesser extent also by tax levels. A number of authors found that TNCs use the Visegrád countries in order to escape the German social model (Meardi and Toth, 2005; Bluhm, 2007). The evidence in the car industry moreover suggests that although shifting production abroad has to date not resulted in an overall reduction of workforce in the sector, firms' current and future investment decisions seem to privilege non-German locations (Jürgens et al., 2006: 24–30).

Second, although much of the job relocation happens below the radar screen of public awareness, a number of spectacular cases have nevertheless had a profound impact on the public perception about the costs of enlargement. The case of Siemens AG threatening in 2004 to close several production units in Germany and shift production to Hungary and China on the grounds of too high labour costs is a case in point. Trade unions could prevent relocation temporarily, in exchange for substantial concessions. Despite all concessions, the failure, selling and finally bankruptcy of the mobile phone division of Siemens was not prevented. The Siemens case has not been an exception: At the end of 2007, white consumer good producer Electrolux closed its location in Nürnberg, and relocated most of the 1,700 jobs to Poland. This happened notwithstanding the readiness of work councils and trade unions to make substantial concessions in terms of wages and working time (FAZ.Net, 2005; ERM database). Most recently, mobile phone producer Nokia decided to close its plant in Bochum, and relocate 3,000 jobs to the ethnic Hungarian part of Romania (*Netzzeitung*, 2008). These and other spectacular cases have resulted in widespread public fear about the threats stemming from their low-wage neighbours. According to the Eurobarometer of 2006, 84 per cent of German respondents state that they fear relocation of jobs to Eastern Europe (*Welt Online*, 2006). Significantly, the perception of the East European competitive threat also puts the German system of industrial relations under pressure. Jürgens et al. (2006: 23) find that in terms of industrial relations, the current balance of power in car enterprises have significantly changed in favour of management, which extensively uses the threat to relocate production to low cost areas in order to gain concessions. Apart from cutting costs, another aim of management has been to decrease employment protection, with outsourcing as a major instrument. Hand in hand with this goes an increased differentiation of the workforce along the production chain, with only core workers keeping their high levels of employment protection (Jürgens et al., 2006).

All in all, then, there are reasons to assume that the competition from the V4 has indeed started to disembed Western embedded neoliberalism by exerting a downward pressure on social standards and wages. The question then is: are there limits to a possible downward spiral? In order to answer this question, the following section will take a closer look at the competitive pressure initiated by TNCs among the four Visegrád countries themselves.

Race to the bottom? II: Locational competition among the Visegrád countries

It is too often overlooked that the competition among the East European countries is much fiercer than competition between East and West countries. Trans-national companies can more easily play out the Visegrád countries against each other than Western against Eastern locations, as these countries crucially depend on capital imports. Moreover, over the past years, a transnational industrial cluster of strategic industries, which covers the south of Poland, the west of Slovakia, east of Czech Republic and the northwest of Hungary, has emerged. In this cluster, it is of minor significance for TNCs which side of the respective national border they ultimately locate the production. It is in this context where 'sweeteners' do indeed make all the difference. If there is the potential of a race to the bottom in the enlarged EU, it should be most virulent among the V4.

The increasing locational competition among the Visegrád countries is closely related to a second generation of economic reforms, which aim at boosting investment O'Dwyer and Kovalčík (2007). These authors define second generation reforms as sharing the following features:

1 Steep tax cuts for business, simplification of the tax code, and a preference for flat-tax systems;
2 Generous incentives to foreign investors, including long tax holidays and land grants;
3 Loosening labour regulations with little consultation from organized labour;
4 Funding tax cuts and incentives through a reduction in the state's commitment to the welfare system. (O'Dwyer and Kovalčík (2007: 8)

How far have these second generation reforms taken hold in the Visegrád countries? Have they led to the dismantling of the Visegrád countries' regime of embedded neoliberalism? How are they related to TNCs playing these countries out against each other?

Tax competition

Tax competition between the Visegrád countries started in earnest towards the end of the 1990s. For a long time, Hungary was leading with its low tax rates. Poland followed with a tax reform in 1999, the Czech Republic in 2000 (Bönker, 2003). A new round in the tax competition among the Visegrád countries was initiated by Slovakia in 2004, when it introduced its flat tax rate regime of 19 per cent for income, corporate and value added tax (VAT). With this step, the corporate income tax (CIT) fell significantly below EU average, and also below the average among the new EU Member States (Moore, 2005: 21), prompting neighbouring countries to lower their corporate taxes in return (see also Chapter 7 in this volume, by Vliegenthart and Overbeek). Hungary reduced its CIT from 18.6 per cent to 17.7 per cent (Moore, 2005: 21). Although Social Democrats in the Czech Republic 'were careful to distinguish themselves from Slovak's tax reforms', with 'Prime Minister Gross declar[ing, D.B.] that his government would not copy Slovakia's flat tax' (O'Dwyer and Kovalčík, 2007: 20), they still reduced CIT from 31 per cent to 28 per cent, and the upper rate of the VAT from 22 per cent to 19 per cent. Poland discussed and ultimately rejected the introduction of a flat tax regime.

There is some evidence that tax competition has been spurred by TNCs. Thus, in an interview conducted in 2003, the then executive director of AmCham in Hungary, Péter Fáth, argued that as EU accession puts limits to tax exemptions for TNCs, the next task for AmCham would be to lobby for a lower corporate tax rate, modelled after the Irish example (Fáth, 2003).

General investment incentives

One of the most striking outcomes of the empirical investigation of investment incentives in Eastern Europe by Cass is that incentive packages have become *more generous* in the period since the late 1990s compared with the early transition. He continues: 'This result is consistent with the extensive accounts of growing competition between countries for relatively mobile efficiency-seeking investments' (2006: 41). This assumption is confirmed by a recent empirical investigation of state–TNC negotiations on three major investment projects: PSA-Peugeot in Trvnava, Slovakia; Hyundai/Kia Motors in Žilina, Slovakia; and Hankook Tire in Dunaujvaros, Hungary (Kolesár, 2006). This study concludes that once locational specificities among competitors are similar, investment incentives play a major role in the TNCs' decision for a specific location. Thus, in the case of Hyundai/Kia the Slovak government outcompeted the Polish in the final round of decision by adding

> special purpose subsidies for the acquisition of further investment property, financial subsidies for professional re-qualification and for the purpose of employment . . . finishing of construction of [a, D.B.] highway . . . English-language education for employee's children, housing, hospital, administrative buildings, support of the Technical University in Žilina specializing in transport, constructing of the railway terminal and a reconstruction of the nearby airport to the general investment stimuli of 15 per cent of the total investment sum as allowed under the EU regulation.
>
> (Kolesár, 2006: 42)

In addition, the Slovak government promised to build a village for the Korean management close to the factory site, as well as luxury houses close to the capital city. It also promised not to increase the corporate tax, or employment and social protection. Kia did not have to give much in return – it neither had to commit itself to a minimum investment nor minimum employment (ibid.: 46). Similarly, in the case of the Korean tyre producer, Hankook Tire, it was investment incentives rather than locational advantages that made all the difference. This became clear when Hankook Tire revised its decision to invest in Slovakia after the Slovak government had to cut back on some of its promised incentives. This situation was swiftly exploited by the Hungarian government, which felt in desperate need of attracting an investor, since the last major investments in the region went to its competitors Slovakia or the Czech Republic (ibid.: 50–3).

The study also argues that the general EU regulations of state aid put only a limited degree of restraints on the Visegrád governments' readiness to offer generous incentives. As demonstrated above, general investment subsidies are typically supplemented by special treatments of strategic investors, including infrastructure provision, educational, medical or housing facilities and the like, which are not covered by EU rules. Finally, in the bargaining process on investments, it is clearly the TNCs that have the upper hand. Kolesár offers ample evidence on the strategic use of misinformation, confusion, prematurely released reports and so on on the part of the TNCs, all of which are tailored towards extorting additional concessions from the competing governments.

All in all, the dynamics of investment competition among the V4 points indeed towards a race to the bottom. Embedding the necessary investments put huge strains on the government's budgets, and ultimately enters in contradiction with the principle of social protection (see below).

Deregulation of the labour market

Since the early 2000s all Visegrád countries with the exception of the Czech Republic fundamentally revised their labour codes. In Hungary, the conservative Fidesz government introduced major changes in the labour code that led to a significant increase of labour market flexibility in 2001. A number of the flexibility measures introduced in 2001 were however curtailed by a revision under the Socialist government in 2002 (Tóth and Neumann, 2002). Slovakia reformed its labour code in 2002, and, after sustained pressure from the employer's side, amended it again in 2003. The main purpose of the 2003 amendment of the labour code was to achieve a higher level of flexibility in labour relations (Munková, 2004). In Poland, in November 2002 a more flexible labour code came into force, which reflected the demands made by employers for a number of years (Czarzasty, 2002). In 2005 proposals for a new Labour Code were presented, which include the establishment of the right of lock-outs for employers and a further deregulation of dismissal protection (Towalski, 2005). Although the right to establish lock-outs has meanwhile been abandoned, the draft of the labour code currently under discussion seeks to increase flexibility in terminating contracts (Towalski, 2006).

Two types of pressures have led to the revision of the labour codes in the V4. On the one hand, during the accession process the countries needed to harmonize their labour codes with the *Acquis Communautaire*. Although the *Acquis* strengthened employees' rights in some places, it also generated heightened debates on labour market flexibility, specifically concerning provisions of working time and dismissals. The revisions of the labour codes in relation to the EU entry provided political opportunities for employers, and specifically foreign direct investors, who had been lobbying for more flexible labour codes for years. In Slovakia, the liberal labour code reflects the preferences of its foreign investors (Munková, 2004: 4; Bohle and Greskovits, 2006). In Poland and Hungary, governments also worked closely together with major employers in order to reform their labour codes.

Table 8.4   Employment protection legislation in the Visegrád countries

	Employment protection legislation (1999)	**Employment protection legislation (2003)**
Czech Republic	1.9	1.9
Hungary	1.5	1.7
Poland	1.9	2.1
Slovakia	2.5	2.0
Germany	2.6	2.5

Sources: OECD, *Employment Outlook*, 2004. This index measures the regulation for regular contracts, temporary contracts and collective dismissals: 1 refers to the most flexible, and 21 to the most protected economy.

Although the reforms were met in some countries with union protests, and trade unions' influence on the legislation process has not been totally absent, it is only in Hungary that trade unions together with a socialist government actually reformed the labour codes to the advantage of employees. Despite this, the current employment protection in Hungary is among the most liberal in Europe (Table 8.4).

Welfare state retrenchment

Finally, with the exception of the Czech Republic, which only very recently embarked on that path, all Visegrád countries have over the last five years been engaged in partly quite radical welfare state reforms. The reforms were triggered by the fact that the regime of embedded liberalism has led in all countries to an accumulation of macroeconomic imbalances. The urge to address these imbalances is strongly related to the requirements of EMU convergence. In contrast with the old EU Member States, the East European newcomers were not granted the possibility of opting out of the EMU, and since their accession to the EU there has been growing pressure on them to meet the convergence criteria.

In 2002–3, together with the reform of its tax system, Slovakia enacted sweeping reforms of its pension and health care systems, and radically decreased social benefits. Recipients of social benefits were asked to participate in 'activation' programmes. Although benefits were significantly lowered for every eligible person, the failure to comply with the activation requirement resulted in having benefits cut in half. Given the unequal distribution of benefit dependency, it is the Roma population, already by far the poorest strata in Slovak society, that is hardest hit by these cuts (Moore, 2005: 25–8).

In Poland, between 2001 and 2004 the socialist government repeatedly attempted to cut public expenditure in order to prepare for EMU accession. In 2001 a package was proposed, which 'provided for a freeze on salaries in the administration and in education, more stringent criteria for awarding many social and pre-retirement benefits, and lower government-subsidized discounts on railway tickets' (Zubek, 2006: 205). Political conflicts within the Socialist Party and radically decreasing popularity among voters led to the reforms being aborted. A second attempt to prepare fast EMU entry through the introduction of a comprehensive stabilization package was rejected on the same grounds. A third package was prepared in January 2004. It 'envisaged a reduction in overall social spending of . . . almost 4 per cent of GDP over four years between 2004 and 2007' (Zubek, 2006: 211). This last package shared the fate of its predecessors – because of the intense struggles within the party, which faced plummeting approval rates, and the resistance of trade unions, the party back-tracked from introducing further reforms.

In Hungary, radical welfare state reforms and EMU convergence have emerged as a top priority under the second socialist government led by Ferenc Gyurcsany. In the face of serious macro-economic imbalances that had accumulated since the socialists' return to power in 2002, in summer 2006 the Gyurcsany administration announced a comprehensive package of tax increases and budget cuts, and structural reforms of the state administration, the health care system and the educational system. A number of stabilization measures have since been introduced, resulting in a plummeting of the government's approval rates (Greskovits, 2007).

All in all, it seems that the priorities of TNCs and the conditions of EMU entry combined with domestic politics have indeed introduced a race to the bottom in the V4 that risks catapulting these states into the neoliberal Baltic camp. The initial latecomer Slovakia has taken the lead in disembedding neoliberalism. Its numerous liberal reforms and its successes in attracting FDI and meeting the EMU convergence criteria have exerted strong competitive pressures on its neighbouring countries. The concluding section explores the social limits to such a race to the bottom.

Conclusion: limits of the race to the bottom

The aim of the paper was to investigate the dynamics and contradictions of the increasing locational competition in the enlarged EU. It argued that the new mode of European integration fosters regime competition and has allowed TNCs to expand significantly their room of manoeuvre. Eastern enlargement of the EU has reinforced these features of European integration, and thus contributed to an accelerating race to the bottom in terms of social standards, labour market flexibility and taxation. The fiercest locational competition is not between East and West, however, but between the four Visegrád countries. As the Visegrád countries can be seen as the weakest and most vulnerable elements in the embedded neoliberal European constellation, this last section asks whether there are limits to a downward spiral in this region. In line with Polanyi's understanding of the countermovement to (neo)liberalism, my answer will take into account economic, social and state actors in their attempts of limiting liberalization.

The analysis argued that industrial TNCs have behaved as forces of the countermovement by seeking state protection from pure market forces, and thus contributed in a limited way to the embedded character of Visegrád capitalism. At the same time, they used their strategic options – most importantly vocal exit and entry – to pressure highly exaggerated subsidies and incentives from governments, which seriously risk to undermine the very capacities of states to provide protection. Although a serious effort to analyse the costs of embedding TNCs in the region is still wanting, the Slovak example gives support to the assumption that in the context of heightened locational competition, attracting TNCs within the supranational EU framework has significant negative repercussions on the public budget, state administration and social welfare programmes.

To counterbalance TNCs' contradictory and ultimately destructive strategies would require a European institutional system that keeps some autonomy from the narrow, short-term interests of capital. The contemporary European system does not allow for this autonomy. Over the last decades, its basis of accountability has strongly shifted in favour of capital. Rather than re-regulating competition in the European common space, EU and state actors are actively involved in the opposite strategy of strengthening regime competition and thus reinforcing the room for manoeuvre for TNCs.

In this constellation, the race to the bottom can only be contained from opposing social forces. As suggested by the theoretical discussion above, there is not much evidence of an organized attempt of resistance among opposing forces in the V4. Rather, with the possible exception of public sector unions, who have been able to mobilize more systematically,[7] trade unions and social movements are engaged in sporadic and isolated cases of social protest. Otherwise, sporadic protest prevailed. As a reaction to the radical Slovak reforms, food riots emerged in several, mostly Roma populated, villages of eastern Slovakia. It took a week before in the largest domestic security operation since 1989 riot police and the army could restore control over the region. In Hungary, protests and riots have never completely stopped since the Gyurcsany package was announced in September 2006.

Overall, voice in forms of strikes and protests have not been able to influence governments' stance on further liberalization significantly. Recently societal dissatisfaction has found another outlet. In three of the four Visegrád countries, new or refashioned nationalist-populist parties have asserted themselves in the political scene, promising encompassing social protection – and partly even sticking to these promises, once in power (Meardi, 2006).[8] The rise of these parties, paradoxically, is as much due to extreme voice as it is to increased silence by those who are not any longer willing to vote for established parties, but out of loyalty consideration prefer not to vote rather than to vote extreme (Greskovits, 2007). In addition, as pointed out by

Meardi (2007), massive silent exit might paradoxically lead to a reversal of the fortune of those who stayed, silently or otherwise. Especially in Poland and Slovakia emigration has led to severe labour shortages, which might open an opportunity for those scarce workers who stayed to get their voices heard.

All in all, then, Polanyi's observation that while liberalization was planned, the countermovement emerges and acts in a spontaneous way seems to be even more true for contemporary capitalism. Limits to liberalization emerge not as a planned attempt of organized forces who aim to resist the direction of change. Rather, they are the result of partly co-ordinated, but mostly individual strategies and their intended as well as unintended consequences.

Notes

1. Loyalty, which he adds, is not a category that describes strategic behaviour.
2. Although I discuss here only strategies open to the countermovement, the state obviously is exposed strongly to forces of the movement, which reinforces its limited accountability to labour.
3. The following is based on Bohle and Greskovits (2007).
4. This is especially visible in the case of EMU accession, where the Baltic states use most consciously the Exchange Rate Mechanism 2 entry as an international pillar of their policies to lock in macroeconomic stability, and acquire credibility in financial markets (Feldman, 2006).
5. The European Monitoring Centre on Change has built a database on restructuring since 2003. Restructuring is defined as bankruptcy, internal restructuring, business expansion, merger and acquisition, offshoring/delocalization (which I refer to here as relocation, which is the more usual terminology) and outsourcing. The information is gathered from press reviews of newspapers and business press. Only instances of restructuring that pass a certain threshold are registered. See http://www.eurofound.europa.eu/emcc/erm/index.php?template=home, accessed 29 February, 2008).
6. The following is based on DB Research (2004); Sachverständigenrat (2004); EIRO (2006); Jürgens et al. (2006); Stettes (2006).
7. I thank Bela Greskovits who brought this to my attention.
8. An interesting example is the fight between the government and foreign investors in Slovakia over a new labour code. See (http://connect.globeforum.com/news/328069/oxford_analytica_update_monday_april_23_2007.html).

9
The Rise of the Competition State in the Visegrád Four: Internationalization of the State as a Local Project

Jan Drahokoupil

An era of rapid internationalization in Central and Eastern Europe (CEE) came to a close in the mid-2000s. A variety of foreign-led economies emerged in the region in the late 1990s and early 2000s (see Myant, 2003; Greskovits, 2005; Vliegenthart, 2007). State economic strategies in the Visegrád Four (V4)[1] region have converged towards a distinct model of the competition state, aiming at upgrading the industrial base in the region by attracting high-value foreign investors (see Drahokoupil, 2007a, 2007b). The 'outsourcing hotspot' has seemed to cool down as the investors have started to complain about wage increases.[2] Yet Eastern European politics is hotter than ever. Politicians mobilizing by appealing to xenophobic and nationalist sentiments were brought right into the political mainstream and governmental offices. In Poland, the Kaczynski 'terrible twins', as foreign journalists would have it, rediscovered Polish national interests and aggravated relations with both Berlin and Brussels. For Kaczynski's 'pig-headed government', 'liberal traitors who want to allow foreign companies to exploit innocent Poland' became the bogeyman of choice.[3] In Hungary, Viktor Orbán, the leader of the Hungarian opposition party Fidesz, rails against 'luxury profits and rapacious foreigners' and calls for 'a national government in Hungary, which sees the world through Hungarian eyes, thinks with a Hungarian mind and senses in its heart a Hungarian beat'.[4] In Slovakia, the nationalistic Movement for a Democratic Slovakia (HZDS) was brought back to government as a minority coalition partner. Finally, the return of the Civic Democratic Party (ODS) to power in the Czech Republic put the Ministry of Industry and Trade, the belly of the beast, firmly in the hands of a major critic of subservience to foreign investors. This led to a major purge in the investment attraction agency CzechInvest.[5]

However, in contrast to the early 1990s, nationalism – as I will argue in this paper – has not provided a major blow to the project of the competition state. What is more, this chapter will show that the externally oriented project of the competition state has solid social bases in the CEE states and beyond. This not only provides strong ground for facing such a challenge, but also makes it less likely that nationalism will succeed. The investors seem to know this. Thus, the business press wonders about the new opportunities of profit extraction based on 'brainpower in the service industries, rather than cheap, nimble fingers in manufacturing'.[6] Exciting dramas of discovery, conquest and eventual incorporation of the region into transnational networks are replaced by mundane challenges of dependent development in the European periphery (analysed by Bohle in Chapter 8). This chapter focuses precisely on these exciting dramas and on the political landscape they gave rise to. It provides an account of the emergence of the externally oriented state strategies, focuses on their political aspects, and identifies political, social and institutional support of the competition state in the V4. I will argue that transnational power blocs organized around a core social group that I call the comprador service sector constitute the political underpinning of the competition state in the region. The hegemony of this domestic social group linked to foreign investors is conditioned on the structural environment, most notably on the form of integration of these economies into globalizing capitalism, and on the institutional and scalar structure of socio-economic governance in the European Union (EU) and within the states. The comprador service sector had a major role in translating structural and external pressures into actual outcomes in the region. It helped to translate the structural power of transnational capital into tactical forms of power that enabled agential power to work in sync with the interests of the multinationals.

The emergence of economies dependent on foreign direct investment (FDI) and FDI-oriented state strategies is far from surprising. What is striking, however, is that internationalization came quite late. The neoliberal rationale that informed transition policies around the region (with the notable exception of Slovenia) and the approach of the West to the region did not render industrial policies to develop endogenous growth potential necessary or desirable. The political economic settings of 'transition' then made pursuit of developmentalist policies particularly difficult (e.g. Amsden, Kochanowicz and Taylor, 1994; Boer-Ashworth, 2000). Indeed, many politicians, policymakers and academics expected FDI and its promotion to play a major developmental and political role in CEE in the 1990s (e.g. Lloyd, 1994; see also Gowan, 1995: 10). Yet the amount of FDI actually attracted by CEE in the early 1990s was very small (Pavlínek, 2004). The V4 states did attract some foreign investment (Sadler and Swain, 1994); nevertheless, with the exception of Hungary and isolated, though important, cases such as the acquisition of Škoda by Volkswagen in the Czech Republic, the FDI inflow into CEE was too small to speed up or deepen industrial restructuring (Pavlínek, 1998) or to have a significant impact on the social structures and politics in the region. What is more, in stark contrast to the globalist spirit of the time, the states in CEE pursued distinct national, inward-oriented strategies in most of the 1990s. Very often explicitly avoiding FDI, CEE states aimed at producing national capitalism and national capitalists. Hungary, of course, was an important exception in this respect (see Drahokoupil, 2007b).

In the process of state internationalization, crucial institutions of the state apparatus become subordinated to the needs and requirements of the global economy (Cox, 1992). The state thus becomes 'increasingly oriented towards facilitating capital accumulation for the most internationalized investors, regardless of their nationality' (Glassman, 1999: 673). I argue that the structural power of transnational capital and integration into the EU had major roles in steering the state in the competitive direction in the V4. The emergence of the competition state, however, cannot be understood without taking account of the agency of domestic social forces. Such forces must come to the forefront if 'structural conditions' or 'structural power' are meant to actually work; they cannot do without. The emergence of the externally oriented competition states has been conditioned on the unfolding hegemonic role of what I call the comprador service sector. The comprador service sector became a nodal point of a wide coalition of forces supporting the competition state. These power blocs did not replace the supporters of the national strategies; the latter were rather transformed and integrated into the transnational coalition of forces underpinning the competition states in the region.

Existing scholarship offers a number of insights to understand the question of convergence in the V4. The debate on the relative importance of internal and external determinations is particularly important in this context. On the one hand, there is a group of scholars emphasizing homogenizing pressures and convergence of state strategies and institutions (Strange, 1996; Cerny, 1997; Jessop, 2002; Van Apeldoorn, 2002). On the other hand, there is an immense body of literature putting emphasis on divergence of outcomes in adapting to manifold and uneven globalization processes (Hall and Soskice, 2001b; Weiss, 2003; Hay, 2004). In the context of the scholarship on the transformations in CEE, institutionalist 'transitology' has attributed analytic primacy to internal determination of post-communist transformation (see Bohle, 2000). By implication, this argument leads us to expect divergence of state transformation. This literature has been later criticized by neo-Gramscian scholars who emphasized the centrality of the global context of transition, underscored its external determination, and pointed to the FDI-dependence it gave rise to (Holman, 1998, 2004b; Van der Pijl, 2001b; Bohle, 2002; Shields, 2003, 2004a).

The moment of convergence towards FDI-dependent social formations provides empirical support to the neo-Gramscian accounts. However, its form and timing does not. By focusing on structural factors and agency of 'external actors', such as transnational capital fractions and the European Commission, the neo-Gramscian accounts have under-estimated the importance of internally oriented projects throughout the 1990s. One could argue that a 'Neo-Gramscian Account Plus', emphasizing external determination, could solve the puzzle of 'belated' emergence of the competition state.

Accordingly, it may be argued that the hyper-globalist discourse of the early 1990s did not reflect real pressures and determinations. Transition strategies reflected what the 'international community' was actually interested in and was capable of achieving, and what the structure of the international political-economy environment allowed for. Thus, the macroeconomic transition policies of the early 1990s followed the developmental panacea of the Washington Consensus (liberalization, stabilization and deregulation). As far as the approach to FDI was concerned, in the context of the economic downturn of the early 1990s, international investors were actually not that interested in investing in the region, or preferred low-involvement strategies. Moreover, in the case of Hungary with substantial FDI penetration and external dependence through debt to private lenders, the investors and international organizations did exert pressure and Hungary indeed followed the externally oriented path. The situation changed in the late 1990s when the international investors became increasingly interested in high-commitment engagement in the region. At the same time, the CEE states were exposed to hard policy constraints in the process of EU enlargement. Thus, FDI-friendly policies could easily be transferred into the region.

However, the Czech case shows that the internal orientation of the early 1990s did not reflect a general lack of interest on the side of foreign investors: the latter were interested in taking over the commanding heights of Czech economy; Czechs, however, turned most of these would-be strategic investors down. On a general level, two most important factors explaining the emergence of externally oriented strategies, neoliberal incorporation of the region into global–European capitalism – what Gowan called the 'American approach' – and an active approach of transnational investors, were present already in the early 1990s. They were translated into actual outcomes only later. I argue that domestic politics played a crucial role in this process. Domestic politics, however, cannot be understood as completely internally determined. I argue that it must be treated as an instantiation of locally materializing transnational processes. This materialization, however, can be reduced neither to an external determination providing just limits and opportunities, nor to the external imposition or coercion itself. Transnationally constituted domestic politics explains both the initial inward-oriented outcomes and later shifts toward the competition state. Thus, while acknowledging local constraints and agency, my argument confirms the importance of the global environment. However, neither the external or internal approach alone, nor their additive combination, provides a satisfactory understanding of the process in which state strategies adapt to the environment in general, and of the moment of convergence in the V4 in particular. In order to understand the global production of local outcomes, we need a relational understanding of the economic policy-making process as part of the reproduction, reconstitution and transformation of hegemony on the regional, national and global scales.

While even the Neo-Gramscian Account Plus does not provide an adequate understanding of transformations in the region, the neo-Gramscian
accounts did grasp many important factors that were ignored by other
approaches. Moreover, (neo-)Gramscian scholarship in general does provide
the conceptual and theoretical apparatus for the relational understanding of
politics I am calling for. I discuss these accounts of CEE developments and
internationalization of the state in the section that follows. Then, I discuss
the emergence of the internally oriented strategies in the V4. In order to
identify the operation of the main mechanisms of state internationalization,
I examine the policy U-turn in the Czech Republic. Finally, I analyse political and institutional underpinnings of the competition state in the region.

I put the Czech case at the centre of my comparative analysis. First, the
Czech Republic actually started the race for greenfield investors in the V4. Its
1999 rolling out of the most generous investment scheme yet seen among
transition countries was followed by the reinvention of the investment scheme
in Hungary and by the introduction of schemes in Poland and Slovakia
(UNCTAD, 2002; Mallya, Kukulka and Jensen, 2004). Second, like Slovakia, the
Czech Republic is an extreme case of discontinuity in state strategy. It at once
experienced a U-turn in which the dominance of the national, internally
oriented strategy was replaced by the hegemony of the externally oriented
competition state. The extremely uneven process of convergence makes the
mechanisms of divergence/convergence and reproduction/transformation
more directly accessible; thus, it allows for exemplifying the theory (Eisenhardt,
1989; Yin, 1989). Third, unlike Slovakia and Poland, the Czech case provides
the opportunity to understand fully the dialectics of external and internal
determination. Foreign investors did show serious interest in high-commitment involvement in the industrial core of the Czech economy. Yet most of
them were turned down by Czech policy-makers.

Neo-Gramscian approaches go east: internationalization of the state in CEE

The post-communist transition was part and parcel of neoliberal globalization. Neo-Gramscian approaches connected the development in the region
to this historical process, dominant social structures and the global political economy. They identified three major implications of the prominence
of global neoliberalism on the world scale for transformations in CEE.
First, the neoliberal design of transition promoted a 'colonial mode of
development' and a peripheral mode of integration of the region into the
international division of labour (Boer-Ashworth, 2000; Bohle, 2006). The
'international community', represented by policies of the USA and the EU,
took the 'American approach' (Gowan, 1995, 1996; see also Van der Pijl,
2006a: 237–47). It promoted abolishment of economic ties between the CEE
states and the USSR and absorption of the region into the Western sphere

through liberalization of trade and investment. Trade with the West was to compensate for the collapse of demand after the abolishment of the Council for Mutual Economic Assistance (Comecon or CMEA). As a result, regional economic relations would be based on the hub-and-spokes structure between the West and CEE, so that each state in the region would relate to the others principally via its relationship with the Western hub. Since higher-value-added goods of CEE producers were not competitive on Western markets, the 'American strategy' effectively destroyed the potential of these sectors and encouraged specialization in labour-intensive, low-tech industries. The structural position of CEE states minimized policy autonomy of national governments and led to competition for subcontracting arrangements with and direct investment by foreign investors. It forced the states to adopt FDI-friendly policies and put downward pressure on wages and taxation (Holman, 2004b). At the beginning of the 1990s, foreign investors pursued low-commitment strategies in CEE. The region was thus integrated more through subcontracting relations than through FDI. This changed by the mid-1990s, when direct investment by (mainly European) corporations into more complex industries took off. This made the investors more involved in direct political influence through lobbying and bilateral negotiations with the governments in order to promote their interests, and it included watering down labour protection and introduction of favourable tax regimes and tax exemptions (see Bohle and Husz, 2005; Bohle and Greskovits, 2006).

Second, foreign advisors, international financial institutions, and the EU played major roles in shaping domestic regulatory frameworks in CEE. It is widely argued that the aim of the EU's strategy has been to promote neoliberal reform and the influence of European transnational capital (Holman, 1998; Bieler, 2002; Bohle, 2006; Shields, 2004b). The EU pushed CEE towards the neoliberal model 'through a mixture of power and conditionality and the promise of membership' (Bohle, 2006: 70; see also Grabbe, 2006). Promotion of foreign investment in industry and finance was one of its major concerns (Vliegenthart and Horn, 2007).

Third, the international environment was 'internalized' within the CEE states. Policy-makers in CEE did not implement policies only because they were forced or advised to do so; they have often actively promoted strategies that corresponded to the preferences and interests of the EU and of the social forces – such as European transnational capital fractions – acting through it (Shields, 2004a). The new power elites internalized the pre-accession strategy of the European Commission (Holman, 2001: 178). The process of transnational class formation incorporating the new power elites was a major vehicle of internalization. The new elites within CEE became integrated, even if in a junior position, into the wider transnational capitalist class, which constitutes an organic base for recent restructuring of capitalism on the global scale (Holman, 2001; Shields, 2004a; Bohle, 2006). Neo-Gramscian scholars put considerable emphasis on the implication of the apparent lack of domestic societal actors, including capital and labour classes (Bieler, 2002; Holman, 2004b; Shields, 2004a). Intellectuals and political elites within the states took charge of the reforms. Weak social embeddedness and weakness of transformational states, according to Bohle, made the reformers eager to secure external assistance. They found the dominant ideas particularly attractive as they represented a radical break with the existing socialist regimes (see Szacki, 1995). In the absence of domestic capitalist classes, various social forces linked to foreign capital were found to have prominent roles. These forces could either benefit directly from alliances with investors or depend on the investment decisions of transnational corporations (TNCs). They then operated as a mechanism translating structural dependence on foreign capital into concrete political processes within CEE states (Shields, 2003; Holman, 2004b: 223).

In order to arrive at an appropriate and comprehensive understanding of the histories of particular cases in CEE, I address and attempt to resolve four problematic aspects of neo-Gramscian accounts. First, it is necessary to specify the particular mechanisms of influence of the EU, international organizations and transnational capital. What is more, the processes in which the structural conditions are translated into policy outcomes have to be identified. The actual operation of these mechanisms – such as the hub-and-spokes relationships of CEE with the EU, the situation of catching up, and uneven development – is often black-boxed (see e.g. Shields, 2004a). A closer analysis of mechanisms of direct influence shows that there is a tendency to overestimate the influence of foreign advisors and international organizations. Despite their heavy presence and vivid activity within various state agencies, independent agency of foreign advisers has not been very influential in many cases, especially in the early years of transition (Meaney, 1995: 298; McDermott, 2002: 91; Appel, 2004, Chapter 2).[7] I will show that the EU and other international organizations, such as the World Bank (WB), provided important financial support for the activities of the comprador service sector within the state. This assistance, however, was largely demand-driven and also included support of the internally oriented strategy (see Appel, 2004; Grabbe, 2006).

Second, the process of transnational class formation and its implications have to be unpacked by means of a careful historical exploration. In order to understand the impact of the structural dependence on foreign capital, it is necessary to provide an account of the process of comprador elite formation, interest articulation and its channels of dominance rather than simply assume their existence from structural features, as indicated by FDI statistics (e.g. Van der Pijl, 2001b) or by linking outcomes to interests (e.g. Shields, 2004a). An organic unity of global elites cannot be assumed, but must be established (Drainville, 1994). Transnational class affiliation, indicated by participation in transnational networks or socialization in different fora associated with the class, cannot account for the fact that some CEE elites promoted interests of transnational capital while others did not (as implied in Van der Pijl, 1998; Shields, 2004a). There may be contradicting preferences among the members of the transnational class even in this respect. The members of the transnational class could be found among both supporters of more nationally oriented policies and among foreign-capital-friendly, externally oriented policies.

Third, the interpretations of CEE transformations focusing on external determination tend to throw out the baby with the bathwater – the baby being the transnationally produced *domestic* strategy. For instance, Gowan's (1995, 1996) account does not deal with the counter-factual. Had the international environment been favourable to more socially inclusive, gradual or statist strategies, would it substantially change the position of social actors promoting them in CEE? There are good reasons to surmise that these actors would have lost – for domestic reasons – the struggle with local neoliberals promoting the 'American strategy' anyway. The neo-Gramscian scholars, then, tend to misinterpret the implications of the lack of societal embeddedness on the side of the political elites. Local elites are considered dependent on external projects, and their autonomy in developing hegemonic projects and ideas is under-estimated. Contrary to neo-Gramscian accounts, FDI has not been the only game in town. Local social forces and locally oriented, anti-FDI projects have been very important throughout the region. In fact, the time of 'foreign investors with their comprador allies' – neo-Gramscians' favoured contenders for the new propertied bourgeoisie, from the list compiled by the seminal study of Eyal et al. (1998) – has come only almost a decade after the region had been well integrated into transnational capitalism.

Finally, fourth, the understanding of CEE transformations has to take the diversity of state strategies and political economies in CEE into account. This relates both to different national projects in the early 1990s and to the variety of competition states and economic integration that crystallized later on (as discussed in Bohle's chapter in this volume). The following sections will show that internationalization and transnational class formation was uneven and unfolded differently around the region.

These problems can be resolved by analyzing the transnationally constituted domestic politics in which the state transnationalization unfolds. As insisted by Poulantzas and other students of peripheral internationalization, the internationalization of the state does not mechanically reflect the economic or class transformations. Instead, economic developments and class transformation have to be understood in the context of the continuing central role of the nation state. Due to 'uneven development and the concrete specificity of each social formation', it is the national form that prevails in social struggles, even if the respective actors are international in their essence (Poulantzas, 1974–78: 78). Although the states take charge of the interest of dominant (foreign) capital, the latter does not constitute a social base of a given national formation directly. The interests of foreign capital are articulated within national social forces in the process of international-ization of domestic social forces (Poulantzas, 1974–78: 8, 70–88; see also Cardoso and Faletto, 1970–79; O'Donnell, 1978; Evans, 1982).

State strategies in the early 1990s: promoting domestic accumulation within the neoliberal framework

The reform strategies throughout the V4 have followed the neoliberal doc-trine of macro-economic stabilization, market liberalization and privatiza-tion in the early 1990s. This reflected the 'American strategy' that materialized in the policies of Western European states and the USA towards the region and in the agency of international financial institutions in CEE states. In this environment, however, Slovenia implemented policies that significantly departed from the global policy orthodoxy. She pursued a much more gradualist strategy, including elements of economic and social protectionism (Mencinger, 1996; Stanojevic, 2003; Pezdir, 2006; Lindstrom and Piroska, 2007). Slovenian exceptionalism shows that it was possible and feasible to pursue more protectionist and gradualist strategies. Thus, the explanation of why the rest of the region jumped on the bandwagon of the Washington Consensus has to go beyond the limits and hostility of the international political economy environment.

The political victory of neoliberal reformers was won through domestic struggles for public support in which the external pressures and support did not play a decisive role (see Appel, 2004: Chapter 2). Anti-communism and delegitimation of the Left provided important political advantages to neoliberals over other forces in the V4; this was not the case in Slovenia, which had a long record of relatively successful reforms implemented by the Communist party (Drahokoupil, 2008a; see also Bohle and Greskovits, 2007; Lindstrom and Piroska, 2007). At the same time, neoliberalism, in both the East and the West, was produced transnationally. neoliberal ideas developed in Western centres of ideational production indeed had important influence on intellectual formation of East European reformers, who were well inte-grated into international networks connecting East and West decades before the transition (Bockman and Eyal, 2002). It is possible, as suggested by Greskovits (1998), that the trust begotten from the international networks provided the reformers in CEE some autonomy – within the margins of the Washington Consensus.

The transnationally connected neoliberals had the upper hand in domes-tic politics all around the V4. At the same time, there was a strong drive for promoting domestic accumulation in all four states, including Hungary.[8] Why did the internally oriented policies prevail in the region? And why did Hungary embark on the externally oriented path? Comparison of the Czech

Republic and Hungary can best illuminate this puzzle. In both of these countries, foreign investors were interested in high-commitment involvement; at the same time, state managers controlled enterprises and could have transferred them to foreign investors if desired. The structural setting thus made both internally and externally oriented scenarios possible. This was not the case in Poland and Slovakia. In Poland, foreign investors were lukewarm to getting involved and the enterprises were largely controlled by insiders. In Slovakia, investors were actually not interested in getting involved at all. These cases thus do not allow for isolating the influence of individual factors that shaped the internally oriented outcomes.

The privatization strategy in Hungary was subordinated to the need of obtaining cash to repay its large external debt to private lenders. Hungarian external imbalances then provided great leverage to international financial institutions that backed the externally oriented strategy. Cash-based privatization provided a huge advantage to foreign investors who, in contrast with local subjects, disposed of capital. The 1990 decision of the government against attempting to renegotiate the debt was influenced by the representatives of TNCs already present in Hungary, by the international financial community, and by foreign private banks (Mihályi, 2001: 63–4). Influential Western companies, including Girozentrale, Siemens, Adidas, Volvo, Ikea, Citibank, Societé Génerale and Creditanstalt, had invested in Hungary even before 1990 on the invitation of Hungarian communist officials (Mihályi, 1993; Stark and Bruszt, 1998: 54).[9] The short-term implications of default on the exchange rate would have had negative implications for the profitability of their local operations. Moreover, privatization through restitution could have questioned the legality of these joint ventures.

The FDI-oriented strategy, however, was not just externally imposed. It was largely shaped by the strategy of internationalized segments of Hungarian elites, most notably financial bureaucrats, industrial managers and economists. The international socialization of state bureaucrats, state financial elites in particular, had an important impact on Hungary's way of debt management. Hungary had bee a member of the International Monetary Fund (IMF) since 1982, and its financial cadre was integrated into the respective international networks. The Hungarian Central Bank pushed the government not to renegotiate the debt and – what is more important – its debt management strategy, which switched a large part of the debt to bonds in 1985–91, making any debt renegotiation particularly difficult, if not impossible (see Piroska, 2002). What is more, the Antall government made it quite clear that the privatization strategy explicitly aimed at attracting foreign capital rather than just reflecting debt-related constraints. The foreign-oriented strategy had broad domestic support. First, some of the Hungarian policy-makers were influenced by a theory of industrial development, such as that articulated by Hungarian expatriate economists Béla Balassa and Nicholas Kaldor. Accordingly, a successful export-led strategy was conditioned by integration into international networks of TNCs. Their advice and recommendations were well received among Hungarian experts already in the 1980s (Csaba, 1997).[10] Second, the exposure to foreign markets, investment, licensing contracts, partnerships and joint ventures of the 1980s produced a significant fraction of the Hungarian managerial elite that was open to co-operation with foreign investors (Greskovits, 2000: 131; King, 2001a, 2001b). Economic openness gave rise to the idea that FDI is needed for Hungarian industry to develop; it also made many managers believe that their career prospects would be higher under a foreign owner.[11]

Czech state strategy was shaped in a struggle between two groups within the state. (Other societal actors were politically weak. Moreover, state managers enjoyed considerable autonomy as the state controlled enterprises and its level of indebtedness was low.) The strategies of the two groups of state managers articulated their (class-relevant) long-term visions, beliefs and 'structural literacy' (see Gramsci, 1971: 113), as well as short-term political considerations. Obviously, their strategies quickly became intertwined with interests of societal actors that benefited from them as well as with their immediate material interests. The 'industrialists', on the one hand, advocated a privatization programme that would find strategic owners, foreign investors, for main enterprises.[12] Most notably, Jan Vrba, then Minister of Industry and Trade, believed that only foreign investors could provide access to new technologies, know-how, distribution networks and capital investment. He planned to bring foreign investors to some 30 to 35 enterprises that he identified as the core of the Czech economy.[13] The externally oriented strategy had wider support within the ministries. It came mainly from the 'business elite', bureaucrats linked to enterprise managers, but not from enterprise managers as a social group. The strategy of the industrialists reflected what seemed to be the realistic reading of the only viable industrial policy under the given conditions (Dittert and Kolanda, 1989; Kolanda, 1989; see also Myant, 1993: 166). It is important to underscore that these conditions were not actually 'given', but rather produced through the 'American strategy' on the international level and through neoliberal strategies within CEE.

On the other hand, neoliberal reformers – who were, in contrast to the industrialists, involved in designing the general transition strategy[14] – promoted a hands-off, voucher-based privatization model.[15] The hands-off model was incompatible with FDI entry, which demanded an active approach by the state to secure contractual commitments required by the investors (McDermott, 2002). What is more, the neoliberals did not favour participation of foreign investors and preferred the creation of a domestic capitalist class.[16] Why did they promote the internally oriented project and how could economic nationalism and neoliberalism go together? First, Czech neoliberals believed that Czech enterprises could compete in an open market. Czech economists held an over-optimistic conception of the general level of development and of the competitiveness of leading enterprises (Myant, 2003: 13–14). Czech reformers also preferred domestic outcomes for nationalistic reasons. Second, the internally oriented strategy was politically superior. In the short term, the voucher method became a flagship of the neoliberal project and substantial political capital was invested in it;[17] the internally oriented project was politically convenient as it went in line with popular fear of foreign ownership. In the long term, the voucher method was seen as the best way to secure political support for capitalism: it guaranteed transfer of property with the greatest speed and certainty,[18] it was expected to change the minds of people who had no experience with the market economy,[19] and it was assumed to create a domestic propertied class, which would provide the social underpinnings for capitalism in general and social and material support for political parties of the reformers in particular.[20]

At a news conference in London in June 1991, Vrba offered more than 50 leading Czech companies for sale to foreign investors.[21] Numerous foreign investors were ready to bid for the commanding heights of the Czech economy (Myant, 1999; McDermott, 2002). For instance, Mercedes signed letters of intent to take stakes in two major truck companies, Avia Praha and Liaz, in March 1992.[22] Very unexpectedly, however, foreign capital was sent home with very little to show for its efforts in the Czech Republic. In the end, foreign participation was more the exception than the rule in privatization outcomes. Mercedes, too, withdrew from both Avia and Liaz. The neoliberals won a path-shaping political struggle. They mobilized enterprise managers, who feared losing their positions after a foreign takeover, to support voucher-oriented strategies in individual enterprises (see Appel, 2004, Chapter 6). More importantly, they marginalized industrialists within the state in a political struggle by making use of anti-communist sentiments (Appel and Gould, 2000). Paradoxically, Czech neoliberals, who could become dominant because of political advantages provided by the anti-communist legacies in one of the most conservative state-socialist regimes in the region, would exploit the same legacies to forge their project of promoting national capitalism and the bourgeoisie.

Czech strategy was thus shaped in a conjunctural domestic struggle and reflected concerns of local neoliberals. The strategy prevented rapid internationalization of the commanding heights of the Czech economy. It produced a distinctive economic dynamic, Czech capitalism (Myant, 2003) and created a coalition of reform winners that provided political support to the internally oriented project (see Gould, 2001; Rao and Hirsch, 2003). At the same time, the neoliberal strategy helped to create conditions providing structural advantages to foreign investors that later, when the economic dynamics of Czech capitalism were exhausted, pushed the state strategy in the externally oriented direction. The next section will show how these structural conditions, which were in place throughout the 1990s, were translated into policy outcomes by the end of the decade.

The moment of convergence: towards the competition state

On 29 April 1998 the Czech Republic rolled out the most generous investment scheme yet seen among CEE countries. This ignited a race for greenfield investors in the V4. The Czech policy U-turn was followed by a reinvention of the investment scheme in Hungary and by the introduction of investment schemes in Poland and Slovakia (Gandullia, 2004: 15–16; Jensen, 2006). The Czech case demonstrates, as if under a magnifying glass, the actual operation of the mechanisms of state internationalization in the region.[23]

The Czech investment scheme was unveiled in 1998. Yet, the turning point had already come in 1997 when the government, led by the major figure of Czech neoliberals, Václav Klaus,[24] reconsidered its hostile approach to FDI. As a part of a policy package reacting to an economic crisis caused by an exhaustion of Czech capitalism, the Minister of Industry and Trade was assigned to draft an investment incentive scheme. Moreover, the government decreed to offer investment packages to Intel and General Motors (GM), which were looking for investment sites in Europe at that time. These decisions came literally days before the government's resignation following a political and economic crisis. Thus it was a new caretaker government that approved the investment schemes in April 1998. This gave rise to the false impression that the policy turn was brought about by political change. Instead, the U-turn has to be linked to the structural dependence on foreign capital, which was heightened by the economic failure of Czech capitalism. During negotiations with Intel and GM, the government got a lesson about the falsity of its belief in the country's 'natural comparative advantage' as an investment site.[25] The cogency of investors' arguments was confirmed by past experiences with investment withdrawals after the government did not offer the incentives that investors requested.[26]

The government's realization of the implication of structural power of transnational capital during negotiations with the investors allowed social forces that had been developing the externally oriented project within the state to come to the fore. There was a group within the state that had been actively working on the promotion of FDI. Located at the Ministry of the Industry and Trade, it faced a hostile environment within the state. Nevertheless, it managed to thrive. In November 1992 it founded the foreign investment promotion agency CzechInvest, then the Czech Agency for Foreign Investment. As recalled by Vladimír Dlouhý, then Minister of Industry and Trade, an Irish adviser financed by EU's PHARE programme had a crucial role in persuading Dlouhý of the utility and necessity of having such an agency.[27] The EU's financial support was vital for the agency in the years that followed. EU-financed advisers used the Irish experience to make the case for the existence of the investment promotion agency and helped with its further development. Ireland was perceived as the first European tiger to emerge to transform its position of being semi-peripheral into that of an export-led 'climber' within the international hierarchy (see Smith, 2005). Many within the EU apparatus and in the CEE states saw CEE as Ireland's natural successor. The region was meant to replicate the Celtic tiger experience within the EU.[28] Along with other foreign donors, the EU provided a crucial source of funding that allowed the agency to develop in the hostile environment.[29] Among other factors, foreign tax-payers' money allowed CzechInvest to open a number of foreign offices around the world.

Throughout the 1990s, CzechInvest worked on winning the government's trust, gaining its support and changing the public's perception of foreign investment. It would organize various public-relations activities, invite bureaucrats on study tours, and try to ally crucial officials by placing them on its Steering Committee, which also included representatives of the FDI-related private sector (see MIGA-FIAS, 2005). However, only the 1997 experience with Intel and GM allowed CzechInvest to push through its project of investment incentives.

In order to demonstrate the positive impact of FDI, the agency needed to show quick results. Greenfield projects were found suitable for this purpose. Such investment projects were considered to have great potential for creating good publicity through job creation. Thus CzechInvest focused on attracting greenfield manufacturing investments in electronics as well as automotive and precision engineering. This reflected interest among investors from these sectors in the region in late 1990s. Just one month after the incentives scheme was introduced, CzechInvest reported 111 applicants.[30] CzechInvest's plan was working. The Social Democrats, who came to power in July 1998, could cash in on the wave of greenfield investors and make foreign investment support the flagship of their industrial policy.

In the mid-1990s CzechInvest became the organizer and a nodal point of various interests linked to FDI. Most notably, these included companies providing legal, administrative and other services to foreign investors. In 1996 CzechInvest established the Association for Foreign Investments (AFI) to serve as an official body representing the interests of investors to the government and to link local service providers with foreign investors. Apart from its business function, AFI proved to be an important vehicle for soliciting and channelling investors' concerns to the government, and it helped CzechInvest to finance activities aimed at promoting investment-friendly policies within the state. The establishment of AFI marked an important moment in the formation of the comprador service sector, a social group that plays a major role in the power blocs underpinning the competition state in the region.

The political and institutional support of the competition state: the comprador service sector, its allies, and their structural advantages

The externally oriented policies of the competition state are pursued by CEE governments regardless of ruling party coalitions (Bohle, 2006). The political support of this state strategy goes beyond narrow short-term interests and immediate material concessions, as was largely the case with the national projects of the early 1990s. Support of this strategy transcends party divisions and party politics, even though it occasionally becomes politicized and connected with the party in power, giving rise to a false impression that the competition state is a project of the ruling party rather than a broader hegemonic project. Thus, even the purge at CzechInvest after ODS's comeback mentioned at the beginning has not led to an abandonment or significant change in the externally oriented strategy; the cleanup was essentially about gaining political control over an important body of the state apparatus.[31] The embracing of the competition state has to be related to the structural environment – material, institutional and ideational – that produces a field of force that not only provides constraints on possible strategies, but also makes the externally oriented strategy a 'comprehensive programme' for societies in the region. The actual policy outcomes, however, have to be understood as products of the agency of particular social forces mediated through structures of representation.

In particular, the competition state is promoted by a power bloc centred around the multinational investors and organized by the comprador service sector. The power blocs underpinning the competition state incorporated significant fractions of domestic capital and labour. Large companies in particular were becoming increasingly integrated into the supply chains of international investors. Thus these comprador power blocs in the V4 did not so much replace the supporters of the national strategies. The latter were gradually transformed and integrated into the transnational coalition of forces underpinning the competition states. While the comprador service sector emerged across the V4, its composition and the importance of individual groups within it vary by country. The comprador service sector is particularly integrated in the Czech Republic and Hungary. In Hungary, the American Chamber of Commerce in Hungary (AmCham Hungary) – along with organizations like the Hungarian European Business Council (HEBC),[32] the Joint Venture Association (JVA),[33] British Chamber of Commerce in Hungary and German–Hungarian Chamber of Industry and Commerce – constitutes the core of the comprador service sector. In Poland, the comprador service sector is more fragmented and organized by region. The Czech case, where the state fraction of the sector had a major political role in the policy U-turn, is exceptional. The importance and consolidation of the state fraction in the Czech Republic can be explained by the necessity of a concerted action in order to be able to deliver some service for the investors within the state, and also by the need to push for a more favourable policy to FDI in an environment that was particularly hostile to such efforts in the political sphere, while, at the same time, being ripe with FDI opportunities in the sphere of accumulation. Given the lack of domestic factors that would hinder or mute the effects of structural factors pushing the states into the competitive direction, there was no such need for a concerted effort and political action by the domestic groups liked to FDI elsewhere.

The literature on (FDI-)dependent development has emphasized the crucial role of domestic actors in the political coalitions underpinning the externally oriented projects (O'Donnell, 1978; Evans, 1979). In the discussion of earlier 'transitions' in Europe incorporating the southern periphery into the European core, Poulantzas identified comprador bourgeoisie as being the dominant class in the peripheral social formations. Comprador bourgeoisie is 'that fraction whose interests are entirely subordinated to those of foreign capital, and which functions as a kind of staging-post and direct intermediary for the implantation and reproduction of foreign capital' (Poulantzas, 1976: 42; see also Baran, 1957). According to Holman, the new power elites in CEE are not propertied comprador bourgeoisie, but managerial and administrative elites with the same position and function as that of Poulantzas' comprador bourgeoisie (Holman, 2004b: 223). I characterize this group as the comprador *service sector*. It is not possible to speak about bourgeoisie, as the comprador service sector is neither a propertied class nor a professional managerial class whose interests are linked to that of company owners. Structurally, the comprador service sector is much closer to what Van der Pijl characterizes as 'cadre' (Van der Pijl, 2004). Yet, recent trends, most notably the emergence of regional developers such as the IPEC Group,[34] indicate the processes of embourgeoisement within this sector. Functionally, this group is *comprador* as it is structurally dependent on transnational capital, whose interests it represents.[35]

The comprador service sector is a nodal point and organizer of transnational power blocs underpinning the competition states in the V4. It represents the interests of multinationals in the region. The comprador service sector had a major role in translating the structural power of multinational into the tactical forms of power. Tactical power refers to the ability to control settings of interaction, or the respective field of force. It enables structural power to work in sync with its agential counterpart (Wolf, 1990).[36] The notion of tactical power introduces an intermediate level between the structural and agential faces of power. Tactical manoeuvring required the multinationals to make alliances with and hire local brokers. In this process of translation, transnational capital became embroiled with local actors embedded in different language jurisdictions, and the comprador service sector became the major organizer of the power bloc centred around the multinational capital. The comprador service sector is constituted by various service providers to FDI in both the public and private sectors. This group includes state officials from FDI-related bodies, local branches of global consulting and legal advisory service firms and their local competitors, and companies providing other services to foreign investors. Such networks of state bureaucrats and the private service sector can be observed across the V4 (see OECD, 2000; Shields, 2003: 236; Drahokoupil, 2008a).[37]

State and corporate fractions of the comprador service sector are linked by the common interest of promoting FDI. They are integrated through personal links, institutional channels, material benefits and recruiting patterns. The externally oriented project provides above-average contracts for the comprador service sector and great potential of material benefits in the form of various commissions and fees for its state fraction. Mutual co-operation allows for more efficient promotion of the externally oriented project within the state, attraction of investors to the respective states and channelling material benefits within the comprador service networks.

The main protagonists would switch from working for the government to jobs in consulting agencies, developers or law offices, and often back. For instance, Jan A. Havelka, founder of CzechInvest, left CzechInvest in 1999 to become the director of corporate and government relations at the Prague office of the global law firm White & Case. While working for White & Case, he chaired the AFI. In 2005 he became a crisis manager of the Slovakian investment promotion agency SARIO and an external adviser to the Ukrainian Center for Foreign Investment Promotion. Quitting White & Case, Havelka took the post of director of international project management and property development corporation IPEC-CZ, which develops industrial sites for foreign investors. A similar phenomenon can be observed in Hungary, where some of the top policy-makers would rotate between public offices and jobs in multinationals, banks and international financial organizations (Greskovits, 1998: 47). Further, recruitment patterns are important mechanisms for comprador service sector integration. In the Czech Republic, a position in CzechInvest, followed by one for a corporate service provider or directly with a multinational, often served as two logical steps on professionals' career ladders, especially for recent graduates.[38]

The state and corporate fractions developed a number of institutional channels and fora for co-operation. The comprador services sector formed networking and lobbying organizations such as AFI. Foreign chambers of commerce, most notably AmCham, constitute major institutional platforms of the comprador service sector in Hungary, Poland and Slovakia. The state-corporate linkages are often organized by including private-sector representatives in supervisory-board structures of investment promotion agencies (McMenamin and Hill, 2004).

Although the comprador service sector serves as a nodal point and organizer of the power bloc underpinning the competition state, the multinational corporations investing in the CEE region represent its main productive element or material base. The structural power of transnational investors was crucial in pushing the states to embark on externally oriented strategies in the late 1990s; however, the actual political agency within the state was left to the comprador service sector. Yet the multinationals do not leave the political agency to the comprador service sector any more. After committing themselves to longer-term activities, such as cost-cutting, efficiency-oriented investment and investment into finance, foreign investors proved to be active in promoting their interests through direct agency (see Bohle and Husz, 2005). They would use various channels of influence – including those created by the comprador service sector, their own business organizations (most notably AmCham), direct negotiations with the government officials and corruption.

Structural dependence on foreign investors, the European regulatory framework and scalar organization of governance are the main structural features that gave rise to the power bloc led by the comprador service sector and provide its externally oriented project with important strategic advantages. Obviously, the influence of foreign investors through agency cannot be seen in isolation from the structural power they continue to exert and make use of. The dramas of bidding for investments keep the state officials involved busy and continue to entertain newspaper readers in the region. After the investment decision is made, the multinationals employ the threat of exit in their negotiations with the governments.[39] European competition regulation could mitigate the competition race through direct subsidies. Yet the impact of the EU's regulation has been much more significant in preventing attempts to promote national accumulation.[40] Finally, rescaling within the states, shifting power to regional bodies, has provided significant advantages to the externally oriented project. It strengthens the representation of actors who are directly exposed to the structural power of capital within the state (Drahokoupil, 2008b).

Conclusion

The neoliberal transition of the early 1990s, a joint project of the 'American strategy' of the West and Eastern European reformers, installed political-economic structures that made the exigencies of global accumulation a political prerequisite for national strategies in the region. Most notably, the peripheral mode of integration made CEE states structurally dependent on foreign capital. These structural exigencies were translated into political outcomes only by the end of the 1990s. Throughout the 1990s, state strategies were relatively hostile to FDI and focused on promoting domestic accumulation. This chapter points to the partial, hesitant and fragmentary nature of neoliberalism. In the Czech Republic, the strategy that was hostile to foreign investors was embraced by neoliberals and became dominant for conjunctural reasons. 'As a political reality, neoliberalism is *both* a broad strategy of restructuring *and* a succession of negotiated settlements, of concessions to the rigidities and dynamics of structures, well as the political possibilities of the moment' (Drainville, 1994: 116, emphasis in original). Establishing the relationship between this broad restructuring and negotiated settlements within national social formations requires a historical exploration.

The Hungarian case showed that the process of transnational class formation and elite socialization did play a major role in putting the country on the externally oriented path. Yet, as the contrasting trajectories of Slovenia and Hungary – the countries that were most internationalized by 1990 – demonstrate, the high degree of transnational integration cannot predict outcomes. The interests and capabilities of domestic allies of the transnational class and/or connected cadres – as well as their structural literacy – are relatively contingent on the domestic context. Internationalization of the state was forged in transnationally constituted domestic politics. The externally oriented strategies were implemented only when both the structural opportunities and the political possibilities of the moment allowed the domestic groups linked to transnational capital to come to the fore in individual social formations.

The eventual convergence towards the competition state in the V4 underscores the importance of the structural constraints. Yet again, the comparison with Slovenia shows that the outcome was relatively open. While the Visegrád states converged towards what I call the Porterian competition state, aiming at upgrading the industrial basis by attracting high-value foreign investors (Drahokoupil, 2007a, 2008a), Slovenia developed a distinctive model of the competition state, putting more emphasis on promoting the competitiveness of domestic capital and on social inclusion (see Bohle and Greskovits, 2007). The Slovenian deviation from the neoliberal strategy, along with its favourable legacies, produced structural preconditions allowing for a different model in the same international political-economic context.

The competition state has solid political, institutional and structural underpinnings within the V4. Politically, it is supported by power blocs organized by the comprador service sector. Institutionally, the EU regulatory framework locks in the state strategies in the direction of competition. Structurally, foreign-led economies have crystallized in the region, with foreign control of leading export industries and most of the public utilities, and unprecedented levels of foreign dominance in the banking sector. The competition state is thus an organic strategy that reflects structural opportunities and constraints. Yet its hegemony is far from unchallenged. Resistance to the competition state comes from small domestic companies that cannot receive investment incentives and do not directly benefit from the presence of multi-nationals. The externally oriented project is also challenged by 'principled NGOs' who object to it primarily on the grounds of environmental damage and human rights violations that the attraction of investment and the operations of multinationals often involve (Drahokoupil, 2005, 2008b). However, occasional moments of resistance do not represent a counter-hegemonic challenge to the competition state.

Notes

1. The Visegrád Four comprises the Czech Republic, Slovakia, Hungary and Poland.
2. 'Outsourcing Hotspot Cools as Wages Rise in Poland', *Deutsche Welle World*, 9 April 2007 (http://www.dw-world.de/dw/article/0,2144,2432641,00.html).
3. Hilary Davies, 'Poland's Terrible Twins', *Prospect Online*, 134 (http://www.prospect-magazine.co.uk/article_details.php?id=8658); 'Turning the Loose Screw', *The Economist*, 382, 17 February 2007, 52. The government was removed from power in November 2007.
4. 'Sense and Nonsense', *The Economist*, 378/8472, 4 August 2006, 50.
5. Jan Drahokoupil, 'Is CzechInvest Facing Extinction?', *Czech Business Weekly*, 7 May 2007 (http://www.cbw.cz/phprs/2007050702.html).
6. 'Shadows at Europe's Heart', *The Economist*, 12 October 2006; 'Rise of a Powerhouse', *Business Week*, 12 December 2005.
7. Even the frequently quoted study by Meaney (1995) actually tells more about the activities than about the impact of foreign 'experts'. Moreover Meaney, too, claims that many of the advisers' activities were not very effective.
8. See Hanley, King and Janos (2002) for the Hungarian case.
9. These companies, however, had stakes in less than 100 joint ventures and their investment had not exceeded $500 million.
10. Confirmed in interview with György Csáki, Budapest, on 15 November 2007.
11. Confirmed in interviews with Péter ákos Bod, Budapest, on 15 November 2007; and György Csáki, Budapest, on 15 November 2007.
12. The industrialists can be understood as embryonic elements of what then became the comprador service sector.
13. Interview with Jan Vrba, Prague, on 21 October 2005, and interview with Vrba in *Listy*, June 1999 (http://www.blisty.cz/2004/4/29/art17878.html).
14. This group was identified as 'neoliberal' in the struggle for the transition strategy in which they promoted a quick market-based policy. The alternative scenario was the gradual reform promoted by more social-democratically minded reformers (see Orenstein, 2001; Myant, 2003).
15. The voucher model of privatization is a market-mediated quick distribution of enterprise shares to the population at large.
16. Confirmed in a number of interviews with direct participants and observers of the privatization struggle (see Drahokoupil, 2008a: Chapter 3).
17. See, inter alia, Orenstein (2001), Mládek (2002), Appel (2004) and Drahokoupil (2008a).
18. Interview with Dušan Tríska in *Respekt*, 45/91, 11 November 1991, 9; Klaus and Tríska (1994, in Appel, 2004: 113).
19. Interview with Karel Dyba, Minister of Economic Policy and Development 1990–2, and Minister of Economics 1992–6, Prague, 21 November 2005. See also Kupka (1992).

20. Speech by Klaus at G30 conference in Vienna on 24 April 1993, 'The Czech Republic's Prospects', published in *Telegraf*, 4 May 1993, cited in Appel (2004: 161); interview with Martin Fassmann, Prague, on 26 October 2005.
21. 'Czechs Head West to Pitch Privatization of Industries', *Washington Post*, 14 June 1991, a23.
22. See 'Mercedes Looks Toward Eastern Europe', *Wall Street Journal*, 9 March 1992, A9B.
23. For further empirical evidence supporting the argument of this section and the one that follows, see Drahokoupil (2008a).
24. A member of the Mont Pelerin Society, Klaus was one of the people who were most strongly integrated into transnational class networks. Paradoxically, the political strategy of Klaus and his peers prevented early internationalization of the state in the Czech Republic.
25. Interviews with Jan A. Havelka, CzechInvest's founder and CEO in 1993–9, Prague, 30 December 2005; Radomil Novák, CzechInvest's adviser to CEO and director in 2004; C. A. Campbell, 29 March 2006; Martin Kavka of the Ministry of Industry and Trade, Prague, 21 November 2005; Martin Jahn, CEO of CzechInvest in 1999–2004, now on the Board of Directors of Škoda-Volkswagen; and Mladá Boleslav, 13 March 2006.
26. Interview with Petr Hájek, then of CzechInvest, Prague, 19 December 2005.
27. Dlouhý's contribution in CzechInvest (2002: 8–10).
28. Confirmed by the experience of officials at a regional development agency in the Czech Republic (various interviews).
29. Interview with Jan Havelka, see note xxv; see MIGA-FIAS (2005).
30. 'Investiční Pobídky Rychle Zabraly [Investment Incentives Work Quickly]', *Hospodárské Noviny*, 29 May 1998.
31. Jan Drahokoupil, 'Is CzechInvest Facing Extinction?'
32. The Hungarian European Business Council (HEBC) was established in 1998 on the initiative of the ERT. It is the business council of the chairmen and CEOs of Hungarian affiliates of ERT enterprises, significant investors of the Hungarian economy such as ABB, Akzo Nobel, BAT, BT, Electrabel, Electrolux, Ericsson, MOL, Nestlé, OMV, Philips, SAP, Suez Environnement and Unilever.
33. Established already in 1986, the JVA aims to 'represent, protect and exert by all legal means the specific interests of partly or wholly foreign-owned companies registered in Hungary' (The JVA's mission statement, available at http://www.jointventure.hu/index.php?cat=intro&lang=en). Its 400-member base includes ABB, Alstrom, Flextronics, Nokia Hungary, Deloitte and PricewaterhouseCoopers.
34. See www.ipec-group.com.
35. Martin Jahn of CzechInvest made quite clear what the role of the agency was. In 1996 he wrote, 'one could get the impression that our agency discriminates against Czech companies. However, our agency represents primarily the interests of foreign investors . . . [In addition, CzechInvest] is the National Contact Centre of the OECD that conveys the demands of the multinationals to Czech authorities' (M. Jahn, 'Investment Produces Higher Competition', *Mladá fronta Dnes*, 8 March 1996, 13).
36. Wolf's notion of tactical power largely corresponds to the agenda-setting face of power as conceptualized by the faces of power debate in political science (see Hay, 2002: 174–8).
37. These networks are more decentralized in Poland, where regional authorities and their investment promotion bodies have more autonomous roles (Capik, 2007).

38. See MIGA-FAIS (2005). Interviews with Martin Kafka, Head of the Investment Support Unit, Ministry of Industry and Trade, Prague, 21 November 2005; Petr Hájek, Prague, 19 December 2005.
39. For example Bohle and Husz (2005), 'Audi Halts Hungarian Investments On New Tax', *BBJ online*, 20 October 2006 (http://www.bbj.hu/news/news_18103.html).
40. For example 'Warsaw–EU Clash Over Stock Exchange Sale', *FT.com*, 14 February 2007.

Part IV Contesting Neoliberal Governance: Resisting Restructuring in National and Transnational Arenas

10
A National Case-Study of Embedded Neoliberalism and its Limits: The Dutch Political Economy and the 'No' to the European Constitution

Bastiaan van Apeldoorn

Introduction

When the Dutch, with an unexpectedly large majority, voted 'Nee' to the European Constitution, it became apparent that even in the traditionally pro-European Netherlands the project of European integration had entered into a serious legitimacy crisis. Many were quick to proclaim that the resounding 'No' vote to a large extent reflected several socio-cultural anxieties over European issues – such as a possible future accession of Turkey – that had little to do with the Constitution as such. Too little attention, however, has so far been paid to underlying socio-economic concerns that may be seen as indicative of an erosion of legitimacy of the output of socio-economic governance at both the national and European Union (EU) levels.[1] In other words, the No vote may have been a manifestation of the legitimacy crisis of embedded neoliberalism as analysed in Chapter 1 of this volume. Whereas the latter chapter analysed the nature, contradictions and limits of this transnational project at the EU level, this chapter takes the Netherlands as a national case study of embedded neoliberalism. Here, I maintain that the rejection of the European Constitution may in part be seen as a manifestation of the failure of this hegemonic project in terms of sustaining the necessary levels of mass legitimacy. The main purpose of this chapter is thus to gain deeper insights into how the contradictions of embedded neoliberalism unfold in a national context. This in turn will help us to understand the limits of the European project as a whole and its likely future *transnational* dynamics.

This chapter is divided into two parts. The first part will analyse the construction and contradictions of embedded neoliberalism in the Netherlands. After examining the origins of the Dutch neoliberal project and its subsequent consolidation in the 1990s, I will argue that what in the 1990s came to be known as the Dutch model (or *polder model*) showed the same contradictions and limits identified with respect to the European embedded neoliberal project (see Chapter 1). In particular, I claim that the Dutch model was in the end much less successful in combining competitiveness with social cohesion than the 'Third Way' discourse at the time made it out to be. In fact, it was neither that competitive nor that socially cohesive, as elements of national embeddedness such as the welfare state were gradually hollowed out within the context of a supranational single market and single currency.

The second part will examine the implications of these limits of the Dutch 'national competitiveness strategy' for the legitimacy of this strategy and of the European socio-economic governance of which it is part and parcel. The focus here is on what I call the political economy of the Dutch 'No' in the referendum. Although the neoliberal nature of European governance was not very well articulated in the public discourse underpinning the referendum debate, the rejection of the Constitution was still a rejection of a treaty that would have further constitutionalized neoliberalism (as argued in Chapter 1 of this volume). The claim I advance here is that it was within the context of the output failure of embedded neoliberalism – the increasingly apparent hollowness of its 'embeddedness', that the 'No camp' could mobilize and activate a latent Euroscepticism among the electorate. Similar to the French 'Non', then, the Dutch referendum result may be seen as an expression of a deeper *multi-level* and *transnational* legitimacy crisis of the European Union (EU), bound up with the political limits of the current integration project as such.

The rise and fall of the Dutch model in European perspective: the limits of 'embedded neoliberalism' re-visited

In the post-war era, the Dutch political economy became firmly anchored in the European integration process, with consecutive Dutch governments consistently favouring a supranational deepening of the European project (see Koch, 2001; Sie Dhian Ho, 2001). At the same time the 'old trade' model (Tsoukalis, 1993: 99) to which European economic integration was initially limited provided ample policy autonomy for the Dutch state to develop and maintain its own distinct welfare state and pursue its own market-correcting and industrial policies. As shown in Chapter 1 of this book, this particular 'corporate-liberal' (Van der Pijl, 1984) configuration of social and political forces began to change in the 1980s with the rise of a neoliberal concept of control, initially vying for hegemony with contending neo-mercantilist and social-democratic projects. In this context, the Internal Market programme launched in the mid-1980s was again enthusiastically supported by the Dutch as dominant sections of Dutch capital – what in Chapter 1 of this volume I called the 'Europeanist fraction' – needed a European home market as a base to successfully confront the increasing global competition, and to serve as a 'springboard' for the world market (Van der Klugt, 1988; see also

Van Apeldoorn, 2002: Chapter 4). Indeed, the Dutch electronics giant Philips played a key role in setting the agenda for Europe's relaunching by presenting a detailed plan for a European home market in late 1984 (Dekker, 1985; Van Apeldoorn, 2002: 129).

Although part of Dutch transnational capital thus promoted a neo-mercantilist strategy, emphasizing in particular the need to protect European industry against US and above all Japanese competition (from which Philips suffered heavily) at the *European* level (Van Apeldoorn, 2002: 124–6), at *home* the 1980s also saw the opening gambits of what became a neoliberal reform strategy in line with, and partly ahead of, what became the dominant market liberalization trend in the then European Community. Nevertheless, inasmuch as these reforms were carried out in concert with the so-called social partners, and inasmuch as these reforms had to accommodate strong continental welfarist traditions, Dutch neoliberalism was an *embedded* neoliberalism in the way that I explained in Chapter 1 of this volume. Moving into the 1990s, then, Dutch socio-economic policies proved to fit perfectly within the new European framework of embedded neoliberal governance.

In fact, what came to be known as the Dutch model or *polder model* was held up as a shining example of socio-economic performance within the academic and public EU policy discourse, while also figuring prominently within the 'Third Way' discourse of the late 1990s.[2] The *polder model,* as it gained fame at the end of the last century, was within this setting analysed as a 'Dutch miracle' (Visser and Hemerijck, 1997; see also Delsen, 2002; Spithoven, 2002; Becker, 2005; Woldendorp, 2005) – a miracle consisting of rapid employment growth on the basis of improved competitiveness, while maintaining relatively high levels of social security, including a generous welfare state A miracle moreover accomplished with the active support of the 'social partners' within the framework of the Dutch system of national-level consultation. It has been thus that Martin Rhodes (2001: 184) has singled out the Netherlands as 'the most advanced example of "competitive corporatism"'.

The Dutch model was, in this discourse, made out to represent a successful case of combining enhanced competitiveness while maintaining social cohesion, that is, the 'hegemonic formula' underpinning the Lisbon reform agenda (see my Chapter 1 and the contribution by Sandy Hager in Chapter 5 of this book). It is hence that we can take the Netherlands as a case of what embedded neoliberalism entails in practice at the national level, and thus gain a fuller understanding of embedded neoliberalism as a project of *multi-level* governance. The limited embeddedness of embedded neoliberalism primarily takes place at the national level, that is, within the context of national state-society relations and their associated institutions. It is at the national level that the social cohesion side of the Lisbon twin strategy needs to be effectuated. It is within this context that I will examine below the rise of embedded neoliberalism in the Netherlands, critically assessing its socio-economic performance and its success as a hegemonic project.

The Dutch variety of embedded neoliberalism

The origins of the Dutch variety of neoliberalism lie in the severe profitability crisis hitting Dutch capital in what for the Netherlands became the deepest post-war recession – with the capital share of income rising to an all time low in 1981 (Delsen, 2002: 28) and GDP growth reaching an all time low of *minus* 1.3 per cent in 1982 (OECD, 2006b). In this context, a political space opened up for a rather drastic reorientation of socio-economic policy-making (Visser and Hemerijck, 1997: 99). Of critical importance here was the power shift in Dutch labour relations that became manifest around the same time (Klandermans and Visser, 1995: 15). The recession, and in particular an unemployment rate reaching 11.4 per cent in 1982 (compared with an EU-15 figure of 8.9 per cent (Delsen, 2002: 2), had seriously weakened the trade unions, who were also confronted with a rapid decline in union density – dropping from 37 per cent in 1979 to 25 per cent in 1985 (Klandermans and Visser, 1995: 15). At the same time, parts of Dutch capital, taking the exit option as a way out of the profitability crisis, had since the 1970s started to deepen its transnationalization strategy (Ruigrok and Van Tulder, 1995: 160–2) and thus enhance its power vis-à-vis labour. It was this reconfiguration of Dutch class relations, then, that undermined the post-war class compromise and laid the basis for the Dutch variety of the neoliberal project.

Although critics have disputed the importance of wage moderation for the subsequent 'Dutch miracle' (Becker, 2005), the so-called 'Wassenaar' agreement of 1982, in which the Dutch trade unions for the first time accepted wage restraint as a *sine qua non* for restoring economic growth and employment (Visser and Hemerijck, 1997: 88), here marks the watershed in Dutch labour relations – reflecting the resurgence of capitalist class power. What the Wassenaar accord also implied was that socio-economic restructuring in the Netherlands would take place with the active involvement of organized labour, articulated in the ideology of social partnership. The particular form in which Dutch neoliberalism took shape also had, albeit limited, implications for its content. In order to gain the consent of labour, a radical neoliberalism of the Thatcherite variety was no option. Apart from the shortening of the working week, labour's main 'reward' for its acceptance of wage restraint was that it kept its seat at the table and remained a key player in Dutch socio-economic governance. Furthermore, although income inequality has risen, the Netherlands remain a more egalitarian society than for instance the Anglo-Saxon political economies, and, in spite of increased labour market flexibility, trade unions have managed to hold on to many of their traditional rights and protections, even if pressures for the further erosion of these rights continue.

The Dutch neoliberal offensive and its consolidation in the 1990s

In terms of government policy, the Dutch neoliberal offensive started in 1982 with the new centre-right coalition starting under the slogan of 'more market, less government' (Delsen, 2002: 37). Under the heading of making government finances 'healthy' again, budget austerity was translated into *inter alia* a lowering of several social benefits (ibid.: 23–4). Privatization also became a central plank of national socio-economic policy in this period (Hulsink and Schenk, 1998).[3] After this 'constructive moment' (Overbeek, 1999: 248) of Dutch neoliberalism, neoliberal restructuring deepened and accelerated in the second half of the 1990s, coinciding with the global post-cold war 'moment of consolidation' of the neoliberal project (ibid.: 249). A critical role here has been played by the so-called 'purple coalition', which from 1994 to 2002 brought together the social-democratic ('red') *Partij van de Arbeid* (Dutch Labour Party; PvdA) and the free market liberals of the ('blue') *Volkspartij voor Vrijheid en Democratie* (Dutch Liberal Party; VVD) and of the smaller Democraten 66 (Dutch Liberal 'Reform' Party; D66). Whereas the latter two parties, in particular the VVD, had neoliberalism wired into their ideological DNA, the Dutch labour party still had to undergo a significant shift towards neoliberalism and away from a more classical notion of social democracy. This neoliberalization of Dutch social democracy of course fitted a pan-European, transnational trend, affecting, albeit in different national colours and at varying speeds, all major European social democratic parties. A traditional commitment to social citizenship and de-commodification was replaced by a Third Way discourse emphasizing the responsibilities and duties of the individual and hence the (partial) privatization of risk and the re-commodification of labour (on this see Ryner, 2002: Chapter 1; see also Hager, Chapter 5 in this volume, and Merkel, 2001).

The neoliberal conversion of the Dutch labour party had already set in in the latter half of the 1980s, but was completed in the 1990s under the party leadership of Wim Kok, the then Prime Minister. In 1995 Kok proclaimed that, in what he called 'a liberating experience', the PvdA had now completed the process of breaking the ideological ties with socialism and 'shaking off' its 'ideological feathers'. Invoking an image of crisis and rapid global change, Kok moreover argued that starting in 1989 (when his party came to power again with the Christian-democratic *Christen Democratisch Appèl*; CDA), 'a policy of austere cutbacks and a reorientation of the welfare state' had become 'inevitable' (Kok, 1995). In seeking a new 'social democratic vision', however, differentiating the PvdA from its market-liberal coalition partners, Kok put forward the idea of a necessary and 'active public sector'. Yet, in a discourse reminiscent of that of European governance at the time, he argued that in order to preserve this public sector, it needed to be 'reformed' and 'modernised' (ibid.).

In the government coalition agreement of 1994, outlining the policy programme for the next four years, the then new Dutch government put forward as its 'guiding principle' the 'necessary rebalancing' of collective arrangements and individual responsibility, following the utilitarian notion that 'more incentives can lead to better performances and higher efficiency' (Regeerakkoord, 1994, my translation). This then translates into a programme of flexibilization of the labour market; adaptation of social security in the sense of a significant retrenchment as well as a (partial) privatization and a marketization of some of its pillars; continuing budget austerity and reduction of the tax burden (in particular the lowering of the highest income tax rates) as well as restructuring of the tax base from direct to indirect taxes such as VAT (ibid.; Delsen, 2002: 24). This programme resulted in a significant retrenchment of the public sector with public expenditure declining by slightly over 5 per cent in just four years during the first purple cabinet, to a level of 42.6 per cent (OECD, 1998: 51, 55). The Kok governments also deepened the commitment to the retreat of government in favour of the market, with deregulation and above all the promotion of what the Dutch call *marktwerking* – which more or less translates as promoting the functioning of the market, or marketization – becoming a key concept in the discourse and practice of Dutch socio-economic governance (Delsen, 2002: 37).

The 1990s also witnessed the further opening of the Dutch market for corporate control to foreign institutional investors and a concomitant marketization of this control (Van Apeldoorn and Horn, 2007b). This changed the traditional Dutch model of corporate governance of managerial control (on the latter see De Jong and Röell, 2005; Gourevitch and Shinn, 2005: 177–87; Heemskerk, 2007: 50–8), buttressed by relatively closed networks of interlocking directorates (Heemskerk, 2007). This national 'corporate community' declined rapidly in the 1990s and virtually disintegrated after the turn of the century (ibid.). At the same time, the influx of foreign, especially Anglo-Saxon, portfolio investors – now making up around 55 per cent of the ownership of firms listed on the Amsterdam stock exchange (Gourevitch and Shinn, 2005: 178) – with a clear financial, short-term perspective, underlines the rise of money capital within Dutch capitalism, reflecting a general trend within European capitalism – that is, the making of a European shareholder capitalism (Van Apeldoorn and Horn, 2007a, 2007b; see also Overbeek et al., 2007).

The contradictions of embedded neoliberalism or why the Dutch model was not so miraculous after all

To what extent have the above policies indeed translated into a 'miraculous' economic performance? Employing standard economic indicators, the performance of the Dutch economy was quite impressive from the late 1980s until the turn of the century. The growth of gross domestic product (GDP) was above the European average, while in a period of 15 years the employment rate went up from 50 per cent to 74 per cent in 2001 (Becker, 2005: 1081; see also Woldendorp, 2005: Chapter 8). Yet after 2001 the trend reversed again. The global economy was hit by a strong recession in the wake of the 9/11 attacks. Yet, like in the early 1980s, the recession was deeper in the Netherlands than the average in the EU-15 – with employment and inflation also rising faster in the Netherlands than in most of the other Member States (OECD, 2006b). The post-2001 downturn clearly signalled the limits of the Dutch model in terms of its socio-economic performance and has led many to question whether the 'Dutch miracle' was really built on a sustainable strategy (see especially Becker, 2005; see for other critical accounts of the Dutch model Delsen, 2002; Spithoven, 2002; Keman, 2003; Woldendorp, 2005). It also raises important questions about the transnational political economy of European integration and the position of the Netherlands within it.

In the dominant explanation of the so-called Dutch miracle in the 1990s, wage restraint, in particular the policy of keeping wages below productivity growth from Wassenaar onwards, was singled out as the key factor (Visser and Hemerijck, 1997; see also Becker, 2005). Another element that has been stressed is the flexibility of the Dutch labour market, although in this account not premised on the deregulated Anglo-Saxon model but combining flexibility with security (Visser and Hemerijck, 1997; see also Remery et al., 2002). Both elements, wage restraint and increased labour flexibility, have been part of negotiated settlements between trade unions, employers and the Dutch government (Visser and Hemerijck, 1997; see also Woldendorp, 2005). Hence these policies have been firmly embedded within Dutch civil society, and as such resting on a broad consensus and a concomitant legitimacy.

The hegemonic view that the Dutch miracle happened because of a 'competitive corporatist' policy of wage restraint is not shared by everyone, however. Uwe Becker (2005) for instance claims that Dutch job growth in the 1990s can be better explained in terms of a big increase in – mainly female and juvenile – part-time employment and a relative decline in the hourly wages of the latter, that is, compared with full-time employment (ibid.: 1086–9).[4] Job growth has thus mainly consisted of the growth of low-paid part-time work. Throughout the 1990s the number of part-time jobs, as well as 'flexible jobs' (fixed-term and temping) rose exponentially whereas the number of full-time jobs virtually stayed the same and its share in total employment declined from 68 per cent to 58 per cent in the period 1987–98 (Delsen, 2002: 41). Rather than a 'jobs machine' (Visser and Hemerijck, 1997), the Dutch model turns out to be about a shift in the nature of employment: from relatively secure full-time jobs, to more precarious, flexible and above all part-time jobs (Becker, 2005; see also Keman, 2003; Woldendorp, 2005). The fact that these new part-time jobs are primarily in the sheltered service sector, rather than in the exposed sectors, would further undermine the claim that it has been enhanced (structural) competitiveness that formed the foundation of the Dutch employment success. Indeed, during much of the period of the Dutch miracle, the performance of the Dutch export sector worsened (Becker, 2005: 1085). Becker therefore concludes that '[t]he Netherlands lost competitiveness during its "miracle" years', this despite the policy of severe wage restraint from the 1980s until 1995 (ibid.: 1094). In terms of labour productivity the Dutch miracle years have not been that wondrous at all – and some would argue that this was actually because of the policy of wage restraint inasmuch as such competition on price (rather than quality) acts as a break on innovation (Kleinknecht and Naastepad, 2002).[5]

Next to the increase in part-time labour, the 'Dutch miracle' also involved significant cutbacks in social security. As Woldendorp concludes: '[T]he Dutch miracle between 1995 and 2000 consisted of a considerable increase in part time participation of women on the labour market, combined with a major retrenchment of the welfare state' (Woldendorp, 2005: 236; see also Keman, 2003). What all of these developments have boiled down to is that overall, even if not reaching the levels of the Anglo-Saxon varieties of capitalism, income and wealth inequality rose significantly in the Netherlands from the 1980s onwards (Delsen, 2002: 69–74).

It turns out that the Dutch model in practice has been far from the successful case of *combining competitiveness with social cohesion* that it has been made out to be. We can observe that the 'embeddedness' of Dutch embedded neoliberalism – which the Dutch state was supposed to provide – was thus increasingly eroded. This erosion is inherent in embedded neoliberalism as a hegemonic project, a project that cannot sustain a genuine embedding of the market as it prioritizes (supranational) market-making policies and the freedom of European and global market forces, over any (national) market-correcting policies (Scharpf, 1999, 2002) and accepts that a transnational neoliberal marketization drive will erode national embeddedness (even if in the shorter run the latter helps to integrate formerly antagonistic social forces into a hegemonic power bloc). Below, then, I will underline the European dimension of the socio-economic governance regime as it had evolved in the Netherlands in the 1990s.

The Dutch model as a national 'supply-side' competitiveness strategy within the context of a supranational market and monetary union

Although, as argued, Dutch embedded neoliberalism clearly also has its specific domestic origins, the subsequent path of its evolution has also been conditioned by the integration into the European framework of a supranational internal market and monetary union. Dutch embedded neoliberalism, then, has to be understood neither as an autonomous national development subsequently shaping European integration nor as simply an outcome of 'top-down' Europeanization (see Cowles et al., 2001), but as a *transnationally constituted* national or local project (on this notion see Chapter 9 in this volume, by Jan Drahokoupil); a transnational constitution in which the EU plays a key role – the transnational here to be seen as taking place at multiple levels *simultaneously* (Van Apeldoorn, 2004a; see also the Introduction to this volume). We must therefore understand how Dutch political and social forces were clearly committed to (and thus helped to constitute) embedded neoliberalism as a European project, while on the other hand their configuration and agency was also to a large extent shaped by it.

With regard to the former, not only did the Dutch government actively support the embedded neoliberal European project (Sie Dhian Ho, 2001), Dutch EU policy in this respect was also well embedded in civil society through Dutch neo-corporatism (ibid.; see also Woldendorp, 2005). Through organizations like the tripartite Social and Economic Council of the Netherlands (SER), not only the Dutch employers associations but, critically, also the Dutch trade unions were firmly tied into a pro-European consensus (see also Pelkmans and Van Kessel, 2006).[6] With regard to the impact of the European project on (the configuration of) Dutch social forces, we can point to how it has empowered neoliberal social forces within the Dutch political economy and thus helped to effectuate a transnationally constituted neoliberal shift within it.

First, the power shift underlying the so-called Dutch model – that is, the weakening of organized labour and the restoration of capitalist class power, as well as a shift within the latter class from industrial to financial capital and from national to transnational capital – is not only a transnational phenomenon that has its roots in global processes of politico-economic restructuring but also one that, in the European context, has been significantly amplified, deepened and institutionalized through the increasingly neoliberal European integration process (see Van Apeldoorn, 2002). The concessions, in particular in the form of wage restraint, that have been made by the Dutch trade unions as part of several national wage deals of which Wassenaar was only the first, were partly made under the (perceived) pressure of rising competition arising both from globalization and Europeanization (Visser and Hemerijck, 1997; Delsen, 2002).

Monetary integration too became a critical factor in restructuring Dutch labour relations, and in shaping the Dutch 'national competitiveness strategy' as premised on a supply-side, 'beggar-thy-neighbour' economic philosophy. This goes back to 1983, when, in the context of the European Monetary System (EMS), the Dutch guilder was pegged to the Deutschmark and monetary policy was in effect set in Frankfurt by the anti-inflationary Bundesbank (Delsen, 2002: 31–4). This amounted to an 'a priori commitment' to monetary austerity as an external constraint on the part of both the

Dutch government and Dutch social partners (De Beus, 2004: 181, 186). With this loss of both the interest rate and the exchange rate instrument as key policy mechanisms of macro-economic adjustment, the burden to adjust came to rest almost entirely on the labour market (ibid.; Delsen, 2002: 34). This made a competitiveness strategy relying mainly on wage restraint as well as on increased labour market flexibility a logical outcome indeed. Although not necessarily, as argued above, translating into any structural improvements in competitiveness, this policy was successful inasmuch as in terms of *relative* prices, that is given the fixed exchange rate with the German Mark, unit labour costs in the Netherlands dropped significantly vis-à-vis its main competitor and export market, Germany (OECD, 1998: 38, 40). The causal mechanism of the external anchor of monetary integration was strengthened from the 1990s onwards with the race to meet the Maastricht convergence criteria and later with the transition to a full monetary union (De Beus, 2004). It was then that aspects of the Dutch supply-side employment strategy became part of a much wider, pan-European phenomenon of social pacts in which labour agreed to carry the burden of adjustment in the face of a rather complete loss of macro-economic policy autonomy (Rhodes, 2001, 2002; Hemerijck, 2002).

With respect to power shifts within the capitalist class, we must note in particular the rise of transnational – Europeanizing and later also increasingly globalizing – capital, as well as of money capital or *rentier* interests vis-à-vis productive capital. With regard to the former, European market integration and monetary union have undoubtedly been a boon to Dutch TNCs such as Philips, Unilever and AKZO-Nobel. Arguably, because of the high degree of transnationalization of these companies (with often up to 90 per cent of their production taking place outside the Netherlands), it is less Dutch society and more the (increasingly foreign) shareholders of these firms that have benefited from this. With regard to the latter, the rise of shareholder capitalism in the Netherlands must of course also be placed in the context of what Van Apeldoorn and Horn (2007b) have identified as the EU's political project of the marketization of corporate control, more broadly enabled by European financial market and monetary integration (ibid.; see also Van Apeldoorn and Horn, 2007a).

Second, the commitment of subsequent Dutch governments since the early 1980s to a programme of privatization, marketization, budget austerity and welfare state retrenchment must not only be understood as national manifestation of a transnational project, but also as ideologically and institutionally reinforced by an emergent European socio-economic governance regime at the supranational level, which can be seen as the EU-level manifestation of this transnational project. Welfare state retrenchment here is a case in point. This too has taken place under the shadow of monetary integration and its competitive austerity (see Cafruny and Ryner, 2007a). If nothing else, the need to reduce the budget deficit to comply with Maastricht helped to legitimate policy choices that arguably were already made. But the role of Economic and Monetary Union (EMU) also went beyond this legitimation function to the extent that, as De Beus (2004: 175) contends, although the Dutch 'trajectory of welfare state reconfiguration had already been set domestically', monetary integration (before and after Maastricht) was nevertheless significant as an external pressure keeping the Dutch policy regime on this path, especially in the latter half of the 1990s (see also OECD, 1998: 51). Next to monetary union, the internal market – and the concomitant regime competition through the enhanced exit power of capital – has also been an important factor in keeping the Dutch government on the path of welfare state retrenchment as well as tax cuts (and a shift in the tax base) that it has followed over the past two decades.

The experiences of the so-called Dutch model may be seen as revealing the limits of national competitiveness strategies within the context of, and partly conditioned by, the EU's asymmetrical socio-economic governance regime, that is, the regime of embedded neoliberalism. As noted in Chapter 1 of this book, (asymmetrical) European economic integration paradoxically fosters an economic nationalism in the sense of national competitiveness strategies that boil down to competition for mobile capital and attempts to shift the burden of adjustment (to the exigencies of European and global competition) on to labour. These strategies not only often fail to raise competitiveness, they also, as I have argued, tend to erode rather than strengthen national social cohesion. The Lisbon promise thus remains unfulfilled. It is partly in this context, then, that we have to understand the growing scepticism in and indeed resistance to the European project within the Netherlands. A resistance that culminated in the massive rejection of the Constitution.

The legitimacy crisis of embedded neoliberalism in the Dutch Polder and the political economy of the 'Nee'

Signs of a weakening pro-European consensus were in fact already visible in the 1990s. In some respects, a more critical attitude could be detected during the 1990s also on the part of the government (Van Keulen, 2004). The main issue through which this transpired was that of the Dutch contribution to the EU budget and the fact that the Netherlands had become the so-called largest net payer per capita (ibid.: 10; Petter and Griffiths, 2005). From the 1990s onwards and into the current decade, the Dutch government time and again publicly complained about this 'unfair' situation (Petter and Griffiths, also Boer, 2005). In this context, the support for European integration on the part of the Dutch political elite became less enthusiastic than was customary in the preceding decades. At the mass level, and partly as a result of this (Petter and Griffiths, 2005), passive consent was also waning.

Arguably, the new Dutch attitude towards the EU as transpired in the 1990s, emphasizing financial costs rather than its benefits, must also be seen in the context of the dominant neoliberal ideology, as particularly (but certainly not exclusively) expressed by the market-liberal VVD (see also Boer, 2005). Paradoxically there tends to be a natural alliance between a particular brand of nationalism and neoliberalism (Streeck, 1996: 305; Hooghe and Marks, 1999; Van Apeldoorn, 2002). Although neoliberals wholeheartedly favour the European project as a project of market liberalization, they are opposed to any European 'state-building' attempt (Ross 1995) that would involve the transfer of other than market-enabling policies to the European level. To this ideological position also belongs a scepticism vis-à-vis a more ambitious federalism as the Dutch government for instance had supported until the Maastricht treaty, and especially vis-à-vis the notion that the EU should have its own budget serving certain redistributive functions. Thus from the 1990s onwards the Dutch government has increasingly sought to put pressure on the EU budget, supporting efforts to make cut-backs in the Common Agricultural Policy (CAP) as well as structural funds (Van Keulen, 2004: 10; Petter and Griffiths, 2005). This serves to underline how the Dutch government has increasingly come to support the European integration project inasmuch as it is primarily a market integration project.

As the primacy of market integration also underpins current EU socio-economic governance in general, with the desire to further trim the European budget also shared by other governments as well as by the Commission, it is perhaps wrong to see this policy as in any sense more eurosceptical, as it is rather about supporting a particular *kind* of Europe. That is, one in which primacy lies on the completion of the internal market and the discipline of monetary union, and where social and employment policies are being relegated to efforts of supply-side policy co-ordination, remaining a competence of the Member States, which are thus facing increasing pressures of regulatory competition in this realm. Another matter, however, is whether consistently hammering home the message that 'we' are paying too much is not feeding into Euroscepticism among the public at large. Although it is impossible to establish causality here, it is noticeable that during the 1990s support for European integration declined more rapidly in the Netherlands than on average in the EU (Netjes, 2004: 6), even if remaining comparatively high. In retrospect, these were 'early warning signs' of a looming legitimacy crisis. Before turning to how this crisis came fully into the open with the 2005 referendum, we should briefly turn to the turbulent political events of 2002 as they will help us understand the prevailing domestic political climate and national mood in the run-up to the vote on the European Constitution.

The discontents of neoliberal restructuring and the populist turn in Dutch politics

In May 2002, the purple coalition that had changed the Dutch political landscape in the 1990s suffered a heavy defeat, with the social-democratic

PvdA losing almost half of their seats in the biggest upset in post-war parliamentary elections. The elections were won by the Christian Democrats and above all by the new party of the far right populist maverick Pim Fortuyn, who had been assassinated weeks before the elections. Although the years of the 'purple coalition' had been marked by a depoliticized climate in which the successes of the *polder model* were celebrated by a power bloc that included both transnational Dutch capital and organized labour, below this elite consensus the end of the 1990s witnessed a 'growing reservoir of discontent' that expressed itself in rising levels of mistrust vis-à-vis political institutions and the political establishment (Bélanger and Aarts, 2006: 16). More substantively, there was a rising discontent with the neoliberal policies of the Kok governments. Concomitant to this, anti-immigrant sentiments, especially in declining inner city areas, were growing and after the attacks of 9/11, ditching multiculturalism in favour of a straight uniculturalism defending 'our culture' against especially the Islam was no longer a taboo (Pellikaan et al., 2003: 36–7).

The growing discontent with over 15 years of neoliberal restructuring was not only related to the retrenchment of the welfare state in a more narrow sense but also to the erosion of the quality of public services (Pellikaan et al., 2003: 36), which after years of privatization, rationalization and marketization had become underfunded as well as paradoxically suffering from heavy bureaucratization as new managers were 'needed' to make the output match quasi-market derived performance targets (with the deterioration of public healthcare high on the lists of popular grievances (Van Praag, 2003: 14–15). Against this background the political entrepreneur Fortuyn could successfully sell his slogan 'the ruins of the purple coalition' (Fortuyn, 2002) – while at the same time skilfully articulating existing worries about a declining public sector with anxieties about immigration and anything foreign in what was an unprecedented Islamophobic and ethno-nationalist discourse (Pels, 2004). In this he was also benefiting from the economic downturn that had set in just around that time and that indicated that the Dutch 'miracle' was indeed over. Although discontent with the neoliberal policies of the 'purple coalition' had become more manifest after the turn of the millennium, the centre-right coalition governments that subsequently assumed power pursued an even more outright neoliberal programme than their predecessors, deepening both privatization (for instance with respect to health care insurance) and welfare state retrenchment (further restricting eligibility and duration of benefits). In the meantime, resistance to these 'reforms' was also growing, with October 2004 witnessing one of the largest (trade-union-led) demonstrations of its kind against the government's socio-economic policies (Kreling, 2004).

The rise of Fortuyn has been interpreted as marking a shift from a 'depoliticized [consensus, BvA] democracy to a centrifugal democracy' (Pellikaan et al., 2003) and as such fits within a larger pan-European pattern of rising populism. More generally, we may interpret the populist turn in Dutch politics (Pennings and Keman, 2003: 64–5) and the 2002 election results in terms of the socio-economic contradictions and subsequent political limits of Dutch embedded neoliberalism, but also as part and parcel of a wider transnational legitimacy crisis of multi-level European governance. Fortuyn not only mobilized discontent against the so-called established political elite in the Netherlands, but also, albeit less prominently, mobilized as well as fuelled growing Eurosceptic sentiments among Dutch voters, claiming that Europe was an elitist, technocratic and fraudulent project that had to be returned to the citizens by creating a union of sovereign states rather than a European super state (Voerman, 2005: 59–60). In this context, it is not surprising that support for European integration declined in the Netherlands, and that in particular voters turned out to be rather sceptical vis-à-vis the alleged need for a European constitution, a constitution for a Europe that, in terms of delivering the public goods that populations had come to expect from their governments (since the post-war era), had increasingly come to be seen as part of the problem rather than as a solution (Scharpf, 1999).

The 2005 turning point: the popular rejection of the Constitutional Treaty

The end to the permissive consensus vis-à-vis the European integration process and the growing Euroscepticism at both the elite and mass levels became visible for all to see when 62 per cent (with an unexpectedly large turn-out of 63 per cent) of Dutch voters rejected the proposed European Constitution on 1 June 2005. Although this resounding 'Nee' came as a shock to the political establishment it was in fact the culmination of some longer structural trends, and indeed can be taken as symptomatic of a deeper legitimacy crisis.

In contrast to France (Storey, 2006; see also Heine, 2006), the public debate in the Netherlands throughout both the 'Yes' and the 'No' campaign leading up to the referendum was rather one-dimensional in the sense that the discourse revolved primarily around the vertical axis (Hooghe and Marks, 1999) of 'more or less Europe' or nationalism (intergovernmental) versus federalism (supranationalism) – excluding a framing along the horizontal left–right axis.[7] In accordance with recent research on the cueing of public opinion by political parties (Edwards et al., 2004; Netjes and Edwards, 2006), parties on the opposing ends (the 'extremes') of the (left–right) political spectrum played a critical role in mobilizing the Dutch 'No' vote. On the right there was the nationalist and xenophobic campaign of (ex-VVD) member of parliament Geert Wilders. In spite of what some had feared beforehand, right-wing nationalists far from dominated the 'No' campaign, and in terms of media exposure Wilders was surpassed by the Socialist Party (SP) in the actual campaign of the final six weeks before the referendum

(Kleinnijenhuis et al., 2005: 134; see also Lucardie, 2005). However, in contrast to what might be the case in other countries, and contrary to what the aforementioned literature on 'party cueing' claims, the SP as an 'extreme left-wing' party did not cue voters primarily on the basis of an opposition to the neoliberal character of the integration project and the latter's (alleged) threat to the welfare state and to jobs (Netjes and Edwards, 2006: 9). Although with respect to the latter, the SP's public discourse did seek to mobilize some feelings of socio-economic insecurity, this was not in any way linked to a fundamental critique of the internal market or the monetary union, and was in any case subordinated to a cueing on the basis of an opposition to an (alleged) further transfer of sovereignty to Brussels, thus tapping into feelings of socio-cultural insecurity. The message here time and again was that with the Constitution the Netherlands would become a 'powerless province of a European super-state'.[8]

All political parties opposing the Constitution were more or less united around the theme of defending the nation-state. In the pro-constitution camp the then centre-right governing coalition as well as the major opposition party, the PvdA, were generally careful to avoid claiming that they favoured 'more Europe', but rather defended the Constitution as a necessary package of institutional reforms making European decision-making more effective and more democratic. Yet, their position was clearly constructed as 'pro-European', especially as the opposition to the Constitutional Treaty was time and again accused of being 'against Europe', and thereby endangering the entire European project on which both peace and Dutch prosperity had always depended (see Lucardie, 2005).

In this discursive setting there was hardly any space for those dissenting voices from civil society that did favour 'another Europe', and did criticize the (socio-economic) content of EU policies, and in that sense sought to go beyond the one-dimensional debate of more versus less Europe.[9] Reinforcing this was the fact that, in line with what had always been the dominant consensus among the elite of the Dutch polder, both social partners were within the 'Yes camp' during the referendum campaign. Although for instance the largest Dutch trade union, the Federatie Nederlandse Vakbeweging (FNV), did not want to give an explicit 'voting advice', its leadership made it clear that it was in favour of the European Constitution and put quite some effort in pointing to its alleged advantages for organized labour.[10] The subsequent landslide victory for the 'No' camp, with an overwhelming majority of their own rank and file having voted No, clearly took the FNV leadership by surprise, and may have served as a warning that it had grown out of touch with its base, at least with regard to European issues. This also showed the limits of a consensus-oriented corporatism in which depoliticization of potentially highly political issues is often the preferred solution (see Pelkmans and Van Kessel, 2006), neutralizing dissenting voices in the short run but arguably not enhancing legitimacy in the longer run. In this respect, the binary framing of the European debate in the Netherlands can also be seen as partly a product of the consensus-oriented way of Dutch EU policy-making, including the role played by Dutch corporatism in creating a rather shallow societal support, and thus effectively keeping the lid on the growing discontent with respect to the EU. The argument here is that once the lid on the discontent is taken off, the politicization then taking place will not be favourable to those supporting European integration. This, then, is precisely what happened with the 2005 referendum. Only with the referendum on the Constitution could Dutch voters express their opinions for the first time, and only *after* the grand intergovernmental bargain had been concluded and signed. In this context, the elitist consensus was about to be derailed by the mass of the population no longer willing to give its 'passive consent' to the European integration project.

The political economy of the Dutch 'No'

The question remains, though, why this consent had apparently broken down. Here I suggest that although, as we have seen, the debate was very much framed along the vertical dimension of more versus less Europe, with concerns about sovereignty dominating much of the 'No' campaign, underlying these issues were also worries about the socio-economic output of both European governance and Dutch governance within it. What follows is not to be taken as suggesting that the Dutch electorate voted against the Constitution either out of a conscious perception of the Constitution as being a neoliberal project (after all, the socio-economic dimension was hardly present in public discourse) nor due to a conscious opposition to neoliberal European governance in general. Rather, the (counterfactual) argument made in this chapter is that we can only make sense of the massive 'No' vote against the Constitution in the context of the contradictions and growing ensuing tensions of Dutch (but transnationally constituted and EU-conditioned) embedded neoliberalism. As the limits of the Dutch model were revealed in the recessionary years of the early 2000s, the limits of the legitimacy of the European project were also reached. The available data indicate that the Dutch voted 'No' for a multitude of reasons but above all because they could no longer identify with this project, the output of which was perceived as a threat to both national identity and national welfare and social security.

The only extensive survey research done on the referendum so far is the one undertaken by Aarts and Van der Kolk (Aarts and Van der Kolk, 2005, 2006; Van der Kolk and Aarts, 2005). According to Aarts and Van der Kolk (2006: 244), the survey shows that Dutch voters were above all concerned with the 'pace and scope' of the integration process, especially with respect to the move to monetary union. This fits the general hypothesis put forward by Hooghe and Marks and others that since the Maastricht Treaty the integration process has become much more *politicized* as it has deepened to such an extent that it intervenes much more directly into people's daily lives and more directly enters into the domestic political arena ('Europeanization'), and that with this politicization contestation of the European project has risen with some political parties and other forces effectively mobilizing against European integration (Hooghe and Marks, 2007a; see also Marks and Steenbergen, 2004; Netjes, 2004; Hooghe and Marks, 2007b; and my Chapter 1 in this volume). Let us now examine more closely the content of this politicization in the Dutch context with regard to the Constitutional Treaty.

First, with regard to the euro, the general perception was that this was the single currency no one had asked for and indeed nobody wanted; it was also consistently held responsible for higher consumer prices in the public discourse. And indeed the survey results of Aarts and Van der Kolk show a 'close association' between negative perceptions about the euro and the 'No' vote in the referendum (Aarts and Van der Kolk, 2006: 243–4). In addition to the pace of deepening, the pace of widening has also led to rising concerns, with citizens in particular expressing worries about the most recent round of enlargement (the 'big bang' of 2004) as well as possible future enlargements, in particular the possible accession of Turkey. Both issues, the 'expensive' euro and possible Turkish membership, figured prominently in the Dutch 'No' campaign in the run up to the referendum (Lucardie, 2005). Negative attitudes about both issues were reinforced by the perception that all of this – monetary union, enlargement, and so on – was the outcome of an elite process about which ordinary voters never had anything to say. It thus reflected a deep gap between the Dutch elite and a majority of the Dutch voters, a gap that according to Aarts and Van der Kolk was not new but was 'fully exposed' for the first time by the referendum instrument, a novelty in Dutch national politics (2006: 243). This might be indicative of a deficit in 'input legitimacy' (on this concept see Scharpf, 1999: 6–13), but at the same time there is evidence that much of the reason why so many voters turned against the Constitution had to do with 'output legitimacy' (ibid.), and that this was also related to the (perceived) socio-economic output of the EU.

In this respect Van der Kolk and Aarts (2005: 206) conclude from their survey that European integration in the Netherlands by the time of the referendum had increasingly come to be perceived as a threat: 'a threat to welfare, a threat to social security and a threat to the national identity'. With respect to the former dimension, they conclude that the Dutch image of the EU has changed from 'one of an institution stimulating international trade for the Dutch open economy [to] an institution costing too much and threatening both our jobs and our social security' (Aarts and Van der Kolk, 2006: 243). In a poll taken shortly after the referendum almost two-thirds of the respondents indicated that that they believed that European integration will *not* increase prosperity whereas 91.7 per cent believed that it will lead to a relocation of production (and thus jobs) out of the Netherlands (ibid.: 245). Even more striking, just before the referendum, 47 per cent of the electorate thought that 'social services' (the welfare state broadly understood) will (probably) disappear due to further integration (Aarts and Van der Kolk, 2005: 177), and 57 per cent expected that Dutch social security would become less extensive if the Constitution were to be adopted (ibid.: 179).[11]

In sum, what the above statistics suggest is that, underlying the more manifest frustrations about the 'rip-off' that many felt EMU was, as well as the sometimes xenophobic worries about enlargement, we find concerns about the social purpose of the current integration process. In particular, the worry that the EU is no longer providing what the legitimacy of the European integration process long rested on, namely a set of institutions and policies supporting national prosperity and welfare, but, on the contrary, helping to undermine these. In other words, Dutch citizens are not only worried about the pace of European integration, but also about its socio-economic content, about the *kind* of Europe that has been, and is being, constructed.

As long as the Dutch economy was still growing relatively fast (especially in the second half of the 1990s) and unemployment remained relatively low, rising negative sentiments about the EU remained relatively subdued. When the socio-economic performance of the Dutch model rapidly deteriorated in the first years of this century, and the effects of the cutbacks made in the welfare state in the preceding decade became more sharply felt by a growing number of people, these negative sentiments increased as well. It was in this context, in which the winners and losers of European integration became more visible, that the referendum was held. Survey data indicate that indeed it was those on the losing side that have voted against the Constitution; those with low education, low income and identifying themselves as working class were all over-represented among the 'No' voters (Van der Kolk and Aarts, 2005: 186).

In sum, the Dutch case has shown how the socio-economic output of the (embedded) neoliberal model of European integration is at least one important source of the growing loss of legitimacy of the European project. Given the fact that a significant majority of Dutch citizens (Van der Kolk and Aarts, 2005: 189) still support EU membership, the conclusion appears justified that the resistance to European governance is not about a rejection of European integration per se but rather of its current particular form and content.

Beyond neoliberal integration?

The latest elections of November 2006 confirmed the earlier noted centrifugal trend with all the major established parties (CDA, PvdA and VVD) losing votes to the new far right and radical anti-Islam party of Wilders (Partij Voor de Vrijheid; PVV), as well as the Socialist Party, which, more than doubling its seats, became almost as big as the PvdA, filling up the ideological vacuum left by the latter as it had abandoned traditional social democracy. In spite of the loss of the PvdA, the Left overall had won slightly. Moreover, the policy manifesto of the new centre-left governing coalition of CDA, PvdA and the small Christian Union to some extent represents a move away from the neoliberalism of the previous governments (Coalitieakkoord, 2007). Indeed, the new government has clearly been affected by the trends analysed above, that is, the rising discontent with the output of Dutch (and hence also European) socio-economic governance. In a remarkably communitarian discourse, the language of marketization (*marktwerking*) has been replaced with an emphasis on solidarity, social cohesion and investment in the quality of public services (ibid.). With regard to Europe, the government has adopted the rhetoric of the SP about the danger of a 'European super-state', pledging that it would not accept a new treaty replacing the Constitutional Treaty that would signal such a move (Ministerie van Buitenlandse Zaken, 2007). Significantly, with regard to the socio-economic dimension, for the first time a notion of limits to the internal market in order to preserve national public services was advanced. In the subsequent intergovernmental bargain Dutch 'demands' in this respect were met, to some extent, by a special protocol annexed to the Lisbon Treaty on 'services of general interest', recognizing their importance, their national diversity, and the 'wide discretion' of state authorities in providing them according to national or local needs and preferences.[12]

At the same time that more social democratic forces are thus seeming to shape the political agenda, a debate has erupted, mirroring that of several other West European states, on the financialization of capitalism, and in particular the spectacular rise of private equity of and activist hedge funds making waves in erstwhile so tranquil Dutch corporate waters.[13] In the wake of several takeovers of Dutch household name corporations by private equity groups as well as several highly publicized battles between Anglo-Saxon hedge funds and the management of other well-known large firms, culminating in the epic takeover battle over Dutch bank ABN AMRO, the choir of critical voices has swelled. These critics include not only trade union leaders (e.g. Tamminga and Wester, 2006), but also, significantly, the president of the Dutch employers' association, who suggested that shareholders might have become too powerful by now (Tamminga, 2007). This, then, is a clear example of rising intra-class tensions and struggles as a result of the ongoing financialization that are, as argued in Chapter 1 of this volume, at the heart of the deepening contradictions of embedded neoliberalism.

Do these developments then mean that we are moving beyond embedded neoliberalism in the sense of witnessing a more substantive (re-)embedding in which the 'principle of social protection' (Polanyi, 1957: 132) would once more trump that of 'economic liberalism'? There are at least two reasons to caution against this conclusion. One is that although the government has changed its discourse and tone, in terms of substance the makeover is less radical. The new government does not intend to reverse any of the neoliberal reforms, whether with regard to privatization, welfare state restructuring or the flexibilization of the labour market, and is in fact planning further advances in some areas. After all, the two main parties of the new government have become ideologically quite wedded to much of the neoliberal paradigm. Second, even if the government were more serious in its ambitions to change course, there would be limits to this within the context of a European governance regime that remains fundamentally asymmetric with the *de facto* constitutional force of its marketization policies. Thus, a political shift at the national level will not be sufficient. In light of the conclusions from Chapter 1 of this volume, the safest prediction for the Dutch case seems to be that we are in for yet more rounds of what will be a protracted legitimacy crisis.

Conclusion

The case of the Dutch political economy as analysed in this chapter can in many ways be taken, and this in spite of the particularities of the Dutch model, as paradigmatic for the transnational dynamics of the European embedded neoliberal project as a whole. Not only does the Dutch case show what embedded neoliberalism means in practice in terms of national restructuring that gradually erodes national arrangement of social protection (thus hollowing out remaining elements of embeddedness), it clearly also demonstrates the contradictions that embedded neoliberalism generates, and thereby also its political limits. Although every national state–society configuration in the EU is always unique in several respects, the general political patterns engendered by the contradictions of embedded neoliberalism are observable in many of the EU's Member States, including rising populism, the (potential) erosion of mass political parties, electoral volatility, xenophobia, as well as rising Euroscepticism and contestation of European (neoliberal) governance (e.g. Mair, 2006; Hooghe and Marks, 2007b). In the Dutch case, this contestation has led to a massive popular rejection of the proposed European constitution. Together with the rejection in France (which of course had even more political weight) this has formed a considerable blow to the neoliberal European project. Although far from a knockout yet, this blow is symptomatic of, while also having contributed to, the unfolding (multi-level) hegemonic crisis of embedded neoliberalism.

Notes

1. On the concept of output legitimacy, see Scharpf (1999: 6–13).
2. As such the Dutch model has been praised inter alia by Third Way luminaries such as US President Clinton, German Chancellor Schröder and UK Prime Minister Tony Blair (Spithoven, 2002: 334).

3. Although in 1989 the Christian Democratic CDA switched coalition partners by substituting the Dutch labour party (PvdA) for the conservative-liberal VVD, the Lubbers III government very much continued on the same 'reform path'.
4. An additional explanation according to Becker lies in some accidental circumstances such as the house price bubble and subsequent 'consumption' of mortgages in the second half of the 1990s (ibid.: 1089).
5. Some Dutch economists (e.g. Witteloostuijn, 1999) have moreover argued that *industrial* competitiveness and innovation have also been sacrificed on the altar of shareholder value and its concomitant corporate strategy of, in the words of Lazonick and O'Sullivan (2000), 'downsize and distribute' (to the shareholders, that is) instead of 'retain and re-invest' in order to promote more organic long-term growth.
6. This way monetary integration has remained effectively depoliticized until very recently (see Engelen, 2006). With regard to the (deepening of) the internal market, both organized capital and labour share the view that that European market integration is a *sine qua non* for a prosperous Dutch economy: it promotes exports, growth and therefore also for jobs (see e.g. SER, 2004).
7. For a more extensive discussion of the Dutch referendum debates see Van Apeldoorn, 2007.
8. As it was *inter alia* phrased in an SP radio commercial, downloadable at http://www. sp.nl/nieuws/actie/grondwet/weblog/2005/05/22/sp-start-ook-radiocampagne/ (accessed 18 July 2006). See also the op-ed articles by party leader Marijnissen (2005a, 2005b).
9. One such voice was the *Comité Grondwet Nee* (Committee Constitution No). This left-wing civil society organisation had close ties to (more internationalist elements of) the Socialist Party but unlike the SP chose to campaign much more explicitly against the Constitution on the grounds that it would consolidate the neoliberal project, at the same time advocating a European project with a different socio-economic content. Although the Committee played a role of some significance in the referendum campaign (Lucardie, 2005: 118), they and other civil society organisations were still overshadowed by the political parties opposing the Constitution, again, in particular the SP, and their substantive objections did not get the attention they might otherwise have received.
10. E.g. *NRC Handelsblad*, 2005.
11. These figures for instance compare, for what it is worth, to 39 per cent of the respondents indicating that because of further European integration 'national identity and culture' will (probably) disappear (Aarts and Van der Kolk, 2005: 177). The argument, therefore, is not to deny the relevance of such identity-related concerns but to argue that contrary to what the public debate suggested, socio-economic concerns may have been at least equally significant and arguably also in part help to explain or at least reinforce socio-cultural worries.
12. Although on these and other points the Dutch government has thus claimed to have met the objections of the Dutch electorate to the Constitution, the government – as in other Member States clearly fearful of another rejection – had decided from the beginning (as this was the outcome of the constitutive coalition negotiations) against holding a second referendum on the renegotiated treaty.
13. Private equity is now accounting for half of the total value of takeovers in the Dutch market (against 6 per cent three years ago) (*NRC Handelsblad*, 2006).

11
Globalization and Regional Integration: The Possibilities and Problems for Trade Unions to Resist Neoliberal Restructuring in Europe[1]

Andreas Bieler

Introduction

Since the mid-1980s, the European Union (EU) has been restructured along neoliberal lines. This is expressed in the deregulation and liberalization of national economies within the Internal Market programme as well as Economic and Monetary Union (EMU), which instructs the European Central Bank (ECB) to make price stability its sole primary objective and constrains Member States' fiscal policy through the neoliberal convergence criteria of the Stability and Growth Pact (SGP), with a focus on low national deficits and debt levels. The flanking social measures of the social dimension do not change this fundamental neoliberal direction (Bieler, 2006: 9–14). The Lisbon Strategy of 2000 has cemented this direction further through its predominant emphasis on monetary price stability (see Hager, Chapter 5 in this volume). While full employment has been made a goal by the Lisbon Council in 2000, employment policy itself remains subordinated to the objective of price stability and, therefore, concentrates on supply-side measures such as life-long learning and labour market deregulation. In other words, 'European employment policy was made to fit the existing integration project and thus became one of the pillars of supply-side-oriented neoliberal restructuring' (Tidow, 2003: 78). Van Apeldoorn calls this arrangement 'embedded neoliberalism', which is mainly pushed by social class forces of transnational capital. Its content is predominantly neoliberal economics, combined with some social and industrial flanking policies to enlist the support of wider social class forces (Van Apeldoorn 2002; see also his Chapter 1 in this volume). In its enlargement to Central and Eastern Europe, the EU exported an even more market-radical variant of neoliberalism to the new Member States, who were not granted immediate labour mobility and full access to the EU's redistributive policies (Bohle, 2006). This course of restructuring, however, has not remained unchallenged. Neoliberal economics has been increasingly criticized within the EU, and the Dutch and French 'No' votes against the EU Constitution are the clearest sign of this multi-level legitimacy crisis (see the Introduction, as well as Chapter 10 by Van Apeldoorn in this volume).

Labour is often overlooked in the analysis of European integration. And yet, it is workers, as well as trade unions as their representatives, who bear the costs of restructuring. Although capital gained flexibility and new room for manoeuvre, states gave up the possibility of stimulating the national economy via currency devaluations and the lowering of interest rates. Moreover, the introduction of a single currency has made cross-border comparisons of wage levels and working conditions easier. This potentially puts national labour movements in conflict with each other. As exchange rates can no longer be adjusted, cuts in wages and working conditions are the only way for countries with lower productivity levels to remain competitive (Martin and Ross, 1999: 345). In short, due to deregulation and liberalization within the Internal Market and EMU there are general pressures to lower conditions and to make labour markets more flexible. 'The logic of "regime competition" . . . has become a main feature and a driving force of current industrial adjustments within the European Union' (Bieling, 2001: 94, see also 103). Second, the general turn towards a low inflation policy and the related austerity budgets and moderate wage increases could imply that demand levels are generally too low within the EU to overcome high unemployment (Martin, 2000: 365). Finally, with economic decisions increasingly taken at the supranational European level as well as within companies, trade unions' traditional position of influence on policy-making at the national level has been undermined.

In response to further European integration around neoliberal restructuring, trade unions regularly responded with a 'yes, but' position (Dølvik, 1999). They supported further integration, but demanded the development of a related Social Dimension. This strategy, however, was not very successful. Rather, social policy developed as a part of the market-building exercise within the EU (Leibfried, 2005). Hence, it is often alleged that the 'yes, but' strategy with its emphasis on a social partnership approach by trade unions has resulted in some kind of symbolic Euro-corporatism, where unions can participate in discussions without having the chance of making a more significant impact on individual proposals (e.g. Schulten and Ryner, 2003). As Taylor and Mathers (2002: 54) put it:

> the 'social partnership' approach that dominates the thinking of leading members of the European labour movement amounts to a strategy that not only further abandons the autonomy of the labour movement but confirms the logic of neoliberalism through 'supply side corporatism' or 'progressive competitiveness'.

Thus trade unions are accused of having been co-opted into neoliberal restructuring and are, therefore, of no importance to anti-neoliberal movements.

The purpose of this chapter is to assess whether labour has emerged as a transnational actor at the European level and, if so, whether it has accepted neoliberalism or continues to resist restructuring. In the first section, based on a neo-Gramscian, historical materialist perspective, a theoretical argument will be developed for why trade unions are potential transnational actors within the EU and how their role can be conceptualized within European integration. Then, with reference to the European Metalworkers' Federation (EMF) and the European Federation of Public Service Unions (EPSU), examples are given of possible trade unions strategies that allow European labour to resist neoliberal restructuring, even though they are disadvantaged within the EU institutional set-up. Nevertheless, as the subsequent section suggests, trade unions are not by default homogeneous actors opposed to neoliberal restructuring. EU enlargement and the Constitutional Treaty provide examples of tensions within the labour movement, also visible within the processes of the European and World Social Forums. The conclusion will summarize trade unions' possibilities to resist neoliberal restructuring within the EU and link up these debates with wider developments at the global level.

Conceptualizing transnational labour

Unlike neorealist international political economy theory, which concentrates on states as the only important international actors, liberal international political economy theory is able to conceptualize trade unions as an international actor next to a range of other actors in a pluralist understanding of policy-making. Smythe's (2000) analysis of the failed OECD negotiations of a multilateral agreement on investment and the struggle against enhanced capital mobility via further deregulation of national financial markets is a good example. Here, the Trade Union Advisory Committee is treated as one interest organization next to its business counterpart and environmental non-governmental organisations (NGOs) such as the World Wide Fund for Nature. As Van Apeldoorn makes clear, however, liberal approaches are actor-centred, conceptualizing 'transnational actors as autonomous entities rather than as embedded in, and indeed constituted by, transnational structures' (Van Apeldoorn, 2004a: 148). In line with the critical political economy perspective of the introduction, this chapter asserts the need to understand labour as a social relation embedded within the underlying power structures, which often give transnational capital a privileged position.

Beverly Silver (2003) captures the international power structure well in her broad historical and geographical analysis of worker movements since 1870. Through a close focus on the social relations of production and the inherent dynamic of capital's relentless search for higher profits, she unravels the links between different instances of labour unrest in diverse geographical locations as well as different industries. During crises of profitability such as the late 1960s and early 1970s, capital can respond through (1) a spatial fix, transferring production to other parts of the world with lower labour costs and less organized working classes; (2) a technological fix, lowering production costs through the innovation of the production process with the help of new technology partly replacing labour; and (3) a product fix, shifting investment from declining industrial sectors to new industrial sectors. Finally, and very similar to the product fix, capital engages in a financial fix, in which financial instruments become the focus of intensified investment and points of accumulation in their own right (Silver, 2003: 132–3). Overall, however, a crisis can never be solved, it is only postponed or transferred elsewhere. Hence, the decline of labour unrest in one area may lead to new unrest in others (Silver, 2003: 41). Nevertheless, while Silver captures well the power structures of the underlying social relations of production at the global level, she overlooks the importance of domestic institutional set-ups, which shape the organization and strategies of individual labour movements. Capitalism emerged in the eighteenth and nineteenth centuries in different ways and at a different pace in individual countries developing different national trajectories. Positions on labour internationalism by trade unions are strongly affected by the possibilities or lack of possibilities to influence policy-making at the national level. Hence, we cannot do without this focus on different national institutional set-ups or forms of state.

A neo-Gramscian perspective (Bieler and Morton, 2004a; Morton, 2007) is able to overcome these limits through a focus – similar to Silver – on the dynamics of global capitalist restructuring, combined with a conceptualization of national institutional set-ups of forms of state with the help of strategic-relational state theory (Bieler, 2005b; see also the Introduction to this volume). It concentrates on the sphere of production as a starting-point for investigation and identifies social class forces as engendered by the production process as the most important collective actors. Capital, the owners of the means of production, is opposed by labour, forced to sell its labour-power. There are, however, further differences within the capitalist mode of production. Due to the transnationalization of production and finance as part of globalization, new, transnational social forces of capital and labour have emerged as significant actors. A basic distinction can be drawn between transnational social forces of capital and labour, engendered by those production sectors, which are organized on a transnational scale, and national capital and labour stemming from national production sectors (Bieler, 2000: 9–14; Van Apeldoorn, 2002: 26–34; Bieler, 2006: 32–5). The role of transnational capital in European integration has been studied widely (e.g. Van Apeldoorn, 2002; Balanya et al., 2003). Little attention has, however, been given to transnational labour, often considered a domestic or weak actor, and thus unimportant at the European level. This overlooks the fact that class is identified by individuals' position in the production process, not whether they have developed a common consciousness and class activity at a political level (Ste. Croix, 1981: 44). As there is a transnational production structure in certain sectors in the EU, there is also a transnational class fraction of labour. In other words, a class may exist as a class-in-itself because of the way production is organized, while it has not yet developed a class consciousness in struggle and, thus, become a class-for-itself (Robinson, 2004: 43). The neo-Gramscian perspective employed in this chapter allows us to understand transnational labour as a class-in-itself in Europe. Whether it has developed a class-consciousness and transformed itself into a class-for-itself needs to be established in an empirical analysis. To avoid economic determinism, neo-Gramscian perspectives focus on class struggle as heuristic explanatory device (Cox with Sinclair, 1996: 57–8). The essence of class struggle is exploitation and resistance to it (Ste Croix, 1981: 57). The focus on class struggle in concrete historical situations implies that there are always several potential strategies actors can choose from and that, by extension, future development is open-ended. Additionally, this focus on exploitation and resistance permits a wider understanding of class struggle. As Van der Pijl outlines, neoliberal capitalist discipline has now been extended to the entire process of social reproduction, involving the exploitation of the social and natural substratum. In response to the commodification of social services, the expanded destruction of the biosphere as well as the disruption of established ways of life, a whole range of new social movements have emerged to resist the latest intensification of exploitation within capitalism (Van der Pijl, 1998: 36–49). Thus, the potential co-operation between trade unions and social movements in resisting neoliberal restructuring can be understood as class struggle as much as the confrontation between employers and employees at the workplace.

In general, transnational social class forces are likely to support regional integration and, by extension, more co-operation at this regional level. Since the production of their sectors is organized across borders, any kind of border barriers are unwelcome. National forces, on the other hand, where production may still depend on subsidies and protection by the state, are probably unlikely to support regional integration, because it undermines national autonomy and sovereignty. In relation to trade union co-operation at the European level, the following hypothesis can be formulated: trade unions organizing workers in transnational production sectors are likely to support European-level co-operation. They do so partly because they rely on the well-being of the companies in their sector, which benefit from a borderless area, partly because they have realized that they have lost control over capital at the national level. Domestic production sector unions, however, tend to concentrate on the national state in their policy-making efforts, since it plays the dominant role in their sector. Nevertheless, class struggle does not only take place within the structure of the social relations of production. Trade unions also operate within different national institutional set-ups and, importantly for this chapter, the increasingly dense institutional arrangement at the European level. The structural impact of this European institutional set-up also needs to be conceptualized.

According to strategic-relational state theory, the form of the state is the framework within which various different strategies are possible. The state in this sense 'can never be considered as neutral. It has a necessary structural selectivity' (Jessop, 1990: 268), favouring certain strategies over others. Institutions select behaviour, but they do not fully determine it. Hence, within a given institutional, structural setting, there are always different possible strategies, from which actors can choose (Bieler and Morton, 2001b: 16–29). Moreover, the state is a generator of strategies in the sense that the political forces in the state – state managers – can develop strategies to achieve unitary action of the state (Jessop, 1990: 261). Thus, 'we must also consider the "state projects" which bond these blocks together with the result that the state gains a certain organizational unity and cohesiveness of purpose' (Jessop, 1990: 353; see also 358). As Ziltener outlines, understood as a system of multilevel governance, the EU institutional set-up constitutes a complex area for strategic-relational decision-making, a form of state with its own inherent strategic selectivity (Ziltener, 2000: 78, 81). Clearly, trade unions' willingness to co-operate at the European level will also depend on their possibilities to influence policy-making within the EU institutional set-up. This leads to a second hypothesis: that trade unions are more likely to co-operate at the European level if they perceive such an engagement as furthering their influence on policy-making. According to Greenwood, increasing EU competencies since the 1980s have made lobbying and working at the European level more attractive to interest groups (Greenwood, 2003: 33). In other words, trade unions in sectors where more EU competencies and more decisions are taken, are more likely to favour a European industrial relations system, even if their production structure is not transnational.

Finally, it is the notion of open-ended struggle that adds a critical dimension to neo-Gramscian perspectives and allows us to analyse the underlying purpose of European integration as well as actors' strategies (Bieler, 2000: 8; Van Apeldoorn, 2002: 11–13, 34–49). As a critical theory, neo-Gramscian perspectives question existing social and power relations with the objective of assessing the possibilities for an emancipatory project (Cox, 1981: 129). This critical theory dimension is here used to assess the social purpose underlying trade unions' strategies at the European level. The reality of operating with a transnational production structure and certain institutions at the European level does not determine trade unions ideological outlook. Hence, the empirical analysis to follow and the conclusion will also include an investigation of the social purpose of trade unions' activities in order to assess whether they have accepted neoliberal restructuring or continue to resist it.

Trade union co-operation at the European level

The structural selectivity of the European Union

When analysing the European form of state, in accordance with the strategic-relational approach, the focus has to be first on the current 'state project'. As briefly outlined above, the EU has been characterized by neoliberal restructuring since the mid-1980s. The new, neoliberal form of state has been institutionally protected by removing monetary and economic policy-making from the wider influence of actors. First, in a move labelled 'new constitutionalism' by Gill (2001), monetary policy-making with a focus on low inflation has been handed over to the ECB, made up of 'impartial' technocrats. Second, the core macroeconomic decisions are taken by the European Council, the meeting of heads of government and heads of state within the EU, which is largely outside lobbying pressure. In June of each year, the European Council passes the so-called broad economic policy guidelines, which must support the low inflation policy of the ECB, therefore regularly re-confirming neoliberal restructuring.

The multilevel nature of governance in the EU provides trade unions as other interest groups with easy access to supranational decision-makers, but with a related much lower chance of making an impact on the outcome of policy-making (Greenwood, 2003: 29, 73). Trade unions have a particularly close contact to the Directorate General (DG) for Employment and Social Affairs, formerly DG V. Overall, however, the Commission has 23 DGs, and not all DGs are equally important. The DG for Competition and the DG for Economic and Financial Affairs are more decisive within the EU. Together with the DG Internal Market and DG Trade they are the hard core of the Commission (Interview No.1), driving the neoliberal project through the discourse of competitiveness (Rosamond, 2002; Van Apeldoorn, 2003: 125–30). In short, trade unions have been too reliant on the DG for Employment and Social Affairs without receiving enough in return (Greenwood, 2003: 47, 151, 170). The European Parliament (EP) has become a focus of interest groups, since it can amend and co-decide legislation. For the European Trade Union Confederation (ETUC), a monthly meeting with the trade union intergroup of the EP is the most crucial contact point. There are also close links between the Socialist Party and the European trade union leaders. 'ETUC has been able to table amendments in the Parliament through this route' (Greenwood, 2003: 159). The overall position of the EP within the EU decision-making process remains weak, however.

Multi-sector social dialogue is one of the core avenues for the ETUC, the trade union peak association at the European level ,which has as its members 82 national confederations from 36 European countries as well as 12 sectoral European industry federations (EIFs), to influence policy-making in the EU (ETUC, 2008). Since the Treaty of Maastricht in 1991, which extended the EU competencies to social policy issues and introduced qualified majority voting for decision-making in this area, the Commission has had the possibility of giving a negotiation mandate to the ETUC and their employers' counterpart Union of Industrial and Employers' Confederation of Europe (UNICE; now Business Europe). Should they agree on a particular issue, this agreement is then passed to the Council of Ministers, which transfers it into a directive without further discussion. First successes include the Parental Leave Directive in 1996 (Falkner 1998). Overall, however, the significance of the Social Dialogue should not be exaggerated. To date, it has concluded only few agreements establishing minimum standards (Greenwood, 2003: 68). The agreement on telework in 2002 is merely voluntary, the implementation of which is not via an EU directive, but remains the task of the social partners themselves (Broughton, 2002a). The same is the case in relation to the latest agreement on work-related stress (Broughton, 2004c). Moreover, the areas covered by the Social Dialogue are compartmentalized and do not include issues of the general macroeconomic direction of the EU. More fundamental issues such as the right to strike, the right to association and wage bargaining have been excluded from European competencies (Greenwood, 2003: 150). In other words, the Social Dialogue is in no position to effect fundamental change of the current neoliberal drive in the EU. Sectoral social dialogue has been even less developed (Keller, 2003: 418–23) and European Works Councils, providing workers with the right to information, while positive at one level could become divisive for European labour (Martin and Ross, 1999: 343–4).

In sum, there are limited structural possibilities for trade unions within the EU. The EU is characterized by a neoliberal 'state project' and the actual institutional set-up structurally disadvantages trade unions. Nonetheless, the strategic-relational approach to the form of state does not only focus on the structural environment. It also concentrates on the rational choice of strategies by agency within specific structural conditions. The next section will analyse trade unions' concrete activities at the European level and investigate whether, and if so how, they overcome these structural limitations.

Concrete examples of European trade union activities

The EMF organizes workers in one of the most transnationalized sectors in Europe, including many transnational companies in consumer electronics, car manufacturing and machinery production. In response to transnationalization, it is argued that the EMF had to follow and internationalize its structure and activities. The crucial turning-point was the early 1990s:

> Under the influence of the opening-up of the European borders, growing international competition, complete Europeanization of the economy and massive unemployment in Europe, [the EMF] had noticed a distinct tendency towards a competition-driven collective bargaining policy.
>
> (EMF, 2001: 1)

Plans for EMU further implied the danger of social dumping through the undercutting of wage and working conditions between several national collective bargaining rounds (EMF, 1998: 1–2). The EMF realized that wage bargaining was no longer a national issue in its sector, characterized by an increasing transnationalized production structure. In response, the EMF started restructuring itself and began to discuss the potential of co-ordinating wage bargaining (Interview No.2). The EMF co-ordination strategy has three main pillars (EMF, 2001: 1): (1) an information exchange system about national collective bargaining rounds, the so-called European Collective Bargaining Information Network (EUCOB@)N); (2) the establishment of cross-border collective bargaining networks including the exchange of observers for collective bargaining rounds (Gollbach and Schulten, 2000: 166–76); and (3) the adoption of common minimum standards and guidelines, of which wage bargaining co-ordination is not the only but arguably the most important aspect. The co-ordination of national wage bargaining was approved in 1998 and the EMF tries to ensure that national unions pursue a common strategy of asking for wage increases along the formula of productivity increase plus inflation rate (EMF, 1998: 3; Schulten, 2005: 274–89). As far as data is concerned, although national negotiators did not refer to the EMF guidelines, the actual bargaining results were pretty much within the formula until 2001. The current results of bargaining are more out of line with the formula, but importantly the guidelines are increasingly used as a political bargaining tool (Interview No.2). The main goal of the co-ordination of collective bargaining is to avoid the downward competition between different national bargaining rounds and to protect workers against the related reduction in wages and working conditions. Thus, 'a co-ordinated European collective bargaining policy will play a major role in intensifying and reinforcing the social dimension of European unity' (EMF, 1998: 1). This, in turn, indicates the EMF's continuing resistance to neoliberal restructuring.

Importantly, the institutional changes have gone hand in hand with an expansion of members of staff. In 1989 the EMF had four full-time members of staff; now it employs 19 (Interview No.2). At the second EMF congress in Prague on 13 and 14 June 2003, internal decision-making was further facilitated by permitting the Executive Committee to adopt recommendations from the policy committees by a two-thirds majority. This introduction of majority voting clearly indicates that the EMF has developed into an independent actor at the European level in accordance with the hypothesis that transnational sector unions are more likely to engage in co-operation at the European level. The example of the EMF highlights that despite structural disadvantages within the EU form of state, the co-ordination of bargaining provides a good, alternative way forward, characterized by the following three advantages: (1) it does not rely on an employers' counterpart, which has not been willing to engage in meaningful social dialogue; (2) the disadvantaged position within the EU institutional framework is of no consequence, since inter-union co-ordination does not rely on the compliance of EU or national institutions; and (3) this strategy allows to take national differences into account, often cited as the core reason of why European-wide union co-operation is impossible. If productivity is lower in one country than another, then the wage increase demands in the former country will be lower than in the latter accordingly.

A second example of European activity is the European Federation of Public Service Unions (EPSU) (Bieler, 2005b: 475–7). It organizes workers in the civil service from local to European government as well as in the health sector and general utilities such as energy and water. Thus, it organizes workers in all those sectors, which were traditionally part of the public sector with a clear national production structure. Nonetheless, EPSU has become increasingly active as an independent actor at the European level since the 1990s. In order to explain EPSU's increased activity, one needs to refer to the second hypothesis and especially the amount of decisions taken at the European level. Deregulation and liberalization of traditionally domestic production sectors such as energy and public procurement has been driven by EU directives including the Services Directive. Moreover, the Commission is the EU's main representative in the negotiations of a General Agreement on Trade in Services (GATS). The European level has, therefore, become more relevant for trade union activity as a result. In a letter to EPSU's affiliated unions, the General Secretary Carola Fischbach-Pyttel herself pointed to the decisions in relation to public services to be taken at the European level in 2003. This included the Commission's position on GATS negotiations, the report by the working group on Social Europe within the Convention on the Future of Europe, the discussion by the EP of draft directives on public procurement and a further opening of the electricity and gas markets, a Green Paper by the Commission on Services of General Interest, as well as a general push by the DG Internal Market towards more deregulation of services of general economic interest (EPSU, 2003a). According to EPSU, the 'liberalization policies of the European Commission with the majority support of the European Council are undermining public services' (EPSU, 2002).

In resistance to neoliberal restructuring, EPSU has engaged to some extent in sectoral social dialogue in the electricity industry, now the most transnationalized sector within the remit of EPSU (Broughton, 2002b, 2004b). Moreover, a new social dialogue committee in the local and regional government sector was established in January 2004, adopting a joint statement on telework as its first measure (Broughton, 2004a). In 2002 the executive committee of EPSU adopted a bargaining information exchange system similar to the EMF and appropriately called it EPSUCOB@, and there is now an annual collective bargaining conference (Interview No.1). A third strategy employed by EPSU has been the lobbying of EU institutions. In relation to GATS, EPSU is concerned that EU public services have become bargaining chips for the Commission in its attempt to open up other countries for European services exporters (EPSU, 2003a). Reservations were expressed by EPSU in a meeting with the Commissioner Pascal Lamy of DG Trade on 17 February 2003 in relation to the tightness of GATS safety clauses, allowing countries to maintain their own regulations, the secrecy of the current negotiations, the pressure applied by institutions such as the World Bank on developing countries to move towards liberalization in these areas, as well as the rights of foreign citizens carrying out contract work within the EU (EPSU, 2003b).

EPSU's most innovative strategy is, however, its increasing co-operation with other social movements. In relation to GATS, additionally to its direct lobbying of the Commission, EPSU has participated in demonstrations organized by Belgian unions and ATTAC on 9 February 2003 to keep public services out of GATS. Furthermore, it took part in the European day of national action on GATS and public services organized by the European Social Forum on 13 March as well as the ETUC European day of national action for a Social Europe on 21 March 2003 (EPSU, 2003a). The link with other social movements is also visible in relation to public procurement. In 2002 and 2003 EPSU and several other EIFs co-operated with a range of environmental and other social movements such as Greenpeace Europe and the Social Platform, itself a network of European NGOs promoting the Social Dimension of the EU, in lobbying the EU Council of Ministers and especially the EP to amend the Draft Directive on Public Procurement towards the inclusion of social, ecological and fair trade criteria in the award of public procurement contracts (Coalition for Green and Social Procurement, 2002; Interview No.1). Most recently, EPSU engaged in close co-operation with other social movements in relation to the Services Directive, aimed at liberalizing the provision of public services. It was top of the union's list of priorities for the period of 2004 to 2009 and the co-operation with NGOs next to the ETUC and other EIFs was identified as part of the overall strategy (EPSU, 2005: 2). The campaign culminated in two large European demonstrations in Brussels and Strasburg in 2005 and early 2006 involving trade unions and other social movements from all over Europe (ETUC, 2006). In the end it was at least successful in preventing the adoption of the initial draft of the directive. EPSU is currently following up these efforts with a campaign for a EU legal framework on public services 'Quality Public Services – Quality of Life' and the Social Platform has publicly declared its support (EPSU, 2007).

In sum, the increasing involvement by the EU in general and the Commission in particular in moves of actual or potential future deregulation and liberalization of national public services, in line with the second hypothesis, has intensified EPSU's engagement at the European level with the aim to counter these measures. The case of EPSU demonstrates again that trade unions are structurally disadvantaged at the European level, but also that there are strategies available that may help to overcome these disadvantages. In all its activities against the further privatization of public services, EPSU has formed close alliances not only with other trade unions, but with wider social movements. These alliances present 'an agreement between trade unions, NGOs and employers, that social Europe is the bridge that connects Europe to the citizen' (EPSU, 2002). Hence, a separate 'social discourse' has emerged in the EU and trade unions have successfully used it to broaden their social basis of the struggle against neoliberal restructuring of the public sector, thereby increasing their impact on EU policy-making.

Tensions within the European labour movement

Both examples of European trade union activities mentioned above demonstrate that unions continue to resist neoliberal restructuring. At the same time, however, resistance to neoliberalism by trade unions is not automatic, nor is it inevitable that all trade unions will act together with the same goals and objectives in mind. EU enlargement to Central and Eastern Europe illustrates the dangers of divisions within the European labour movement. It was West European trade unions that – through the Economic and Social Committee of the EU, research by the ETUC, as well as through pressure by the German DGB and Austrian ÖGB on their respective governments – pushed successfully for a transition period of up to seven years in relation to the free movement of labour. There was a clear lack of transnational solidarity, which may result in long-term divisions between the Eastern and Western labour movements and thereby weaken European labour overall (Bohle and Husz, 2005: 108–9).

The EU constitution provides another good example for the tensions within the European labour movement (see the previous chapter by Van Apeldoorn in this volume). On the one hand, the ETUC strongly argued in favour of a 'yes' in the various national referenda on the Constitution, as this 'is the most pro-Social Europe treaty that Europe has ever had' (ETUC, 2005a). On the other hand, critics singled out especially Part III of the Constitutional Treaty as enshrining the predominance of neoliberal economics within the EU (Cassen, 2005a: 30–1). The 'No' camp in the French referendum campaign included radical trade unions such as the G10-Solidaires, which argued that 'this "constitution" sets in stone an anti-democratic institutional mechanism, the primacy of competition law, the weakening of public services. The principles of an economic liberalism without limits is the backbone of the text and makes free and unhindered competition the supreme value of the European Union' (G10-Solidaires, 2005). Similarly, Force Ouvrière openly defied the ETUC, of which it is a member, and rejected the Constitution as yet another example of how economic interests would be the predominant driving force behind European integration (Force Ouvrière, 2005). In other EU member countries too, trade unions adopted positions on the EU constitution. In the UK, the confederation Trades Union Congress (TUC) published an information document on the Constitution in September 2004 arguing that it would only adopt a decision on whether to support it closer to the referendum initially scheduled for 2005 or 2006 (TUC, 2004). In the document itself, however, the TUC highlighted the inclusion of the Charter of Fundamental Rights, including the right to join a union and the right to strike, the emphasis on a social market economy, the specification of the role of the social partners within EU decision-making as well as the Social Chapter as important positive aspects, while only a short section was dedicated to the case against the Constitution. This mild support for the Constitution was even more explicit in a speech by Brendan Barber, TUC General Secretary at the time, in which he concluded that 'not everything [the Constitution] does is right. But at its core remains a social bargain that is anathema to the alternative US model of capitalism' (Barber, 2004: 3). Of course, after the Dutch and French 'No', the Constitution was shelved and the British referendum never held. Hence, a full debate leading to potential divisions within the British labour movement did not take place. The main German confederation DGB welcomed the Constitution, although it acknowledged that not all trade union demands had been met. In particular, it positively pointed to the inclusion of the Charter of Fundamental Rights into the Constitution (DGB, n.d.). In its position paper on the German EU presidency during the first half of 2007, the DGB strongly urged the German government to overcome the stalemate within the EU after the Dutch and French referenda and to provide a new initiative towards a European constitution (DGB, 2006: 15). The large German services sector union Ver.di had also welcomed the draft Constitution and did not accept criticisms that the Constitution would simply reflect a neoliberal market economy. The emphasis would be on a social market economy including many important trade union demands such as the inclusion of the Charter of Fundamental Rights (Ver.di, 2004). The IG Metall, the German metalworkers' union, was slightly more critical. In its assessment of the Lisbon Treaty of 2007, which replaced the draft Constitution, it criticized that the period since the negative referenda had not been used sufficiently to correct the social imbalance of the Constitution and to bring the EU as a whole closer to its citizens (IG Metall, 2007: 4). Its President Jürgen Peters had already declared in 2004 that neither the commitment to a neoliberal economic policy nor the task of strengthening the military should be part of a Constitution (Peters, 2004). In short, while the positions of the TUC, DGB and Ver.di reflect the ETUC's endorsement of the Constitution, the IG Metall's position indicates the potential for divisions. These tensions within the European labour movement over the Constitutional Treaty, explicit especially in France, signify that rather than providing common ground for joint resistance the Constitutional Treaty split trade unions.

Similar tensions between established and more radical trade unions are also visible within the European Social Forum (ESF) and the World Social Forum (WSF) gatherings, bringing together anti-neoliberal globalization movements in Europe and at the global level respectively. At the first ESF in Florence in November 2002 these tensions were visible as a result of the different histories, internal structures and strategies of these unions (Bieler and Morton, 2004b). Historically, the new, radical European unions emerged as a reaction to, or even a split from, the established trade unions in the late 1980s and early 1990s due to discontent over the accommodationist position of mainstream unions *vis-à-vis* neoliberal restructuring. For example, the French union Solidaires, Unitaires et Démocratiques (SUD-PTT), organizing workers in the postal services and telecommunications industry, emerged in 1988 after a split from the Confédération Française Démocratique du Travail (CFDT) over the support for strikes in the postal services and hospitals. After SUD-PTT became a member of G10-Solidaires, the latter confederation became the focal point for radical, progressive unions in France (G10-Solidaires, 2002: 9–14). As for the internal structure, G10-Solidaires as well as the individual SUD unions define themselves as rank and file unions, which 'is concretized by the idea that all decisions are the result of a consensus, where each rank-and-file union has one vote regardless of its size' (G10-Solidaires, 2002: 13).

This different history and structural development of union activities has implications for questions of strategy. Having mainly emerged as a reaction to established trade unions' accommodationist positions, these new unions reject tripartism with employers and the state, be it at the national or European level. They define their struggle in a wider sense and are almost by definition more open to interaction with social movements. SUD unions and the G10-Solidaires recognize that neoliberal exploitation goes beyond issues of the workplace. 'It is, therefore, necessary to operate in relation to all these consequences in partnership with social movements, which also struggle on this terrain' (G10-Solidaires, 2002: 29–30). Hence these groups do not only raise demands related to the workplace, they also ask for the right to work, to accommodation and to health alongside raising ecological concerns. Established trade unions at the ESFs, on the other hand, continue to concentrate on the defence of core labour rights with an emphasis on collective bargaining with employers supported by the state in tripartite institutions. The ETUC in particular emphasizes its role within the European level social dialogue.

Similar tensions were noticeable at the WSF in Nairobi, Kenya, in January 2007. On the one hand, there was a group of established trade unions around the International Trade Union Confederation (ITUC). It used the WSF to launch its Decent Work Campaign with the aim to achieve 'decent work' for all, consisting of 'equal access to employment, living wages, social protection, freedom from exploitation and union rights' (ITUC, 2007). The main strategies adopted include (1) a recognition of trade unions as the main actor for progressive reform; (2) a focus on improvements in the work place; and (3) an emphasis on tripartite relationships with employers, states and international organizations. On the other hand, there was a group of more radical trade unionists and social movement activists who focused on establishing a 'Labour Network on and in the World Social Forum process'. Here, it is argued that in order to respond to the vicious attack on labour by neoliberal globalization, new alliances of forces are necessary, including unions, social movements and intellectuals. One would need to accept that globalization has led to the extension of exploitation beyond the work place into the sphere of social reproduction. Hence, issues to be dealt with needed to go beyond the work place and include problems such as the division of society along gender lines. Instead of interacting with employers and state officials, the focus should be on co-operation with social movements, which are precisely able to organize within the informal working sector as well as the sphere of social reproduction (Bieler, 2007).

Conclusion

This chapter has shown, first, that some trade unions have emerged as independent actors at the international and European level. The EMF, in line with the first hypothesis, expanded its activities at the European level, after it was acknowledged that the transnational structure of the metalworking industrial sector made national action increasingly less meaningful. The example of EPSU, in turn, confirmed the second hypothesis. Although the union's national member federations organize predominantly in domestic production sectors, the very fact that more and more initiatives within the public and private service sectors are taken at the supranational level led to a more co-ordinated response by the European trade union. At the same time, however, we need to remember that a neo-Gramscian perspective, employed in this chapter, is a critical, post-positivist approach, which does not aim at identifying causal relationships in an objective reality. Hence, the task is not to verify or falsify hypotheses, but the hypotheses developed in this chapter have to be understood as research questions, allowing us to guide the research and order empirical material. By extension, this also implies that economic determinism is avoided in the analysis. The first hypothesis states that it is more likely that unions in transnational production sectors will emerge as independent actors at the European level. From a post-positivist point of view, however, this does not imply that we expect this to be inevitably the case. Rather, this hypothesis can be used as a research question to establish whether concrete transnational EIFs have actually developed an independent actor capacity such as the EMF, or whether they still operate more like a secretariat co-ordinating the activities of their national member unions. Here, the European Mine, Chemical and

Energy Workers' Federation (EMCEF) is a good example. Despite the transnational structure of the chemical industry, EMCEF has advanced its independent activities much less in comparison with the EMF (Bieler, 2005b: 473–4).

Second, both the EMF and EPSU represented examples of continuing resistance to neoliberal restructuring. The attempt to co-ordinate national collective bargaining at the European level by the EMF is clearly directed against the neoliberal logic of regime competition, driving down wages and working conditions across Europe to make companies more competitive on the global market. EPSU's initiatives, together with other social movements, to preserve an integrated public sector confronts the latest neoliberal efforts to extend restructuring beyond private sector industry into the traditionally decommodified realm of public services. Nevertheless, it was also shown that labour is not by default a homogenous actor of resistance. Especially a division between established unions such as the ETUC on the one hand and radical trade unions such as the French G10-Solidaires on the other could be identified. These differences, however, should not make us overlook the commonalities and resulting possible joint activities. Despite different structures and strategies, all movements and unions present at the ESF in Florence in 2002 identified neoliberal globalization, in its economic, deregulatory form as well as militaristic version (as embodied in the war on Iraq) as the main target for resistance. Hence a convergence of opinions emerged around several areas for joint activities, including the call to hold worldwide demonstrations against the impending war on Iraq on 15 February 2003 as well as joint activities in defence of the public sector against neoliberal restructuring. Similar co-operation efforts were initiated and/or deepened in relation to the demand for a European minimum income, the combat of tax evasion, as well as the co-ordinated demands for the introduction of a Tobin Tax on currency speculations (Bieler and Morton, 2004b: 312–19). Although the second ESF in Paris in November 2003 was a disappointment as far as the co-operation between social movements and trade unions was concerned, these links experienced renewed emphasis at the third ESF in London in October 2004. British trade unions were especially out in force for the first time. Moreover, resistance to neoliberal restructuring in general and the privatization of public services in particular was still the main priority that brought together this wide range of different movements (Bieler and Morton, 2007). Within the EU itself, an engagement with the Community's institutions and a push for a growth and employment oriented macroeconomic policy-mix, including an equal emphasis on low inflation, growth and wage increases in line with productivity gains, does not automatically imply having been co-opted into neoliberal restructuring. Nevertheless, this strategy must not be seen as an endpoint, but as a start towards more dramatic demands such as a renewed push for economic democracy (Bieler, 2006: 208–19).

It was indicated above how it proved to be impossible to establish transnational solidarity between Eastern and Western European labour over EU enlargement. In a protectionist move, Western European trade unions attempted to defend the jobs and higher wealth levels of their members against cheaper labour from the new members through the seven-year transition period. This divide between more affluent workers and poorer workers is even more pronounced in the differences between workers in the North and those in the Global South. As Silver has indicated, contemporary capitalist restructuring has not resulted in a homogenization of workers' conditions. Instead, 'while spatial fixes tended to erode the North-South divide, technological fixes, product fixes and protectionism tended to reconstitute the divide continually' (Silver, 2003: 170). This divide does not imply that transnational solidarity cannot be established and that co-operation between mainstream trade unions, radical unions and social movements at the international level is impossible. Joint initiatives may well be feasible, but they need to keep the tensions resulting from the North–South divide in mind (Bieler, Lindberg and Pillay, 2008). In this respect, the possibilities of the Decent Work Campaign should not be underestimated. First, because the ITUC is a comparatively powerful actor, officially representing over 168 million workers worldwide across this divide. Second, this initiative speaks to the concerns of workers around the world and provides the opportunity to garner support. If short-term gains are obtained in some industrial sectors in some parts of the world, then this offers the possibility to recruit new members and involve the rank and file more actively in struggles. Of course, the Decent Work initiative must not be the endpoint of the strategy. Only if it is regarded as a first step towards a more drastic challenge to neoliberal restructuring can it actually challenge global capitalism more directly. As indicated in relation to the European level, established labour rejects the neoliberal rationale currently driving globalization. It is this rejection that can provide a common basis for co-operation with the second group, consisting of radical trade unions and social movements. The very fact that the Decent Work initiative was launched at the WSF indicates that established trade unions are at least in principle open to this form of co-operation. If successful, this would allow labour to broaden the social basis for resistance against neoliberal globalization and in favour of an economy where production is no longer organized around private property and wage labour. If one takes into account that labour's structural power based on workers' location in the production process has decreased as a result of the shift from manufacturing to a range of different service sectors as the new leading industries in the 21st century, a strengthening of associational power through co-operation with other social movements and the integration of campaigns within the wider community (Silver, 2003: 170–3) is an absolute precondition for a successful countering of neoliberal restructuring. To conclude, many trade unions continue to contest neoliberalism and are, therefore, potential participants in the wider movement of resistance against restructuring. Intensified co-operation with social movements has the potential to expand the counter-neoliberal social basis, creating a powerful movement for progressive change. Trade unions have the capacity to play a significant role in these processes at the European, but also national and global level. Whether they pursue these opportunities is an issue of open-ended class struggle.

Interviews

Interview No.1: Deputy General Secretary, European Federation of Public Service Unions (EPSU); Brussels, 22 January 2003.
Interview No.2: Deputy General Secretary, European Metalworker's Federation (EMF); Brussels, 23 January 2003.

Notes

1. I am indebted to the editors of this volume as well as two anonymous reviewers for comments on earlier drafts.

References

Aarts, K. and van der Kolk, H. (2005) 'Op weg naar 1 Juni', in K. Aarts and H. van der Kolk (eds), *Nederlanders en Europa: Het Referendum over de Nederlandse Grondwet* (Amsterdam: Bert Bakker), pp. 158–82.

Aarts, K. and van der Kolk, H. (2006) 'Understanding the Dutch 'No': The Euro, the East, and the Elite', *PS: Political Science & Politics*, 39, pp. 243–6.

Abdelal, R. (2006) 'Writing the Rules of Global Finance: France, Europe, and Capital Liberalization', *Review of International Political Economy*, vol. 13, pp. 1–27.

Adler, E. and Haas, P. (1992) 'Conclusion: Epistemic Communities, World Order, and the Creation of A Reflective Research Program', *International Organization*, vol. 46 (1), pp. 367–90.

Agence Europe (1995), No. 6478, 11 May.

Aglietta, M. (1987) *A Theory of Capitalist Regulation: The US-Experience* (London: Verso).

Aglietta, M. (1998) 'Capitalism at the Turn of the Century: Regulation Theory and the Challenge of Social Change', *New Left Review*, vol. 232, pp. 41–90.

Aglietta, M. (2000) *Ein neues Akkumulationsregime. Die Regulationstheorie auf dem Prüfstand* (Hamburg: VSA).

Aglietta, M. and Rebérioux, A. (2005) *Corporate Governance Adrift: A Critique of Shareholder Value* (Cheltenham: Edward Elgar).

Agnew, J. (2001) 'How Many Europes? The EU, Eastern Enlargement, and Uneven Development', *European Urban and Regional Studies*, vol. 8 (1), pp. 29–38.

Albo, G. (1994) '"Competitive Austerity" and the Impasse of Capitalist Employment Policy', in R. Miliband and L. Panitch (eds), *Between Globalism and Nationalism: The Socialist Register* (London: Merlin Press), pp. 471–504.

Ali, M. (2007) 'New "Strategic Partnership" Against China', *BBC News*, 3 September, (http://newsvote.bbc.co.uk).

Altvater, E. (1996) 'Westeuropäische Integration und osteuropäische Transformation in der globalen Standortkonkurrenz' in M. Jachtenfuchs and B. Kohler-Koch (eds), *Europäische Integration* (Opladen: Leske und Budrich), pp. 531–58.

Amable, B. (2003) *The Diversity of Modern Capitalism* (Oxford: Oxford University Press).

Amsden, A. H., Kochanowicz, J. and Taylor, L. (1994) *The Market Meets its Match: Restructuring the Economies of Eastern Europe* (Cambridge, MA and London: Harvard University Press).

Anderson, R. (2006) 'A Bumpy Ride For Flat Taxes', *Business Week*, 29 November.

Appel, H. (2004) *A New Capitalist Order: Privatization and Ideology in Russia and Eastern Europe* (Pittsburgh: University of Pittsburgh Press).

Appel, H. (2006) 'International Imperatives and Tax Reform: Lessons from Postcommunist Europe', *Comparative Politics*, vol. 1, pp. 43–62.

Appel, H. and Gould, J. (2000) 'Identity Politics and Economic Reform: Examining Industry-State Relations in the Czech and Slovak Republics', *Europe-Asia Studies*, vol. 52 (1), pp. 111–31.

Arnold, M. (2007) 'Unions vow to fight the "cancer" of hedge funds', *Financial Times*, 17 March, p. 6.

Arrighi, G. (2005) 'Hegemony Unravelling–2', *New Left Review*, vol. 33, pp. 83–117.

Atkins, R. (2007a) 'Interview: Business grows in confidence', *Financial Times*, 4 June.

Atkins, R. (2007b) 'Dollar's role is seen as safe from challenge of the Euro', *Financial Times*, 23 November, p. 8.

Atkins, R. and Parker, G. (2007) 'Sarkozy told to lay off ECB', *Financial Times*, 9 May, p. 1.

Baghat, G. (2002) 'Pipeline Diplomacy: The Geopolitics of the Caspian Sea Region', *International Studies Perspectives*, vol. 3 (3), pp. 310–27.

Bajpaee, C. (2007) 'Strategic Interests Pull Japan and India Together', *Power and Interest News Report*, 16 February.

Baker, A. (2006a) 'American Power and the Dollar: The Constraints of Technical Authority and Declaratory Policy in the 1990s', *New Political Economy*, vol. 11, pp. 23–46.

Baker, R. (2006b) 'The New Old Face of Asia', *Stratfor Geopolitical Intelligence Report*, 16 November.

Balanyá, B., Doherty, A., Hoedeman, O., Maánit, A. and Wesselius, E. (2003) *Europe Inc.: Regional and Global Restructuring and the Rise of Corporate Power*, 2nd edn (London: Pluto Press).

Balcet, G. and Enrietti, A. (1997) 'Regionalization and Globalization in Europe: The Case of Fiat Auto Poland and its Suppliers', *Actes du Gerpisa*, vol. 20 (available from: http://www.univ-evry.fr/labos/gerpisa/actes/20/article2.html).

Balibar, E. (1991) 'Es Gibt Keinen Staat in Europa: Racism and Politics in Europe Today', *New Left Review*, vol. 186, pp. 5–19.

Balibar, E. (2004) *We the People of Europe? Reflections on Transnational Citizenship* (Princeton: Princeton University Press).

Baran, P. (1957) *The Political Economy of Growth* (New York: Monthly Review Press).

Barber, B. (2004) 'Judge the constitution, not Labour's stance' (available from: http://www.tuc.org.uk/international/tuc-8566-f0.pdf).

Barber, T. and Parker. G. (2004) 'Prodi says European efforts to catch US "a failure"', *Financial Times*, 25 October.

Barnard, C. and Deakin, S. (1999) 'A Year of Living Dangerously? EC Social Rights, Employment Policy, and EMU', *Industrial Relations Journal*, vol. 30 (4), pp. 355–72.

Barroso, J. M. (2004) 'Speaking Points By President-Designate Barroso – Lisbon Strategy', Speech to the European Council, 4 November (available from: http://www.europa.eu.int/comm/commission_barroso/president/speeches/speech_20041104_ en.pdf).

Barroso, J. M. (2005a) 'Choosing to Grow – a New Agenda for Growth and Jobs', Speech/05/188, Warsaw.

Barroso, J. M. (2005b) 'The Lisbon Strategy – a Key Priority of the European Commission', Speech/05/125, Brussels.

Barroso, J. M. (2005c) 'Growth and Jobs: A New Start for the Lisbon Strategy', Speech/05/152, Strasbourg.

Barroso, J. M. (2005d) 'Key Challenges for the European Union: Enlargement and Governance', Speech/05/195, 1 April, Madrid.

Barroso, J. M. (2005e) 'Working Together for Jobs and Growth: A New Start for the Lisbon Strategy', Speech/05/67, 2 February, Brussels.

Bartlett, D. and Seleny, A. (1998) 'The Political Enforcement of Liberalism: Bargaining, Institutions, and Auto Multinationals in Hungary', *International Studies Quarterly*, vol. 42 (2), pp. 319–38.

Basel Committee on Banking Supervision (1999) 'A New Capital Adequacy Framework', Basel (available from: http://www.bis.org/publ/bcbs50.pdf).

Basel Committee on Banking Supervision (2004a) 'Basel II: International Convergence of Capital Measurement and Capital Standards: A Revised Framework', Basel (available from: http://www.bis.org/publ/bcbs107.pdf).

Basel Committee on Banking Supervision (2004b) 'Consensus achieved on Basel II proposals', 11 May (http://www.bis.org/press/p040511.htm).

Baumol, W. (1967) 'The Macroeconomics of Unbalanced Growth', *American Economic Review*, vol. 52 (3), pp. 415–26.

Becht, M. and Da Silva, L. C. (2007) 'External Financial Markets Policy: Europe as Global Regulator?', in A. Sapir (ed.), *Fragmented Power: Europe and the Global Economy* (Brussels: Bruegel), pp. 200–25.

Becker, U. (2005) 'An Example of Competitive Corporatism? The Dutch political Economy 1983–2004 in Critical Examination', *Journal of European Public Policy*, vol. 12 (6), pp. 1078–1102.

Becker, U. and Schwartz, H. (eds) (2005) *Employment 'miracles': A Critical Comparison of the Swiss, Dutch, Scandinavian, Australian and Irish Cases Versus Germany and the US* (Amsterdam: Amsterdam University Press).

Beckfield, J. (2006) 'European Integration and Income Inequality', Luxembourg Income Study, Working Paper No. 447.

Beckmann, M. (2007) *Das Finanzkapital in der Transformation der europäischen Ökonomie* (Münster: Westfälisches Dampfboot).

Beland, D. and Hansen, R. (2000) 'Reforming the French Welfare State: Solidarity, Social Exclusion and the Three Crises of Citizenship', *West European Politics*, vol. 23 (1), pp. 47–64.

Bélanger, E. and Aarts, K. (2006) 'Explaining the Rise of the LPF: Issues, Discontent, and the 2002 Dutch Election', *Acta Politica*, vol. 41 (1), pp. 4–20.

Bellak, C., Leibrecht, M. and Römisch, R. (2005) 'New Evidence on the Tax Burden of MNC Activities in Central- and East-European New Member States', SFB International Tax Coordination Paper No. 2 (http://ssrn.com/abstract=869222).

Benoit, B., Condon, C. and Parker, G. (2005) 'Juncker achieves "small miracle" as deal is rewritten: The Luxembourg prime minister's more flexible agreement has handed a political victory to Germany and France', *Financial Times*, 22 March.

Berle, A. A. and Means, G. C. (1991 and 1967 [1932]) *The Modern Corporation and Private Property* (New York: Transaction Publishers, New Brunswick, Harcourt, Brace and World).

Beunderman, M. (2006) 'Poland Compares German—Russian Pipeline to Nazi-Soviet Pact', *EUObserver*, 2 May.

Bhagwati, J. (1998) 'The Capital Myth', *Foreign Affairs*, vol. 77, pp. 7–12.

Bhaskar, R. (1979) *The Possibility of Naturalism. A Philosophical Critique of the Contemporary Human Sciences* (Brighton: Harvester Press).

Bieler, A. (2000) *Globalisation and Enlargement of the European Union: Austrian and Swedish Social Forces in the Struggle over Membership* (London: Routledge).

Bieler, A. (2002) 'The Struggle of EU Enlargement: A Historical Materialist Analysis of European Integration', *Journal of European Public Policy*, vol. 9 (4), pp. 575–97.

Bieler, A. (2005a) 'Class Struggle over the EU Model of Capitalism: Neo-Gramscian Perspectives and the Analysis of European Integration', *Critical Review of International Social and Political Philosophy*, vol. 8 (4), pp. 513–26.

Bieler, A. (2005b) 'European Integration and the Transnational Restructuring of Social Relations: The Emergence of Labour as a Regional Actor?', *Journal of Common Market Studies*, vol. 43, pp. 461–84.

Bieler A. (2006) *The Struggle for a Social Europe: Trade Unions and EMU in Times of Global Restructuring* (Manchester: Manchester University Press).

Bieler, A. (2007) 'Labour at the world social forum 2007 in Nairobi/Kenya' (http://www.choike.org/nuevo_eng/informes/5380.html).

Bieler, A. and Morton, A. D. (eds) (2001a) *Social Forces in the Making of the New Europe. The Restructuring of European Social Relations in the Global Political Economy* (Basingstoke: Palgrave Macmillan).

Bieler, A. and Morton, A. D. (2001b) 'The Gordian Knot of Agency-Structure in International Relations: A Neogramscian Perspective', *European Journal of International Relations*, vol. 7 (1), pp. 5–35.

Bieler, A. and Morton, A. D. (2004a) 'A Critical Theory Route to Hegemony, World Order and Historical Change: Neo-Gramscian Perspectives in International Relations', *Capital & Class*, vol. 82, pp. 85–113.

Bieler, A. and Morton, A. D. (2004b) '"Another Europe is Possible?" Labour and Social Movements At the European Social Forum', *Globalizations*, vol. 1 (2), pp. 303–27.

Bieler, A. and Morton, A. D. (2007) 'Canalising Resistance: Historical Continuities and Contrasts of "Alter-Globalist" Movements At the European Social Forums', in A. Gamble et al. (eds), *Labour, the State, Social Movements and the Challenge of Neoliberal Globalisation* (Manchester: Manchester University Press), pp. 204–22.

Bieler, A., Lindberg, I. and Pillay, D. (2008) 'What Future Strategy for the Global Working Class? The Need for a New Historical Subject', in A. Bieler, I. Lindberg and D. Pillay (eds), *Labour and the Challenges of Globalisation: What Prospects for Transnational Solidarity?* (London: Pluto Press), pp. 264–85.

Bieling, H. -J. (2001) 'European Constitutionalism and Industrial Relations', in A. Bieler and A. D. Morton (eds), *Social Forces in the Making of the New Europe: The Restructuring of European Social Relations in the Global Political Economy* (Basingstoke: Palgrave Macmillan), pp. 93–114.

Bieling, H. -J. (2003a) 'European Employment Policy Between Neo-Liberal Rationalism and Communitarianism', in H. Overbeek (ed.), *The Political Economy of European Employment* (London: Routledge), pp. 51–74.

Bieling, H. -J. (2003b) 'Social Forces in the Making of the New European Economy: The Case of Financial Market Integration', *New Political Economy*, vol. 8, pp. 203–24.

Bieling, H. -J. (2005) 'Finanzmarktintegration und transnationale Interessengruppen in der Europäischen Union', in R. Eising und B. Kohler-Koch (eds), *Interessenpolitik in Europa* (Baden-Baden: Nomos), pp. 179–201.

Bieling, H. -J. (2006a) 'EMU, Financial Integration and Global Economic Governance', *Review of International Political Economy*, vol. 13, pp. 420–48.

Bieling, H. -J. (2006b) 'Implikationen der neuen europäischen Ökonomie', *Prokla*, vol. 36 (3), pp. 325–42.

Bieling, H. -J. and Deppe, F. (2003) 'Die neue europäische Ökonomie und die Transformation von Staatlichkeit', in M. Jachtenfuchs and B. Kohler-Koch (eds), *Europäische Integration*, 2nd edn (Opladen: Leske and Budrich), pp. 513–39.

Bieling, H. -J. and Steinhilber, J. (2002) 'Finanzmarktintegration und Corporate Governance in der Europäischen Union', *Zeitschrift für Internationale Beziehungen*, vol. 9 (1), pp. 39–74.

Blanke, J. and Lopez-Claros, A. (2004) *The Lisbon Agenda 2004: An Assessment of Policies and Reforms in Europe* (Geneva: World Economic Forum).

Blažienė, I. (2006) 'Relocation of production and industrial relations – case of Lithuania' (http://www.eiro.eurofound.eu.int/2005/11/study/index.html).

Bluhm, K. (2007) *Experimentierfeld Osteuropa? Deutsche Unternehmen in Polen und der Tschechischen Republik* (Wiesbaden: VS-Verlag).

Blyth, M. (2002) *Great Transformations: Economic Ideas and Institutional Change in the Twentieth Century* (Cambridge: Cambridge University Press).

Bockman, J. and Eyal, G. (2002) 'Eastern Europe as a Laboratory for Economic Knowledge: The Transnational Roots of Neoliberalism', *American Journal of Sociology*, vol. 108 (2), pp. 310–52.

Boer, B. (2005) 'Euroscepsis en Liberalisme in Nederland', in: B. Boer and H. Vollaard (eds), *Euroscepsis in Nederland* (Utrecht: Lemma), pp. 129–49.

Bohle, D. (2000) 'Internationalisation: An Issue Neglected in the Path-Dependency Approach to Post-Communist Transformation', in M. Dobry (ed.), *Democratic and Capitalist Transitions in Eastern Europe: Lessons for the Social Sciences* (Dordrecht and London: Kluwer Academic Publishers), pp. 235–61.

Bohle, D. (2002) *Europas Neue Peripherie: Polens Transformation und transnationale Integration* (Münster: Westfälisches Dampfboot).

Bohle, D. (2005) 'The EU and Eastern Europe: Failing the Test as a Better World Power', in L. Panitch and C. Leys (eds), *The Empire Reloaded, Socialist Register* (London: Merlin Press), pp. 301–12.

Bohle, D. (2006) 'Neoliberal Hegemony, Transnational Capital and the Terms of the EU's Eastward Expansion', *Capital & Class*, vol. 88, pp. 57–86.

Bohle, D. (2007) 'The New Great Transformation: Liberalization and Social Protection in Central Eastern Europe', Paper prepared for presentation at the second ESRC seminar: (Re)distributions of Uncertainty, Warwick Business School, University of Warwick, Coventry, 2 November.

Bohle, D. and Greskovits, B. (2006) 'Capitalism Without Compromise: Strong Business and Weak Labor in Eastern Europe's New Transnational Industries', *Studies in Comparative International Development*, vol. 4 (1), pp. 3–25.

Bohle, D. and Greskovits, B. (2007) 'Neoliberalism, Embedded Neoliberalism and Neocorporatism: Towards Transnational Capitalism in Central-Eastern Europe', *West European Politics*, vol. 30 (3), pp. 443–66.

Bohle, D. and Husz, D. (2005) 'Whose Europe is it? Interest Group Action in Accession Negotiations: The Cases of Competition Policy and Labor Migration', *Politique Européenne*, vol. 15, pp. 85–112.

Bolkestein, F. (2000) 'The Lisbon European Council: A New Stimulus Towards the Integration of European Financial Markets', Speech read at Formum Financiere Belge, 4 May, Brussels (available from: http://europa.eu.int/rapid/pressReleases Action.do?reference=SPEECH/00/163&format=HTML&aged=1&language=EN&guiLanguage=en).

Bolkestein, F. (2001) 'European competitiveness', Ambrosetti Annual Forum, 8 September, Cernobbio (available from: http://europa.eu.int/comm/internal_market/en/speeches/spch373.htm).

Bolkestein, F. (2003) 'Corporate Governance in Europe', Speech at FESE Conference at Clifford Chance, 30 January, Amsterdam.

Boltho, A. (ed.) (1982) *The European Economy: Growth and Crisis* (Oxford: Oxford University Press).

Bönker, F. (2003) 'Steuerpolitische Aspekte der EU-Osterweiterung', *Vierteljahreshefte zur Wirtschaftsforschung*, vol. 72 (4), pp. 522–34.

Bordonaro, F. (2005) 'Intelligence Brief: U.S. Military Bases in the Black Sea Region', *Power and Interest News Report*, 19 November.

Bordonaro, F. (2006) 'Kazakhstan and the "New Great Game"', *Asia Times*, 10 March.

Böröcz, J. (2004) 'Foreign Direct Legislation, Informality, and the Iron Fist of Liberal Capitalism After the End of European State Socialism', Paper presented at the ARC-CGOR Inaugural Workshop, Amsterdam, December.

Borrás, S. and Jacobsson, K. (2004) 'The Open Method of Co-ordination and New Governance Patterns in the EU', *Journal of European Public Policy*, vol. 11 (2), pp. 185–208.

Bounds, A., Buck, T. and Thornhill, J. (2007) 'A dynamic Sarkozy profits from liberal preoccupation: Could the French president's summit victory presage an EU retreat from market reform?', *Financial Times*, 28 June.

Bourdieu, P. (1989) 'The Corporatism of the Universal: The Role of Intellectuals in the Modern World', *Telos*, vol. 81, pp. 99–110.

Bouwen, P. (2001) 'Towards a Theory of Access', European University Institute Working Paper, SPS 2001/5.

Bouwen, P. (2002) 'Corporate Lobbying in the European Union: The Logic of Access', *Journal of European Public Policy*, vol. 9 (3), pp. 365–90.

Boyer, R. (1995) 'Capital-Labour Relations in OECD: From the Fordist Golden Age to Contrasted Trajectories', in J. Schor and J. Il You (eds), *Capital, the State and Labour: A Global Perspective* (Aldershot: Edward Elgar), pp.18–69.

Boyer, R. (2000) 'Is a Finance-Led Growth Regime a Viable Alternative to Fordism? A Preliminary Analysis', *Economy and Society*, vol. 29, pp. 111–45.

Boyer, R. (2004) *The Future of Economic Growth: As New Becomes Old* (Cheltenham, UK: Edward Elgar).

Boyer, R. (2005) 'Les crises financières contemporaines: entre nouveauté et repetition', *La lettre de la regulation*, vol. 52, pp. 1–6.

Boyer, R. and Petit, P. (1991) 'Technical Change, Cumulative Causation and Growth', in OECD Technology and Productivity Programme, *Technology and Productivity: The Challenge of Economic Policy* (Paris: OECD), pp. 47–67.

Broughton, A. (2002a) 'Social partners sign teleworking accord', *Eironline*, 23 July (http://www.eiro.eurofound.ie/2002/07/Feature/EU0207204F.html).

Broughton, A. (2002b) 'Social dialogue conference held in electricity sector', *Eironline*, 8 November (http://www.eiro.eurofound.ie/2002/11/inbrief/eu0211203n.html).

Broughton, A. (2004a) 'New social dialogue committee in local and regional government', *Eironline*, 23 March (http://www.eiro.eurofound.eu.int/2004/03/feature/eu0403203f.html).

Broughton, A. (2004b) 'Electricity partners agree joint statement on skills needs', *Eironline*, 6 July (http://www.eiro.eurofound.eu.int/2004/07/inbrief/eu0407201n.html).

Broughton, A. (2004c) 'Social partners sign work-related stress agreement', *Eironline*, 20 October (http://www.eiro.eurofound.eu.int/2004/10/feature/eu0410206f.html).

Brzezinski, Z. (1997a) 'A Geostrategy for Eurasia', *Foreign Affairs*, vol. 76 (5), pp. 78–89.

Brzezinski, Z. (1997b) *The Grand Chessboard: American Primacy and its Geostrategic Imperatives* (New York: Basic Books).

Brzezinski, Z. (2004) *The Choice: Global Domination or Global Leadership* (New York: Basic Books).

Buch-Hansen, H. (2006) 'Beyond Rationalism and Constructivism: Towards a Critical Realist Intervention in EU studies', Paper presented at the ESA Critical Political Economy Workshop in Amsterdam, August–September.

Buck, T. (2005) 'Brussels seeks to streamline EU's Lisbon agenda for economic reform', *Financial Times*, 18 January.

Buck, T. (2006) 'EU waters down services market law', *Financial Times*, 9 February.

Buck, T. (2007) 'Brussels resists clampdown on hedge funds', *Financial Times*, 9 May.

Buck, T. and Benoit, B. (2007) 'Dismay over competition shift', *Financial Times*, 23 June.

Buehler, K., Da Silva, V. and Pritsch, G. (2004) 'The Business Case for Basel II', *The McKinsey Quarterly*, vol. 1 (available from: http://www.mckinseyquarterly.com/article_page.aspx?ar=1396).

Burba, A. J. (1999) 'Emerging Leader of the Tax Avant-Garde: Poland's Proposal to Institute a Flat Tax on Individual and Corporate Incomes', *Vanderbilt Journal of Transnational Law*, vol. 32 (5), pp. 1402–1442.

Cafruny, A. (2003) 'The Geopolitics of U.S. Hegemony in Europe: From the Break-Up of Yugoslavia to the War in Iraq', in A. Cafruny and M. Ryner (eds), *A Ruined Fortress: Neoliberal Hegemony and Transformation in Europe* (Lanham, MD: Rowman and Littlefield), pp. 95–122.

Cafruny, A. and Ryner, M. (eds) (2003) *A Ruined Fortress?* (Lanham, MD: Rowman and Littlefield).

Cafruny, A. and Ryner, M. (2007a) 'Monetary Union and the Transatlantic and Social Dimensions of Europe's Crisis', *New Political Economy*, vol. 12 (2), pp. 141–66.

Cafruny, A. and Ryner, M. (2007b) *Europe at Bay: In the Shadow of U.S. Hegemony* (Boulder, CO: Lynne Rienner Publishers).

Campbell, J. L. (1998) 'Institutional Analysis and the Role of Ideas in Political Economy', *Theory and Society*, vol. 27 (3), pp. 377–409.

Capik, P. (2007) 'Organising FDI Promotion in Central-Eastern European Regions', *Place Branding and Public Diplomacy*, vol. 3 (2), pp. 152–63.

Caporaso, J. A. (1996) 'The European Union and Forms of State: Westphalian, Regulatory or Post-Modern?', *Journal of Common Market Studies*, vol. 34 (1), pp. 29–51.

Carchedi, G. (2001) *For Another Europe: A Class Analysis of European Economic Integration* (London: Verso).

Cardoso, F. and Faletto, E. (1979) *Dependency and Development in Latin America* (M. M. Urquidi, translation) (Berkeley and Los Angeles: University of California Press).

Cass, F. (2006) *Attracting FDI to Transition Countries: The Role and Impacts of Incentives and Promotion Agencies*. Manuscript.

Cassen, B. (2005a) 'ATTAC against the Treaty', *New Left Review*, vol. 33 (2), pp. 27–33.

Cassen, B. (2005b) 'Ce "non" qui redistribuerait les cartes en Europe', *Le Monde Diplomatique*, April, pp. 4–5.

Center for Strategic and International Studies (2005) *European Defense Integration: Bridging the Gap Between Strategy and Capabilities* (CSIS: Washington, DC).

Center for Strategic and International Studies (2007) *Towards a Grand Strategy for an Uncertain World: Renewing Transatlantic Partnership* (CSIS: Washington, DC).

Cerny, P. G. (1997) 'Paradoxes of the Competition State: The Dynamics of Political Globalization', *Government and Opposition*, vol. 32 (2), pp. 251–74.

Chesnais, F. (ed.) (2004) *La finance mondialisée: Racines sociales et politiques, configuration, conséquences* (Paris: La Découverte).

Chown, J. (2000) 'Monetary Union and Tax Harmonization', *International Tax Review*, vol. 28 (3), pp. 102–9.

Clayton, R. and Pontusson, J. (1998) 'Welfare State Retrenchment Revisited', *World Politics*, vol. 51 (1), pp. 67–98.

Coalitieakkoord (2007) 'Coalitieakkoord tussen de Tweede Kamerfracties van CDA, PvdA en ChristenUnie', 7 February (available from: http://www.regering.nl/dsc?c= getobject&s=obj&objectid=74638).

Coalition for Green and Social Procurement (2002) 'Proposal for a directive on the coordination of procedures for the award of public supply contracts, public service contracts and public works contracts', COM 275 (available from: http://www.eeb. org/activities/product_policy/Coalition-PP-April-2002-v3.pdf).

Coates, J. C. (2003) 'Ownership, Takeovers and EU Law: How Contestable Should EU Corporations Be?', ECGI Law Working Paper 11/2003.

Cohen, B. (2003) 'Global Currency Rivalry: Can the Euro Ever Rival the Dollar?', Global and International Studies Program, Paper No. 8, University of California at Santa Barbara.

Commission Européenne (2000) *La politique fiscale dans l'Union européenne* (Luxembourg: Office des Publications Officielles des Communautés Européennes).

Council of the European Union (1997) *Consolidated Version of the Treaty on European Union* (Luxembourg: Office for Official Publications of the European Communities).

Cowles, M. G. (1995) 'Setting the Agenda for a New Europe: The ERT and EC 1992', *Journal of Common Market Studies*, vol. 33 (4), pp. 501–26.

Cowles, M. G. (2001) 'The Transatlantic Business Dialogue: Transforming the New Transatlantic Dialogue', in M. A. Pollack and G. C. Shaffer (eds), *Transatlantic Governance in the Global Economy* (Lanham, MD: Rowman and Littlefield), pp. 213–33.

Cowles. M. G., Caporaso, J. and Risse, T. (eds) (2001) *Transforming Europe: Europeanization and Domestic Change* (Ithaca, NY: Cornell University Press).

Cox, R. W. (1981) 'Social Forces, States and World Orders: Beyond International Relations Theory', *Millennium,* vol. 10 (2), pp. 126–55.

Cox, R. W. (1992) 'Global Perestroika', in R. Miliband and L. Panitch (eds), *Socialist Register 1992* (London: Merlin Press), pp. 26–43.

Cox, R. W. and Sinclair, T. (1996) *Approaches to World Order* (Cambridge: Cambridge University Press).

Crouch, C. (2000) 'Introduction: The Political and Institutional Deficits of European Monetary Union', in C. Crouch (ed.), *After the Euro* (Oxford: Oxford University Press), pp. 1–23.

Csaba, L. (1997) 'Transformation in Hungary and (in) Hungarian Economics (1978–96)', Frankfurter Institut für Transformationsstudien, Discussion Paper 6/97.

Czarzasty, J. (2002) 'Amended labour code adopted', *Eironline*, 7 October (http://www. eurofound.europa.eu/eiro/2002/09/feature/pl0209107f.html).

Czech Radio 7 (2007) *Government reportedly set to push for 15-percent flat income tax rate,* Czech Radio 7, Radio Prague, 19 March (www.radio.cz/en/article/89462).

CzechInvest (2002) *CzechInvest: The investment gateway to the Czech Republic, 1992–2002* (Prague: CzechInvest).

DB Research (2004) 'Automobilmarkt Osteuropa: Produktionsstandort dauerhaft wichtiger als Absatzstandort', *EU Monitor*, vol. 15, pp. 16–20.

De Beus, J. (2004) 'The Netherlands: Monetary Integration and the Polder model', in A. Martin and G. Ross (eds), *Euros and Europeans: Monetary integration and the European Model of Society* (Cambridge: Cambridge University Press), pp. 174–200.

De Boer-Ashworth, E. (2000) *The Global Political Economy and Post-1989 Change: The Place of the Central European Transition* (New York: Palgrave Macmillan).

De Corbière, C. (2007) 'Le G-8 des patrons rêve d'un nouveau dialogue avec les politiques', *Le Figaro*, 26 April.

De Graaff, N. and Van Apeldoorn, B. (2008) 'The Making of the "Long War": Neo-conservative Networks and Continuity and Change in US Grand Strategy', Paper presented at the 49th Annual Convention of the International Studies Association, San Francisco, 24–9 March.

De Grauwe, P. (2006a) 'What Have We Learnt About Monetary Integration Since the Maastricht Treaty?', *Journal of Common Market Studies*, 44 (4), pp. 689–715.

De Grauwe, P. (2006b) 'Germany's pay policy points to Eurozone design flaw', *Financial Times*, 5 May, p. 11.

De Jong, A. and Röell, A. (2005) 'Financing and Control in the Netherlands: An Historical Perspective', in R. K. Morck (ed.), *A History of Corporate Governance around the World* (Chicago: University of Chicago Press), pp. 467–516.

De la Porte, C. and Pochet, P. (2001) 'Social Benchmarking, Policy Making and New Governance in the EU', *Journal of European Social Policy*, vol. 11 (4), pp. 291–307.

De Mooij, R. (2005) 'Will Corporate Income Taxation Survive?', *De Economist*, vol. 153 (3), pp. 277–301.

De Ste. Croix, G. E. M. (1981) *The Class Struggle in the Ancient Greek World from the Archaic Age to the Arab Conquests* (London: Duckworth).

Dekker, W. (1985) 'Europe 1990', Speech by the President of Phillips at the Centre for European Policy Studies in Brussels, 11 January.

Delors, J. (1992 [1988]) *Our Europe* (London: Verso).

Delsen, L. (2002) *Exit Polder Model? Socioeconomic changes in the Netherlands* (Westport, CT and London: Praeger).

Deutsche Welle (2005) 'Rumania, U.S. Sign Military Base Agreement', 7 December.

Deutschmann, C. (2005) 'Finanzmarkt-Kapitalismus und Wachstumskrise', in P. Windolf (ed.), *Finanzmarkt-Kapitalismus: Analysen zum Wandel von Produktionsregimen* (Wiesbaden: VS Verlag), pp. 58–84.

DGB (2006) 'Anforderungen des DGB and die Deutsche EU-Ratspräsidentschaft 2007: Beschluss des DGB-Bundesvorstandes vom 05, September 2006' (http://www.einblick.dgb.de/hintergrund/2006/16/text01/).

DGB (n.d.) 'Europäische Verfassung' (http://www.dgb.de/themen/europa/europ_verfassung.htm).

Diamantopoulou, A. (2000) 'Europe, Globalisation, and Social Policy', Speech/00/166, Brussels.

Dinan, D. (1999) *Ever Closer Union. An Introduction to European Integration*, 2nd edn (Boulder, CO and London: Lynne Rienner Publishers).

Dittert, J. and Kolanda, M. (1989) 'Worry Rather than Pride' (Spíše starost než chlouba), *Hospodářské noviny*, vol. 35.

Dølvik, J. E. (1999) *An Emerging Island? –ETUC, Social Dialogue and the Europeanisation of Trade Unions in the 1990s* (Brussels: ETUI).

Dombey, D. (2007) 'America Faces a Diplomatic Penalty as the Dollar Dwindles', *Financial Times*, 27 December, p. 9.

Domhoff, G. W. (1996) *State Autonomy or Class Dominance? Case studies on Policy Making in America* (New York: Aldine de Gruyter).

Dörre, K. and Brinkmann, U. (2005) 'Finanzmarkt-Kapitalismus: Triebkraft eines flexiblen Produktionsmodells?', in P. Windolf (ed.), *Finanzmarkt-Kapitalismus. Analysen zum Wandel von Produktionsregimen* (Wiesbaden: VS Verlag), pp. 85–116.

Drahokoupil, J. (2005) 'From Collectivization to Globalization: Putting Populism in Its Place', *Slovak Foreign Policy Affairs*, Spring, pp. 65–74.

Drahokoupil, J. (2007a) 'Analyzing the Capitalist State in Post-socialism: Towards the Porterian Workfare Postnational Regime', *International Journal of Urban and Regional Research*, vol. 31 (2), pp. 401–24.

Drahokoupil, J. (2007b) 'The State of the Capitalist State in East-Central Europe: Towards the Porterian Workfare Post-National Regime?', in B. S. Sergi, W. T. Bagatelas and J. Kubicová (eds), *Industries and Markets in Central and Eastern Europe* (Aldershot, UK: Ashgate), pp. 175–96.

Drahokoupil, J. (2008a) *Globalization and the State in Central and Eastern Europe: The Politics of Foreign Direct Investment* (London: Routledge).

Drahokoupil, J. (2008b) 'The Investment Promotion Machines: The Politics of Foreign Direct Investment Promotion in Central and Eastern Europe', *Europe-Asia Studies*, vol. 60 (2), pp. 199–227.

Drainville, A. C. (1994) 'International Political Economy in the Age of Open Marxism', *Review of International Political Economy*, vol. 1 (1), pp. 105–32.

Dulleck, U., Foster, N., Stehrer, R. and Woerz, J. (2004) 'Dimensions of Quality Upgrading in CEECs', Vienna, WIIW Working Paper 29.

Duménil, G. and Lévy, D. (2001) 'Costs and Benefits of Neoliberalism: A Class Analysis', *Review of International Political Economy*, vol. 8 (4), pp. 578–607.

Duménil, G. and Lévy, D. (2004a) *Capital Resurgent: Roots of the Neoliberal Revolution* (Cambridge, MA: Harvard University Press).

Duménil, G. and Lévy, D. (2004b) 'The Economics of US Imperialism at the Turn of the 21st Century', *Review of International Political Economy*, vol. 11 (4), pp. 657–76.

Dunford, M. (2005) 'Old Europe, New Europe, and the USA: Comparative Economic Performance, Inequality, and Market-Led Models of Development', *European Urban and Regional Studies*, vol. 12 (2), pp. 149–76.

Eamets, R. and Philips, K. (2006) 'Relocation of production and industrial relations – case of Estonia' (http://www.eiro.eurofound.eu.int/2005/11/study/index.html).

Easson, A. (1998) 'Tax Competition Heats Up in Central Europe', *Bulletin of the International Bureau of Fiscal Documentation*, May, pp. 192–7.

Eberlein, B. and Kerwer, D. (2004) 'New Governance in the European Union: A Theoretical Perpspective', *Journal of Common Market Studies*, vol. 42 (1), pp. 121–42.

EBRD (1994) *Transition Report 1994* (London: European Bank for Reconstruction and Development).

EBRD (2001) *Transition Report 2001: Energy in Transition* (London: European Bank for Reconstruction and Development).

ECB (2004) 'Enlargement and "old" Europe: Blow or blessing?', Speech by Tommaso Padoa-Schioppa, Member of the Executive Board of the ECB, Frankfurt am Main, 21 October (available from: http://www.ecb.int/press/key/date/2004/html/sp041021_1.en.html).

Economist, The (2004a) 'The Lisbon lament; Charlemagne', 6 November.

Economist, The (2004b) 'Je t'aime, ich auch nicht', 6 June, p. 371.

Economist, The (2005) 'The case for flat taxes: Pioneered in Eastern Europe, flat tax systems seem to work because they are simple', 14 April.

Economist, The (2006a) 'Special Report: European Energy Markets', 11 February (Oxford: Oxford University Press).

Economist, The (2006b) 'BAE Systems', 28 October.

Economist, The (2007) 'Eastern Europe economy: Are flat-rate tax systems here to stay?', The Economist Intelligence Unit Viewswire, 16 January.

Edwards, E., Netjes, C. E., and Steenbergen, M. R. (2004) 'Who's Cueing Whom? Assessing the Relationship between Electorate Opinion and Party Positions on the European Union', Paper presented at the Annual Meeting of the American Political Science Association, Washington, D.C., September 1–4, forthcoming in *European Union Politics*.

Eichengreen, B. (2003) *Capital flows and crisis* (Cambridge, MA: University Press).

EIRO (2006) 'Relocation of Production and Industrial Relations: Summary Report', *Eironline* (http://www.eiro.eurofound.eu.int/2005/11/study/index.html).

Eisenhardt, K. M. (1989) 'Building Theories from Case Study Research', *Academy of Management Review*, vol. 14, pp. 532–50.

EMF (1998) 'Collective bargaining with the Euro', 3rd EMF Collective Bargaining Conference, Frankfurth, 9–10 December (http://www.emf-fem.org/index.cfm?target=/default.cfm).

EMF (2001) 'EMF position on the European industrial relation system', adopted by the EMF Executive Committee, Luxembourg, 3–4 December (http://www.emf-fem.org/index.cfm?target=/default.cfm).

Engelen, E. R. (2006) 'How to solve the riddle of belated Euro contestation in the Netherlands?', Wetenschappelijk Raad voor het Regeringsbeleid, W26 (The Hague: WRR) (available from: http://www.wrr.nl/content.jsp? objectid=4043).

EPSU (2002) 'Services of General interest and the Convention on the future of Europe – You can shape the future of Europe!', EPSU General Circular No. 13 (http://www.epsu.org/Campaigns/sgi/gen13.cfm).

EPSU (2003a) '2003: A crucial year for public services in Europe', letter by the EPSU General Secretary Carola Fischbach-Pyttel to all affiliated unions (available from: http://www.epsu.org/gen1.cfm).

EPSU (2003b) 'GATS, PSI-EPSU and Pascal Lamy' (http://www.epsu.org/Campaigns/GATS/Lamy.cfm).

EPSU (2005) 'Public services – Europe's strength: EPSU priorities 2004–9', adopted by the EPSU Executive Committee, 7 June (available from: http//www.epsu.org/IMG/pdf/EN_Outline_EPSU_priorities_2004-2009_upd.pdf).

EPSU (2007) 'Social platform signs up to EPSU campaign for public services', 21 February (http://www.epsu.org/a/2775).

ERT (1983) 'Foundations for the Future of European Industry', Memorandum to EC Commissioner Davignon, 10 June.

ERT (1989) *Education and European Competence* (Brussels: European Round Table of Industrialists).

ERT (1991) *Reshaping Europe* (Brussels: European Round Table of Industrialists).

ERT (1992) *Lifelong Learning* (Brussels: European Round Table of Industrialists).

ERT (1994) *European Competitiveness: The Way to Growth and Jobs* (Brussels: European Round Table of Industrialists).

ERT (1995) *Education for Europeans – Towards the Learning Society* (Brussels: European Round Table of Industrialists).

ERT (1996) *Benchmarking for Policy-Makers: The Way to Competitiveness, Growth and Job Creation* (Brussels: European Round Table of Industrialists).

ERT (1999) *The East-West Win-Win Business Experience* (Brussels: European Round Table of Industrialists).

ERT (2001a) *Opening up the Business Opportunities of EU Enlargement: ERT Position Paper and Analysis of the Economic Costs and Benefits of EU Enlargement* (Brussels: European Round Table of Industrialists) (available from: http://www.ert.be/doc/0038.pdf).

ERT (2001b) *Actions for Competitiveness through the Knowledge Economy in Europe* (Brussels: European Round Table of Industrialists).

ERT (2002) *Will European Governments in Barcelona keep their Lisbon promises?* (Brussels: European Round Table of Industrialists).

ERT (2003) *The European Challenge. Message from the European Round Table of Industrialists to the Spring European Council* (Brussels: European Round Table of Industrialists).

ERT (2004a) *ERT's Vision of a Bigger Single Market* (Brussels: European Round Table of Industrialists).

ERT (2004b) *Letter to the March 2004 European Council* (Brussels: European Round Table of Industrialists) (available from: http://www.ert.be/doc/01663.pdf).

ERT (2004c) *Message on eve of Council Spring Summit* (Brussels: European Round Table of Industrialists).

ERT (2005) *The Chairmanship of Morris Tabaksblat* (Brussels: European Round Table of Industrialists).

Eschweiler, B. (2007) 'Don't Blame the Central Banks for the Falling Dollar', *Financial Times*, 4 December, p. 28.

Esping-Andersen, G. (1990) *The Three Worlds of Welfare Capitalism* (Cambridge: Polity Press).

ETUC (2000) 'Memorandum on the Lisbon European Council', March, (http://www.lex.unict.it/dml-online/archivio/numero4/online/ces.htm).

ETUC (2004) 'ETUC and the Lisbon Mid-Term Review: A Discussion and Background Document', Executive Committee, 13–14 October (Brussels: European Trade Union Confederation).

ETUC (2005a) 'ETUC hails victory over Bolkenstein and calls for "Yes" votes on the Constitution', 23 March (http://www.etuc.org/a/1018).

ETUC (2005b) '"Revitalize the Lisbon strategy" by keeping the balance between the economic, social and environmental pillars and by the reform of the macroeconomic policy framework', Resolution adopted by the ETUC Executive Committee in their meeting in Brussels on 15–16 March 2005 (available from: http://www.etuc.org/a/1006?var_recherche=lisbon+agenda).

ETUC (2006) 'Euro-demonstration: Strasbourg 14/02/2006' (available from: http://www.etuc.org/a/1581).

ETUC (2008) *ETUC members – List of National Trade Union Confederations* (http://www.etuc.org/a/82).

ETUC /UNICE/UEAMPE/CEEP (2005) 'Joint declaration on mid-term review of Lisbon strategy: Social partners agree on the way forward', 15 March, Brussels (available from: http://www.etuc.org/IMG/pdf/Joint_declarationspring_sumita.pdf).

EUObserver (2006) 'EU energy policy encounters difficulties', Brussels, 8 February.

EUObserver (2007) 'EU summit paper sparks clash over taxation', Brussels, 27 February.

EurActiv (2007) 'Debate over tax sovereignty heats up in Slovakia', 11 April, updated 31 May.

European Commission (1988) 'Europe 1992: The Overall Challenge', SEC 524 final, 13 April (Brussels: European Commission).

European Commission (1995a) 'Preparation of the Associated Countries of Central and Eastern Europe For Integration into the Internal Market of the Union', Commission's White Paper, COM 163 final, 3 May (Brussels: European Commission).

European Commission (1995b) 'Teaching and Learning: Towards the Learning Society', White Paper on Education and Training, COM 590 final, 29 November (Brussels: European Commission).

European Commission (1996a) 'Taxation in the European Union', SEC 487 final, 20 March (Brussels: European Commission).

European Commission (1996b) 'Taxation in the European Union: Report on the Development of Tax Systems', COM 546 final, 22 October (Brussels: European Commission).

European Commission (1997) 'Benchmarking: Implementation of an Instrument Available to Economic Actors and Public Authorities', COM 153/2 final, 16 April (Brussels: European Commission).

European Commission (1999a) 'A Review of Regulatory Capital Requirements for Credit Institutions and Investment Firms', Consultation Document, MARKT/1123/99-EN, 22 November (available from: http://ec.europa.eu/internal_market/bank/docs/regcapital/1999-consult/1999-consult_en.pdf).

European Commission (1999b) 'Implementing the Framework for Financial Markets: Action Plan', COM 232, 11 May (Brussels: European Commission).

European Commission (2000) 'Innovation in a Knowledge-Driven Economy', COM 567 final, 20 September (Brussels: European Commission).

European Commission (2001a) 'Company law: Commission Creates High Level Group of Experts', IP/01/1237, 4 September, Brussels.

European Commission (2001b) 'Towards an Internal Market Without Tax Obstacles. A Strategy for Providing Companies with a Consolidated Corporate Tax Base for their EU-Wide Activities', 23 October, COM 582 final (Brussels: European Commission).

European Commission (2002a) 'Proposal for a Directive on Takeover Bids', COM 534 final, 2 October *Official Journal of the European Union 45 E.*

European Commission (2002b) 'The Lisbon Strategy: Making Change Happen', COM 14 final, 15 January (Brussels: European Commission).

European Commission (2003a) 'An Internal Market Without Company Tax Obstacles: Achievements, Ongoing Initiatives and Remaining Challenges', Communication form the Commission to the Council, the European Parliament and the European Economic and Social Committee, 24 November, COM 726 final (Brussels: European Commission).

European Commission (2003b) 'Choosing to Grow: Knowledge, Innovation and Jobs in a Cohesive Society', COM 5 final, 14 January (Brussels: European Commission).

European Commission (2003c) 'European Defence – Industrial and Market Issues: Towards an EU Defence Equipment Policy', COM 133 final, 11 March (Brussels: European Commission).

European Commission (2003d) 'Modernising Company Law and Enhancing Corporate Governance in the European Union – A Plan to move Forward', 21 May, COM 284 final (Brussels: European Commission).

European Commission (2003e) *The European Economy* No. 6 (January) (Brussels: European Commission).

European Commission (2004a) 'A Common Consolidated EU Corporate Tax Base', Commission Non-Paper to informal Ecofin Council, 10–11 September, (Brussels: European Commission), 7 July (available from: http://europa.eu.int/comm/taxation_customs/resources/documents/ CCTBWPNon_Paper.pdf).

European Commission (2004b) 'Delivering Lisbon: Reforms for the Enlarged Union', Report from the Commission to the Spring European Council, 20 February, COM 29 final/2, (Brussels: European Commission).

European Commission (2005a) 'Commission Staff Working Document' (in Support of the Report from the Commission to the Spring European Council, 22–3 March 2005, on the Lisbon Strategy of Economic, Social and Environmental Renewal), 28 January, SEC 160 (Brussels: European Commission).

European Commission (2005b) 'Communication to the Spring European Council: Working Together for Growth and Jobs – A New Start for the Lisbon Strategy', 2 February, COM 24 (Brussels: European Commission).

European Commission (2005c) *Eurobarometer 64: Public Opinion in the European Union* (Brussels: European Commission), December (available from: http://europa.eu.int/comm/public_opinion/archives/eb/eb64/eb64_first_en.pdf).

European Commission (2005d) 'Integrated Guidelines for Growth and Jobs', COM 141 final, 12 April (Brussels: European Commission).

European Commission (2006a) 'A European Strategy for Sustainable, Competitive and Secure Energy', COM 105 final, 8 March (Brussels: European Commission).

European Commission (2006b) *The European Economy,* No. 6 (January) (Brussels: European Commission).

European Council (2000) 'Presidency Conclusions: Lisbon European Council 23 and 25 March 2000', DOC/00/8, 24 March.

European Parliament (2003) 'Taxation in Europe: Recent developments', European Parliament Directorate-General for Research Working Paper, Economic Affairs Series, ECON 131 EN 01-2003.

European Parliament (2005) 'Basel II directives on track', (http://www.europarl.europa.eu/news/expert/infopress_page/042-1444-238-08-34-907-20050826IPR01426-26-08-2005-2005-false/default_en.htm).

European Parliament (2006) 'Directive 2006/48/EC of the European Parliament and of the Council of 14 June 2006', *Official Journal of the European Union* (available from: htttp://eurlex.europa.eu/LexUriServ/site/en/oj/2006/l_177/l_17720060630en00010200.pdf).

European Restructuring Monitor Database (http://www.eurofound.europa.eu/emcc/erm/index.php?template=stats).

Evans, E. and Strasburg, J. (2008) 'Soros Sees End of Dollar-Backed Credit Expansion', 23 January (www.bloomberg.com).

Evans, P. (1979) *Dependent Development: The Alliance of Multinational, State, and Local Capital in Brazil* (Princeton: Princeton University Press).

Evans, P. (1982) 'Reinventing the Bourgeoisie: State Entrepreneurship and Class Formation in Dependent Capitalist Development', *American Journal of Sociology*, vol. 88, S210–47.

Evans, P. (1995) *Embedded Autonomy: States and Industrial Transformation.* (Princeton, NJ: Princeton University Press).

Evans, P., Rueschemeyer, D. and Skocpol, T. (eds) (1985) *Bringing the State Back in* (Cambridge and New York: Cambridge University Press).

Eyal, G., Szelenyi, I. and Townsley, E. R. (1998) *Making Capitalism Without Capitalists: Class Formation and Elite Struggles in Post-Communist Central Europe* (London and New York: Verso).

Falkner, G. (1998) *EU Social Policy in the 1990's: Towards a Corporatist Policy Community* (London: Routledge).

Farrell, D. (2005) 'The U.S. Trade Deficit Does Not Spell Doom', *Financial Times*, 10 February, p. 13.

Fáth, P. (2003) 'Interview with Péter Fáth, Executive Director of the American Chamber of Commerce', 20 February (Interview conducted together with Dóra Husz).

Faz.Net (2005) 'Electrolux schliesst AEG-Werk in Nürnberg', 12 December (http://www.faz.net/s/RubC9401175958F4DE28E143E68888825F6/Doc~EDF92DA1B513F41DCBC5B86446FF4ED37~ATpl~Ecommon~Scontent.html).

Feldmann, M. (2001) 'The Fast Track from the Soviet Union to the World Economy: External Liberalization in Estonia and Latvia', *Government and Opposition*, vol. 36 (4), pp. 537–58.

Feldmann, M. (2006) 'The Baltic States: Using Pace-Setting on EMU Accession to Consolidate Domestic Stability Culture', in K. Dyson (ed.) *Enlarging the Euro-Zone: The Euro and the Transformation of East-Central Europe* (Oxford: Oxford University Press), pp. 127–44.

Ferrera, M. (2005) *The Boundaries of Welfare. European Integration and the New Spatial Politics of Social Protection* (Oxford: Oxford University Press).

Ferrera, M. (2006) 'Friends, not Foes: European Integration and National Welfare States', URGE Working Paper, 10/2006.

Ferrera, M., Hemerijck, A. and Rhodes, M. (2000) 'The Future of Social Europe: Recasting Work and Welfare in the New Economy', Report for the Portuguese Presidency of the European Union (available from: http://www.iue.it/SPS/People/Faculty/Current Professors/PDFFiles/RhodesPDFfiles/report.pdf).

Fielder, N. (1997) *Western European Integration in the 1980s: The Origins of the Single Market* (New York: Peter Lang).

Fielder, N. (2000) 'The Origins of the Single Market', in V. Bornschier (ed.), *State-building in Europe: The Revitalization of Western European Integration* (Cambridge: Cambridge University Press), pp. 75–92.

Financial Times (2004a) 'Europe's tax rivalry', 24 November, p. 10.

Financial Times (2004b) 'Listless Lisbon: Europe needs all hands to prime the economic reform pump', *Editorial*, 26 March.

Financial Times (2007a) 'Finland joins the retreat of Nordic social democracy', 21 March, p. 11.

Financial Times (2007b) 'It's a multi-currency world we live in: The dollar is becoming merely the first among equals', 27 December, p. 8.

Financial Times (2008) 'Euro-US coupled', 22 February, p. 8.

Fligstein, N. and Stone Sweet, A. (2002) 'Constructing Politics and Markets: An Institutionalist Account of European Integration', *American Journal of Sociology*, vol. 107 (5), pp. 1206–43.

Fondazione Rodolfo Debenedetti (2008) *FRDB Social Reforms Database* (available from: http://www.frdb.org/documentazione/scheda.php?id=55&doc_pk=9027).

Force Ouvrière (2005) 'Europe – FO confirme qu'elle n'est pas engagée par la position de la CES', Communiqué Force Ouvrière, 21 January (http://www.force-ouvriere.fr/).

Fortuyn, P. (2002) *De Puinhopen van acht jaar Paars* (Uithoorn: Karakter Uitgevers).

Freyberg-Inan, A. (2005) 'World System Theory: A Bird's-Eye View of the World Capitalist Order', in J. Sterling-Folker (ed.), *Making Sense of International Relations Theory* (Boulder, CO: Lynne Rienner Publishers), pp. 225–41.

Frieden, J. and Rogowski, R. (1996) 'The Impact of the International Economy on National Policies: An Analytical Overview', in R. O. Keohane and H. V. Milner (eds), *Internationalization and Domestic Politics* (Cambridge and New York: Cambridge University Press), pp. 25–47.

G10-Solidaires (2002) *Qu'est-ce que SUD Solidaires* (Paris: L'Archipel).

G10-Solidaires (2005) 'La Constitution européenne: Une constitution libérale contre les peuples – Votez NON!', 23 February (http://solidaires.org/article2170.html?var_recherche=Constitution).

Galbraith, J. K. (2004) 'Rising inequality within countries under globalization', paper presented at the annual meeting of the American Political Science Association, Chicago, September.

Gandullia, L. (2004) 'Tax systems and reforms in EU new member countries: An overview', Università di Genova DISEFIN, Working Paper 10/2004.

Ganghof, S. (1999): *Adjusting National Tax Policy to Economic Internationalization: Strategies and Outcomes*, MPIfG Discussion Paper 99/6, Cologne: Max Planck Institut für Gesellschaftsforschung, December 1999.

Gardner, D. (1991) 'Crisis in Yugoslavia; EC dashes into its own backyard – Ministers making fresh trip in attempt to salvage peace package', *Financial Times*, 1 July, p. 1.

Gill, S. (1998) 'European Governance and New Constitutionalism: Economic and Monetary Union and Alternatives to Disciplinary Neolibealism in Europe', *New Political Economy*, vol. 3 (1), pp. 5–26.

Gill, S. (2001) 'Constitutionalising Capital: EMU and Disciplinary Neoliberalism', in A. Bieler and A. D. Morton (eds), *Social Forces in the Making of the New Europe: The Restructuring of European Social Relations in the Global Political Economy* (London: Palgrave Macmillan), pp. 47–69.

Glassman, J. (1999) 'State Power Beyond the "Territorial Trap": The Internationalization of the State', *Political Geography*, vol. 18, pp. 669–96.

Glick Schiller, N. (2006) 'What Can Transnational Studies Offer the Analysis of Localized Conflict and Protest?', *Focaal – European Journal of Anthropology*, vol. 47, pp. 3–17.

Global Risk Regulator (2007a) 'FDIC's Bair fears Basel II impasse; Fed's Bies urges forward movement, says market risk timetable could be pushed back', June (http://www.globalriskregulator.com/grrnews0041.htm).

Global Risk Regulator (2007b) 'Turmoil shows up Basel II model weaknesses, says FDIC's Blair; Australia names banks for advanced approach', December (http://www.globalriskregulator.com/article.php?pgkey=1600).

Gollbach, J. and Schulten, T. (2000) 'Cross-Border Collective Bargaining Networks in Europe', *European Journal of Industrial Relations*, vol. 6 (2), pp. 161–79.

Gompert, D. (1996) 'The United Nations and Yugoslavia's Wars', in R. Ullman (ed.), *The World and Yugoslavia's Wars* (New York: Council on Foreign Relations), pp. 122–44.

Goodman, P. and Story, L. (2008) 'Overseas Investors Buy Aggressively in U.S', *New York Times*, 20 January, p. B1.

Goul Andersen, J. (2007) 'The Danish Welfare State as "Politics for Markets": Combining Equality and Competitiveness in a Global Economy', *New Political Economy*, vol. 12 (1), pp. 71–8.

Gould, J. (2001) *Beyond Creating Owners: Privatization and Democratization in the Slovak and Czech Republics, 1990–8*. Unpublished PhD, Columbia University.

Gourevitch, P. A. and Shinn, J. (2005) *Political Power and Corporate Control* (Princeton and Oxford: Princeton University Press).

Gowan, P. (1995) 'Neo-Liberal Theory and Practice for Eastern Europe', *New Left Review*, vol. 213, pp. 3–60.

Gowan, P. (1996) 'Eastern Europe, Western Power and Neo-Liberalism', *New Left Review*, vol. 216, pp. 129–40.

Gowan, P. (1999) *The Global Gamble: Washington's Faustian Bid for World Dominance* (London: Verso).

Grabbe, H. (1999) 'A Partnership for Accession? The Implications of EU Conditionality for the Central and East European Applicants', European University Institute, Robert Schuman Centre Working Paper 12/99.

Grabbe, H. (2006) *The EU's Transformative Power: Europeanization Through Conditionality in Central and Eastern Europe* (Basingstoke: Palgrave Macmillan).

Grahl, J. (2001) 'Globalized Finance: The Challenge to the Euro', *New Left Review. Second Series*, vol. 8, pp. 23–47.

Grahl, J. (2004) 'The European Union and American Power', in L. Panitch and C. Leys (eds), *The Empire Reloaded, Socialist Register 2005* (London: Merlin Press), pp. 284–300.

Grahl, J. (2005) 'Europe's Inflexible Bank', *Le Monde Diplomatique*, July, pp. 7–8.

Grahl, J. and Teague, P. (1989) 'The Cost of Neoliberal Europe', *New Left Review*, vol. 174, pp. 33–50.

Grahl, J. and Teague, P. (1990) *1992 – The Big Market: The Future of the European Community* (London: Lawrence and Wishart).

Grahl, J. and Teague, P. (1994) 'Economic Citizenship in the New Europe', *Political Quarterly*, vol. 64 (4), pp. 379–96.

Gramsci, A. (1971) *Selections from the Prison Notebooks* (translation Q. Hoare and G. Nowell Smith) (New York: International Publishers).

Greenwood, J. (2003) *Interest Representation in the European Union* (London: Palgrave Macmillan).

Greskovits, B. (1998) *The Political Economy of Protest and Patience: East European and Latin American Transformations Compared* (Budapest: Central European University Press).

Greskovits, B. (2000) 'Hungary's Post-Communist Development in Comparative Perspective', in W. Baer and J. L. Love (eds), *Liberalization and its Consequences: A Comparative Perspective on Latin America and Eastern Europe* (Cheltenham: Edward Elgar), pp. 126–49.

Greskovits, B. (2005) 'Leading Sectors and the Variety of Capitalism in Eastern Europe', *Actes du GERPISA*, vol. 39, pp. 113–28.

Greskovits, B. (2007) 'Terminating Social Contracts: Mass Exit, Extreme Voice, and Regime Destabilization in Central and Eastern Europe', Conference paper presented at Political Turbulences in Central Europe: Symptoms of a Post-accession Crisis? Friedrich Ebert Stiftung, Budapest, 25–7 February.

Griffith, R. and Klemm, A. (2004) 'What has been the Tax Competition Experience of the Last 20 Years?', Institute for Fiscal Studies, Working Papers 04/05.

Griffith-Jones, S. (2003) 'How to prevent the New Basel Capital Accord harming developing countries', IDS, Sussex (available from: http://www.wadmo.net/Basel2_Griffith Jones.pdf).

Groenendijk, N. S. (1999) 'Tax Co-ordination and the Enlargement of the European Union', *Journal for Institutional Innovation, Development and Transition*, vol. 3, pp. 55–73.

Groenendijk, N. S. (2006) 'Enhanced Cooperation in Corporate Taxation: Possibilities and Possible Effects', Paper presented at EUSA Economics Interest Section Research seminar 'Whither EU integration and cooperation?', Viessmann Research Centre on Modern Europe, Laurier Waterloo, 28 April, Ontario, Canada.

Grunberg, G. (2005) 'Le referendum français de ratification du traite constitutionnel européen du 29 mai 2005', *French Politics, Culture, and Society*, vol. 23 (3), pp. 128–45.

Guha, K. (2007) 'The world's currency could become America's problem', *Financial Times*, November 10, p. 13.

Guha, R. (1992) 'Dominance Without Hegemony and its Historiography', in R. Guha (ed.), *Subaltern Studies VI* (New Delhi: Oxford University Press India), pp. 20–38.

Haas, E. B. (1968 [1958], with 1968 preface) *The Uniting of Europe. Political, Social and Economic Forces*, 1950–7 (Stanford: Stanford University Press).

Haas, P. M. (1992) 'Epistemic Communities and International Policy Coordination', *International Organization*, vol. 46 (1), pp. 1–35.

Haba, K. (2004) 'The EU and NATO enlargement and Central Eastern European's EU Policy under the Influence of the USA Non-European Perspective', Paper presented at the SGIR Pan-European International Relations Conference, The Hague, 9–11 September.

Habermas, J. and Derrida, J. (2003) 'February 15, or What Binds Europeans Together: A Plea for a Common Foreign Policy, Beginning in the Core of Europe', *Constellations*, vol. 10(3), pp. 291–97.

Haggard, S. (1990) *Pathways from the Periphery: The Politics of Growth in the Newly Industrializing Countries* (Ithaca and London: Cornell University Press).

Hall, B. and Parker, G. (2007) 'Paris urged to learn from history', *Financial Times*, 6 June.

Hall, P. and Soskice, D. (2001a) 'An Introduction to Varieties of Capitalism', in P. Hall and D. Soskice (eds), *Varieties of Capitalism. The Institutional Foundations of Comparative Advantage* (Oxford: Oxford University Press), pp. 1–68.

Hall, P. and Soskice, D. (eds) (2001b) *Varieties of Capitalism. The Institutional Foundation of Comparative Advantage* (Oxford: Oxford University Press).

Hamilton, D. S. and Quinlan, J. P. (eds) (2005) *Deep Integration. How Transatlantic Markets are Leading Globalization* (Washington, DC and Brussels: CTR and CEPS).

Hanley, E., King, L. and Janos, I. T. (2002) 'The State, International Agencies, and Property Transformation in Postcommunist Hungary', *American Journal of Sociology*, vol. 108 (1), pp. 129–67.

Hansen, P. (2000) 'European Citizenship: Or Where Neoliberalism Meets Ethnoculturalism', *European Societies*, vol. 2 (2), pp. 139–65.

Hansen, P. (2005) 'Still a *European* Social Model? From a Vision of a "Social Europe" to the EU Reality of Embedded Neoliberalism' (in co-operation with Carl-Ulrik Schierup), *Themes: Occasional Papers and Reprints on Ethnic Studies*, No. 26, Norrköping: Centre for Ethnic and Urban Studies (CEUS) (http://www.ceus.nu/ themes/THEMES262005.pdf).

Hanson, B. T. (1998) 'What Happened to Fortress Europe?: External Trade Policy Liberalization in the European Union', *International Organization*, vol. 52 (1), pp. 55–85.

Harcourt, A. and Radaelli, C. (1999) 'Limits to EU Technocratic Regulation?', *European Journal of Political Research*, vol. 35, pp. 107–22.

Harvey, D. (2003) *The New Imperialism* (Oxford: Oxford University Press).

Harvey, D. (2005) *A Brief History of Neoliberalism* (Oxford: Oxford University Press).

Haseler, S. (2004) *Superstate: The New Europe and its Challenge to America* (London: I. B. Taurus).

Häusler, J. and Hirsch, J. (1989) 'Political Regulation: The Crisis of Fordism and the Transformation of the Party System in West Germany', in M. Gottdiener and N. Komninos (eds), *Capitalist Development and Crisis Theory* (New York: St Martin's Press), pp. 300–27.

Hay, C. (2002) *Political Analysis* (Basingstoke and New York: Palgrave Macmillan).

Hay, C. (2004) 'Common Trajectories, Variable Paces, Divergent Outcomes? Models of European Capitalism Under Conditions of Complex Economic Interdependence', *Review of International Political Economy*, vol. 11 (2), pp. 231–62.

Heemskerk, E. M. (2007) *The Decline of the Corporate Community. Network Dynamics of the Dutch Business Elite* (Amsterdam: Amsterdam University Press).

Heine, S. (2006) 'Ideological Analysis of the Alterglobalists' Euroscepticism: Attac-France and Attac-Germany's Critiques against the "European Constitution"', Paper presented at ESA Critical Political Economy Workshop, Amsterdam, 31 August–2 September.

Helleiner, E. (1994) *States and the Re-emergence of Global Finance: From Bretton Woods to the 1990s* (Ithaca, NY: Cornell University Press).

Hemerijck, A. (2002) 'The Self Transformation of the European Social Model(s)', *International Politics and Society*, vol. 4, pp. 1–24.

Higgott, R. (2000) 'Contested Globalization: The Changing Context and Normative Challenges', *Review of International Studies*, vol. 26, pp. 131–54.

High Level Group Chaired by Wim Kok (2004) *Facing the Challenge: The Lisbon Strategy for Growth and Employment* (Luxembourg: Office for Official Publications of the European Communities).

High Level Group of Company Experts (2002) *Report of the high level group of company law experts on issues related to takeover bids* (available from: http://ec.europa.eu/ internal_market/company/docs/takeoverbids/2002-01-hlg-report_en.pdf).

Hirschman, A. O. (1970) *Exit, Voice and Loyalty. Responses to Decline in Firms, Organization, and States* (Cambridge: Harvard University Press).

Hofheinz, P. (2005) cited in an LCEC press release entitled 'A New Beginning', 2 February, Brussels, LCEC.

Hollinger, P., Laitner, S. and Mulligan, M. (2006) 'France fearful over deal's effects', *Financial Times*, 30 January.

Holman, O. (1992) 'Transnational Class Strategy and the New Europe', *International Journal of Political Economy*, vol. 22 (1), pp. 3–22.

Holman, O. (1998) 'Integrating Eastern Europe: EU Expansion and the Double Transformation in Poland, the Czech Republic, and Hungary', *International Journal of Political Economy*, vol. 28 (2), pp. 12–43.

Holman, O. (2001) 'The Enlargement of the European Union Towards Central and Eastern Europe: The Role of Supranational and Transnational Actors', in A. Bieler and A. D. Morton (eds), *Social Forces in the Making of the New Europe: The Restructuring of European Social Relations in the Global Political Economy* (Basingstoke: Palgrave Macmillan), pp. 161–84.

Holman, O. (2004a) 'Asymmetrical Regulation and Multidimensional Governance in the EU', *Review of International Political Economy*, vol. 11 (4), pp. 714–35.

Holman, O. (2004b) 'Integrating Peripheral Europe: The Different Roads to "Security and Stability" in Southern and Central Europe', *Journal of International Relations and Development*, vol. 7 (2), pp. 208–36.

Holman, O. and Van der Pijl, K. (1996) 'The Capitalist Class in the European Union', in G. Kourvetaris and A. Moschonas (eds), *The Impact of European Integration: Political, Sociological and Economic Changes* (London: Pinter), pp. 55–74.

Holmquist, J. (2007) 'Implementation of Basel II. Challenges and Opportunities', Speech for Institute of International Bankers, 5 March (available from: http://ec.europa.eu/internal_market/speeches/docs/2007/jh05032007.pdf).

Holtz-Eakin, D. (2006) 'How to determine whether the War is worth it', *Financial Times*, 14 February.

Hooghe, L. and Marks, G. (1999) 'The Making of a Polity: The Struggle over European Integration', in H. Kitschelt, P. Lange, G. Marks and J. Stephens (eds), *Continuity and Change in Contemporary Capitalism* (Cambridge and New York: Cambridge University Press), pp. 70–97.

Hooghe, L. and Marks, G. (2007a) 'A Postfunctional Theory of European Integration: From Permissive Consensus to Constraining Dissensus', *British Journal of Political Science*, forthcoming.

Hooghe, L. and Marks, G. (2007b) (eds) *Understanding Euroscepticism*, Special Issue of *Acta Politica*, vol. 42 (2–3).

Höpner, M. (2003) *Wer beherrscht die Unternehmen? Shareholder Value, Managerherrschaft und Mitbestimmung in Deutschland* (Frankfurt: Campus Verlag).

Hossein-Zadeh, I. (2006) *The Political Economy of U.S. Militarism* (New York: Palgrave Macmillan).

Horkheimer, M. (1982 [1939]) 'The Social Function of Philosophy', in *Critical Theory: Selected Essays* (London: Continuum).

Hulsink, W. and Schenk, H. (1998) 'Privatisation and Deregulation in the Netherlands', in D. Parker (ed.), *Privatisation in the European Union: Theory and Policy Perspectives* (London: Routledge), pp. 242–57.

Hunter, R. and Shapiro, R. (2000) 'Reform of the Polish Tax System: Triumph of Politics over Policy?', *International Tax Journal*, vol. 26, pp 79–85.

Husson, M. (2008) *Un pur capitalisme* (Paris: Page Deux).

IG Metall (2007) 'Übersicht "Vertrag von Lissabon" und erste Bewertung', 22 October (available from: http://www.igmetall.de/cps/rde/xbcr/SID-0A456501-2E99F2F2/internet/1_0028712.pdf).

Irish Times (2004) 'Barroso intent on shifting EU to the right', *Editorial*, 7 February.

ITUC (2007) 'Decent work campaign launched in Nairobi', 13 February (http://www.ituc-csi.org/spip.php?article583).

Ivanova, M. (2007) 'Why There Was No "Marshall Plan" for Eastern Europe and Why This Still Matters', *Journal of Contemporary European Studies*, vol. 15 (3), 346–74.

Iversen, T. and Wren, A. (1998) 'Equality, Employment and Budgetary Restraint: The Trilemma of the Service Economy', *World Politics*, vol. 50 (4), pp. 507–46.

Iversen, T. (2005) *Capitalism, Democracy and Welfare* (Cambridge: Cambridge University Press).

Jackson, B. (2006) 'The "Soft" War for Europe's East', *Policy Review*, vol. 137, pp. 3–14.

Jäger, J. (2004) 'Basel II: Ökonomische Regulation, Finanzsystemstabilität und Realwirtschaft', *WISO*, vol. 27, pp. 127–46.

Jäger, J. and Redak, V. (2006) 'Austrian Bank's Lending and Loan Pricing Strategies against the Background of Basel II', *OeNB Financial Stability Report*, vol. 12, pp. 92–103.

Jenkins, P. (2005) 'Hedge funds spark Berlin's ire', *Financial Times*, 20 April.

Jensen, C. (2006) 'Foreign Direct Investment and Economic Transition: Panacea or Pain Killer?', *Europe-Asia Studies*, vol. 58 (6), pp. 881–902.

Jessop, B. (1983) 'Accumulation Strategies, State Forms, and Hegemonic Projects', *Kapitalistate*, vol. 10 (11), pp. 89–111.

Jessop, B. (1990) *State Theory: Putting the Capitalist State in its Place* (Cambridge: Polity).

Jessop, B. (2002) *The Future of the Capitalist State* (London: Polity Press).

Jessop, B. (2003) 'Changes in Welfare Regimes and the Search for Flexibility and Employability', in H. Overbeek (ed.), *The Political Economy of European Unemployment. European Integration and the Transnationalization of the (Un)employment Question* (London: Routledge), pp. 29–50.

Jessop, B. (2007) *State Power* (Cambridge: Polity Press).

Jones, S. and Larrabee, F. (2006) 'Arming Europe', *The National Interest*, vol. 82, pp. 62–8.

Judt, T. (2005) *Postwar: A History of Europe Since 1945* (New York: Penguin).

Jürgens, U., Krzywdzinski, M. and Teipen, C. (2006) 'Changing Work and Employment Relations in German Industries – Breaking Away from the German Model', WZB-Discussion Paper, SPIII-2006-302.

Kader, M. (2005) 'Risiko, Rating, Rendite: Zur Reorganisation der Kreditvergabe durch Basel II', *Kurswechsel*, vol. 3, pp. 80–9.

Kalb, D. (1997) *Expanding Class: Power and Everyday Politics in Industrial Communities, The Netherlands, 1850–1950* (Durham: Duke University Press).

Kapstein, E. B. (1994) *Governing the Global Economy: International Finance and the State* (Cambridge and Massachusetts: Harvard University Press).

Karnite, R. (2006) 'Relocation of Production and Industrial Relations – Case of Latvia', *Eironline* (http://www.eiro.eurofound.eu.int/2005/11/study/index.html).

Keen, M., Kim, Y. and Varsano, R. (2006) 'The "Flat tax(es)": Principles and Evidence', IMF Working Paper 06/218 (Washington, DC: International Monetary Fund).

Keller, B. (2003) 'Social Dialogues – the State of the Art a Decade after Maastricht', *Industrial Relations Journal*, vol. 34 (5), pp. 411–29.

Keman, H. (2003) 'Explaining Miracles: Third Ways and Work and Welfare', *West European Politics*, vol. 26 (2), pp. 115–35.

Kindleberger, C. (1973) *The World in Depression* (Berkeley: University of California Press).

King, L. P. (2001a) *The Basic Features of Postcommunist Capitalism in Eastern Europe: Firms in Hungary, the Czech Republic, and Slovakia* (London and Westport, CT: Praeger).

King, L. P. (2001b) 'Making Markets: A Comparative Study of Postcommunist Managerial Strategies in Central Europe', *Theory and Society*, vol. 30 (4), pp. 493–538.

King, M. R. and Sinclair, T. (2003) 'Private Actors and Public Policy: A Requiem for the New Basel Capital Accord', *International Political Sciences Review*, vol. 24, pp. 345–62.

Klandermans, B. en Visser, J. (1995) *De vakbeweging na de Welvaartsstaat* (Assen: Van Gorcum).

Kleinknecht, A. and Naastepad, C. W. M. (2002) 'Is loonmatiging goed voor de export?', *Economisch Statistische Berichten*, vol. 87, pp. 624–6.

Kleinnijenhuis, J., Takens, J. and Atteveldt, W. H. (2005) 'Toen Europa de dagbladen ging vullen', in K. Aarts, and H. van der Kolk (eds), *Nederlanders en Europa: Het Referendum over de Nederlandse Grondwet* (Amsterdam: Bert Bakker), pp. 123–44.

Koch, K. (2001) 'De valse tweedeling van federalism en intergouvermentalisme: Terughoudendheid als traditie in Nederlands Europees beleid', *Internationale Spectator*, vol. 55 (9), pp. 429–43.

Kok, W. (1995) 'Sociaal Nederland kan niet zonder publieke sector', *NRC Handelsblad*, 12 December, p. 10.

Kolanda, M. (1989) *Ke strategii rozvoje čs. strojírenství v letech 1990–2010 [Strategy of Development of Engineering and Electrotechnical Industry 1990–2010].* Prague: Prognostický ústav ČSAV (Institute for Economic Forecasting, Czech Academy of Science).

Kolesár, P. (2006) 'Race to the Bottom? The Role of Investment Incentives in Attracting Strategic Automotive Foreign Direct Investment in Central Europe', MA Thesis, Central European University, Budapest, Department of International Relations and European Studies.

Korpi, W. (2003) 'Welfare-State Regress in Western Europe: Politics, Institutions, Globalization and Europeanization', *Annual Review of Sociology*, vol. 29, pp. 589–609.

Kovács, L. (2006) 'Making the EU Tax-Competitive', Speech of Commissioner László Kovács, First Business Round Table with the European Commission hosted by The Economist, 10 October, Brussels.

Kreling, T. (2004) 'Iedereen zijn eigen reden voor protest', *NRC Handelsblad*, 4 Oktober.

Kuhn, T. (1962) *The Structure of Scientific Revolutions* (Chicago: Chicago University Press).

Kupchan, C. (2002) *The End of the American Era: U.S. Foreign Policy and the Geopolitics of the Twenty-First Century* (New York: Vintage).

Kupka, M. (1992) 'Transformation of Ownership in Czechoslovakia', *Soviet Studies*, vol. 44 (2), pp. 297–311.

Kvist, J. (2004) 'Does EU Enlargement Start a Race to the Bottom? Strategic Interaction among EU Member States in Social Policy', *Journal of European Social Policy*, vol. 14 (3), pp. 301–18.

Laar, M. (2005) 'The impact of Central Europe's tax revolution', *The Economist*, 5 March.

Laclau, E. and Mouffe, C. (1985) *Hegemony and Socialist Strategy* (London: Verso).

Lafontaine, O. (2000) *The Heart Beats on the Left* (Cambridge: Polity Press).

Lagace, M. (2007) 'All Eyes on Slovakia's Flat Tax', *Harvard Business School Working Knowledge*, 30 April.

Langley, P. (2002) *World Financial Orders: An Historical International Political Economy* (London: Routledge).

Lazonick, W. (2003) 'The Theory of the Market Economy and the Social Foundations of Innovative Enterprise', *Economic and Industrial Democracy*, vol. 24, pp. 9–44.

Lazonick, W. and O'Sullivan, M. (2000) 'Maximizing Shareholder Value: A new Ideology for Corporate Governance?', *Economy and Society*, vol. 29, pp. 13–35.

LCEC (2004) *A Social Contract for the 21st Century* (Brussels: Lisbon Council for European Competitiveness).

LCEC (2005) *Open Letter to the European Council. Reform Leaders Demand: Make Europe Social Again!* (Brussels: Lisbon Council for European Competitiveness).

Leibfried, S. (2005) 'Social Policy', in H. Wallace and W. Wallace (eds), *Policy-Making in the European Union*, 5th edn (Oxford: Oxford University Press), pp. 243–78.

Len, C. (2006) 'The Growing Importance of Japan's Engagement in Asia', *Power and Interest Report*, 17 February.

Leonard, M. (2005) *Why Europe Will Run the Twenty-First Century* (London: Fourth Estate, Ltd).

Leonard, M. and Popescu, N. (2007) *A Power Audit of EU-Russia Relations* (Brussels: European Council on Foreign Relations).

Levey, D. and Brown, S. (2005) 'The Overstretch Myth: Can the Indispensable Nation Be a Debtor Nation?', *Foreign Affairs*, vol. 84 (2), pp. 2–7.

Lim, E. (2006) 'The Euro's Challenge to the Dollar: Different Views from Economists and Evidence from COFER and Other Data', IMF Working Paper 06/153 (Washington, DC: International Monetary Fund).

Lindstrom, N. (2005) 'Contesting Europe from its Margins: Domestic Politics of Europeanization in Estonia and Slovenia', Paper presented at the Capstone Conference of the Cornell/CEU Mellon-Sawyer Group on a Transnational and Transcultural Europe, Budapest, 17–18 June.

Lindstrom, N. and Piroska, D. (2007) 'The Politics of Privatization and Europeanization in Europe's Periphery: Slovenian Banks and Breweries for Sale?', *Competition and Change*, vol. 11 (2), pp. 115–34.

Lipietz, A. (1987) *Mirages and Miracles: The Crises of Global Fordism* (London: Verso).

Lipietz, A. (1993) 'Social Europe, Legitimate Europe: The Inner and Outer Boundaries of Europe', *Environment and Planning D: Society and Space*, vol. 11, pp. 501–12.

Lloyd, J. (1994) 'How to Make a Market', *London Review of Books*, 10 November.

Lorentowicz, A., Marin, D. and Raubold, A. (2002) 'Ownership, Capital or Outsourcing: What Drives German Investment to Eastern Europe', Centre for Economic Policy Research Discussion Paper No. 3515, July.

Lucardie, P. (2005) 'De campagne: David tegen Goliath?', in K. Aarts, and H. van der Kolk (eds), *Nederlanders en Europa: Het Referendum over de Nederlandse Grondwet* (Amsterdam: Bert Bakker), pp. 104–22.

Lundvall, B.-Å. (ed.) (1992) *National Systems of Innovation: Towards a Theory of Innovation and Interactive Learning* (London: Francis Pinter).

Lütz, S. (2002) *Der Staat und die Globalisierung von Finanzmärkten: Regulative Politik in Deutschland, Großbritannien und den USA* (Frankfurt am Main: Campus).

Lütz, S. (2004) 'The Political Economy Approach to Financial Reform', Paper presented at the Workshop on the Political Economy of International Financial Governance, Austrian Central Bank, Vienna, 26 November.

Mahon, R. (1977) 'Canadian Public Policy: The Unequal Structure of Representation', in L. Panitch (ed.), *The Canadian State: Political Economy and Political Power* (Toronto, Buffalo and London: University of Toronto Press), pp. 165–98.

Mahon, R. (2007) 'Swedish Model Dying of Baumols? Current Debates', *New Political Economy*, vol. 12 (1), pp. 79–86.

Mair, P. (2006) 'Ruling the Void? The Hollowing of Western Democracy', *New Left Review*, vol. 42, pp. 25–51.

Majone, G. (1996) *Regulating Europe* (London: Routledge).

Mallya, T. J. S., Kukulka, Z. and Jensen, C. (2004) 'Are Incentives a Good Investment for the Host Country? An Empirical Evaluation of the Czech National Incentive Scheme', *Transnational Corporations*, vol. 13 (1), pp. 109–48.

Manne, H. (1965) 'Mergers and the Market for Corporate Control', *The Journal of Political Economy*, vol. 73 (2), p. 113.

Mannheim, K. (1976 [1936]) *Ideology and Utopia. An Introduction to the Sociology of Knowledge* (London: Routledge and Kegan Paul).

Marginson, P. (2006) 'Europeanisation and Regime Competition: Industrial Relations and EU Enlargement', *Industrielle Beziehungen*, vol. 13 (2), pp. 97–117.

Marijnissen, J. (2005a) 'De ene Eurostaat komt er in een snel tempo aan', *Trouw*, 21 May, p. 16.

Marijnissen, J. (2005b) 'Europese Grondwet is een gedrocht', *NRC Handelsblad*, 18 April, p. 7.

Marks, G., and Steenbergen, M. (eds) (2004) *European Integration and Political Conflict* (Cambridge: Cambridge University Press).

Marshall, T. H. (1950) *Citizenship and Class and Other Essays* (Cambridge: Cambridge University Press).

Marshall, T. H. (1992) 'Citizenship and Social Class' in T. H. Marshall and T. Bottomore (eds), *Citizenship and Social Class* (London: Pluto Press), pp.3–49.

Martin, A. (2000) 'Social Pacts, Unemployment and EMU Macroeconomic Policy', in G. Fajertag and P. Pochet (eds), *Social Pacts in Europe – New Dynamics* (Brussels: ETUI), pp. 365–400.

Martin, A. and Ross, G. (1999) 'In the Line of Fire: The Europeanization of Labor Representation', in A. Martin and G. Ross (eds), *The Brave New World of European Labor: European Trade Unions at the Millennium* (New York and Oxford: Berghahn Books), pp. 312–67.

Martin, A. and Ross, G. (2004) (eds) *Euros and Europeans: Monetary Integration and the European Model of Society* (Cambridge: Cambridge University Press).

Martinez-Vasquez, J. and McNab, R. (2000) 'The Tax Reform Experiment in Transitional Countries', *National Tax Journal*, vol. 53 (2), pp. 273–98.

McCormack, G. (2005) 'Koizumi's Coup', *New Left Review*, vol. 35, pp. 5–18.

McCormick, J. (2007) *The European Superpower* (New York: Palgrave Macmillan).

McDermott, G. A. (2002) *Embedded Politics: Industrial Networks and Institutional Change in Postcommunism* (Ann Arbor: The University of Michigan Press).

McMenamin, P. and Hill, S. (2004) 'Survey of Performance of Investment Promotion agencies', in *Promoting Foreign Direct Investment in Central and Eastern Europe and the CIS* (Geneva: United Nations Publications), pp. 25–38.

Meaney, C. S. (1995) 'Foreign Experts, Capitals, and Competing Agendas: Privatization in Poland, the Czech Republic, and Hungary', *Comparative Political Studies*, vol. 28 (2), pp. 275–305.

Meardi, G. (2002) 'The Trojan Horse for the Americanization of Europe? Polish Industrial Relations Towards the EU', *European Journal of Industrial Relations*, vol. 8 (1), pp. 77–99.

Meardi, G. (2004) 'Short Circuits in Multinational Companies: The Extension of European Works Councils to Poland', *European Journal of Industrial Relations*, vol. 10 (2), pp. 161–78.

Meardi, G. (2006) 'Social Pacts on the Road to EMU: A Comparison of the Italian and Polish Experiences', *Economic and Industrial Democracy*, vol. 27 (2), pp. 197–222.

Meardi, G. and Toth, A. (2005) 'Who is Hybridising What? Insights on MNCs' Employment Practices in Central Europe', in A. Ferner, J. Quintanilla and C. Sanchez-Runde (eds), *Multinationals and the Construction of Transnational Practices: Convergence and Diversity in the Global Economy* (Basingstoke: Palgrave Macmillan), 155–83.

Mencinger, J. (1996) 'Privatization Experiences in Slovenia', *Annals of Public and Cooperative Economics*, vol. 67, pp. 415–28.

Merkel, W. (2001) 'The Third Ways of Social Democracy into the 21st Century', in A. Giddens (ed.), *The Global Third Way Debate* (Cambridge: Polity), pp. 50–73.

Merkt, H. (2004) 'European Company Law Reform: Struggling for a more Liberal Approach', *European Company and Financial Law Review*, vol. 1, pp. 3–35.

Merril Lynch (2004) *EU Enlargement: Western European Companies to See Further Benefits* (Merril Lynch: Global Fundamental Equity Research Department).

Mettler, A. (2005) 'A Two-Speed Europe, At Last', *Wall Street Journal Online Edition*, 9 June.

Metzger, M. (2006) 'Basel II. Benefits for Developing Countries?', *Intervention*, vol. 3, pp. 131–50.

MIGA-FIAS (2005) *Competing for FDI: Inside the Operations of Four National Investment Promotion Agencies* (Washington: Multilateral Investment Guarantee Agency and Foreign Investment Advisory Service).

Mihályi, P. (1993) 'Hungary: A Unique Approach to Privatization – Past, Present and Future', in I. Székely and D. M. G. Newbery (eds), *Hungary: An Economy in Transition* (London: The Centre for Economic Policy Research), pp. 84–117.

Mihályi, P. (2001) 'The Evolution of Hungary's Approach to FDI in Post-Communist Privatization', *Transnational Corporations*, vol. 10 (3), pp. 61–73.

Miliband, R. (1969) *The State in Capitalist Society* (London: Quartet Books).

Milne, R. (2008) 'Europe's executives gloomy on prospects', *Financial Times*, 14 April, p. 1.

Milward, A. S. and Sørensen, V. (1994) 'Interdependence or Integration? A National Choice', in A. S. Milward, F. M. B. Lynch, F. Romero, R. Raineri, and V. Sørenson, *The Frontier of National Sovereignty: History and Theory 1945–92* (New York: Routledge), pp. 1–32.

Ministerie van Buitenlandse Zaken (2007) 'Kamerbrief inzake EU-verdragswijziging', 19 March (available from: http://www.minbuza.nl/nl/actueel/brievenparlement, 2007/03/Kamerbrief-inzake-EU-verdragswijziging.html).

Ministry of Foreign Affairs of Japan (2005) 'Security Consultative Committee Document – U.S.-Japan Alliance: Transformation and Realignment for the Future', Tokyo, 29 October.

Mitchell, D. J. (2005) 'Will Europe's Flat Tax Revolution Spread from East to West?', *European Affairs*, Fall (available from: http://www.europeanaffairs.org/current_issue/2005_winter/2005_winter_12.php4).

Mitchell, D. J. (2007) *The IMF's Remarkably Shoddy Flat Tax Study*, The Heritage Foundation, 6 January.

Mládek, J. (2002) 'Kupónová privatizace: Politický úspech, ekonomické selhání' [Voucher privatization: Political success, economic failure], *Kupónová privatizace* (Prague: Centre for Economics and Politics).

Monks, J. (2007) 'Europe should not give in to casino capitalists', *Financial Times*, 4 June, FT Report – The Future of Europe, p. 6.

Moore, D. (2005) 'Slovakia's 2004 Tax and Welfare Reforms, IMF Working Paper WP/05/133 (Washington, DC: International Monetary Fund).

Moravcsik, A. (1998) *The Choice for Europe: Social Purpose and State Power from Messina to Maastricht* (Ithaca, NY: Cornell University Press).

Moravcsik, A. and Vachudova, M. A. (2003) 'National Interests, State Power, and EU Enlargement', *East European Politics and Societies*, vol. 17 (1), pp. 42–57.

Morton, A. D. (2007) *Unravelling Gramsci: Hegemony and Passive Revolution in the Global Political Economy* (London: Pluto Press).

Mosher, J. S. and Trubek, D. M. (2003) 'Alternative Approaches to Governance in the EU: EU Social Policy and The European Employment Strategy', *Journal of Common Market Studies*, vol. 41 (1), pp. 63–88.

Mouffe, C. (1992) 'Democratic Citizenship and the Political Community', C. Mouffe (ed.), *Dimensions of Radical Democracy: Pluralism, Citizenship, Community* (London: Verso), pp. 225–39.

Mülbert, P. O. (2003) 'Make It or Break It: The Break-Through Rule as a Break-Through for the European Takeover Directive?', ECGI Law Working Paper No. 13/2003.

Munková, M. (2004) 'Fundamental changes made to Labour Code', *Eironline* (http://www.eurofound.europa.eu/eiro/2003/12/feature/sk0312103f.html).

Myant, M. (1993) *Transforming Socialist Economies: The Case of Poland and Czechoslovakia* (Aldershot: Edward Elgar).

Myant, M. (1999) 'Inward Investment and Structural Transformation', in A. Lorentzen, B. Widmaier and M. Laki (eds), *Institutional Change and Industrial Development in Central and Eastern Europe* (Aldershot: Ashgate), pp. 61–84.

Myant, M. (2003) *The Rise and Fall of Czech Capitalism: Economic Development in the Czech Republic Since 1989* (Cheltenham, UK and Northampton, MA: Edward Elgar).

Netjes, C. E. (2004) 'All Aboard? Explaining Public Support for European Integration in a Post-Maastricht Era', Paper presented at the 2nd Pan-European Conference, Bologna, Italy, 24–6 June.

Netjes, C. E. and Edwards, E. E. (2006) 'Taking Europe to its Extremes: Extremist Parties and Public Euroskepticism', Paper presented at the Midwest Political Science Association Annual Conference, Chicago, 20–3 April.

Netzzeitung (2008) 'Nokia will Werk in Bochum schliessen', 15 January (http://www.netzeitung.de/wirtschaft/879872.html).

Newsweek (1999) 'New World Disorder', 31 May, p. 22.

Nölke, A. (2003) 'The Relevance of Transnational Policy Networks: Some Examples from the European Commission and the Bretton Woods Institutions', *Journal of International Relations and Development*, vol. 6 (3), pp. 267–98.

Nölke, A. and Perry, J. (2007) 'The Power of Transnational Private Governance: Financialization and the IASB', *Business and Politics*, vol. 9 (3), pp. 1–25.

Norris, R. and Kristensen, H. (2006) 'Where the Bombs Are, 2006', *Bulletin of the Atomic Scientists*, vol. 62 (6), pp. 57–8.

North Atlantic Treaty Organization (2007) 'NATO and Egypt Conclude Individual Cooperation Agreement', Press Release, Brussels, 10 October.

NRC Handelsblad (2005) 'Arbeid en kapitaal eensgezind vóór', 14 May, p. 2.

NRC Handelsblad (2006) 'Te koop: B.V. Nederland. Golf van buitenlandse overnames komt welvaart ten goede maar werknemers niet', 25 November, p. 23.

Nugent, N. (2004) *European Union Enlargement* (Houndmills: Palgrave Macmillan).

Nye, J. S. (1990) *Bound to Lead: The Changing Nature of American Power* (New York: Basic Books).

Nye, J. S. (2003) 'Europe is too powerful to be ignored', *Financial Times*, 14 January.

Nye, J. S. (2004) *Soft Power: The Means to Success in World Politics* (Cambridge, MA: Public Affairs).

O'Donnell, G. (1978) 'Reflections on the Patterns of Change in the Bureaucratic-Authoritarian State', *Latin American Research Review*, vol. 13 (1), pp. 3–38.

O'Dwyer, C. and Kovalčík, B. (2007) 'And the Last shall be the First: Party System Institutionalization and Second-Generation Economic Reforms in Postcommunist Europe', *Studies in Comparative International Development*, vol. 41 (4), pp. 3–26.

OECD (1998) *OECD Economic Surveys. 1997–8. The Netherlands.* (Paris: Organisation for Economic Co-operation and Development).

OECD (2000) *OECD Reviews of Foreign Direct Investment: Hungary* (Paris: Organisation for Economic Co-operation and Development).

OECD (2006a) *Economic Outlook* (Paris: Organisation for Economic Co-operation and Development).

OECD (2006b) *Factbook 2006: Economic, Environmental and Social Statistics* (Paris: Organisation for Economic Co-operation and Development).

Open Europe (2008) 'The Lisbon treaty and the European constitution: A side-by-side comparison', January (available from: http://www.openeurope.org.uk/research/comparative.pdf).

Orenstein, M.A. (2001) *Out of the Red: Building Capitalism and Democracy in Postcommunist Europe* (Ann Arbor: The University of Michigan Press).

Ost, D. (2000) 'Illusionary Corporatism in Eastern Europe: Neoliberal Tripartism and Post-communist Class Identities', *Politics and Society*, vol. 28 (4), pp. 503–30.

Ost, D. (2005) *The Defeat of Solidarity. Anger and Politics in Postcommunist Europe* (Ithaca, NY and London: Cornell University Press).

Overbeek, H. (1990) *Global Capitalism and National Decline: The Thatcher Decade in Perspective* (London: Unwin Hyman).

Overbeek, H. (1999) 'Globalisation and Britain's Decline', in R. English and M. Kenny, (eds), *Rethinking Decline: Britain Towards 2000* (London: Macmillan), pp. 231–56.

Overbeek, H. (2000) 'Transnational Historical Materialism', in R. Palan (ed.), *Global Political Economy: Contemporary Theories* (London: Routledge), pp. 168–83.

Overbeek, H. (2003) 'Globalization, neoliberalism and the employment question', in H. Overbeek (ed.), *The Political Economy of European Employment: European Integration and the Transnationalization of the (Un)Employment Question* (London: Routledge), pp. 13–28.

Overbeek, H., Nölke, A. and van Apeldoorn, B. (eds) (2007) *The Transnational Politics of Corporate Governance Regulation* (London and New York: Routledge).

Overbeek, H., and van der Pijl, K. (1993) 'Restructuring Capital and Restructuring Hegemony: Neoliberalism and the Unmaking of the Post-war Order', in H. Overbeek (ed.), *Restructuring Hegemony in the Global Political Economy: The Rise of Transnational Neoliberalism in the 1980s* (London: Routledge), pp. 1–27.

Palan, R. (2006) 'Is the Competition State the New, Post-Fordist, Mode of Regulation? Regulation Theory from an International Political Economy Perspective', *Competition and Change*, vol. 10 (2), pp. 246–62.

Panitch, L. and Gindin, S. (2003) 'Euro-Kapitalismus und Amerikanischer Imperialismus', in M. Beckmann, H. -J. Bieling and F. Deppe (eds), *Euro-Kapitalismus und globale politische Ökonomie* (Hamburg: VSA), pp. 113–43.

Panitch, L. and Gindin, S. (2005) 'Superintending Global Capital', *New Left Review*, vol. 35, pp. 101–23.

Pant, H. (2006) 'U.S.-India Nuclear Deal: The End Game Begins', *Power and Interest Report*, 27 January.

Parker, G. (2006) 'Barbed response: How Europe could be rent asunder by barricades to business', *Financial Times*, 22 March, p. 15.

Parker, G. and Benoit, B. (2007) 'Key clause dropped from draft EU treaty', *Financial Times*, 22 June.

Parts, Juhan (2004), *Competition and Competitiveness in Europe* (Natolin: College of Europe), 29 September, p. 4 (available from: http://www.coleurop.be/template.asp?pagename=speeches (accessed 27 July 2008).

Pateman, C. (1988) *The Disorder of Women* (Princeton, NJ: Princeton University Press).

Pavlínek, P. (1998) 'Foreign Direct Investment in the Czech Republic', *Professional Geographer*, vol. 50 (1), pp. 71–85.

Pavlínek, P. (2004) 'Regional Development Implications of Foreign Direct Investment in Central Europe', *European Urban and Regional Studies*, vol. 11 (1), pp. 47–70.

Pelkmans, J. and van Kessel, S. (2006) 'Encapsulating Services in the 'Polder': Processing the Bolkestein Directive in Dutch Politics', Paper commissioned by the WRR (Dutch Scientific Council for Government Policy) for the project The Political and Societal Embedding of Dutch EU Policy, Mimeo, June.

Pellikaan, H., van der Meer, T. and de Lange, S. (2003) 'The Road from a Depoliticized to a Centrifugal Democracy', *Acta Politica*, vol. 38 (1), pp. 23–50.

Pels, D. (2004) *De Geest van Pim. Het gedachtegoed van een politieke dandy* (Amsterdam: Anthos).

Pennings, P. and Keman, H. (2003) 'The Dutch Parliamentary Elections in 2002 and 2003: The Rise and Decline of the Fortuyn Movement', *Acta Politica*, vol. 38 (1), pp. 51–68.

Perry, J. (2006) 'Goodwill Hunting: Fair Value Accounting, Financialisation and the Knowledge Economy', Paper presented at the workshop of the Critical Political Economy Research Network of the European Sociological Association, Free University of Amsterdam, 31 August–2 September.

PES (2007) *Hedge Funds and Private Equity: A Critical Analysis* (available from: www. socialistgroup.eu/gpes/media/documents/33841_33839_hedge_funds_executive_ summary_070329.pdf).

Peters, J. (2004) 'Perspektiven eines neuen Europäischen Sozialmodells – Strategien der IG Metall in und für Europa' (http://www.uni-kassel.de/fb5/frieden/themen/ Gewerkschaften/peters-eu-verf.html).

Petter, I. and Griffiths, R. (2005) 'Gekke Henkie in Europa? Financiële euroscepsis in Nederland', in B. Boer and H. Vollaard (eds), *Euroscepsis in Nederland* (Utrecht: Lemma), pp. 45–69.

Pezdir, R. (2006) 'Thirteen years of gradualism – Inhibiting transition in Slovenia?', *Post-Communist Economies*, vol. 18 (1), pp. 51–68.

Pierson, P. (1994) *The Dismantling of the Welfare State? Reagan, Thatcher and the Politics of Retrenchment* (Cambridge: Cambridge University Press).

Pierson, P. (1998) 'Irresistable Forces, Immovable Objects: Post-Industrial Welfare States Confront Permanent Austerity', *Journal of European Public Policy*, vol. 5 (4), pp. 539–60.

Pierson, P. (2001a) 'Coping with Permanent Austerity: Welfare State Restructuring in Affluent Democracies', in P. Pierson (ed.), *The New Politics of the Welfare State* (Oxford: Oxford University Press), pp. 410–56.

Pierson, P. (2001b) 'Post-Industrial Pressures on Mature Welfare States', in P. Pierson (ed.), *The New Politics of the Welfare State* (Oxford: Oxford University Press), pp. 80–104.

Piroska, D. (2002) 'Varieties of Debt Management in Central and East European Countries: An Institutional Investigation of International Financial Transactions', Copenhagen Business School Intercultural Management and Communication Department Working Paper 1029.

Platform of European Social NGOs (2005) *From a strategy to a tragedy: Social NGOs call on political leaders to reject the Barroso approach to Lisbon and reaffirm the European model of society* (available from: http://www.socialplatform.org/module/FileLib/ ENSpringSummit2005resolution.pdf).

Polanyi, K. (1957) *The Great Transformation: The Political and Economic Origins of Our Time* (Boston: Beacon Press).

Politi, J. and Saigol, L. (2006) 'Rise in hostile bids pushes M&A to record – Unsolicited approaches double last year's figure: Switch to shorter-term views fuelling the boom', *Financial Times*, 29 September.

Pollack, M. A. (1998) 'Beyond Left and Right? Neoliberalism and Regulated Capitalism in the Treaty of Amsterdam', Working Paper Series in European Studies, vol. 2 (2), University of Wisconsin-Madison.

Pontusson, J. (2005) *Inequality and Prosperity: Social Europe vs. Liberal America* (Ithaca, NY: Cornell University Press).

Poulantzas, N. (1978 [1974]) *Classes in Contemporary Capitalism* (London: New Left Books).

Poulantzas, N. (1976) *The Crisis of the Dictatorships* (London: New Left Books).

Poulantzas, N. (1978) *State, Power, Socialism* (London: New Left Books).

Power and Interest News Report (2005) 'Bulgaria, Rumania and the Changing Structure of the Black Sea Geopolitics', 20 May.

Prague Post (2004) 'Czech or Slovakia', 21 October.

Prodi, R. (2000a) 'Europe's Renaissance', Speech/00/441, 17 November, Frankfurt am Main.

Prodi, R. (2000b) 'The Road to Europe's Future', Speech/00/416, 7 November, Brussels.

Prodi, R. (2001a) 'Are We Really on the Road to European Integration?', Speech/01/187, 26 April, Munich.

Prodi, R. (2001b) 'A New Economic Policy for a New European Economy', Speech/01/194, 2 May, Brussels.

Prodi, R. (2003) 'Investment in Knowledge – The Way Forward', Speech/03/4/, 14 January, Strasbourg.

Purcell, M. (2002) 'The State, Regulation, and Global Restructuring: Reasserting the Political in Political Economy', *Review of International Political Economy*, vol. 9 (2), pp. 298–332.

PWC (2004) 'Study on the financial and macroeconomic consequences of the draft proposed new capital requirements for banks and investment firms in the EU: Final Report' (http://europa.eu.int/comm/internal_market/regcapital/index_en.htm# consequences.).

Rabushka, A. (2005) 'The Flat Tax Gathers Momentum in Western Europe', *Hoover Institution Comments, Essays and Speeches*, 30 August.

Radaelli, C. (1999) 'The Public Policy of the European Union: Whither Politics of Expertise?', *Journal of European Public Policy*, vol. 6 (5), pp. 757–74.

Ramet, S. (1996) *Balkan Babel: The Disintegration of Yugoslavia from the Death of Tito to Ethnic War* (Boulder, CO: Westview).

Rao, H., and Hirsch, P. (2003) '"Czechmate": The Old Banking Elite and the Construction of Investment Privatization Funds in the Czech Republic', *Socio-Economic Review*, vol. 1 (2), pp. 247–69.

Reid, T. R. (2004) *The United States of Europe: The New Superpower and the End of American Supremacy* (New York: Penguin).

Regeerakkoord (1994) 13 August (Coalition Agreement of the PVDA-VVD-D'66 coalition) (available from: http://www.minaz.nl/regeringsbeleid/regeerakkoord/pdfs/regeerakkoord1994.pdf).

Remery, C., van Doorne-Huiskes, A. and Schippers, J. J. (2002) 'Labour Market Flexibility in the Netherlands: Looking for Winners and Losers', *Work, Employment and Society*, vol. 16 (3), pp. 477–96.

Rhodes, M. (2000) 'Lisbon: Europe's Maastricht for Welfare?', *ECSA Review*, vol. 13 (30), pp. 2–7.

Rhodes, M. (2001) 'The Political Economy of Social Pacts: Competitive Corporatism and European Welfare States', in P. Pierson (ed.), *The New Politics of the Welfare State* (Oxford: Oxford University Press), pp. 165–94.

Rhodes, M. (2002) 'Why EMU Is – or May Be – Good for European Welfare States', in K. Dyson (ed.), *European States and the Euro* (Oxford: Oxford University Press), pp. 305–33.

Risse-Kappen, T. (1996) 'Exploring the Nature of the Beast: International Relations Theory and Comparative Policy Analysis Meet the European Union', *Journal of Common Market Studies*, vol. 34 (1), pp. 53–80.

Robinson, W. I. (2004) *A Theory of Global Capitalism: Production, Class, and State in a Transnational World* (Baltimore and London: John Hopkins University Press).

Rogoff, K. (2008) 'Dog Days for the Super Dollar', December (http://www.project-syndicate.org/commentary/rogoff37).

Rosamond, B. (2002) 'Imagining the European Economy: "Competitiveness" and the Social Construction of "Europe" as an Economic Space', *New Political Economy*, vol. 7 (2), pp. 157–77.

Roseberry, W. (1994) 'Hegemony and the Language of Contention', in G. M. Joseph and D. Nugent (eds), *Everyday Forms of State Formation: Revolution and the Negotiation of Rule in Modern Mexico* (Durham: Duke University Press), pp. 355–66.

Ross, G. (1995) *Jacques Delors and European Integration* (Cambridge: Polity Press).

Ross, G. (2004) 'Monetary Integration and the French Model', in A. Martin and G. Ross (eds), *Euros and Europeans: Monetary Integration and the European Model of Society* (Cambridge, UK: Cambridge University Press), pp. 76–102.

Roubini, N. (2008) 'Can the Fed and Policymakers Avoid a Systemic Financial Meltdown? Most Likely Not', 8 February (http://www.rgemonitor.com/blog/roubini/242906/).

Rügemer, W. (2005) 'Investitionen ohne Arbeitsplätze', *WSI Mitteilungen*, vol. 58, pp. 49–54.

Ruggie, J. G. (1982) 'International Regimes, Transactions and Change: Embedded Liberalism in the Postwar Economic Order', *International Organisation*, vol. 47 (1), pp. 379–416.

Ruigrok, W. and van Tulder, R. (1995) *The Logic of International Restructuring* (London and Oxford: Routledge).

Ryner, M. (2002) *Capitalist Restructuring, Globalisation and the Third Way: Lessons from the Swedish Model* (London: Routledge).

Ryner, M. (2003) 'Disciplinary Neoliberalism, Regionalization and the Social Market in German Restructuring', in A. Cafruny and M. Ryner (eds), *A Ruined Fortress? Neoliberal Hegemony and Transformation in Europe* (Lanham, MD: Rowman and Littlefield), pp. 201–27.

Ryner, M. (2004) 'Neo-Liberalization of Social Democracy: The Swedish Case', *Comparative European Politics*, vol. 2 (1), pp. 97–119.

Ryner, M. (2007a) 'U.S. Power and the Crisis of Social Democracy in Europe's Second Project of Integration', *Capital & Class*, vol. 93, pp. 101–20.

Ryner, M. (2007b) 'The Nordic Model: Does It Exist? Can It Survive?', *New Political Economy* 12 (1), pp. 61–70.

Sabatier, P. A. (1998) 'The Advocacy Coalition Framework: Revisions and Relevance for Europe', *Journal of European Public Policy*, vol. 5 (1), pp. 98–130.

Sachverständigenrat zur Begutachtung der gesamtwirtschaftlichen Entwicklung (2004) 'Jahresgutachten 2004–5 – Erfolge im Ausland, Herausforderungen im Inland', Berlin, pp. 165–87.

Sadler, D. and Swain, A. (1994) 'State and Market in Eastern Europe: Regional Development and Workplace Implications of Direct Foreign Investment in the Automobile Industry in Hungary', *Transactions of the Institute of British Geographers (NS)*, vol. 19 (4), pp. 387–403.

Sayer, A. (1992) *Method in Social Science: A Realistic Approach* (London: Routledge).

Scharpf, F. W. (1999) *Governing in Europe: Effective and Democratic?* (Oxford, NY: Oxford University Press).

Scharpf, F. W. (2002) 'The European Social Model: Coping with the Challenges of Diversity', *Journal of Common Market Studies*, vol. 40 (4), pp. 645–70.

Schmitter, Ph. C. (1996) 'Imagining the Euro-Polity with the Help of New Concepts', in G. Marks, F. Scharpf, Ph. C. Schmitter, and W. Streeck (eds) *Governance in the European Union* (London: Sage), pp. 121–50.

Schmitthoff, C. (ed.) (1973) *The Harmonisation of European Company Law* (London: The United Kingdom National Committee of Comparative Law).

Schulten, T. (2005) 'Foundations and Perspectives of Trade Union Wage Policy', in E. Hein, Niechoj, T., Schulten, T. and Truger, A. (eds), *Macroeconomic Policy Coordination in Europe and the Role of the Trade Unions* (Brussels: ETUI), pp. 263–92.

Schulten, T. and Ryner, M. (2003) 'The Political Economy of Labour Market Restructuring and Trade Unions in the Social Democratic Heartland', in H. Overbeek (ed.) *The Political Economy of European Employment: European Integration and the Transnationalization of the (Un)Employment Question* (London and New York: Routledge), pp. 176–98.

Schwartz, H. (1994) *States versus Markets* (London: Macmillan).

Scott-Smith, G. (2003) 'Cultural Policy and Citizenship in the European Union: An Answer to the Legitimation Problem?', in A. Cafruny and M. Ryner (eds), *A Ruined Fortress? Neoliberal Hegemony and Transformation in Europe* (Lanham, MD: Rowman and Littlefield), pp. 261–84.

Seabrooke, L. (2001) *US Power in International Finance: The Victory of Dividends* (Basingstoke: Palgrave Macmillan).

Seabrooke, L. (2006) 'The Bank for International Settlements', *New Political Economy*, vol. 11, pp. 141–9.

Sell, S. K. (2000) 'Big Business and the New Trade Agreements: The Future of the WTO', in R. Stubbs and G. Underhill (eds), *Political Economy and the Changing Global Order* (Oxford: Oxford University Press), pp. 174–83.

SER (2004) *Met Europa meer groei* (Den Haag: Sociaal-Economische Raad).

Shields, S. (2003) 'The "Charge of the Right Brigade": Transnational Social Forces and the Neoliberal Configuration of Poland's Transition', *New Political Economy*, vol. 8 (2), pp. 225–44.

Shields, S. (2004a) 'Global Restructuring and the Polish State: Transition, Transformation, or Transnationalization?', *Review of International Political Economy*, vol. 11 (1), pp. 132–54.

Shields, S. (2004b) 'Neoliberalisation Through Depoliticisation: Transnational Governance and the Political Economy Implications of Eastwards Enlargement of the EU', Paper presented at the Amsterdam Research Centre for Corporate Governance Regulation (ARCCGOR) Inaugural Workshop, Vrije Universiteit Amsterdam, 17–18 December.

Shields, S. (2007) *The International Political Economy of Transition* (London: Routledge).

Sie Dhian Ho, M. (2001) 'Federatiekampioen of trouwe bondgenoot: Het Nederlandse beleid ten aanzien van Europese en Atlantische samenwerking', in R. E. van Ditshuyzen (ed.), *Tweehonderd jaar Ministerie van Buitenlandse Zaken* (Den Haag: SDU), pp. 286–304.

Silver, B. J. (2003) *Forces of Labor: Workers' Movements and Globalization since 1870* (Cambridge: Cambridge University Press).

Skog, R. (2002) 'The Takeover Directive – an endless Saga?', *European Business Law Review*, vol. 13 (4), pp. 301–12.

Slate, D. (2005) 'Fair and Flat: The European Flat Tax Revolution', *The Stanford Review*, 11 November.

Slovak Spectator (2004a) 'Finance Ministry rejects German criticism', 5 April.

Slovak Spectator (2004b) 'French tax talk soundly rejected', 13 September.

Smith, G. (2004a) 'Hegemony: Critical Interpretations in Anthropology and Beyond', *Focaal – European Journal of Anthropology*, vol. 43, pp. 99–120.

Smith, H. (2004b) 'The Politics of "Regulated Liberalism": A Historical Materialist Approach to European Integration', in M. Rupert and H. Smith (eds), *Historical Materialism and Globalization* (London: Routledge), pp. 257–83.

Smith, N. J. -A. (2005) *Showcasting Globalisation? The Political Economy of the Irish Republic* (Manchester: Manchester University Press).

Smith, A., Rainnie, A. and Dunford, M. (2001) 'Regional Trajectories and Uneven Development in the "New Europe": Rethinking Territorial Success and Inequality', in H. Wallace (ed.), *Interlocking Dimensions of European Integration* (Basingstoke: Palgrave Macmillan), pp. 122–44.

Smythe, E. (2000) 'State Authority and Investment Security: Non-state Actors and the Negotiation of the Multilateral Agreement on Investment at the OECD', in R. Higgott, G. R. D. Underhill and A. Bieler (eds), *Non-State Actors and Authority in the Global System* (London: Routledge), pp. 74–90.

Špidla, V. (2005) 'The 2005 Jean Jacque Rousseau Lecture for the Lisbon Council: Modernizing the European Social Model', 20 June, Brussels.

Spithoven, A. H. G. M. (2002) 'The Third Way: The Dutch experience', *Economy and Society*, vol. 31 (3), pp. 222–68.

Stanojevic, M. (2003) 'Worker's Power in Transition Economies: The Cases of Serbia and Slovenia', *European Journal of Industrial Relations*, vol. 9 (3), pp. 283–301.

Stark, D. and Bruszt, L. (1998) *Postsocialist Pathways: Transforming Politics and Property in East Central Europe* (Cambridge and New York: Cambridge University Press).

Stettes, O. (2006) 'Relocation of production and industrial relations – case of Germany', *Eironline*, February (http://www.eiro.eurofound.eu.int/2005/11/study/index.html).

Stone Sweet, A. and Sandholtz, W. (1998) 'Integration, Supranational Governance and the Institutionalization of the European Polity', in W. Sandholtz and A. Stone Sweet (eds), *European Integration and Supranational Governance* (Oxford: Oxford University Press), pp. 1–26.

Storey, A. (2006) 'The Struggle for Europe: Resistance to Neoliberalism', *IPEG papers in Global Political Economy*, no. 22.

Storrie, D. and Ward, T. (2007) *ERM Report 2007: Restructuring and Employment in the EU: The Impact of Globalization* (Dublin: European Foundation for the Improvement of Living and Working Conditions).

Strange, S. (1988) *States and Markets* (London: Pinter).

Strange, S. (1996) *The Retreat of the State: The Diffusion of Power in the World Economy* (Cambridge: Cambridge University Press).

Strange, S. (1998) *Mad Money: When Markets outgrow Governments* (Ann Arbor: University of Michigan Press).

Streeck, W. (1996) 'Public Power Beyond the Nation-State: The Case of the European Union', in R. Boyer and D. Drache (eds), *States Against Markets: The Limits of Globalization* (London: Routledge), pp. 299–314.

Streeck, W. (1997) 'German Capitalism: Does it Exist? Can it Survive?', *New Political Economy*, vol. 2 (2), pp. 237–56.

Streeck, W. (1998) 'The Internationalization of Industrial Relations in Europe: Prospects and Problems', MPIfG Discussion Paper 98/2, Cologne: Max Planck Institute for the Study of Societies.

Streeck, W. and Trampusch, C. (2005) 'Economic Reform and the Political Economy of the German Welfare State', Max Planck Institut für Gesellschaftsforschung, Working Paper 05/2.

Szacki, J. (1995) *Liberalism after Communism* (Budapest: Central European University Press).

Tabb, W. K. (2003) *Economic Governance in the Age of Globalization* (New York: Columbia University Press).

Tagliabue, J. (2002) 'Poland to Buy Lockhead Jets', *New York Times*, 28 December, Section C, p. 1.

Tamminga, M. (2007) 'Behoud hoofdkantoren ook zaak voor premier', *NRC Handelsblad*, 30 April.

Tamminga, M. and Wester, J. (2006) 'Voorzitter FNV Bondgenoten wil actie tegen uitwassen van private equity en hedgefondsen', *NRC Handelsblad*, 26 August, p. 21.

Taylor, G. and Mathers, A. (2002) 'The Politics of European Integration: A European Labour Movement in the Making?', *Capital & Class*, vol. 78, pp. 39–60.

Teslik, L. H. (2008) 'Recession, beyond the economy', *Council on Foreign Relations, Daily Analysis*, 22 January (http://www.cfr.org/publication/15287/recession_beyond_the_economy.html?breadcrumb=%2F).

Thacker, S. C. (2000) *Big business, the State, and Free Trade: Constructing Coalitions in Mexico* (Cambridge, UK and New York, NY: Cambridge University Press).

Tidow, S. (2003) 'The emergence of European employment policy as a transnational political arena', in H. Overbeek (ed.), *The Political Economy of European Employment* (London: Routledge), pp. 77–98.

Tiits, M. (2006) 'Industrial and Trade Dynamics in the Baltic Sea Region – The Last Two Waves of EU Enlargement from a Historical Perspective', IDEUNIS Papers, March.

Tóth, A. and Neumann, L. (2002) 'Major amendment of Labour Code comes into effect', *Eironline*, 29 October (http://www.eurofound.europa.eu/eiro/2002/10/feature/hu0210101f.html).

Towalski, R. (2005) 'New Labour Code proposed', *Eironline*, 31 October (http://www.eurofound.europa.eu/eiro/2005/10/feature/pl0510105f.html).

Towalski, R. (2006) 'Proposed amendments to Polish Labour Code under review', *Eironline*, 19 December (http://www.eurofound.europa.eu/eiro/2006/10/articles/pl0610069i.html).

Tsoukalis, L. (1993) *The New European Economy* (Oxford: Oxford University Press).

TUC (2004) 'The EU Constitutional Treaty – a briefing for trade unionists' (available from: http://www.tuc.org.uk/international/tuc-8564-f0.pdf).

Turner, B. (1993) 'Contemporary Problems in the Theory of Citizenship', in B. Turner (ed.), *Citizenship and Social Theory* (London: Sage), pp. 1–18.

Twining, D. (2007) 'America's Grand Design in Asia', *The Washington Quarterly*, vol. 30 (3), pp. 79–94.

UNCTAD (2002) *World Investment Report: Transnational Corporations and Export Competitiveness* (New York and Geneva: United Nations Conference on Trade and Development).

Underhill, G. (1997) 'Private Markets and Public Responsibility in the Global System: Conflict and Cooperation in Transnational Banking and Securities Regulations', in

G. Underhill (ed.), *The New World Order in International Finance* (Basingstoke: Macmillan), pp. 17–49.

Underhill, G. (2004) 'Theorising Governance in a Global Financial System', Paper presented at the workshop on the Political Economy of International Financial Governance, Austrian Central Bank, 26 November, Vienna.

Unger, R. M. (1976) *Law in Modern Society* (New York: The Free Press).

U.S. Department of Defense (2006) *Quadrennial Defense Review Report* (Washington, DC: Office of the Undersecretary of State for Defense (Policy)).

US Treasury (2007) 'Report to Congress on International Economic and Exchange Rate Policies', December (available from: http://www.treas.gov/offices/international-affairs/economic-exchange-rates/pdf/Dec2007-Report.pdf).

Van Apeldoorn, B. (2000) 'Transnational Class Agency and European Governance: The Case of the European Round Table of Industrialists', *New Political Economy*, vol. 5 (2), pp. 157–81.

Van Apeldoorn, B. (2001) 'The Struggle over European Order: Transnational Class Agency in the Making of "Embedded Neoliberalism"', in A. Bieler and A. D. Morton (eds), *Social Forces in the Making of the New Europe: The Restructuring of European Social Relations in the Global Political Economy* (Basingstoke, UK: Palgrave Macmillan), pp. 147–64.

Van Apeldoorn, B. (2002) *Transnational Capitalism and the Struggle over European Integration* (London and New York: Routledge).

Van Apeldoorn, B. (2003) 'European Unemployment and Transnational Capitalist Class Strategy', in H. Overbeek (ed.), *The Political Economy of European Employment: European Integration and the Transnationalization of the (Un)Employment Question* (London: Routledge), pp. 113–34.

Van Apeldoorn, B. (2004a) 'Theorizing the Transnational: A Historical Materialist Approach', *Journal of International Relations and Development*, vol. 7 (2), pp. 142–76.

Van Apeldoorn, B. (ed.) (2004b) *Transnational Historical Materialism: The Amsterdam International Political Economy Project*, Special Issue of *Journal of International Relations and Development*, vol. 7 (2).

Van Apeldoorn, B. (ed.) (2007) *The political economy of European integration in the polder: Asymmetrical supranational governance and the limits of legitimacy of Dutch EU Policy-making*. Wetenschappelijke Raad voor het Regeringsbeleid, W15 (The Hague: WRR), (available from: http://www.wrr.nl/content.jsp?objectid=4034).

Van Apeldoorn, B. and Horn, L. (2007a) 'The Marketisation of Corporate Control: A Critical Political Economy Perspective', *New Political Economy*, vol. 12, pp. 211–35.

Van Apeldoorn, B. and Horn, L. (2007b) 'The Transformation of Corporate Governance Regulation in the European Union: From Harmonisation to Marketisation', in H. Overbeek, A. Nölke and B. van Apeldoorn (eds), *The Transnational Political Economy of Corporate Governance Regulation* (London and New York: Routledge), pp. 77–97.

Van Apeldoorn, B., Overbeek, H. and Ryner, M. (2003) 'Theories of European Integration: A Critique', in A. Cafruny and M. Ryner (eds), *A Ruined Fortress?*, (Lanham: Rowman and Littlefield), pp. 17–45.

Van der Klugt, C. J. (1988) 'Why Wait for 1992? Agenda for Immediate Action in Europe', Speech by the president of Philips, June, Brussels.

Van der Kolk, H. and Aarts, K. (2005) 'Opkomst en uitslag', in K. Aarts and H. van der Kolk (eds), *Nederlanders en Europa: Het Referendum over de Nederlandse Grondwet* (Amsterdam: Bert Bakker), pp. 183–206.

Van der Pijl, K. (1984) *The making of the Atlantic Ruling Class* (London: Verso).

Van der Pijl, K. (1996) *Vordenker der Weltpolitik* (Opladen: Leske and Budrich).

Van der Pijl, K. (1998) *Transnational Classes and International Relations* (London: Routledge).

Van der Pijl, K. (2001a) 'From Gorbachev to Kosovo: Atlantic Rivalries and the Reincorporation of Eastern Europe', *Review of International Political Economy*, vol. 8 (2), pp. 275–310.

Van der Pijl, K. (2001b) 'What Happened to the European Option for Eastern Europe?', in A. Bieler and A. D. Morton (eds), *Social Forces in the Making of the New Europe* (Basingstoke and New York: Palgrave Macmillan), pp. 185–204.

Van der Pijl, K. (2004) 'Two Faces of the Transnational Cadre Under Neoliberalism', *Journal of International Relations and Development*, vol. 7 (2), pp. 177–207.

Van der Pijl, K. (2006a) *Global Rivalries from the Cold War to Iraq* (London: Pluto Press).

Van der Pijl, K. (2006b) 'Lockean Europe?', *New Left Review*, vol. 37, pp. 9–37.

Van Kersbergen, K. (1995) *Social Capitalism: Study of Christian Democracy and the Welfare State* (London: Routledge).

Van Keulen, M. (2004) 'The Netherlands 2004 EU Council Presidency: Dutch EU Policy-making in the Spotlights', Sieps Occasional Paper, 1, Stockholm: Swedish Institute for European Policy Studies.

Van Praag, P. (2003) 'The Winners and Losers in a Turbulent Political Year', *Acta Politica*, vol. 38 (1), pp. 5–22.

Van Witteloostuijn, A. (1999) *De anorexiastrategie: over de gevolgen van saneren* (Amsterdam: De Arbeiderspers).

Vanhuysse, P. (2006) *Divide and Pacify: The Political Economy of Welfare State in Hungary and Poland, 1989–96* (Budapest: Central European University Press).

Verdun, A. (1999) 'The Role of the Delors Committee in Creating EMU: An Epistemic Community?', *Journal of European Public Policy*, vol. 6 (2), pp. 308–28.

Ver.di (2004) 'Entwurf für eine Europäische Verfassung' (http://international.verdi. de/europapolitik/europaeische_verfassung_und_europaeischer_konvent).

Visser, J. (2004) 'Patterns and Variations in European Industrial Relations', Paper prepared for the European Commission.

Visser J. and Hemerijck, A. (1997) *A Dutch Miracle. Job Growth, Welfare reform, and Corporatism in the Netherlands* (Amsterdam: Amsterdam University Press).

Voerman, G. (2005) 'De Nederlandse politieke partijen en Europese integratie', in K. Aarts and H. van der Kolk (eds), *Nederlanders en Europa: Het Referendum over de Nederlandse Grondwet* (Amsterdam: Bert Bakker), pp. 44–63.

Vliegenthart, A. (2007) 'EU Membership and the Rise of a Foreign-Led Type of Capitalism in the Czech Republic', in J. Pickles (ed.), *State and Society in Post-socialist Economies* (Basingstoke: Palgrave Macmillan), pp. 47–68.

Vliegenthart, A. and Horn, L. (2007) 'The Role of the EU in the (Trans)Formation of Corporate Governance Regulation in Central Eastern Europe – The Case of the Czech Republic', *Competition and Change* (forthcoming).

Vliegenthart, A. and Overbeek, H. (2007) 'Corporate Governance Regulation in East Central Europe: The Role of Transnational Forces', in B. Van Apeldoorn, A. Nölke and H. Overbeek (eds), *The Transnational Politics of Corporate Governance Regulation* (London and New York: Routledge), pp. 177–97.

Walters, W. and Haahr, J. H. (2005) *Governing Europe: Discourse, Governmentality and European Integration* (London: Routledge).

Watson, M. (2006) 'Whither Financialisation? The Contradictory Microfoundations of Finance-Led Growth Regimes', Paper presented at the annual meeting of the British International Studies Association, University College of Cork, 19 December.

Watson, M. and Hay, C. (2003) 'The Discourse of Globalisation and the Logic of no Alternative: Rendering the Contingent Necessary in the Political Economy of New Labour', *Policy and Politics*, vol. 31 (3), pp. 289–305.

Weiss, L. (ed.) (2003) *States in the Global Economy: Bringing Domestic Institutions Back in* (Cambridge: Cambridge University Press).

Welt Online (2006) 'Angst vor Arbeitsplatzverlagerung', 27 January (http://www. welt.de/print-welt/article193866/Angst_vor_Arbeitsplatzverlagerung.html).

Williams, R. (1977) *Marxism and Literature* (Oxford: Oxford University Press).

Wincott, D. (2003) 'Beyond Social Regulation? New Instruments and/or a New Agenda for Social Policy at Lisbon', *Public Administration*, vol. 81 (3), pp. 533–53.

Windolf, P. (1994) 'Die neuen Eigentümer: Eine Analyse des Marktes für Unternehmenskontrolle', *Kölner Zeitschrift für Soziologie*, vol. 23 (2), pp. 1–36.

Winter, J. (2004) 'EU Company Law on the Move', *Legal Issues of Economic Integration*, vol. 31 (2), pp. 97–114.

Wissen, M. (2005) 'Europäische Wettbewerbsstaatlichkeit: Die Rolle der EU im Prozess der neoliberalen Restrukturierung', *Widerspruch*, vol. 25 (48), pp. 31–8.

Woldendorp, J. J. W. (2005) *The Polder Model: From Disease to Miracle? Dutch Neo-Corporatism 1965–2000*. Doctoral Dissertation (Amsterdam: Vrije Universiteit).

Wolf, E. R. (1990) 'Facing Power – Old Insights, New Questions', *American Anthropologist*, vol. 92 (3), pp. 586–96.

Wolf, K. D. (2000) *Die Neue Staatsräson- Zwischenstaatliche Kooperation als Demokratieproblem in der Weltgesellschaft. Plädoyer für eine geordnete Entstaatlichung des Regierens jenseits des Staates* (Baden-Baden: Nomos).

Wood, D. (2005) *Governing Global Banking: The Basel Committee and the Politics of Financial Globalization* (Aldershot: Ashgate).

World Bank (2007) *International Comparison Program—Preliminary Results*, 17 December (Washington, DC: World Bank), pp. 24–5 (available from: http://siteresources.world bank.org/ICPINT/Resources/ICPreportprelim.pdf).

Yin, R. K. (1989) *Case Study Research: Design and Methods*, 2nd edn (Thousands Oaks, CA: Sage).

Zängle, M. (2004) 'The European Union Benchmarking Experience: From Euphoria to Fatigue?', *European Integration online Papers* (EIoP), vol. 8 (5) (available from: http://eiop.or.at/eiop/texte/2004–005a.htm).

Zelikow, P. and Rice, C. (1995) *Germany Unified and Europe Transformed* (Cambridge: Harvard University Press).

Ziltener, P. (1999) *Strukturwandel der Europäischen Integration* (Münster: Westfälisches Dampfboot).

Ziltener, P. (2000) 'Die Veränderung von Staatlichkeit in Europa – regulations- und staatstheoretische Überlegungen', in H. -J. Bieling and J. Steinhilber (eds), *Die Konfiguration Europas: Dimensionen einer kritischen Integrationstheorie* (Münster: Westfälisches Dampfboot), pp. 73–101.

Zubek, R. (2006) 'Poland: Unbalanced Domestic Leadership in Negotiating Fit', in K. Dyson (ed.), *Enlarging the Euro Area: External Empowerment and Domestic Transformation in East Central Europe* (Oxford: Oxford University Press), pp. 197–214.

Index